The Red Lancers

The Red Lancers

Anatomy of a Napoleonic Regiment

RONALD PAWLY

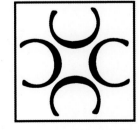

The Crowood Press

ACKNOWLEDGEMENTS

First published in 1998 by
The Crowood Press Ltd
Ramsbury, Marlborough
Wiltshire SN8 2HR

www.crowood.com

This impression 2017

© Ronald Pawly

British Library Cataloguing-in-Publication Data
A catalogue record for this book is available
from the British Library

ISBN 978 1 78500 336 3

Cover picture: Chef d'escadron Jan Post (1778-1841);
portrait by Louis Moritz (1773-1850),
private collection, Holland.

Edited by Martin Windrow
Designed by Frank Ainscough, Compendium
Printed and bound in India by
Replika Press Pvt Ltd

The author wishes to record his gratitude to all those
who have assisted in the preparation of this book:

Mr Jacques Bartels,
    Member of the Committee of the Dutch Army Museum, Delft
Mr & Mrs Bernard Quintin,
    authors of *Dictionnaire de Colonels de Napoléon*, France
Mr Robert Chénier, President, Association pour la
    Conservation des Monuments Napoléoniens, France
Mr Alain Chappet, co-author of *Répertoire Mondial
    des Souvenirs Napoléoniens*, France
Mr Otto Schutte, Secretary, Hoge Raad van Adel, The Hague

The staff of the following institutions:
Royal Army Museum, Brussels, Belgium
Army Museum, Les Invalides, Paris, France
Army Museum, Holland
Museum de l'Empéri, Salon-de-Provence, France
French Army Historical Service, Vincennes, France
Dutch Army Historical Service, The Hague, Holland

I also wish to express special gratitude to those private
collectors who have done me the honour of granting access
to their collections.

For their kind assistance and valuable information,
I wish to record my thanks to:

Ms Jenny Spencer-Smith, National Army Museum, London
Historical Museum, Berne, Switzerland
Royal Collection Enterprises, Windsor, England
Mrs Roberts and son, Hambledon, England
Miss Jones, Cheltenham, England
Countess R. de Warren, Switzerland
Countess L. de Warren, France
The von Tscharner family, Switzerland
The van Hasselt family, South Africa & Hong Kong
The Post family, Holland
Count & Countess de Peyronnet, d'Ainay-le-Vieil, France
Count & Countess d'Ursel, Ecaussinnes-Lalaing, Belgium
Count François de Colbert, Les Echelles, France

Personally, I wish to emphasise my debt of gratitude to:
Mr Yves Meessen, Thimister, Belgium
Mr & Mrs Hoogstoel-Fabri, Brussels, Belgium
Mr Jean-Jacques Pattyn, Chairman,
    Société Belges d'études Napoléoniennes, Brussels, Belgium
Mr André Sadzo, Antwerp, Belgium
Mr Alistair McGregor, Kapellen, Belgium

CONTENTS

FOREWORD

BY HH THE PRINCE MURAT

To recall the magnificent epic of the 2nd Light Horse Lancers of the Imperial Guard - the legendary Red Lancers - is to evoke the French First Empire at its moment of greatness. This is a splendid enterprise, which Ronald Pawly has undertaken with precision, scholarship, talent and passion. The milestones along the march of this crack regiment shine from the very heart of the Napoleonic saga, and form part of the most glittering military heritage in history. Smolensk, Borodino, Lützen, Bautzen, Reichenbach, Leipzig, La Rothière, Champaubert, Montmirail, Saint Dizier - these were the triumphs and tragedies along the Red Lancers' journey, taken at a breathtaking rush through the campaigns of Russia in 1812, Saxony in 1813, and France in 1814.

Ronald Pawly displays a deep understanding of the many facets of this dazzling, intoxicating story: its chronology, its delights and sufferings, its sacrifices and triumphs. He has mastered the everyday facts of the Lancers' story as well as their days of glory: their uniforms and equipment, their regulations and procedures, and - most fascinating of all - the individual service records of many of the actors in this five-year drama. He portrays, through the detailed facts of their careers and through their own words, a gallery of authentic and often highly coloured personalities. He shines a light onto this exceptional cavalry regiment; and the seductive picture which emerges is perhaps unprecedented in its depth and in the valuable richness of its details.

The common denominator linking these heroic individuals was a courageous faith in their mission. This being so, I hope I may be forgiven for my pride in recalling the fact that in 1812 the Red Lancers served as scouts and flank guards for the Cavalry Corps of Joachim Murat, King of Naples, called by his brother-in-law Napoleon "the bravest man in the world". In his day this victor of Aboukir, Jena and Eylau was the army's idol, "the god of cavalry", a paladin who could galvanize thousands of mounted men and lead them to victory - lead them from the front, sword in hand, like a crusader king. Personalities of such size surely cannot be judged against any narrow matrix, but only against the dimension of centuries.

Ronald Pawly has researched this story marvellously - set it in place, filled it out, and brought it to life. He deserves our warm thanks and respectful admiration.

Joachim MURAT

Garde Impériale.

2ᵉᵐᵉ Régiment de Chevau-Légers Lanciers.

INTRODUCTION

On Sunday 18 June 1815, under a leaden sky, Captain Baron Antonie van Omphal, adjutant to Lieutenant-General Baron Chassé, was following the mud-splashed columns of that commander's 3rd Dutch Division as they marched east from Braine l'Alleud to take up position on the field of Waterloo among the British, Netherlands and German formations of Wellington's Allied army.

Drawn up facing them a few hundred yards to the south, Napoleon's Armée du Nord presented an impressive sight. At the age of 27 Antonie van Omphal was already a cavalry veteran of seven years' fighting in Spain, Russia, Germany and France; and as he cast an experienced eye along the ranks of the enemy one corps in particular drew his attention. Dressed in red, its front ranks bearing lances tipped with white and red pennons, it was clearly distinguishable against the mostly blue and green mass of the Imperial army. Van Omphal was deeply moved by the sight: for four unforgettable years he had served with that regiment, sharing their bivouacs and their saddle-sore marches, their moments of glory and their defeats. Today many of his old comrades were still serving in the corps which he now faced as an enemy.

A few days after the battle van Omphal was one of the first officers of the Dutch army to enter Paris. He made his way to the Palais Royal, where he met several of his former comrades in arms; despite his Dutch uniform, they welcomed him with great affection. Regimental esprit de corps was stronger than the political forces which had divided them: above everything, they were all survivors of the legendary Red Lancers of the Imperial Guard.

Formed in September 1810, they were - after the Polish Lancers - the second cavalry regiment of the Guard composed entirely of foreigners, in this case Dutchmen passing from the Royal Guard of the former King Louis, brother of the Emperor. Eighteen months later the 2nd Regiment of Light Horse Lancers of the Imperial Guard marched out for an unknown destination; in the ranks they argued whether it was to be Rome or Warsaw, but in the end the road would lead them all the way to Moscow.

The retreat from Russia would pass into Europe's shared legend as a byword for privation and suffering. Starving and freezing, the men and horses of the Red Lancers dwindled away as the Cossack wolfpacks harried them across the endless snows. Yet in 1813 the Regiment was rebuilt stronger than ever - ten squadrons, each 250 strong. This was achieved by drawing in men from all over the Empire, and apart from its officer corps the Regiment lost its specifically Dutch character.

The 1813 campaign in Saxony began victoriously, but ended on the frontiers of France, where Napoleon strove to hold the Allies back beyond the Rhine. Despite some strokes of brilliance worthy of the high noon of Empire, the French campaign in the spring of 1814 ended with Napoleon's first abdication.

The First Restoration saw the Red Lancers pass into the Guard of the returned but insecure Bourbon monarchy as the Royal Corps of Light Horse Lancers of France. When Napoleon escaped from Elba in 1815 most of the Regiment rallied to the Eagle and tricolour. Under its wings they followed him to Waterloo that June, charging the British squares and batteries as the last afternoon of Empire wore away in frustration and carnage. There was to be no forgiveness under the Second Restoration; and in December 1815 the Red Lancers were finally disbanded.

Years later some of the former officers of the Regiment - such as Dumonceau, van Omphal and de Stuers - began to set down their memoirs. In some cases the letters which members of the Regiment had sent home to their families were and are preserved, and the present writer has been enabled to quote verbatim from many of these in this account. The former squadron commander Jan Post had actually kept a small notebook in which he had recorded all the places where he had spent a night. Some accounts have been the subject of study and publication, such as the memoirs of Dumonceau, the life of de Watteville, and the works of Rembowski on the history of the Polish Lancers. The regimental muster rolls and a range of other official correspondence and records have been preserved in the French military archives. It is this whole spectrum of documents, preserved by the descendants of the actors in this story or - sometimes by the blessing of "benign neglect" - in national or regional archives, which have made it possible to reconstruct the history of the Regiment.

Ronald Pawly
Antwerp 1997

1810-1811: The Birth of the Regiment

The Low Countries in 1810

On 9 July 1810, at the Castle of Rambouillet, Napoleon Bonaparte, Emperor of the French and in that year at the height of his power, signed the decree by which Holland was annexed to the Empire and, as a consequence, by which the Red Lancers were born.

The Netherlands or Low Countries had been for centuries one of the cockpits in which the contending European powers had struggled for advantage, and their history presented a complex sequence of occupation and liberation, combination and separation. In the late 18th century they had been divided between the United Provinces (roughly, modern Holland) and the Austrian Netherlands (roughly, modern Belgium).

In 1794, during the Revolutionary Wars, France overran the Netherlands. The former Austrian provinces effectively remained part of France until 1814. The former United Provinces became the Batavian Republic, under French control; the Dutch ruler, the Prince of Orange, fled to England early in 1795. By the subsequent Treaty of the Hague the Dutch States General ceded to France the provinces of Flanders, Maastricht, Venlo, and part of Walcheren with Flushing; the Batavian Republic would subsequently consist of Ems, Old Yssel, Rhein, Texel, Delft, Scheldt and Maas (Seeland), and Dommel. From 1803 the president ("Pensioner of the Council") was Jan Rudiger Schimmelpenninck.

The Batavian Republic contributed troops for French campaigns in Germany in 1796, 1800-01, 1803, 1805 and 1806, forming divisions commanded by Generals Beurnonville, Daendels, Dumonceau and Bonhomme. In 1806, in the aftermath of Napoleon's crushing defeat of Austria and Russia at Austerlitz on 2 December 1805, the Emperor set about redrawing much of the map of Europe. He amalgamated a number of cowed German states into his client Confederation of the Rhine; and he raised the Batavian Republic to the status of a Kingdom of Holland, placing on the throne his brother Louis.

Later that year Napoleon turned on Prussia, winning major victories at Jena and Auerstädt on 14 October; in the winter of 1806-07 he occupied Poland, and on 7 February drove a Russian army from the field at Eylau. In April a Dutch contingent served under Marshal Mortier in Swedish Pomerania, Prussia and Poland. On 14 June 1807 Napoleon smashed Bennigsen's Russians at Friedland; and at Tilsit in July both Tsar Alexander I of Russia and King Frederick William III of Prussia were obliged to agree to more or less humiliating peace terms, including the partial restoration of Polish national identity in France's client Grand Duchy of Warsaw. Napoleon was now the acknowledged master of most of Europe; and his domination was apparently sealed by his second great victory over Austria in the Wagram campaign of 1809.

Unable to invade Great Britain - his last implacable enemy - due to her supremacy at sea, Napoleon sought to starve her into making terms by instituting a commercial quarantine. By his Berlin and Milan decrees of 1806 and 1807 he forbade any trade contact between the Continental nations and Britain, closing every port on the European coastline to British ships and citizens. This dictat confronted some regions with the prospect of commercial ruin, and clandestine trade continued despite his efforts to enforce the embargo.

Colonel-Major Charles Dubois (1772-1829), wearing the uniform of a colonel of the Dutch Hussars of the Royal Guard. The decorations were added to the portrait at a later date. (Photograph from the former collection of Georges Englebert, Austria)

The weak Spanish monarchy was manipulated into allowing a French army to march through Spain to occupy Portugal, Britain's long-time trading partner, in October 1807. Reinforcements followed, taking control of strategic points along their routes; but in spring 1808 the Spanish people rose spontaneously against a de facto French occupation of their homeland, which was followed that June by Napoleon's installation of his brother Joseph on the Spanish throne. The ensuing Peninsular War - involving conventional campaigns against a background of constant guerrilla activity - was to last until 1814, and gave Britain the opportunity to intervene directly by landing an army in the Iberian Peninsula.

Napoleon obliged many of his client states to provide troops for the occupation armies in Portugal and Spain, among them a Dutch brigade led by General Chassé which served with the French VI Corps (Marshal Lefebvre) and I Corps (Marshal Victor) in 1808-10. They were present at the battles of Durango (31 October 1808), Mesa de Ibor and Ciudad Real (17 & 27 March 1809), the defence of Merida (15 May-13 June 1809), Talavera (28 June 1809), Almonacid (11 August 1809), Daymiel (15 October 1809), Dos Barros (9 November 1809), and Ocana (19

Madame Dubois, née Catherine Agnes Scheuss von Ravensbergh (1765-1842), with their children Henri François Joseph Auguste (b.1798) and Amélie Philippine (b.1803). Charles Dubois married Catherine while in garrison at Urdingen in Germany in 1796. She had already refused the hands of the future Marshals Bernadotte and Soult, rejecting the latter with the words, "Do you think I could marry a Sansculotte?" - to which Soult replied, "Ah, but we shall not be Sansculottes forever." (Portrait by Alexandre J.Dubois, 'Dubois-Drahonet', 1791-1834; Château d'Ecaussinnes-Lalaing, Belgium)

November 1809). The cavalry of this formation was provided by the Dutch 3rd Regiment of Hussars.

Meanwhile, Louis Bonaparte had been showing signs of an ambition to rule in fact rather than merely in name as his brother's puppet. All the occupied or client states with access to the open sea had become centres of secret traffic with Britain, and Napoleon's "Continental system" blockade was proving both unenforceable and ruinous. A powerful British expedition landed at Walcheren in August 1809 with the objective of seizing Flushing and Antwerp; although it was mishandled, and withdrew ravaged by fever, it did manage to stay ashore for some months, and Napoleon began to harbour suspicions about Dutch loyalty.

Finally, overruling his brother's strong objections, Napoleon decided simply to annexe to France a large area of the Low Countries and northern Germany: Holland, parts of Westphalia, the Duchy of Oldenburg, and the Hanseatic cities of Hamburg, Bremen and Lubeck. In early 1810 French troops gradually moved into Dutch territory, and on 1 July King Louis was forced to abdicate in favour of his son. He left his residence at Haarlem

that night, fleeing incognito in fear of imprisonment at his brother's hands. Crossing Holland and Germany, he made his way to Töplitz in Bohemia, where he obtained permission to stay from the Emperor of Austria. On 2 July 1810 the troops of Marshal Oudinot occupied Amsterdam. On 10 July the decree of the previous day appeared in the *Moniteur*. Holland had become part of France; and much of her 27,000-strong army was absorbed into the French forces.

The arrival of the Dutch Hussars

As a compliment to the Dutch contingents which had served him bravely in the 1806-07 campaigns, Napoleon proclaimed in the same decree:

"The officers of the land and sea services, whatever their ranks, are confirmed in their posts. They will be issued certificates signed by my hand. The Royal Guard will be united with our own Imperial Guard."

On 31 July Napoleon ordered General Clarke (the Duke of Feltre, and Minister of War since 1807) to send the Royal Guard to Paris; this consisted of the 1st Grenadier Regiment, 1st Jaeger

A miniature of a Hussar of the Dutch Royal Guard. The dolman jacket is dark blue faced with scarlet, the pelisse scarlet trimmed with black, the lace yellow; his hair is shown red-blond, the sideburns and moustache a darker natural colour, and note the earring. (Collection of Belgian Royal Army Museum, Brussels)

Battalion, 1st Cuirassiers and 1st Hussars of the Guard. It was stipulated that these troops would be paid by the Treasury of Holland until 1 September 1810 and from that date on by the French Treasury.

Before leaving for Paris the Royal Guard was inspected one last time by Marshal Oudinot in front of the Royal Palace in Amsterdam. From there, under the orders of Colonel Charles Dubois, the Hussars of the Guard marched for Utrecht, where they stayed for a few days. A delegation formed from officers of the different corps of the Guard was ordered to report to Paris at once to render homage to the Emperor; among these was a Captain Abraham Calkoen of the Hussars of the Guard.

The morale of the troops who followed them at a steadier pace was mixed; there was an air of depression over the loss of their national independence, but some among them were proud at the thought of joining Napoleon's Imperial Guard - perhaps the most prestigious military organisation in Europe at that date - and hopeful of a glittering career.

The march carried them through Gorkum, Breda and Hoogstraten, where they crossed the frontier onto French territory. Here an officer of the Chasseurs à cheval (Mounted Chasseurs) of the Imperial Guard was waiting for them, to instruct them in the procedures and requirements of the French administration. Travelling via Lier and Mechelen, where they halted to rest, the former Royal Guard Hussars finally arrived in Brussels. While in the Belgian capital they were drawn up for inspection on the Place Royale.

Braine-le-Compte was the next halt, then Mons, Valenciennes, Cambrai, and Péronne. There they celebrated the Emperor's birthday on 15 August with a regimental dinner; and there they were joined by the wife and two children of their colonel, who travelled with the Regiment thereafter along the dusty roads from Roye to Gournay, Pont Ste Maxence, Louvres

and Le Bourget. Leaving Le Bourget early on a beautiful summer's morning the Dutch Guard Hussars bypassed Paris on the west, passing round the foot of the Butte de Montmartre to follow the exterior boulevards to Neuilly, through the Bois de Boulogne and across the Seine on the Pont de St Cloud, then following the Left Bank through Sèvres until they finally reached Versailles at the end of August.

Meanwhile, Captain Calkoen had arrived in Paris on 5 August with the delegation of Royal Guard officers. On the 15th he wrote to his father that they had been presented to His Majesty, sitting on the throne surrounded by the great dignitaries of the court in full dress - a most impressive spectacle. The Empress was not pretty but, as far as he could judge, appeared very kind.

The Dutch officers were not allowed to feel socially neglected. On 16 August they were invited to the Palace of St Cloud; on the 17th they dined at the palace of Grand Marshal Duroc, together with an Illyrian delegation. On the 18th they visited Arch-Chancellor Cambacérès, who invited them to dinner on the following day; that evening they paid their respects to Marshal Berthier.

On 20 August the officers were each presented individually to the Emperor. Calkoen was told that the Hussars of the Guard would be quartered at Versailles, and would be maintained within the Imperial Guard.

On its eventual arrival at Versailles the Regiment was welcomed and congratulated on the Place d'Armes in front of the château by the officers of the Guard regiments then in garrison. When the necessary administrative details of duties and quartering had been settled, the officers of the other Guard corps offered their new-found comrades a magnificent dinner, which gave all present an opportunity to get to know one another in a convivial atmosphere.

Two companies, including that of acting Captain Dumonceau with 200 horses, occupied a large barracks near the Barrière de Satory. The others were dispersed as follows : two and a half companies at the Stables of Madame with 250 horses; one and a half companies at the Stables of Monsieur with 150 horses; and two companies at the Limoges Stables with 218 horses and some surplus.

The next day the troops in their turn were treated to a lavish meal prepared in the various barracks of the Dragoons, Mounted Grenadiers and Mounted Chasseurs of the Guard. As among their officers, fraternisation was encouraged; and such lubricated harmony was achieved between the Dutch and French troopers that many of the Hussars exchanged uniforms with the vélites of the Chasseurs, later scattering about the town in these disguises. Vélites were officer-candidates, young men who paid for their place in the corps and were trained in the ranks while hoping for an eventual commission. It was perhaps the thoughtless high spirits of youth which prompted the revellers to take certain liberties with the good citizens of Versailles. Their sense of humour went largely unappreciated, to judge by the storm of indignant paperwork which followed. The Prefect of Seine-et-Oise reported on 1 September:

"On 31 August a regiment of the Dutch Guard arrived in Versailles. This corps was received by the Imperial Guard stationed in this town, who treated the newcomers to a fraternal banquet. At the end of this a large number of these soldiers scattered about the town under the influence of wine, particularly in the neighbourhood where a fair was taking place, where they caused great disorder and fear. Men and women alike were grossly insulted. A police superintendent, unrecognized, was outraged while attempting to carry out his duties; shops suffered considerable damage; and it was not until about eleven o'clock at night that peace began to be restored.

"There was no way of suppressing the disorder; the town remains without an armed force, and the commander of the Subdivision has no authority over the Imperial Guard. Since the depots of the Line troops have left the National Guard is entrusted with guarding the main posts,

On arrival at their new garrison in Versailles the Dutch officers were invited to a dinner organised by the officers of the other Guard regiments. (Marius Roy, 1833-post 1880; author's collection)

but their resources were inadequate to control the numerous soldiers who ignored any kind of restraint. The town Mayor and the police superintendents did their duty, but lacked the means to enforce respect of the law. The commanding officers of the various units have expressed their deep regrets to the Mayor, however; they have promised to search out and punish the offenders, and to take the necessary measures to prevent any repetition of such disorder."

On 3 September the Minister of Police, the Duke of Rovigo, wrote to the Minister of War, the Duke of Feltre:

"I beg to communicate to your Excellency an extract from a report by the Prefect of Seine-et-Oise dated the first of this month concerning severe disorder provoked on 31 August in the town of Versailles by soldiers of a regiment of the Dutch Guard. May I ask you, M.le Duc, to inform me of His Majesty's intructions bearing on this incident..."

Clearly at least a show had to be made of punishing the offenders - although any military man could have predicted the blank impenetrability of soldiers faced with such enquiries. On 6 September the Duke of Feltre wrote to the Duke of Istria (Marshal Jean-Baptiste Bessières, Colonel-General commanding the Cavalry of the Guard):

"I have received notice from the General commanding the 1st Military Division that on the 31st of last month a regiment of the Dutch Guard which had arrived in Versailles broke out into the most severe excesses, following a banquet to which it had been invited by the Imperial Guard. Since the town of Versailles no longer has a garrison, it was impossible for the public authorities to restore law and order.

"His Excellency the Minister of Police, to whom various reports have been addressed on this matter, has invited me to let him know the measures which should be taken for the punishment of the disorders committed on this occasion..."

Once tranquility had returned, however, and the officers had made ostensible but no doubt fruitless enquiries after the culprits, they turned their attention to more urgent matters.

At 6p.m. on 2 September the Emperor and Empress, in residence at St Cloud and accompanied by a large court, reviewed all the regiments of the Imperial Guard and the Dutch Guard between the bridges of Sèvres and St Cloud. The review

did not take long. After having passed at a gallop along the front of the ranks the Emperor had the columns formed for a march past. Behind the infantry, the cavalry preceded by Marshal Bessières and his staff moved off towards the Emperor in order to carry out a manoeuvre in front of him. To reach the road the Dutch Hussars had to cross in front of the Dutch Grenadiers; apparently this evolution did not work smoothly, causing certain comments to be passed between their respective leaders. At this moment a storm broke out. Their Majesties, the courtiers and the spectators hastened away across the Bois de Boulogne to return to Paris.

The episode did not leave a good impression. Taken together with the incident following the Versailles banquet, and some minor disturbances now reported caused by stragglers from the Dutch Grenadiers left behind on the march, it did not reflect well on these new troops of the Guard. Irreproachable behaviour in future would be needed to overcome this first bad impression.

As soon as the troops of the ex-Royal Guard of his exiled brother had been settled in their new garrisons, Napoleon proceeded with the organisation of the new corps. On 13 September the Emperor signed his next decree on the subject:

Palace of St Cloud, 13 September 1810
Napoleon, Emperor of the French, King of Italy, and Protector of the Confederation of the Rhine. We have decreed and we decree as follows:
Chapter 1: Organisation
Article 1
The four companies of the Dutch Bodyguard are disbanded; the NCOs and soldiers will be incorporated as Vélites, viz:
1st and 2nd Companies in the Dutch Infantry Regiment
3rd and 4th Companies in the Regiments of Chasseurs and Grenadiers of the Imperial Guard

Article 2

The Grenadier Regiment of the Dutch Guard will take the title 2nd Foot Grenadiers of our Imperial Guard. This regiment will consist of two battalions, each battalion of four companies and each company of 200 men, all organised in the manner of the Foot Grenadier Regiment of our Guard.

Article 3

The Hussar Regiment of the Dutch Guard will take the title 2nd Light Horse Lancers of the Guard. They will be armed with lances. It will be composed of eight companies. The men of this regiment who are German by birth will be incorporated into the Light Horse Lancers of Berg. Those who would prefer to serve in the four Dutch regiments will be free to choose.

Article 6

The Marshal Duke of Istria and his Chief Inspector of Reviews of our Guard will proceed by 15 September at the latest with the organisation of the Dutch Guard and the assignment of the officers. No officer may remain in the corps who is not Dutch by birth. The officers will be selected without distinction, either in the Bodyguard or the Foot Guards.

Chapter 2: Pay and allowances

Article 7

The pay and allowances, of all kinds, of NCOs and soldiers will remain the same as those stipulated in Dutch regulations; the officers will receive the same pay as the officers of our Imperial Guard, on and after 1 September 1810.

Article 9

Eagles will be presented to this new unit of our Guard.

A brief recapitulation on the lineage of these hussars is in order at this point.

In 1809 the Dutch 3rd Hussars, who had distinguished themselves in battle in the Peninsula, passed from the Line into the Dutch Royal Guard under the title "Hussar Regiment of the King's Guard". By reason of the heavy casualties suffered in Spain, however, their Colonel van Merlen asked permission to send the cadres of two squadrons, the sick and the disabled back to Holland. Following agreement at the beginning of 1810, the cadres of the 2nd and 3rd Squadrons returned to their depot at Deventer in June 1810; a single squadron remained in Spain under the command of Colonel van Merlen. By a decree of 16 June 1810 King Louis stipulated that:

(1) The squadron remaining in Spain was to take the designation 2nd Division of Horse Guards, but would be administered separately until it returned to Holland to be definitively re-organised.

(2) All officers, NCOs and troopers of the former 3rd Hussars present in Holland would be temporarily assigned to the Guard, but would retain their former uniforms and pay scales.

(3) From among the officers of the two elements the Captain of the Guard would submit to His Majesty recommendations as to whom to appoint immediately as regular Guardsmen and whom to incorporate subsequently.

(4) Finally, during July, a selection would be made of NCOs, troopers and horses to be assigned permanently to the Guard, in order to complete its establishment. Those excess to establishment would be dispersed between the two other cavalry regiments.

No sooner had these changes been announced than King Louis abdicated; as a result the provisions of the decree of 16 June were not fulfilled exactly. The Horse Guard Regiment - former Cuirassiers of the Guard - took in a number of officers and many NCOs, troopers and horses from the depot of the disbanded 3rd Hussars. This was done on the initiative of Colonel Charles Dubois of the Horse Guards, who thought them fit to be permanently incorporated in his regiment. Under the command of Major van Hasselt, 25 officers and a certain number of troopers and horses who were considered ill-qualified to join the Horse Guards were left at the 3rd Hussars' old depot at Deventer.

Consequently the Hussars forming part of the Dutch Royal Guard would be admitted into the French Imperial Guard. The

Colonel Jean B. van Merlen (1773-1815), who continued to command the remainder of the 3rd Hussars in Spain until March 1812 when they too passed into the 2nd Light Horse Lancers of the Imperial Guard. He wears here the uniform of a general in the Netherlands army, 1814; he would be killed at Waterloo the following year. (Photo © Stichting Iconographisch Bureau, The Hague)

squadron of Dutch Hussars left in Spain continued to be treated as troops of the Line. Colonel van Merlen, commanding this nominal 2nd Division of Horse Guards according to the decree of 16 June, was refused a Guard pay scale by the Minister of War on 29 March 1811.

* * *

On 18 September 1810 the Regiment was reviewed by the Inspector of Reviews of the Imperial Guard, Baron Félix. Its strength was noted as 58 officers, of whom 12 were absent in Holland; 865 troopers, of whom 149 were in Holland, and 28 in hospital (of whom four were in Holland); one trumpet major and 15 trumpeters. The effectives thus totalled 939 men, with 865 horses.

On the 21st of that month the composition of the 2nd Light Horse Lancers of the Imperial Guard was established as the regimental staff and four squadrons each of two companies, totalling 58 officers and 881 enlisted men, the latter total including one trumpet major, two trumpet corporals and 21 trumpeters. On 1 October the staff establishment - *Etat-Major* - was increased from eleven to twenty officers: one colonel, two majors, four chefs d'escadron, one quartermaster, one captain instructor, two captain adjutant-majors, four lieutenant sub-adjutant-majors, one Eagle (standard) bearer, two surgeon-majors and two sub-assistant surgeon-majors. Twelve enlisted men were attached to the staff.

At that time the Regiment included 48 Germans, who were to be transferred to other units according to Article 3 of the decree of 13 September. Thirty of them wanted to transfer to other regiments formed from former Netherlands corps, such as

JAN HENDRIK CORNELIS VAN HASSELT,
Colonel-Majoor by het 2'. Reg'
Chevau Legers Lanciers de la Garde Imperiale
le Cibicie 20 Dec. 1812

A highy stylised equestrian study of Colonel-Major Jan H.C. van Hasselt (1776-1812) in the uniform of a senior officer of the Hussars of the Dutch Royal Guard; he would distinguish himself during the Russian campaign. (Private collection, South Africa)

the latter was a highly regarded tactical instructor - there was no contradiction between social rank and a serious application to the profession of arms).

On 23 September the entire Imperial Guard, with the Dutch Guard, the marching battalion of the Rearguard Division of the Army of Spain, and the Portuguese Legion were present at the Sunday parade at the Tuileries. On that day the officer corps of the new regiment was formally presented to the Emperor for the first time. After having dismissed the Portuguese officers Napoleon approached them, inquiring about their quartering in Versailles, and asking about the recent disorders which had taken place in their garrison. Colonel Dubois confined himself to an apology, attributing the episode to the effects of the hospitality lavished on them by their new brothers in arms. The Emperor retorted, "Well, if your men can't withstand the effects of wine they will have to be satisfied with drinking beer in future."

The practical business of organising the Regiment proceeded with some urgency; until it was completed neither officers nor men could take leave to see their families in Holland. At this date the unit was 143 short of establishment, lacking ten officers (out of 59), seven NCOs (of 163) and 126 troopers (of 816). In order to fill the ranks, and to mark the previous services performed by soldiers of German nationality, Napoleon signed a new decree on 30 October; at the same time he commissioned most of the officers of the corps:

Palace of Fontainebleau, 30 October 1810
Napoleon, Emperor of the French, King of Italy, Protector of the Confederation of the Rhine, Mediator of the Swiss Confederation. We have decreed and we decree as follows:
Chapter 1
Article 1
All officers, NCOs and soldiers of the former Dutch Royal Guard who where born in the territory of the Hanseatic cities, in Oldenburg, Osnabrueck (Duchy of Berg) and in Westphalia will be considered as Dutch.
Article 2
All Germans who have served without interruption since at least 1800 in the former Dutch Royal Guard, either on foot or mounted, who have never deserted and who enlisted of their own free will in the Dutch forces, will be considered as Dutch.
Article 3
All Germans and individuals of all other nationalities at the present time forming part of the former Dutch Guard who were present at the battles of Ulm or at the actions in Stralsund will equally be considered Dutch.
Article 4
Inquiries will be made as to the nationality of all those who, by virtue of preceeding arrangements, have been confirmed into the Guard, and information about them will be gathered at the place of their residence. Our Minister of War will make a special register of those who are Prussian.
Chapter 3
2nd Light Horse Lancers of the Guard
Article 7
The 2nd Light Horse Lancers of the Imperial Guard will be commanded by a major. He will be under the orders of the Marshal Duke of Istria, commander of the cavalry of the Guard.
Article 8
The following are commissioned into the 2nd Light Horse Lancers of our Guard:
Major - Dubois, Colonel of Hussars of the former Dutch Guard
Second Major - van Hasselt, Major id.
Chef d'escadron - Coti, Chef d'escadron id.
Lieutenant Quartermaster - Dufour, QM, 6th Mounted Chasseurs
Sub-Adjutant-Majors - Royen, 1st Lt, Hussars of the Dutch Guard; Fallot, id.
Surgeon-Major - Mergell, Surgeon-Major id.;
Sub-Assistant Surgeon-Major - Stutterheim, Sub-Asst S-M id.
Captains - van der Meulen, Captain id.; Post, id.; Calkoen, id.; Schneither, id.; Tulleken, id.; Werner, id.

the 14th Cuirassiers and 11th Hussars; four requested transfer to the Light Horse Lancers of Berg (a German unit provided to the Imperial Guard by Marshal Murat in his capacity as Grand Duke of Berg and Cleves). The remainder, non-French speakers, applied for retirement or honourable discharge.

Finally, there were still fifteen officers of the former 3rd Hussars who had been taken into the Dutch Horse Guards by Colonel Dubois, and who were "placed at the disposal of the Minister of War".

It should be noted that almost all the officers of the Regiment, on its formation and for at least two years, were drawn from aristocratic families. Captain Abraham Calkoen, whom we have already met, lived in the style natural to the heir of the Lord of Kortenhoef; his needs were attended to by a suite of personal servants, and he was in the habit of inviting senior officers to dine. (We should recall that in this period military rank was not the simple measure of a man's status in the army which it has since become; outside the exercise of their professional functions, gentlemen did not define their relationships by their place in the military hierarchy.)

Lieutenant Fréderic Chomel was the son of the King of Prussia's consul to the court of Holland; Lieutenant Charles Mascheck was the son of a general, Lieutenant Count Dumonceau the heir of a former marshal of King Louis; Lieutenant Count Duranti was a former page to King Louis; and Sub-lieutenant Albert Frank was the son of a senior court official to the Sovereign of Anholt. Lieutenants van Zuylen van Nyevelt and van Haersolte and Captain van Balveren were all barons (and

Captain Abraham Calkoen (1780-1830), wearing the Cuirassier uniform of an officer of the Dutch Royal Guard, 1809. A prolific correspondent, Calkoen left a series of letters from his service with the Red Lancers upon which the present author draws heavily. (Johannes Hari the Elder, 1772-1849; photo © Stichting Iconographisch Bureau, The Hague)

1st Lieutenants - Manheim, 1st Lieutenant id.; Vermaesen, id.; Dumonceau, id.; Chomel, id.; Zuylen van Nyevelt, id.; de Mey, id.; Böcher, id.; Sterke, id.; Mascheck, id.; de Stuers, id.; Verhaegen, id.; Mascheck, id.[note that two cousins of this name both served - see Appendix III]; Haersolte, id.; Heshusius, id.; Delafargue [sic], id.; van Heiden, id.

2nd Lieutenants - Weerts, 2nd Lieutenant id.; van Doorn, id.; Frank, id.; Geubels, id.; de Wacker van Son, id.; Brepoels, id.; van der Linden, id.; van Omphal, id.; Leutner, id.; Ziegler, id.[note that father and son both served - see Appendix III]; Wijchgel, id.; de Jongh, id.; Das, id.; Delaizement, id.; Willich, id.

On 14 November the officers received personal notification of their commissions in the Guard; for instance, Captain Jan Post received the following letter from the Duke of Feltre, Minister of War:

"I inform you, Monsieur, that by a decree of 30 October 1810, the Emperor has nominated you as captain in the 2nd Light Horse Lancers of the Guard. I will notify His Excellency the Marshal Duke of Istria, Colonel-General of the Guard, of your nomination and will request that he makes you welcome in our Guard."

At the end of November the officers, NCOs and troopers were still being brought up to strength. Chefs d'escadron Tiecken and Hoevenaar of the former Royal Guard were commissioned into the 2nd Light Horse Lancers in that rank, despite the fact that the confident Captain Calkoen had already - unwisely - written to his father that the colonel intended to promote him. (Hardly installed in his quarters at Versailles, Tiecken would receive news that his brother, a first lieutenant with the 1st Provisional Chasseur Regiment, had been killed in Spain.) Hennige became surgeon-major and Steenis sub-assistant surgeon-major. Captain van Balveren was appointed captain instructor. The ranks were finally

Study of a Red Lancer by Théodore Géricault (1791-1824). In 1813 the painter made many studies of horses at Versailles, where the Red Lancers were quartered. (Photo © Réunion des Musées Nationaux, Paris)

filled with former members of the Dutch Bodyguard and the 3rd Hussars, and by vélites.

On 1 January 1811 all officers of the Imperial Guard and of the Guard of Paris were admitted to the court to pay their respects to the Emperor and Empress. They gathered in the Marshals' Hall at the Palace of the Tuileries; and there they came forward one by one, in front of the entire Imperial court ranked in full ceremonial dress in the Diana Gallery - an imposing assembly, which could not fail to make an impression on the Dutch officers.

Although Napoleon had originally intended to commission only Dutch officers into the Regiment, he was obliged to appoint some Frenchmen to attend to the administration and paperwork; the procedures differed from those to which the Dutch officers were accustomed. Among these were Lieutenant, later Captain Quartermaster Dufour; and Baron Albert de Watteville, a Swiss by birth. Appointed chef d'escadron on 13 January 1811, de Watteville, formerly an orderly officer to the Emperor, announced to his parents on 15 March 1811 that he was now a lieutenant-colonel, and chef d'escadron in the Red Lancers of the Guard (Guard ranks counted as one grade higher than the Line equivalent).

Orders of 29 January and 8 February confirmed the composition of the squadrons. Each of the four squadrons, commanded by chefs d'escadron, comprised two companies. Each company, divided into two troops *(pelotons)*, had an establishment of four officers - the captain commanding, one (1st) lieutenant, and two (2nd or sub-) lieutenants leading troops; one sergeant-major and six sergeants; one quartermaster corporal and ten corporals; three trumpeters - one for the company commander

and one each for the two troop subalterns; and 99 lancers, of whom two were farriers.

The uniform

At the same time the question of new uniforms was being addressed. Initially it had been intended to manufacture uniforms *à la Chasseur* for the Regiment, so as to remove as soon as possible the spectacle of Guardsmen walking around in their worn Dutch Hussar uniforms. Officers, at least, seem to have complied (see de Watteville's letter below); however, it was subsequently decided that since the Regiment was organised in every respect similarly to the Polish (now, 1st) Light Horse Lancers of the Guard, so their uniform should be the same as that of their fellow lancers. This would mean their adopting the Polish style of square-topped lancer's *czapska* headgear, a short-tailed *kurtka* jacket with broad buttoned-back lapels and cord aiguillettes at one shoulder, and tight-fitting trousers reaching the instep.

Palace of the Tuileries, 10 February 1811
Napoleon, Emperor of the French, King of Italy, Protector of the Confederation of the Rhine, Mediator of the Swiss Confederation. We have decreed and we decree the following:
Article 1
The 2nd Light Horse Lancers of the Guard will have the same cut of

jacket and the same headdress as the 1st Regiment. It will keep the colour scarlet for the jacket, with yellow buttons and distinctions. The distinctive colour for lapels, collars and cuff facings will be sky blue.
Article 2
These changes will be made gradually as replacements are issued, so that they do not occasion any extraordinary expenditure.
Article 3
Our Minister of War is charged with the execution of the present decree.
Signed: Napoléon
Duke of Bossano
Duke of Feltre

The reference to keeping (*"il conservera..."*) the colour scarlet indicates that the former 3rd Hussars (whose regimental uniform was light blue) had received the red uniform of the Dutch 1st, former "Guards" Hussars when raised to Royal Guard status in 1809. Bravely coloured against the more understated glamour of the Polish Lancers in their dark blue and crimson trimmed with silver, the Dutch were inevitably nicknamed "the Red Lancers".

The Emperor, who took a great interest in the uniforms of his Guard, asked to see a model. General of Brigade Edouard Colbert, a former commander of the 7th Hussars who had earned the nickname "Iron Man" on many battlefields, was appointed as colonel commandant of the Regiment on 6 March; and he had Lieutenant Adjutant-Major Fallot dressed in the new uniform for the Emperor's inspection. Apart from being one of the handsomest officers in the unit, "Bear" Fallot was luxuriantly hirsute, and made a strikingly martial figure; Napoleon was apparently delighted, and the new uniform was adopted. The collars, lapels, cuffs and turnbacks were in fact produced in dark blue; General Colbert believed that sky blue would show dirt too easily.

Every rose has its thorn. The Dutch officers had already had to provide themselves with two new uniforms in a very short time; at a period when officers wore superfine woollen fabrics and Morocco leather, richly embellished with heavy gold bullion wire, this was a major expense. Many of them were plunged into serious debt - as were the parents to whom they had appealed for help. Chef d'escadron de Watteville explained all this in a relentlessly detailed letter to his father, which usefully mentions both the initial Chasseur and later Polish styles of uniform:

"I have been commissioned in my unit for a month. This Regiment, although admitted to the Guard with all the privileges of the Old Guard, had already undergone various changes by subsequent decrees and the details of its formation were still not positively known. The pay for a lieutenant-colonel is 500 francs instead of the 333 francs for an orderly officer. But this new posting also carries with it new expenses.

"It is necessary, first, to order from the tailors a red uniform of chasseurs cut, royal blue collar and trimmings, a braided blue hussar-style waistcoat,

gold epaulettes and aiguillettes, and a round shako. The saddler will provide a tigerskin shabraque edged with gold lace, and yellow-trimmed bridles.

"The second uniform will have a red Uhlan jacket with sky blue lapels, and trousers of the same colour worn over boots. It was the officers who had been asking for this blue colour, less expensive than the red and more mud-proof. A golden sash in the Prussian fashion will complete this uniform, along with a square cap bearing a plate showing an eagle on a sunburst, an 'esprit' [lion's mask boss with hook for chin chains] for the senior officers, and finally a cartridge pouch and a belt laced with gold."

The well-connected young de Watteville borrowed the necessary money against his income as a Baron of the Empire, which amounted to 4,000 francs, and against an annuity of a thousand francs which he had left untouched and of which a whole year was due to him.

The Emperor, aware of his officers' financial problems, granted them the pay scale of the Polish Lancers of the Guard, and an advance payment of 584 francs per man. This was still insufficient, however, and General Colbert asked for grants of 1,000 to 1,200 francs for each of his officers to compensate them for the expense of the three changes of uniform in succession. (Napoleon agreed to this request in August 1811.)

The Regiment's remounts came from the regions of the Orne, Calvados, the Manche and the Ardennes. Measuring 1.46m to 1.50m (between 14 and 14.75 hands), they cost 460 francs each. Draught horses for the regimental transport cost 600 francs each - an excessive price, but approved by Commissioner of War Dufour. The depot which had remained in Holland under the command of Major van Hasselt was now brought up to Versailles, leaving Deventer on 8 April 1811 and arriving on 3 May. Once he had installed his command van Hasselt obtained leave in August to go and fetch his wife and five children. Versailles was to be not merely a barracks, but the new home town of the Dutch officers and their families.

Garrison life
From this new garrison Albert de Watteville would write:
"If Versailles were not such a horribly sad place I would feel very comfortable here. Although there are a lot of people here it is not very agreeable for the officers. Everyone here affects the style of the Faubourg St Germain of about eight years ago, and casts disapproving eyes upon anything to do with the new regime. And there can be no provincial town in France which is more given to small-minded gossip and criticism. One would believe oneself a hundred leagues from Paris."

De Watteville's lodgings cost him 80 francs; he took his meals in a *pension* together with the other chefs d'escadron and captains - dinner cost him another 80 francs a month.

The reaction of Albert de Watteville - born into the nobility of the city of Berne, a former aide to a marshal and orderly officer

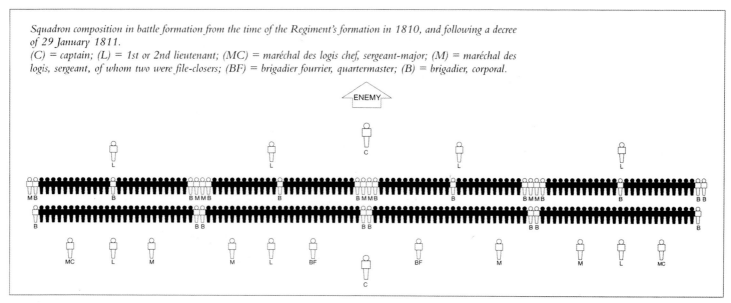

Squadron composition in battle formation from the time of the Regiment's formation in 1810, and following a decree of 29 January 1811.
(C) = captain; (L) = 1st or 2nd lieutenant; (MC) = maréchal des logis chef, sergeant-major; (M) = maréchal des logis, sergeant, of whom two were file-closers; (BF) = brigadier fourrier, quartermaster; (B) = brigadier, corporal.

to Napoleon himself – was perhaps not entirely typical, and most of the Dutch officers seem to have taken to Versailles happily enough. In the early months they spent a lot of time visiting Paris and enjoying its historic monuments, its theatres and other places of amusement. Before long, however, they were increasingly accepted by what passed for society in Versailles, and they did not take long to establish their own networks of social relationships.

Nevertheless, some of the officers' wives complained about the prices in the local shops, and claimed that when they were accompanied by their husbands prices were systematically raised at the sight of the uniform. They also seem to have regarded French servants with suspicion. The officers' children attended the local school, but fortunately were in no danger of forgetting their mother tongue; the language of Vondel was as much spoken in Versailles as that of Molière.

The families of Hoevenaar, van Hasselt, Dubois and other Dutch officers soon created their own small personal circles. Versailles was the capital of the Department of Seine-et-Oise; and luckily for the newcomers the Prefect was none other than the Prince of Gavre, Belgian by birth and belonging to one of the most prominent noble families of the Netherlands. The officers of the Lancers found a good friend in the Prince, who paid them a lot of attention; Dumonceau, van Omphal and Chomel saw him frequently on social occasions. As for de Watteville – the regimental dandy, with his whiskers cut in the latest fashion and his little waxed moustache – he almost became a member of the family. The discovery of a fairly remote blood connection earned him the affectionate nicknames "Cousin Lancer", "Cousin Colonel" or "Little Cousin", and the chef d'escadron visited his new friends almost every day. (One is tempted to wonder if his friendly attention was attracted more by the Prefect or by his wife....)

During wintertime the Lancers were on duty in Paris every second week, taking part in the great Sunday parades and in the other ceremonies which were popular at this period. The Guard troops assembled at 11a.m. on the Place de la Concorde. At about noon General Colbert, who resided in Paris, joined his regiment and led them towards the outer area of the Carrousel. Once the parade was over they returned to Versailles at around 7p.m. or 8p.m. in the evening.

In barracks the day started for the regimental duty officer at 2a.m., inspecting the four barracks located at different points around the town to ensure that all officers were present and ready to supervise their men's fatigues and exercises. Drill exercises lasted for four hours, those on foot for two hours. The officers would return at about 10a.m. having worked up a considerable appetite. After taking refreshment they reported to the colonel, whose quarters were about a mile and a half away in the Avenue de St Cloud. Immediately thereafter they went on parade, which occupied from 11a.m. to noon; this was followed by a rollcall, and then the men were set to grooming their horses. This was followed by the officers' *"promenade des casernes"* – a tour of inspection of the four separate barracks, which lasted until 3p.m.; and the officers' dinner was served half an hour later. At 6p.m., in warm weather and when there was no rain, the horses were taken out in order to air the stables and to change their litter. "Retreat" was sounded at 9p.m., and fifteen minutes later the final rollcall of the day was held.

The ceremonial duties which punctuated the daily routine

A trooper of the 2nd Light Horse Lancers in full dress, by Louis F.Lejeune (1775-1848). The crown of the czapska lancer cap is scarlet, the sunburst plate of brass alloy with a brass crowned N on a silver ground; the chinstrap rosettes, brass; the skull, black leather with a yellow lace band, the peak black leather with brass binding, the plume white. The kurtka lancer jacket and the trousers are scarlet; the facings, stripes and piping are dark blue; the cap cords and aiguillette are yellow, and all metal is brass alloy. The belt, slings and sword knot are white leather; the Chasseur sabre and scabbard have brass furniture. (Collection of Belgian Royal Army Museum, Brussels)

throughout the month alternated with field exercises on the training ground called "du Grand Maître". One of the instructors was Lieutenant Fallot, who was detached with eight regimental NCOs to the Polish Lancers at Chantilly on 27 November 1810 to learn the handling of the lance. Although Poland had a lancer tradition the Polish Light Horse of the Guard had only received the weapon in 1809 after the battle of Wagram.

In recent years Napoleon had been unpleasantly impressed by the effectiveness of this weapon - then a novelty in Western Europe - in the hands of Austrian and Russian Uhlans and Cossacks, and 1811 would see his final decision to form a new lancer branch within the French cavalry. That May, at Albuera in Spain, Polish lancers of the Vistula Legion in French service took part in one of the most bloodily successful cavalry charges of the Napoleonic Wars: together with the French 2nd Hussars they rode right over a British infantry brigade, caught unprepared in a rainstorm. The following month Napoleon signed a decree transforming six Dragoon regiments into Lancers, and three more would follow.

Fallot's party spent six weeks at Chantilly learning this demanding new skill. The safe and effective handling of the heavy wooden lance - 2.26m long with a 21cm iron head - took a great deal of practice, the rudiments being taught on foot for some time before any attempt was made to master mounted drill. The lancer in full field equipment also carried a Chasseur-style sabre dangling from the left side of his waist belt; and during the course of 1811-12 the Regiment received an issue of carbines - the An XIII (1803-04) flintlock light cavalry musketoon - which were carried hanging at the right hip clipped to a crossbelt, with a cartridge pouch in the small of the back. Thus encumbered, it took a thoroughly trained trooper to handle the lance in action; to a poor horseman it was an impediment, even a danger, as a mistake could

tip or knock a man out of the saddle all too easily. That said, a competent lancer enjoyed great tactical advantages in battle. His long reach allowed him to engage sabre-armed cavalry with confidence, and his weapon was absolutely deadly to infantry in open order - indeed, with courage and luck he could even shake the cohesion of infantry packed into defensive formation.

★　　★　　★

Not long after the birth of Napoleon's longed-for heir, the King of Rome, in March 1811, a detachment of the Regiment received orders to set out for Tours, capital of the Indre-et-Loire department; Dumonceau commanded the party, in which van Omphal also served. At Tours they joined elements of the 26th Mounted Chasseurs, 113th Line Infantry and Departmental Gendarmes to form the 4th Mobile Column under the orders of General Colbert. Their mission was to comb the 22nd Military Division for men evading conscription and for deserters from the Belle-Île regiment. The lancers left Versailles on 26 March and reached Tours on 2 April. After six weeks in the Indre-et-Loire they moved on into the department of Maine-et-Loire; later the column marched via Laval, capital of Mayenne, into the department of Sarthe, where its inglorious "campaign" ended in the 12th Military Division in early August. Another part of the Regiment was meanwhile fulfilling a more attractive function, escorting the Emperor on his progress to Cherbourg and Caen during May and June.

Meanwhile the regimental Aministrative Council - formed by Coti, de Watteville, Post, Dubois and Sergeant-Major Veldhuys - were ordering the new uniforms; further ceremonial duties loomed, and particularly the Emperor's birthday parade in mid-August. The order included 95 lancer caps for NCOs and trumpeters at a price of 40 francs each; 874 for corporals and lancers, at 32 francs; five hats for the specialist craftsmen (maîtres-ouvriers), one trumpeter's bearskin at 51 francs, lancer cap cases, lance pennons - all these from M.Chardon, master hatter, with cap cords, aiguillettes, etc. ordered from M.Hebert.

Messieurs Muraines and Lesage received the order for 3,235 meters of scarlet cloth in three qualities, 7,150 meters of royal blue cloth in three qualities, yellow, black and iron-grey cloth. M.Destort junior was to provide 200 pairs of socks, drawers of Flanders linen and linen cloths; a healthy order for 10,974 dozen buttons and 978 copper belt buckles went to the premises of M.Mionnet. A total of 978 pairs of enlisted men's boots were ordered at 19 francs the pair, and 63 pairs for officers at 22.50 francs, from M.Eysenbach; 970 pairs of iron spurs and 57 pairs in copper at 2.50 francs a pair from M.Stratemacker, master armourer; M.Gérel was to provide 962 pairs of buckskin gauntlets and 38 pairs of buckskin wrist-length gloves all at 3.50 francs a pair.

No less than 1,041 black calfskins at 7.75 francs each were to be supplied by M.Fossey. Saddles, bridles, sword belts, shoulder belt pouches, etc., were ordered from M.Wilmotte, master saddler, and 400 horse-cloths at 11.90 francs each. Later six baggage wagons with all harness and saddles would also be ordered.

By a decree of 22 June the Emperor appointed and promoted more officers: de la Fargue was named captain adjutant-major and Jean Joseph Courbe was transferred from the 6th Hussars with that rank, Dumonceau and Sterke were named captains, and de Stuers and Heshusius lieutenant adjutant-majors.

On the 30th the Regiment was presented with an Eagle

The nephew of General Edouard Colbert in the uniform of a junior officer of the Red Lancers, by Mademoiselle Chaudet. The boy Napoléon Auguste, born in 1805, was the son of Edouard's brother General Auguste Colbert, killed in Spain on 3 January 1809. Note that senior officers wore fringed gold epaulettes on both shoulders, junior officers a single epaulette on the left, and all officers a gold aiguillette on the right; rankers wore a yellow epaulette with dark blue crescent on the right and a yellow aiguillette on the left. (Château d'Ainay-le-Vieil, France)

A Red Lancer with his horse, by Géricault. Notwithstanding artistic licence, it is a fact that the horses originally provided as remounts for the Regiment were too small for the tall Dutch troopers, and when the disproportion was noticed these had to be replaced with taller mounts. The regulation size for a lancer's mount was 14 to 14.2 hands. (Photo © Musée de l'Armée, Paris)

Three trumpeters of the Red Lancers in full dress, by Géricault. This uniform was white faced with scarlet and trimmed with gold braid; there was a long tradition of dressing cavalry trumpeters in expensive and highly visible uniforms. (Photo © Musée de l'Armée, Paris)

standard - cast in bronze in handsome imitation of the eagles of Imperial Rome, with a 60cm-square flag in national colours bearing gold inscriptions. (Originally each squadron of a cavalry regiment had carried one, but by 1811 a single Eagle was entrusted to the 1st Squadron for campaign service.) As July passed the officers and NCOs ran their subordinates ragged; the Regiment had to be in perfect order for the Emperor's birthday parade on 15 August.

On 29 July Napoleon wrote to Grand Marshal Duroc from St Cloud:

"I wish you to bring together the Generals and Colonels of the Guard to lay down the following rules:

(1) On and after 1 July this year no more vélites will be admitted to the Chasseurs, Grenadiers and Dragoons of the Guard. Those who have been admitted before 1 July will be kept.

(2) All cavalry vélites will form part of the 2nd Light Horse of the Guard, in order that this regiment shall be brought up to strength by vélites.

(3) The admission fee they have to pay is to be no more than 200 francs. They will receive pay and allowances such that they will cost no more than in the Regiments of the Line, discounting their admission fees.

(4) The positions of officers and NCOs will be filled by officers and NCOs of the Guard."

On 4 August 1811, 80 lancers led by Chef d'escadron Coti and under the orders of Royen, van der Meulen, Charles Mascheck, van Zuylen van Nyevelt, Frank, and Leutner accompanied by Assistant Surgeon Stutterheim delivered a train of horses to the 13th Cuirassiers at Niort, where they arrived on 16 August. In their absence Captain Dumonceau's detachment with the 4th Mobile Column hurried back from their hunt for draft-dodgers, returning to Versailles in time to satisfy General Colbert's

request that they be re-equipped before 15 August. On that day most of the Regiment appeared resplendent in the new lancer uniform at Napoleon's birthday parade, to the admiration of the people of Paris. The Red Lancers even had a kettledrummer.

The Imperial visit to Holland

Shortly afterwards each Guard regiment was ordered to provide two squadrons to escort the Emperor on a progress through the new Belgian and Dutch departments in September, October and November 1811. The Regiment contributed men at a rate of 25 to 30 from each company to form its two squadrons. General Colbert appointed Chef d'escadron de Watteville as detachment commander; also taking part would be Captains de la Fargue, Post, Calkoen and Sterke; Lieutenants Fallot, de Stuers, Vermaesen, Böcher, van Heiden and Chomel; 2nd Lieutenants Weerts ten Brink, de Bellefroid, Brepoels, van Omphal and J.C.Spies (the youngest of three brothers who would serve with the Regiment), as well as Surgeon-Major Mergell assisted by his deputy Gerhard Stutterheim.

During the first days of September 250 to 300 of the Regiment's horses were sent to Brussels and Antwerp where they stayed for a few days. The escorts which would follow the Emperor and Empress were organised from those cities - detachments each of one officer and 25 lancers dispersed among relay stations all along the route. Van Omphal, who commanded one of the first escorts, was to await the Empress at Oosterhout. It was then discovered, however, that the Old Meuse could not be crossed at Raamsdonck for lack of the number of boats needed to build a bridge there; he was sent to Heusden and escorted the Empress, accompanied by the Duchess of Montebello, to

Study of a Red Lancer, by Géricault. (Photo © Musée de l'Armée, Paris)

Gorkum. The next day he marched his detachment to Utrecht to join the other troops of his Regiment. Another detachment under the orders of Captain Calkoen waited from 22 September at Breskens - "one of the ugliest places in the world", according to a letter to his father. On the 23rd he passed the Emperor through on his way to Flushing.

By 26 September the main body of the detachment had reached Utrecht, a garrison town of about 13,500 men. There, as at every relay station, de Watteville was snowed under by paperwork as he tried to keep up to date with the required accounts and reports. He wrote home to Switzerland about the countryside in which he found himself:

"Although it is one of the most beautiful towns in Holland, I find it very dull. The country is very odd, but monotonous: nothing but canals, dikes, and pretty, tidy villages which all look the same. The country houses are charming, but all alike, as are their gardens. The houses are low and built like houses of cards: an outer tidiness which becomes mesmerising, and finally almost unbearable. Given this, the filthiness of the Dutch as to their own persons is inexplicable. All around is flat country, far inferior to any other I have ever seen.

"As to the cooking, it bears a close resemblance to ours but vegetables are not cooked enough. Wine is very expensive, always adulterated and consequently unwholesome. Bread and cakes are badly baked; but the potatoes are excellent, and we almost live on them. I am convinced that this way of life and feeding themselves contributes as much as the climate to the fevers which prevail in this region. One is forced to admire its industry, and one wonders how - since it is constantly threatened by the waters - it is carried on. The steadiness with which they constantly win and re-win their land from the sea, the confidence with which they rebuild

their homes again and again, seems inexplicable. It is a country I am delighted to have seen, but in which I would never wish to live."

In time the order came to take the road for Amsterdam, third city of the Empire. On 9 October Napoleon and Marie-Louise made a processional entrance; all the regiments of the Guard were represented there by detachments, as well as several units of the Line. The festivities would cost the town one and a half million francs.

Forty trumpeters of the Red Lancers led the way under the command of Lieutenant de Stuers, followed in order by a mounted detachment of the Guards of Honour of Amsterdam; a detachment of Red Lancers under General Colbert; a detachment of Polish Lancers; five coaches, the fourth being that of the Empress, drawn by eight horses and accompanied by eight pages; the Master of the Horse and his officers; 25 Mounted Grenadiers of the Guard; the 4th, 6th and 14th Cuirassiers under the orders of General Baron de Berckheim; a detachment of the Foot Guards of Honour of Amsterdam; the Emperor's orderly officers; the Emperor's aides-de-camp; the Emperor; Roustam, the Emperor's personal Mameluke attendant; the marshals, generals and staff officers, four by four; a detachment of Mounted Grenadiers of the Guard; a detachment of Dragoons of the Guard; and the 7th Cuirassiers.

(Among the cavalry of the Guard of Honour of Amsterdam Captain Abraham Calkoen met his brother Piet, who shortly afterwards gave way to his elder brother's urging and became a vélite of the Regiment.)

In Amsterdam three weeks passed in a succession of Imperial inspections and festivities. Although they were proud to be riding close to the Emperor in the old capital of their native country the Lancers were not used to acting as an escort, which takes practice for both horse and man to achieve smoothly when on public show; and on 23 October Napoleon asked Marshal Bessières to send him some 50 Mounted Chasseurs of the Guard, who had long experience of such duties.

The return leg of the Imperial tour was now at hand, and Lieutenant van Omphal was selected to await the Emperor in Leiden with a train of horses from the Imperial stables. During the night he received orders to set out with the horses to a stipulated place to await the Emperor's arrival. At 10a.m. the next morning Napoleon arrived at the rendezvous, mounting a horse to gallop towards Rijnsburg to visit the sluices of Katwijk. After this visit the party had breakfast on the beach before heading back to Leiden. A short distance from the town a coach was waiting to carry the Emperor for the remainder of the journey. The Emperor's convoy halted at Rapenburg at the house of one Markus, where the Empress was already staying; it was a short visit, and after granting a few audiences the Emperor took the road for The Hague. For lack of any other escort, van Omphal's detachment was compelled to accompany the Imperial party on their way; he and his men were exhausted, and their horses worn out, by the time he had the pleasure of recognising a detachment of his own Regiment led by Captain Jan Post waiting at Huis ten Deyl. Thereafter van Omphal could go on in shorter stages and spare the horses.

Napoleon and Marie-Louise entered The Hague under escort by the Mounted Guards of Honour of the town commanded by van Bijlandt, and detachments of various regiments of the Imperial Guard, all under the orders of General Colbert. The population received the sovereigns with a lack of enthusiasm so coldly noticeable that Prefect de Stassart felt distinctly uncomfortable. The Emperor visited the coastal quarter of Scheveningen and received local dignitaries; not wishing to waste time, he left the next day without attending the ball which had been arranged in his honour, which made an unfortunate impression on the authorities and the townspeople.

Rotterdam was the next scheduled halt; and here Napoleon cut his visit from three days to one. Once more it was van Omphal who had to hold himself in readiness to escort their Majesties, this time from Montfoort back to Utrecht. After that march the detachments which had been escorting the Emperor and Empress from Amsterdam to The Hague received orders to make their way to Brussels where they would join up with the other troops of the Guard for the return to Versailles. Some officers obtained leave to visit their families in Holland; de Stuers was able to see his mother again, and van Omphal received permission to absent himself for two weeks to visit his father, the Sub-Prefect of Deventer. On 10 November the other detachments - from Nijmegen, Cleves, Wesel, Achen and Liège - assembled at Namur. From there they made their way back via Dinant, Mézières, Soissons, Louvres and St Dizier to Versailles.

Lieutenant van Omphal returned to Versailles on 20 November to discover that he had been placed under the orders of Captain van Balveren as an instructor to the new vélites. The winter routine resumed, with major parades at the Tuileries every second Sunday, although gossip in the messes was enlivened by rumours of active service before too long. Some familiar faces had disappeared during van Omphal's absence: Lieutenants Charles Maschek and Michel Manheim had been promoted to captaincies in the 20th and 22nd Mounted Chasseurs respectively - their pleasure no doubt modified by the thought of purchasing yet more new uniforms. In November one of the assistant adjutants, Lieutenant Henri Royen, was sent to Hamburg to instruct the newly created 9th Lancers of the Line in the handling of the lance. Although Dutch born and bred, he settled in so happily among the officers of this German regiment (recently formed from the 30th Mounted Chasseurs) that he applied for a permanent transfer. His application was turned down; and on his return to the Regiment the following spring in Germany he was cold-shouldered by his brother officers for what they considered a slur on the Red Lancers and the Guard itself.

The Regiment still needed a few men and horses. On 21 December 1811 Napoleon wrote to Marshal Bessières:

"My Cousin, I see that thanks to your efforts the cavalry strength of the Guard amounts to 6,450, or 400 men short of establishment. I have decreed that the following regiments shall each provide ten men of the required quality, to wit the 1st, 2nd, 3rd, 4th and 10th Hussars, and the 10th, 13th, 14th, 15th, 22nd, 26th, 27th, 29th and 30th Mounted Chasseurs, totalling 140 men. These men will be taken from the regimental depots, and if enough men of the required quality are not available at the depots then the shortfall will be made up from the combat squadrons in Spain. The twenty Dragoon regiments serving in Spain will each provide ten men, making another 200. The sixteen regiments of Cuirassiers and Carabiniers will each provide six men, making another 96. As for the 60 men needed to complete the 2nd Light Horse, the vélites will provide them. The cavalry of the Guard will thus be complete, that is to say brought up to 6,800 men.

"We are short of 543 horses; I have issued a decree to raise them, to wit: 188 for the Mounted Chasseurs, 65 for the Mamelukes, 176 for the Mounted Grenadiers, 22 for the Élite Gendarmes and 13 for the 2nd Light Horse."

★   ★   ★

For a year and a half the new Dutch corps of the Imperial Guard had been occupied in its formation, quartering and organisation, its clothing and equipment, weapons training, drill and field exercises. Its skills had been practised and displayed during ceremonial parades; but the officers and men had been entrusted only with escort duties, and with scouring the countryside for deserters, during their weeks away from their garrison. As yet the Regiment had been given no opportunity to show their true qualities as soldiers in the arena of war. That was now going to change, and change abruptly. In a year's time the Red Lancers would be unrecognisable.

A miniature of Captain-instructor Walvaren E.J. van Balveren (1784-1865), here in the uniform of an officer of the Dutch Royal Guard. This officer was responsible for the training, among others, of the Regiment's vélites - aspiring officers who paid for a place in the ranks while hoping to be selected for eventual commission. (Photo © Stichting Iconographisch Bureau, The Hague)

Captain Henricus Royen (1788-1859), who served on the regimental staff during the Russian campaign. He is shown in the dark green and orange uniform of an officer of the Dutch 10th Lancers, raised by Colonel Dubois in 1819, of which Royen became the lieutenant-colonel on 16 April 1830. (Photo © Stichting Iconographisch Bureau, The Hague)

CHAPTER II

1812: The Invasion of Russia

The march into Germany

As in the previous year, 1 January 1812 was celebrated with a state reception at the Tuileries. The winter season in Paris was a succession of banquets, concerts, balls and receptions where the great dignitaries of the Empire mingled with the young military men. Although the rumours of a coming campaign were officially denied, to the point that open discussion was forbidden, it was - of course - the major topic of conversation among the regimental officers. They looked forward to the prospect with eager confidence, as if it were to be no more than a six-month hunting party. For those with eyes to see, a succession of events seemed to confirm the rumours of war, denied or not.

On 19 January 1812 two officers of the Red Lancers, Captain van der Meulen and 2nd Lieutenant de Bellefroid, left Versailles for the remount depot at Hanover; they were followed on the 23rd by a cavalry detachment of the Guard consisting of 40 Grenadiers, 95 Dragoons, 91 Chasseurs and 49 Lancers. Over a period of time the Lancers had received an issue of carbines. A few days later, on 27 January, Napoleon wrote asking Bessières: *"The 2nd Light Horse is commanded by General Colbert; I think there is a Dutch major; but who is second major? Can I trust the Dutch major ?"* This question clearly implies that the Guard would play a prominent part in the coming campaign, if the Emperor needed reassurance about the cadres of his new regiments. On 8 February Napoleon wrote again to Bessières - a letter which would change the lives of the Dutch lancers irrevocably:

"...Finally, you will also order the 2nd Light Horse Lancers to leave on the 10th; they will not travel via Paris, and you will trace a route so that this movement may be carried out with as much concealment as possible - they will set out for Brussels. By this means there will be a Guard division in Brussels by 20 February. It will be termed 1st Division of the Guard, and will consist of four regiments with eight battalions forming a Corps of 6,000 men with eight pieces of artillery, cartridges, ambulances and all other necessities. My 2nd Light Horse will also be present...Recommend to General Colbert that he vanishes, saying goodbye to nobody."

The officers of the Regiment received this order the next morning, and the time of departure was set for midnight on the 9th; they were forbidden to pass the news on to their men. Some officers took the chance to pen a few lines to their loved ones - Captain Abraham Calkoen wrote to his father: *"We have just received the order to march, my dear father, and I believe that we will go first to Brussels...."* Piet Calkoen would also be riding in the scarlet column, in the ranks of the vélites; we may wonder whether his elder brother sought him out for a whispered word. If discipline was stronger than blood, then Piet heard of the Regiment's marching orders only at rollcall that evening, along with the rest of the lancers. Naturally, the troopers were not told the itinerary of the march, but Russia had already been mentioned in barracks and tavern gossip as one of the possible destinations.

Vélite Geesteranus was on leave in Paris with two comrades; he returned to his barracks at 10p.m. to find that his brothers-in-arms, formed in companies, had already left. He ran into his barrackroom to clamber into marching dress and snatch up his belongings. At midnight the Regiment formed up on the Avenue St Cloud, and set out through a dark and foggy night for an unknown destination. Latecomers like Vélite Geesteranus had to catch up with their unit on the road.

The wife of Jan van Hasselt, the second ranking Dutch

A ball at the Imperial Court, by F. de Myrbach (1853-post 1900). (Author's collection)

officer, was pregnant; worried by her husband's mood as he set out, she wrote to her sister: *"He was so restless and depressed, I hardly recognised him anymore. There is one stroke of luck, which is that his friend Dubois is also going...between ourselves, the general [Colbert] is not an agreeable man, but haughty and tactless."*

The Regiment had been on a war footing for some time, each company having 125 mounted men and a depot; the sabre squadrons totalled more than 1,000 mounted men. A short time before the marching orders came through General Colbert had ordered a rigorous inspection of his men drawn up in marching dress on the Grand-Maître exercise ground, though even its wide extent could hardly hold them. The Regiment's officer corps was then as follows:

Regimental Staff
General of Brigade Colbert, Colonel commanding
Colonel-Majors Dubois & van Hasselt
Chefs d'escadron de Tiecken, Coti & de Watteville
Captain Adjutant-Majors Courbe & de la Fargue (the latter acting as paymaster)

Lieutenant Sub-Adjutant-Majors Fallot, de Stuers (responsible for quartering throughout the march to the Niemen), Heshusius and Royen (the first and last named would join the regiment later in Germany)

2nd Lieutenant Verhaegen, standard bearer (the Eagle itself would be left in Paris)

Surgeon-Major Mergell & Assistant Surgeon-Major Hennige

1st Squadron:

1st Company	Captain van der Meulen
	1st Lieutenant Böcher
	2nd Lieutenants Weerts ten Brink & Geubels
5th Company	Captain Sterke
	1st Lieutenant Vermaesen
	2nd Lieutenants van Doorn & van der Linden

2nd Squadron:

2nd Company	Captain Post
	1st Lieutenant Chomel
	2nd Lieutenants Frank & J.W.Spies
6th Company	Captain Dumonceau
	1st Lieutenant Vacant
	2nd Lieutenants de Wacker van Son & P.A.Ziegler

3rd Squadron:

3rd Company	Captain Calkoen
	1st Lieutenant van Zuylen van Nyevelt
	2nd Lieutenants Brepoels & J.C.Spies
7th Company	Captain Tulleken
	1st Lieutenant van Heiden
	2nd Lieutenants Das & de Bellefroid

4th Squadron:

4th Company	Captain Schneither
	1st Lieutenant van Haersolte
	2nd Lieutenants van Wijchel & van Omphal
8th Company	Captain van Balveren (who asked permission to follow the Regiment as he had to remain at Versailles)
	1st Lieutenant le Sueur
	2nd Lieutenants Leutner & Delaisement

Temporarily remaining at the depot would be: Chef d'escadron Hoevenaar, Captain Werner, Captain Quartermaster Dufour, Lieutenants Manheim, Willich, Bredenbach, Doyen, de Jongh, and Assistant Surgeon-Major Stutterheim; these were later joined by the newly arrived Chef d'escadron de Verdière.

Chef d'escadron de Watteville was also obliged, most unwillingly, to remain at the depot. He was in the grip of a fever which had been gradually undermining his health for months, and wrote in frustration to his parents: *"Anyone who does not take part in a campaign like this will be forgotten."* He pressed ahead with arrangements to rejoin his comrades; but General Colbert appointed him as commander of the depot, giving him to believe that this was simply because he was the most junior of the chefs d'escadron. Ill and depressed, he wrote:

"Although only temporary, this appointment caused me such resentment that I have suffered many worries and annoyances, and my fever returned three days later. Thought had not been taken beforehand to forming the depot; I found it without organization or any means to carry out the ambitious tasks demanded. With the greatest difficulty I have obtained two French NCOs for the company administration, and after much hard work I have got the job under control; everything is now going well. Can you see me in charge of administration, acting as a major? I ask you - is this my kind of work? Do I love paperwork so much? I am worn out with it.

"I hope to have two or three hundred horses leaving within six weeks. If only my colleague would arrive so that I could rejoin my regiment! If he does not come soon they will be too far away and the journey will be too expensive. My own horses have followed the regiment with my new servants. They are under the supervision of a captain and an old lancer, a

Bust of a Lancer of the Imperial Guard, 1812, by Maurice Orange (1868-1916); Salon of 1909. (Collection Alain Chappet)

decent man who always stays close to them. I will wait and buy some other horses in Germany if I can find any suitable ones."

The Princesse de Gavre, wife of the Prefect under whose roof he had spent so many happy days, realised that she could not keep the dashing young officer at Versailles; so she commissioned a portrait of him from the painter van Dorne, so as to have at least a remembrance of him when he was gone. She wanted to keep a copy of it for herself and would send the original to de Watteville's parents. He wrote to them: *"My portrait has been a success, contrary to all expectations. Everyone pays me compliments about it. Van Dorne finished it within two days. As I needed my uniforms he painted them in one day, more especially as it was not always possible to send them to Paris and as I could not go myself whenever I wished. I spent a whole day at his studio with a raging fever."*

From Versailles the Regiment rode down past Sèvres to the bridge of St Cloud and made a first halt on the outskirts of the Bois de Boulogne, then a second at daybreak before St Denis. The infantry regiments of the Young Guard - the 5th and 6th Tirailleurs and Voltigeurs - were marching with them but following a slightly different route. These formed the 1st Infantry Division of the Guard under the orders of General of Division Delaborde and of General Lanusse, Adjutant-General of the Guard and detachment commander. Also marching with them were 150 Mounted Chasseurs, the 4th Artillery Company with eight guns, ammunition caissons, two commissaries, surgeons and ambulances.

On the afternoon of 10 February they halted at Luzarches; the next morning they left for Clermont where they were to spend the night. Passing through Chantilly at daybreak they rode close to the stables of their brothers-in-arm, the 1st Light Horse Lancers of the Guard; the surprised Poles shouted out to ask them the reason for this manoeuvre, but no one could satisfy their curiosity. At Creil they were joined by General Colbert - they had left Versailles under the orders of Colonel-Major Dubois. Bringing his captains together to address them, the general announced that he was taking back direct command of the corps and explained his requirements concerning the daily assemblies before departure, the marching order and all other normal details.

Taking sideroads, the Lancers passed by Gournay-sur-Aronde, Roye and Péronne; on the 15th they passed the night at Cambrai, leaving very early the next day for Valenciennes. On the 17th they reached Condé-sur-l'Escaut where Dumonceau's company was quartered at Anzin. The march continued via Ath and Enghien, and the Regiment reached Brussels on 21 February; surrounded by a huge crowd, they entered the city by the Porte d'Anderlecht. For the next ten days they stayed in Brussels; garrison discipline was observed, and Dumonceau took his turn on military police duties. Necessary repairs were made, and sabres and lances were already being sharpened. Many of the horses were exhausted; Vélite Geesteranus had to exchange his sick mount, but the replacement was itself a worn-out nag which did not look as if it would make old bones.

On a bitterly cold morning shortly before marching orders were given General Colbert, who was staying at the Hotel d'Angleterre, made a close inspection of the Regiment on the Rue Royale facing the park. The sabre squadrons recorded present 42 officers and 668 lancers, with 803 horses; three lancers were missing. On 1 March the Regiment's strength was, in Brussels, 43 officers and 723 lancers with 811 horses; at the Versailles depot, ten officers and 197 lancers with 306 horses; and 26 lancers were listed missing.

From Brussels Captain Calkoen wrote to his father: *"First they talked of a congress at Erfurt; then, it was to be a trip to Rome..."*. By 2 March he was able to add, *"We are leaving tomorrow for Magdeburg via Maastricht and Wesel."* Departure was originally planned for the 5th, but was brought forward two days at the last minute.

On 3 March, under a cold rain, the Regiment rode to Leuven. Marching via Sint-Truiden they reached Tongeren on the 5th. This was the home town of Chef d'escadron de Tiecken, who took his friend Jan Post to lodge at his father's house; Captain Dumonceau and his lieutenants were accommodated at the castle of the Count de Renesse. The next morning Dumonceau and his company took a wrong turn on their way to the assembly area, and only managed to catch up with the Regiment at the gates of Maastricht after a wretched day on muddy roads under flurries of wet snow. They were the very last to arrive, and could not get into their assigned place before the Regiment formed up on Vrijthof Square for the captains to receive their orders as usual. Dumonceau was reprimanded for having lost his way; that evening the entire Regiment had to attend a general rollcall on the town hall square, watched by a large crowd of civilians.

As they passed through Holland some officers took the fleeting opportunities which offered to see their families. Lieutenant van Omphal, accompanied by Colonel-Major van Hasselt, visited his father; it would be their last meeting - the old baron would die on 5 April 1813. After a stay of two or three days they rejoined the Regiment at Osnabrück. On the 7th the Lancers were at Susteren, the next day at Roermond. On the 10th Napoleon wrote to Bessières on the subject of Guard regiments taking their Eagle standards on campaign: *"The Chasseurs will have only one Eagle; the Grenadiers will have only one Eagle, which must always be carried by the 1st Old Guard Regiment of each arm; the Horse Grenadiers will have only one Eagle; the Dragoons, one Eagle; the Mounted Chasseurs, one Eagle; the Light Horse regiments will have no Eagles."*

By 10 March the Regiment's sabre squadrons in the field numbered 41 officers with 119 horses, and 649 lancers with 662 horses. One horse had died at Tongeren; nine lancers had been sent to hospital. That day, in severe cold and lashed by icy winds, they arrived at Venlo, where Jan Post lodged with a parish priest at Beringen. The march continued via Gelderen, Wesel, Dorsten, Dulmen and Munster, where they arrived on 15 March; again,

HENRI-FRANÇOIS DELABORDE

COMTE DE L'EMPIRE

GÉNÉRAL DE DIVISION, GRAND-OFFICIER DE LA LÉGION D'HONNE

Né le 21 Décembre 1764, à Dijon, Dép' de la Côte-d'Or

à Paris, chez l'Auteur, rue de Touraine, No 5, Faub. St-Germain

(Collection du Colonel Sadi-Carnot)

General of Division Henri François Delaborde (1764-1833), Count of the Empire, Grand Officer of the Legion of Honour. On 8 February 1812 he was ordered to Brussels to take command of the 1st Division of the Imperial Guard and to get it on the march towards an unknown destination. (La Sabretache)

some officers had been able to avail themselves of overnight hospitality offered by local aristocrats. The cold, wet roads stretched on across the winter landscape, with no known end; the 17th and 18th were spent at Osnabrück, the night of the 19th at Oldendorf and the 20th at Minden.

Vélite Geesteranus was not happy with his horse. The remount he had been given in Brussels was in no fit state for this sort of service, and he fell from the saddle on three occasions. Eventually he had to abandon it at Minden, and marched on foot until he got another horse at Magdeburg. In a letter to his sister he wrote that they had weapon inspections every day; we may presume that this was to foil any troopers who planned to "lose" their unwieldy lances along the road. From repeated references in his letters to his wife, Captain Adjutant-Major de la Fargue was missing his children badly.

On 21 March the column reached Stadhagen, and Hanover the next day. There they met up again with the troopers who had been sent on to Hanover the winter before; each of these men had been provided with two excellent horses by the good offices of General Bourcier, director of the general remount depot. They were the envy of the rest of the Regiment, who halted at Brunswick on 24-26 March to try to spare their own tired mounts.

After six weeks on the march many of the horses were in bad condition. Every company had horses injured by the pressure of the saddle or equipment, and particularly by the combined weight of the lance and carbine, both carried on the right side of the horse. The weight of the lance bore down on the stirrup, where its lower end fitted into a small "bucket"; carried on the march slanting back from a small sling around the rider's arm, it was also liable to cause chafing. They tried to solve the problem at first by moving the lance from the right to the left side. It is also mentioned that the carbine was ordered worn hanging from the swivel hook of the shoulder belt, as it would be on outpost duty in the field; this suggests that it was previously carried slung to the saddle when on the march. It was no real solution, in any case, since the rider more or less buckled under the weight of his arms, which in turn caused other injuries.

*   *   *

Back in Paris, the Emperor decided to reinforce the units of his Guard including the Red Lancers. A 5th Squadron was created by a decree of 11 March 1812; from that date the rank and file of the Regiment were deemed part of the Middle Guard, while the officers retained their status as members of the Old Guard.

The Elysée, 11 March 1812
Napoleon, Emperor of the French, King of Italy, Protector of the Confederation of the Rhine, Mediator of the Swiss Confederation. We have decreed and we decree the following:
Article 1
A fifth squadron of two companies will be formed within the 2nd Light Horse Lancers of the Guard.
Article 2
This fifth squadron will have the same organisation as the first four squadrons.
Article 3
The 1st, 2nd, 3rd, 4th and 5th Light Horse [Lancers]; 1st, 2nd, 3rd, 4th and 10th Hussars; 5th, 10th, 13th, 14th, 15th, 21st, 22nd, 26th, 29th and 31st Chasseurs; and 4th, 5th, 6th, 11th, 15th, 16th, 17th, 18th, 21st, 22nd, 24th, 25th, 26th and 27th Dragoons, are each to provide fifteen men for the recruitment of the above-mentioned 2nd Light Horse Lancers of our Guard. These men must have completed between two and four years of service, and will be selected from among the best remaining at the depots in France.

The results were not very convincing; with great difficulty, 431 men of the required 510 were scraped together. The remainder were taken from the former Dutch Hussars still serving in Spain. A nominal roll dated at Versailles on 8 April 1812 lists the following officers, who were still in Spain, as admitted to the 2nd Light Horse Lancers:

van Merlen	Colonel	supernumerary officer
Timmerman	Captain	9th Company
Macare	Captain	10th Company
Ziegler A.J.	Lieutenant	9th Company
le Sueur	Lieutenant	10th Company
Hannemann	Lieutenant	supernumerary officer
Fischer	2nd Lieut	9th Company
Vanderbruggen	2nd Lieut	10th Company
Doyen	2nd Lieut	9th Company
Duranti	2nd Lieut	10th Company

Chef d'escadron de Watteville had been ordered to Caen on detached duty from 25 March; his orders were swiftly changed, and he was entrusted with organising the new 5th Squadron. *"We are going to be stronger than the Guard!"*, he exclaimed proudly.

In order to dress and equip the newcomers the regimental Administrative Council, under de Watteville's chairmanship, ordered on 21 March: 450 lancer caps, of which 27 for NCOs, 12 for trumpeters and the rest for troopers; 450 lance pennons, 450 pairs of gauntlets, boots and spurs, with the necessary buttons, aiguillettes, epaulettes, lace, and so on.

Even though the Emperor had confided the administration

and accounts of the Regiment to French officers using the French system, the inspectors were unable to verify the books turned over to them, since they were written in Dutch. Marshal Bessières wrote on 18 March to Minister of War Clarke:

"...Sub-inspector Lasalle has advised the depot commander of the 2nd Light Horse Lancers of the Imperial Guard that he has received an order from Your Excellency to proceed with the verification of the Dutch regiment's bookkeeping. General Colbert draws our attention to the departure with the combat squadrons of the persons who, having run the former administration, are the only ones able to provide the necessary information. It is impossible for the verification to be made at Versailles unless Major Dubois, who understands the matter perfectly, could temporarily leave the combat squadrons and return to process it. General Colbert adds that the depot commander and the present quartermaster are unable to give any information about book-keeping according to methods with which they are unacquainted, written in a language they do not understand.

"If Your Excellency wants this verification to be made at the combat squadrons' location he should appoint an inspector for this purpose; but neither of these two solutions is without some disadvantages - the first removes a senior officer whose presence is needed, and a satisfactory result of the second is difficult to guarantee in time of war. I hope Your Excellency will let me know the decision that he will be taking on this matter."

*   *   *

In Germany, the Regiment (from which Charles Dubois would *not* be withdrawn to sort out the accounts...) left Brunswick for Königslutter and Helmstedt on 26 March; they spent from 28 March to 3 April at Magdeburg. From there Abraham Calkoen told his father that his brother Piet *"has marched on foot from Brussels to Magdeburg leading his horse, which was injured by saddle galls...quite a stroll!"* In the same letter he listed all the recent and anticipated stages on the march so that his father could trace his sons' route with pins on the map.

He also mentioned that the Lancers had been forbidden to wear the insignia of the Order of the Union until further notice. This Dutch order had been founded by the former King Louis as an equivalent to the Legion of Honour. On 18 October 1811 Napoleon had founded the Order of the Reunion; members of his brother's order could apply by 1 March 1812 (later extended to 9 March) to Nompère de Champagny, Duke of Cadore and Grand Chancellor of the Order of the Reunion, to be incorporated in it, exchanging their former insignia; after 1 March King Louis' order was not to be displayed. Decrees of 22 and 29 February for the Grand Cross and Commanders and of 7 March for the Knights confirmed these nominations. Those affected within the Regiment were Colonel-Majors Dubois, van Hasselt and van Merlen; Chefs d'escadron de Tiecken, Coti and Hoevenaar; Captains Calkoen and van Balveren, and 2nd Lieutenant van der Linden.

A veterinary depot for sick and injured horses was established at Magdeburg. Despite his heroic efforts to spare it Vélite Piet Calkoen's mount was so exhausted that it was put down, and he was issued a replacement. The weather was abominable, the ground so saturated with rain that it was only with difficulty that a large enough area of passable "going" was found on which to hold regimental rollcalls.

At Magdeburg on 1 April 1812 the sabre squadrons of the Red Lancers numbered 690 men. The total effectives of the Regiment at that date were as follows, the figures expressed as "at Magdeburg/at Versailles":

	Officers	Horses	Troops	Horses	Hospital	Leave
1st Sqn	23/5	78/24	189/54	178/72	7	1
2nd Sqn	7/-	16/21	70/60	162/75	5	-
3rd Sqn	7/1	16/2	178/42	170/65	5	-
4th Sqn	8/5	17/14	178/60	161/75	7	-
5th Sqn	-/-	-/-	-/108	-/-	-	-

Official squadron strengths were:

	Commander	Personnel	Horses
1st Sqn	de Tiecken	279	352
2nd Sqn	Coti	242	255
3rd Sqn	de Watteville	240	253
4th Sqn	Verdière	258	267
5th Sqn	Hoevenaar	108	–
Total		1,127	1,127
Shortfalls were thus		168	259

From the Elbe to the Niemen

In leaving Magdeburg for Mokeren on 3 April the Regiment crossed the Elbe into Prussia. Not surprisingly given that kingdom's recent defeat by France, the inhabitants were noticeably cooler, more reserved and less obliging than those of the lands to the west. On 4 April they spent the night at Ziesar, on the 5th at Brandenburg, the 6th at Nauen and the 7th at Oranienburg.

The King of Prussia, on learning that the Imperial Guard was passing through Potsdam, asked Marshal Oudinot about the Lancers, and for the sake of diplomacy Oudinot asked General Colbert to present some of his officers. Adjutant-major Courbe and Lieutenant van Heiden were assigned to represent the Regiment and were given permission for a 24-hour visit to the castle of Potsdam. The king, accompanied by his two sons, expressed his satisfaction; he admired their uniforms, and congratulated them on belonging to such a distinguished corps. One of his adjutants was instructed to show the two officers round the royal residence.

The next day the Regiment rode through a dry, sandy countryside dotted with lakes; the road led via Zehdenick, Templin, Prenzlau and Löcknitz to Stettin on 12 April. The Lancers rested more than two weeks in this fortified town, where a French garrison was quartered; one company was accomodated in the small village of Damm east of the town, on the right bank of the Oder. During this halt the Regiment's tradesmen busied themselves with all kinds of running repairs, and the officers inspected their troops. On the 16th the Regiment was reviewed by Colonel-Major van Hasselt, and on Sunday 19 April by General Colbert; at that date the unit strength was recorded as 42 officers with 121 horses, and 637 lancers with 645 horses; 20 lancers were in hospital, and three were en route. Orders arrived for the Regiment to leave Stettin on 1 May; the 1st Guard Division was to be in Posen by 10 May. On 22 April Lieutenant Frederick van Heiden of Captain Tulleken's 7th Company wrote from Nemitz, near Stettin:

"Here we are, ten days since arrival, still not knowing where we are going. It is likely that this will soon be decided, however.... We had a pleasant enough march, and here I am, thank God, safe and sound despite cold and fatigue.... I am very comfortable here in the home of a miller, who serves me coffee from morning to night. I am enjoying the good times while they last; as they say in German, Heute Rot, Morgen Tot [rosy today, dead tomorrow]."

"I think that we are going to Warsaw and that the entire Guard will be assembled there", wrote Captain Calkoen on 28 April. *"The number of troops and different nations represented is incredible - Swiss, Corsicans, Croats, Dutch, French, Prussians, Hessians, Bavarians, Austrians, etc... all are coming together."*

"To the Emperor and the ladies" - a pleasing study of a sergeant-major of the Red Lancers in marching order, by Louis Vallet (1856-?). Typical of the appearance of the Regiment on campaign, he has a black oilcloth cover protecting his cap, the plastron lapel buttoned over to his left to show scarlet only, and riding overalls; the rear corners of the yellow-trimmed dark blue shabraque are hooked up to keep the embroidered eagle badge away from thorns and mud. As a senior NCO he is not armed with a lance, only with his sabre and a pistol in a saddle holster under the front of the shabraque. (Collection of the Belgian Army Museum, Brussels)

The Regiment prepared to continue their march towards the Vistula, but there followed an infuriating series of contradictory orders. On 24 April the word came down to postpone the anticipated movement until further notice. A few days later the Lancers set off, with a strength of 45 officers and their 126 horses, and 681 lancers with 668 horses; 38 men were in hospital, and one was still on the road trying to catch up.

Their itinerary was Neumark, Pyritz, Soldin, Landsberg, Friedberg, Driesen, Zirke, Ostrooy, Samter, and finally Posen; but they had not completed the first day's march before the Regiment was ordered to turn back to Stettin.

The Lancers marked time at Greiffenhage, a small country town a few miles from the city, from 1 to 28 May. The time passed pleasantly enough. To entertain their comrades and the villagers the men of Captain Calkoen's 3rd Company put on a comic cabaret, with soldiers playing all the characters including "peasant girls". The show was a huge success, and the amateur actors even discussed repeating the performance at future halts; unfortunately, time would be too short to allow this.

A letter from Marshal Bessières at St Cloud to Colonel van Merlen at Versailles on 22 April appointed him commander of the regimental depot:

"The intention of the Emperor is that you should take command of the depot of the 2nd Light Horse Lancers. Occupy yourself with the arms, the clothing of the men and the harnessing of the horses. It is necessary that every unmounted man at the depot should be ready to leave at short notice. These men must take their carbines and their saddles with them on the vehicles. Concerning the transport of the saddles you will have to apply to the Minister of War Administration; the safest way is to send them by wagon to Hanover, where the horses assigned to these men of the regiment are grouped. Do not waste any time; everyone has to be ready to march as soon as the order is given. Let me know when everyone is ready to leave."

The reinforcements were soon ready to start their journey eastwards, directly to the Regiment or to local depots in Germany. On 1 May a detachment of 200 lancers left St Avold; they were at Saarbrücken on the 2nd, at Homburg on the 3rd, and at Kaiserslautern on the 5th; after a brief rest they moved on, to Winweiler on the 7th and Mainz on the 9th.

On 5 May, another 240 lancers under the command of Captain Timmerman set off from Versailles for Hanover, where they arrived on 6 June. On 26 May a detachment of 25 lancers and 26 horses left Mainz to arrive in Berlin on the 14th, and at Marienwerder on 1 July.

Along all the roads of Europe that spring soldiers, horses, guns and wagons were converging like columns of ants on the staging area of the Grande Armée. Men from every client state of Napoleon's continent, speaking scores of languages and dialects, clothed in every colour imaginable, trudged eastwards in their tens of thousands. Endless convoys of horse-drawn wagons creaked through the mud or the dusty ruts, loaded with every kind of equipment and munitions from cannon balls to bridging pontoons, from shoe nails to shovels, from spare musket flints to officers' private rations. Bone-weary columns of infantry, months on the march, scattered out of the path of the jingling, rumbling artillery trains; herds of remounts grazed in every roadside meadow and poached the ground around every spring and well; and everywhere flustered commissaries, adjutants and aides-de-camp galloped up and down the columns, brandishing handfuls of paperwork at one another as they strove to match reality to staff plans, in an army whose means of communication were little swifter than those of Augustus Caesar.

Chef d'escadron Albert de Watteville, relieved at last of the command of the Red Lancers' depot, greeted the arrival of his comrade Colin de Verdière with delight and rushed to arrange his own departure; at last, on 23 April, came the impatiently awaited order for the 5th Squadron to join the Regiment. After an inspection at the depot Marshal Bessières announced that Chef d'escadron de Verdière would lead the detachment while de

Naïf portrait of an unidentified member of the Red Lancers wearing the cross of the Legion of Honour. While epaulette and aiguillette are depicted on the "non-commissioned shoulders" they are in gold; this, with apparently gold laced, silver furnished pouch and waist belts, suggests an officer. (Photo © Musée Napoléonien d'Art et d'Histoire Militaire, Fontainebleau)

Watteville would have to follow by mail coach. He could not believe his ears:

"Departure day for the squadron arrives. I tell my comrade that I am taking command of it. I arrive at the Military School and announce my arrival to the Marshal, claiming to be the squadron leader. He answers that I should take care of quartering and would receive my orders tonight. I have been waiting for them from nine to eleven, and have heard nothing."

The next day the Emperor himself reviewed the column with great ceremony, and asked the marshal if de Watteville commanded this squadron. The reply was no, that de Verdière would lead the squadron and de Watteville would travel by mail coach. The Swiss officer, deciding to risk everything, went to the palace and took up a position where Napoleon could not fail to notice him.

- *"You are leaving?"*
- *"Sire, I am asking permission to leave."*
- *"So you are at the depot?"*
- *"No, Sire, I am here at the marshal's orders."*
- *"Very well, agreed."*

Bessières eventually instructed de Watteville to leave at the first favourable opportunity, travelling via the remount depot at Hanover with a letter from the marshal to General Bourcier before rejoining his regiment. With his marching orders firmly clasped in his hand at last the delighted de Watteville returned to Versailles - only to fall ill again immediately....

"I am so agitated by all these emotions that I have come down with a new bout of fever - it seems that pleasure can have the same results as

pain. This will not prevent me from leaving. Doctor Bourdois, doctor to the King of Rome, has examined me thoroughly. He has advised me that I can travel, although he does not consider me cured. The remedies have upset my liver, but the doctor assures me that movement and exercise will be of great benefit to me; I will, however, continue to suffer from intermittent fevers until I am able to take the ferruginous waters for six weeks to two months."*

Before leaving de Watteville gave the fond Princesse de Gavre a lock of his hair; she was heartbroken at their parting, believing that he was quite unfit to withstand the hardships of campaigning. Indeed, upon his arrival in Hanover he fell sick again. His business on behalf of Marshal Bessières and General Bourcier compelled him to stay there for more than a week, and during this enforced delay he took the opportunity to try the spa cure recommended by Dr Bourdois. Travelling on via Berlin, Posen and Danzig, he arrived early in June at Outzschopemen some three miles from Insterburg. (The French *lieue*, league, is used in most sources for this text; this was equivalent to 2.76 miles.) There he was overjoyed to hear that the Red Lancers were at Braunsberg, between Elbing and Königsberg.

★   ★   ★

On 20 May the Regiment was ordered to head for Danzig. The sabre squadrons in the field had 45 officers with 126 horses, and 692 lancers with 699 horses; 21 lancers were in hospital (and that one nameless lancer to whom we have grown accustomed was still trying to catch up). The next day, at Marienberg south of Elbing, the orders were changed: to avoid crowded roads and consquent delays each squadron was to take a different route. The major concentration points were to be Pyritz, Friedland, Neu-Stettin, Konitz and Dirschau.

On the night of 4 June a courier brought orders to send several detachments to various points on the Vistula to serve as escorts to the Emperor, who had been at Thorn since 2 June. These parties set off early on the morning of the 5th by forced marches for destinations between Graudentz and Danzig. The rest of the Regiment continued the march towards Elbing, where they remained for a few days to assemble once more. On 10 June Ambraham Calkoen mentioned one of the consequences of their progress north-eastwards:

"It has been a long time since I wrote to you, my dear father, but this is only owing to our marches and countermarches, not knowing where we were going or if my letters would reach you. This has been made especially difficult as we have been passing through provinces where they do not understand what a mail service is once you stray from the main highways.

"You cannot imagine these countries, especially northern Poland. These are real deserts. You can march ten leagues over sandy heathland without even seeing a house. The villages you find at the end of the day are just miserable hamlets of "Noah's Arks" where the host, his guests, his oxen, his pigs, his lice and his chickens all live in the same room. The pigs eat under the table just like dogs. You can imagine what the beds are like - one is absolutely devoured by fleas. The food is of a similar standard; there is no wine, just a miserable, sour black beer, and the high point is a disgusting sort of brandy. The crowning misfortune is a language that was invented by the devil, and a nation so stupid that they can't even understand sign language. All this only applies to the country bumpkins - the inhabitants of Warsaw and Posen are very friendly and speak French well.

"The Emperor is in the neighbourhood and we are impatiently awaiting his arrival from Danzig. Tomorrow we are going to Braunsberg and from there to Königsberg; it seems now that the cards have been shuffled thoroughly, and that we are soon going to start fighting.... We march 10 to 15 hours a day in suffocating heat, but then yesterday we had the first rain and hail, and it was very cold. I hope we have some decent weather at the bivouac, which cannot be far away."

The Regiment did indeed march via Braunsberg to Königsberg, where the Imperial Guard assembled around their Emperor during a three-day halt. Before entering the city the troops were told to re-whiten their leather equipment and to tidy up their uniforms; once inside Königsberg they immediately had

Light Horse Lancer of the 2nd Regiment, Imperial Guard, by Bellangé (1800-1866). Although Dumonceau does mention in his memoirs an 'N' badge on the shabraques - oddly reversed here - they cannot be found in the orders placed for equipment between 1811 and 1814, and most sources show a yellow Imperial eagle badge. Again, Bellangé has made a common error in showing the lance pennon with scarlet over white - white over scarlet was a distinction of the Red Lancers. (Author's collection)

Chevau-Légers Lanciers.

DEUXIÈME RÉGIMENT. GARDE IMPÉRIALE

to provide a mounted detachment for the Emperor's service. During their stay each company's quartermaster-corporal was issued one large felling axe, and eight hatchets for the corporals, so that trees could be cut down.

The Guard detachment at the castle was relieved daily at noon, and accompanied the Emperor each day on his tours of inspection. During these tours he was escorted by two lancers very slightly in front of him, and Marshal Bessières a little behind him on his left side; the rest of the entourage and escort followed further behind. Sometimes the Emperor used the Dutch officers as interpreters, since many of them spoke German. On Sunday 14 June, in the grounds of Königsberg palace, the Young Guard Division under General Delaborde, and the Red Lancers, were paraded in front of the Emperor and his suite.

During the three days' stay Lieutenant van Omphal received orders to await the Emperor with an escort at Insterburg; they were to escort him during his inspections of the troops gathered along the river Pregel. After one of these inspections, being too far away from a bridge crossing the river, Napoleon ordered the escort commander to ford and swim the river, and he would follow.

Leaving Königsberg with enough bread for four days and two rations of oats, the Regiment began the last stage of their long march to the Niemen, via Tapiau, Insterburg and Gumbinnen, finally reaching Vilkoviski in extremely hot weather.

After four exhausting months on the road the Red Lancers had reached their objective. Their destination was to be neither Rome, nor Erfurt, nor Warsaw. On the far bank of the Niemen lay Russian territory.

★   ★   ★

The Grande Armée which Napoleon assembled for the actual invasion of Russia was some 450,000 strong, of whom a minority were Frenchmen. It was to advance across the Niemen in one main army flanked by two supporting forces. In the north the German and Polish X Corps (Marshal Macdonald) would strike up towards the Baltic at Riga; in the south Prince Schwarzenburg's Austrians would cover Russia's southern armies. The main invasion army led by Napoleon himself consisted of the Imperial Guard (Bessières and Mortier); I Corps (Davout), II

Corps (Oudinot), III Corps (Ney), 1st (Nansouty) & 2nd (Montbrun) Corps of the Reserve Cavalry led by Marshal Murat, King of Naples; Prince Eugène de Beauharnais' Army of Italy, consisting of IV Corps (Eugène), the Bavarian VI Corps (Gouvion St Cyr) and 3rd Reserve Cavalry Corps (Grouchy); and the Second Support Army, initially led by Napoleon's brother King Jerome of Westphalia, with the Westphalian VIII Corps, Polish V Corps (Poniatowski), Saxon VII Corps (Reynier), and 4th Reserve Cavalry Corps (Latour-Maubourg).

In its simplest terms, Napoleon's plan was to force a decisive action on the Russians as soon as possible so that he would not have to march too deep into their limitless territory, straining his vulnerable logistics and communications. Confident that he could smash Russia's field armies if he could bring them to battle, he believed that he could force Tsar Alexander to submit to terms thereafter.

The enemy he faced were patriotic, brave and enduring, but inefficient and disorganised. The only available field armies were the 130,000-strong First West Army led by the Minister of War, Barclay de Tolly, facing the northern element of Napoleon's army; the Second West Army of Prince Bagration, with 50,000-60,000 men, in the centre; and Tormasov's Third West Army with some 45,000 men south of the Pripet Marshes.

The march on Moscow

On 24 June 1812 the trumpeters sounded *Reveille*, and shortly afterwards *Boots and saddles*; the order to *Mount* was not sounded until later in the course of the morning. The general had the Regiment drawn up under arms and in square. A solemn trumpet call alerted the troops; then Adjutant Fallot read aloud the Emperor's proclamation, dated 22 June, announcing the outbreak of war:

"Soldiers: The second Polish War has begun. The first ended at Friedland and Tilsit. At Tilsit, Russia swore eternal alliance with France and war against England. Today she is breaking her oaths. She chooses not to give any explanation for her strange behaviour as long as French troops have not crossed back over the Rhine, thus leaving our allies at her mercy. Russia is being carried away by a sense of inevitability - her destiny

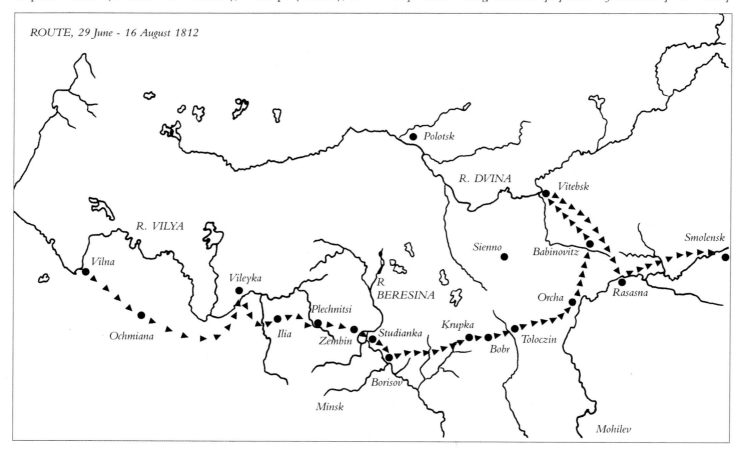

ROUTE, 29 June - 16 August 1812

must be fulfilled. Does she think we are degenerates? Are we no longer the soldiers of Austerlitz? She gives us a choice between dishonour and war - which is no choice at all. So let us march forward! Let us cross the Niemen, and carry the fight onto her own territory. The second Polish War will be as glorious to French arms as the first. When it is concluded it will bring a guaranteed peace, ending the arrogant influence which Russia has been excercising over European affairs for fifty years."

The proclamation was greeted by cheers of *"Vive l'Empereur!"*

Marching dismounted, the Red Lancers crossed the Niemen over the right hand bridge, following the leading Corps and followed by the rest of the Guard. During their first day in Russia the Regiment followed the Niemen and marched towards wooded heights to reach Kovno, where the army's General Headquarters was located. The Guard infantry were also quartered in this town; the cavalry were accomodated nearby under the town walls. From this time on the horses had to remain saddled and packed almost day and night, and their riders dressed and armed.

On the morning of the next day the trumpeters of the various Guard regiments sounded the order to mount as urgently as if the enemy were falling upon them by surprise. The Guard was drawn up in a very short time; and Marshal Bessières led them in column in the direction of Vilna, following Marshal Murat's 1st and 2nd Reserve Cavalry Corps and Marshal Davout's I Corps.

From the earliest weeks of the campaign weather which alternated between choking heat and rain, and a shortage of forage which meant that the horses had to feed themselves on green grass along the route, led to a very high death rate among the army's mounts. (After only 24 days in Russia Murat would be able to mount only some 14,000 of his 22,000 Reserve Cavalry.) The withdrawing Russian troops practised the "scorched earth" policy, burning almost every store or source of forage which might provide feed for the Grande Armée. This obliged the cavalry to spread out to seek forage over ever wider areas each side of the line of march; the scores of thousands of horses concentrated in the army "ate out" a huge swathe of countryside daily. Sometimes the French vanguard troops managed to extinguish the fires set by the retreating enemy and to save part of the stores, which were distributed; but even then the damage caused by the flames and smoke rendered the forage hardly edible, which worsened the condition of the horses. The rate of injury and sickness was naturally aggravated by the practice of keeping horses saddled for all except a very few hours a day, with the inevitable result of suppurating saddle sores which seldom had a chance to heal; and by their repeated exposure to rainstorms while picketed in the open.

On the morning of 26 June the Red Lancers were used as outposts and scouts, with orders to link up with the vanguard of Murat's cavalry marching on Vilna and to protect his right flank. That night they made their bivouacs at Zismoroui. The next day Murat had to send a detachment of the 7th Hussars to find them and warn them that they had passed beyond the vanguard of his army by about six miles. They reached Vilna on the evening of 28 June in pouring rain, to find, nevertheless, that all the magazines were in flames - the same sight which would greet them in almost every Russian town. Albert de Watteville wrote to his parents:

"Our reconnaissance tells us that the Russians are still withdrawing. The most important part has already crossed the Duna. A small part of Bagration's Corps has joined the Corps which is withdrawing on Vilna after being defeated at Swinziani. We are told that Counts Orloff and Roumiantzeff have already been sent to parley with us. All the information we are gathering and the reports that reach us seem to correspond: the Russians have suffered a disaster and their army has been dispersed. Napoleon is reorganising Poland, appointing a prefect and sub-prefect at Vilna and setting up units of Gendarmes. Everyone is coming to General Colbert asking him for passports to take up service at Vilna; Polish deserters from the Russian Army are flooding here every day. We have found some Russian magazines with provisions of all kinds and hospital stores, as well as a tax chest - though we would have preferred it to be a military chest. If we do not receive the order to march our provisioning will be assured for a fortnight.

"The countryside is very good, but we are eaten up by insects of all kinds and overwhelmed by the extreme heat. Luckily storms come to refresh us every night."

On the night of the 28th the Regiment made their bivouacs in a Vilna suburb well supplied with kitchen gardens; but the ground was one huge mud puddle in which horses and lancers alike sank knee deep. They had no straw to sleep on, and no firewood to warm them; that night's "refreshing" storm completed their misery, especially as they knew that the other cavalry regiments of the Guard had gone into billets. They believed that their hardships were due to a caprice of General Colbert, who was treating them like unwanted bastards and outcasts. The sullen mood of the troops and company officers alike became even worse when they realised that the regimental staff officers were comfortably lodged in nearby houses.

That night the adjutants distributed billeting orders for the whole unit; but they had hardly begun to enjoy being under cover when the trumpets called the Regiment to arms. They assembled very slowly and in a foul temper, harried by repeated trumpet calls; when the cursing Lancers prepared to get on the road at midnight they were still missing two officers and a hundred men. These latecomers caught up with the army the following day, 30 June, led by Lieutenant Hubert le Sueur. Sharply reprimanded by Marshal Bessières, the stragglers were attached temporarily to the Mounted Chasseurs, only rejoining the Regiment at Vitebsk in early August.

The effects of the lack of forage were beginning to make themselves felt; the Red Lancers had to leave 30 out of 750 horses behind at their bivouac. The rest of the army was suffering equally, and the losses among draught horses forced the artillery to leave a hundred guns together with their caissons at Vilna.

At the time of departure the Regiment - including the depot and detachments on the march towards Russia - numbered 57 officers, 1,095 lancers and 1,264 horses. They had a detachment of 25 lancers and 27 horses at Marienwerder and a detachment of 210 lancers at Hanover.

From Vilna the Emperor wrote to Marshal Davout on 1 July 1812: *"Cousin, there is no doubt today that Bagration has made off from Brzesc to Grodno, and from Grodno has passed Vilna, six leagues away, on the way to Sventsiany. I have organised three strong columns to follow him. As soon as you can establish communications with them all three will fall under your command. The right column is commanded by General Grouchy and consists of Bordesoulle's brigade, Dessaix's infantry division and the light cavalry brigade of Castex. The second column is under your orders; you have Pajol's brigade, Compans' division, the Cuirassier division of Valence, and the Lancers of the Guard. The third column will debouch by Mikhalichki; it consists of Morand's division, the two brigades of Bruyère's division, and Saint Germain's division. General Nansouty will command this column."*

The Regiment was now temporarily attached to Davout's command, whose mission was to isolate the left wing of the Russian army under Prince Bagration and frustrate his attempts to join up with the main army of Barclay de Tolly, which was retiring to the north. (In the event Davout's planned right flank movement was to be frustrated partly by the pricked vanity of King Jerome, who chose to return to Westphalia; left without orders, his Corps failed to fix Bagration, who managed to withdraw once again.)

That afternoon the horizon cleared, the sun shone again and it became very hot. Marshal Davout gave his orders and, from Miedniki, wrote that day to General Colbert: *"The Russians have established communications between the roads from Grodno to Vilna and from Vilna to Polotsk, leading from the first at the Posy of Lachounoui to the second at Lavarichki, passing near Miedniki. It seems necessary to me that you bring this route under observation, since there are Russian columns roaming in the neighbourhood which could be trying to make use of this road. If this were to happen His Majesty should be informed and I should be warned so that I could place troops to oppose them."*

On 2 July the Regiment arrived at Ochmiana. From Olchanouï Marshal Davout wrote to General Colbert the next day: *"This morning at 3a.m. I received your letter of 3 July. The enemy is no longer taking the direction of Boronouï. I suppose that there will not even be a large force at Smorgouï. Reconnoitre this point extensively. Get in touch with General Nansouty. who is at Mikhaïlichki; it was mainly to establish communications with him that I left you at Ochmiana."*

Shortly afterwards the Regiment took up a position between Davout's I Corps, heading for Mohilev, and the main force under the direct orders of Napoleon, thus forming an additional column.

On 7 July a furious General Colbert wrote from Raschowtski (Radozkowicze) to Marshal Bessières: *"I have the honour to request the dismissal from my regiment of Monsieur Weerts, lieutenant of the 1st Company. This officer may serve in the Guard no longer, since he has made remarks unforgivable in a soldier, and has shown insubordination. I feel obliged, Monseigneur, to ask you for this punishment as a fundamentally necessary measure. A bad mood reigns among the officers, and it could spread to the soldiers if one should be indulgent. I have had Monsieur Weerts sent back to Vilna and have suspended him from duty until Your Excellency has decided upon his fate."*

By a decree dated at Vilna on 9 July, Lieutenant Jacob Weerts ten Brink - a veteran of two campaigns, characterised by his superiors as competent enough but lazy - was dismissed the Regiment. He had been caught leaving a cellar followed by two lancers carrying bottles of wine. It was strictly forbidden to steal the smallest thing from civilian homes in this region, whose population Napoleon wished to persuade that they were being liberated. Weerts ten Brink's superior, Captain Jan Post, reprimanded him on the spot. If Weerts had apologised appropriately the matter would have gone no further; instead he flew into a temper, completely disregarding the respect due to rank. Captain Post calmly warned him to be careful if he wanted to avoid a crushing report. Far from getting himself under control, Weerts hurled the bottles down at the captain's feet in full view of witnesses.

Without further ado a report was drawn up, and Weerts was brought before the permanent court martial sitting at Vilna. The court showed indulgence, merely sentencing the lieutenant to fifteen days' arrest. He reported back to the Red Lancers, but General Colbert refused to readmit him. The outcast Weerts took refuge with some friends of his in the formerly Belgian and Dutch 11th Hussars, and spent the rest of the campaign in their company (he would eventually disappear during the winter retreat). As for the unfortunate accomplices who had no doubt believed that the presence of an officer was an absolute defence, Lancer van Geffen was expelled from the Guard by order of Bessières on 28 July 1812, and Lancer Blinkman was "placed at the disposal of the Minister of War" on the same day.

Even on campaign the Emperor had time to pay attention to conditions of service in his Guard; on 10 July he raised the pay of the trumpet corporals and company corporals. By a decree of 8 February 1811 Napoleon had approved the Regiment's pay scales without noticing an error which gave these NCOs less than the common trumpeters; now the corporals' pay was raised from 1.20 to 1.50 francs, and that of the trumpeters was cut from 1.50 to 1.20 francs. (The veterinarians had to wait until the end of the year until their underpayment compared with their colleagues of the Line was corrected.)

★   ★   ★

On 8 July, after two forced marches, the Lancers captured Vileyka from its Russian garrison, taking the bridge over the Vilya before the enemy could burn it. This swift advance and attack saved for the French important magazines and convoys of stores and forage (2,000 quintals of flour, 30,000 to 40,000 biscuit rations and large quantities of oats). The Regiment left the town on 11 July to proceed to Plechnitsi.

To ensure communication between the Lancers and Davout,

Lancer of the 2nd Regiment in full dress. Again, the lance pennon colours are reversed; and the lance seems to be rather too short - it actual length was over nine feet. (Author's collection)

Lieutenant van Omphal had been detached to the marshal's staff as an orderly officer since the Regiment was at Ochmiana. In this function he had to make his way between the Regiment and the Corps headquarters a number of times - dangerous journeys, and the more dangerous the further one moved from the Corps. Russian Cossacks ranged the countryside between the various advancing French columns for the express purpose of killing or capturing such couriers; and even the peasants hiding in the woods would take any opportunity which offered to kill isolated French soldiers. Van Omphal remained detached to Davout's staff for two months, returning to the Regiment on 14 August.

On the morning of 11 July General Colbert received orders from Marshal Davout to aid General Grouchy's 3rd Corps of the Reserve Cavalry in the attempted capture of well-supplied magazines at Borisov. General Bordesoulle was to support this operation; he was sent four Red Lancer despatch riders to keep him in touch with General Colbert and to give him Marshal Davout's letter. Setting out immediately, the Regiment headed for Zembin via Ilya, where they had an engagement with a force of Cossacks. They crossed the Beresina river in the early morning of 13 July - at exactly the same spot where they would recross it four months later, the ford of Studianka. (Local peasants told them that this was the same ford where King Charles XII of Sweden had crossed during his wars against Peter the Great a hundred years before. One wonders if any well-read Dutch officer allowed himself to muse upon the utter ruin of the encircled Swedish army at Poltava in 1709.) At Borisov on the left bank they joined Grouchy's Corps, who had taken the town too late to save the food and ammunition depots.

After these forced marches General Colbert rested his regiment for a day; they pitched camp near a pleasant farm where they found plenty of forage, meat and vegetables. On the night of the 14th fresh orders arrived to set out for Orcha, crossing the Dnieper and pressing ahead fast to capture Russian depots. On their way the Lancers passed by Krupka, Bobr and Toloczin; in the latter town they seized Russian despatches, and also a convoy of 100 ox-wagons loaded with provisions. Their continuing thrust brought them to Kokanov, a major crossroads on the route between Sienno in the north and Mohilev in the south. They were marching so fast that they found themselves more than 20 miles ahead of Grouchy, following with his cavalry Corps at a day's interval. They were running a considerable risk of being cut off by enemy forces converging from north and south; it was for this reason that on 16 July Marshal Davout ordered Grouchy to put his foreign brigade, as well as the French 6th Hussars, under Colbert's command.

The priority was to reach the Orcha magazines before they could be destroyed. At Kokanov on the night of 18 July General Colbert gave Colonel-Major van Hasselt two squadrons to accomplish this mission. Leaving the bulk of the Regiment behind Jan van Hasselt led his troopers in a single-minded dash for Orcha, where at 2a.m. on the morning of the 20th they seized depots full of hay, oats, flour and brandy - and also captured the Russian colonel who had been ordered to burn them. Meanwhile the rest of the Regiment stayed in its bivouacs until the 3rd Cavalry Corps arrived to relieve them, which was accomplished on the morning of the 20th. From Orcha Captain Calkoen wrote to his father on 21 July:

"Here we are at Orcha on the Dnieper, a little above Smolensk [sic].... Since Königsberg I have not taken off my boots; we have always been in the vanguard, always trailing at the Russians' heels without ever being able to catch them. They retreat at an unbelievable speed, and all we have been able to capture so far are several depots just as they were about to set them on fire, and a number of wagons loaded with powder, arms and baggage which were following their army. We have not given them a single sabre cut yet, and we do not understand it. The Russians must be retreating in terrible disorder, or rather they must have completely lost their heads. Their army seems to be split up by our forces, one part of it at Riga and all along the Dvina, and the other towards the Ukraine, and both are retreating.

"We are still marching as friends in this country, promising freedom to the peasants and consideration to the nobles. The Emperor has already installed a prefecture at Vilna, and we keep organising Lithuania as we did the Grand Duchy of Warsaw. It is presumed that the Emperor will have himself crowned King of Poland and will leave a viceroy in this country - but you do not want to hear idle speculation.

"This country is dreadful - a desert. One can march 15 or 20 miles in a day without encountering a village, only some poor hamlets with houses built from unsawn pine, the roofs from planks. The men look like savages, their wives like monkeys; they are all the slaves of their lords, compelled to work for them all the time simply in return for food. Judging by their industry, without the Jews who play an important role in this country we would have plenty to complain about. These all speak German, are very diligent and very anti-Russian.

"Since Königsberg we have been constantly in bivouac; but although we are always at the ready, our horses saddled and bridled day and night, unfortunately our precautions have been pointless up to now. I must confess to you that this campaign is very tiresome; no other campaign has been as wearying as this without coming to a conflict. It's such bad luck; our regiment has such a need to distinguish itself and we are all looking

for any opportunity, but in vain. I still cannot foresee when we will return. It is quite impossible that this campaign should last less than a year, and spending the winter in this country of bears and wolves is quite a prospect.

"You can still write to me as usual by adding 'to the Grande Armée'. We are both very well and want for nothing but rest. We have been separated from the Guard to form a Light Horse Division which has been ordered to search for the enemy until we find them. If they keep retreating like this we may well pass the winter at St Petersburg or Moscow, à la bonne heure...

"I have lost all my belongings but what I stand up in. My portmanteau and the company's caisson, forced to stay behind because of bad roads, have been plundered by marauders. We have taken a convoy of 14 wagons loaded with sugar, coffee, pepper and ginger going from Riga to Moscow and have shared it out between the troops, so we are all drinking coffee day and night."

★   ★   ★

The Regiment stayed at Orcha for a few days, and slipped once more into their routine daily tasks. The troops fell in, mounted and under arms, early each morning, and waited upon the duty captain's report to General Colbert after the inspection of the outlying pickets. After that they were allowed to dismount and take their horses to drink. Scouting patrols were sent out every day towards Babinovitz, Smolensk, Sienno and Mohilev.

The Russians under Barclay de Tolly were withdrawing from Kamen to Vitebsk in the face of the leading columns of the French main force led by Napoleon; to the south Davout was exerting pressure on Prince Bagration before Mohilev. The situation in the north made the advanced position of the Red Lancers somewhat hazardous, and measures were taken; one was the despatch of a scouting detachment of 50 lancers under Lieutenants van Zuylen and van Wijchel towards Babinovitz. On 26 July a patrol reported to General Colbert that they had been forced to flee from a Russian cavalry force around Sienno. The next day came the news that Marshal Davout had just beaten Prince Bagration before Mohilev when he attempted a move to join up with the northern army. Any immediate danger lay in the north, from around Babinovitz and Vitebsk.

Barclay de Tolly had reached the latter town, and he in his turn was eager to re-establish communications with Bagration before deciding whether to stand and fight there. He sent the Uhlan Brigade of the Russian Guard to Babinovitz under the command of Grand Duke Constantine; and it was in that small town on 27 July that the Uhlans surprised the Red Lancers scouting party as they searched for food and forage. Taking refuge in an inn where Lieutenants van Zuylen and van Wijchel had been playing billiards, the Lancers tried in vain to defend themselves. Outnumbered and trapped, too far away from their regiment to make a run for it, too isolated for there to be any hope of holding out until reinforcements arrived, they were forced to surrender. Only an NCO and three troopers, posted on the far edge of the town from the direction of attack, managed to escape and return to the Regiment. The wounded 2nd Lieutenant Adriaan Paats van Wijchel was to die in captivity on 17 January 1813 at Sarratov; Lieutenant Baron van Zuylen van Nyevelt, also wounded, was taken prisoner together with the other 48 lancers of the detachment.

As soon as news reached them the Regiment mounted and sent off a scouting squadron. It returned that night without having met the enemy, who must have been retreating to escape IV Corps (commanded by Eugène de Beauharnais, Napoleon's stepson). On that day Chef d'escadron de Watteville wrote from Orcha:

"We have constantly been out in front of the whole Army Corps, sometimes 25 to 30 miles. The campaign continues to be murderous. Except for the Prince of Eckmühl [Davout], who has defeated Bagration at Mohilev, I do not believe that there has been any fighting other than by the vanguard, and then only occasionally. The Emperor has crossed the Düna at Ouhla [Orcha] at the time when the Russians were leaving their camp to take refuge in Vitebsk; they must have found themselves in even

A pleasing drawing by JOB (Jacques Onfroy de Bréville, 1858-1931) of Red Lancers on the march in full dress; although the pennon colours are, as usual, reversed, this does show convincingly the appearance of the lance carried slung from the arm with its ferrule on the stirrup. (René Chartrand collection)

greater difficulties. I fear, however, that things are coming to a head. I have made good progress with my squadron, taking the magazines which the Russians had assembled here - I carried out my mission successfully.

"We have been at Orcha for ten days now, using food from the Russian supplies. The enemy's manoeuvres at Vitebsk compel us to bring together all our forces before moving forwards. If, when we first reached this town, we had had half the cavalry that is here now and a little artillery, we could have reached Moscow without firing a shot; and we could as easily have spread terror to Vitebsk. They are completely routed."

The next day the scouting patrols were unable to find any enemy; even so, the Red Lancers felt a certain reassurance with the arrival that afternoon of troops of the 3rd Cavalry Corps to relieve them in the advanced outposts. The regimental officers were presented to General Grouchy, who congratulated them on their services in the vanguard of the Grande Armée. Subsequently VIII Corps also arrived in the region. The Red Lancers accompanied Grouchy's cavalry corps towards Babinovitz, following General Gerard's brigade. While on the march they were ordered to proceed immediately to Vitebsk, where battle seemed imminent. Excited by the prospect of a general engagement at last, the Red Lancers were moving up in column when they met a detachment of Mounted Chasseurs accompanied by a staff officer who informed them that the enemy had refused battle once again and were falling back towards Smolensk. The Regiment were to continue their march to Vitebsk, where the Emperor was assembling the whole Guard.

"We had thought that we were about to find the enemy and engage them, but they had made off. The Emperor has entered Vitebsk, where we are hoping that a decisive battle may bring the war to an end", wrote de Watteville. *"We have passed from abundance to hardships, but we are still alive. The heat is insupportable. It is said that when you meet with misfortune everything goes wrong at the same time, and I can vouch that this is true. One of my servants has been ill for some time. Coming onto the camping ground the day before yesterday the other one was also taken ill, with a hernia. I found myself left alone with six horses and one lancer, my orderlies being on duty. In the morning one of my horses pulled out his picket pin; my lancer tried to bring him back but, wild as he was, the horse sped away like lightning through the bivouac and nobody could catch him again. As a result I have lost beyond hope of recovery my best charger complete with saddle, coat, pistols and full equipment. One must resign oneself to make the best of it, and be glad to remain in good health."*

On 31 July Lieutenant-Adjutant de Stuers came back from a meeting with Marshal Bessières bearing orders for a move to Terespol. All the houses in Vitebsk and its immediate surroundings were already occupied by Guard troops, and the Regiment was unpleasantly surprised to find itself quartered on a sandy plain before the village. Predictably, General Colbert and the regimental staff were accomodated in houses near the bivouac, which reminded the junior officers and troops of the Vilna camp ground.

The Lancers' task at Terespol was to guarantee the security of the General Headquarters and to provide outposts. Although this duty was honourable, the soldiers tended to grumble that brothers-in-arms of the other Guard regiments were enjoying a well-deserved rest while the Lancers had to watch over their safety. Detachments were sent out every day, both for reconnaissance and to bring back food and forage to contribute to the provisions of the army at Vitebsk.

Shortly thereafter they were joined by the latecomers who had got themselves separated at Vilna, under command of Hubert le Sueur; and also by a reinforcement of 200 mounted men coming directly from Versailles under Chef d'escadron Colin de Verdière. Upon his arrival in Vitebsk the regiment numbered about 600 horses - a shortfall of 400, of which only 50 losses were due to enemy action and the rest to sickness, injury and exhaustion. Consisting mainly of ex-members of the former Dutch 3rd Hussars, these were the first party of the reinforcements brought back from active service under Colonel van Merlen in Spain to form the 5th Squadron. Among the officers of this detachment were the 48-year-old Lieutenant Arend Ziegler, who was assigned to the same company as his 25-year-old son 2nd Lieutenant Pieter Ziegler; Lieutenants Hanneman, Doyen, Duranti and Deban de Laborde; Assistant Surgeon-Major Stutterheim; and Lieutenant Hubert de Stuer's brother Leopold, who was serving as a vélite. The Regiment were well provided with food and forage at this time, and fresh bread arrived regularly from the bakeries in the town.

On 9 August they received orders to leave the next day for Vitebsk, which they would pass on their way to Smolensk. The march began in rainy weather, and they soon found themselves plunging along narrow, swampy, and barely visible roads. On 12 August Marshal Bessières inspected the Regiment as he passed them with his staff. (It was also on that date that the other half of the 5th Squadron set out from Berlin with 194 troopers and 200 horses, to reach Königsberg on 20 September.) In a note dated from Rasasna on 13 August Chef d'escadron de Watteville wrote:

"We have left the Army Corps of the Prince of Eckmühl [Davout] and General Grouchy to rejoin the Guard at Vitebsk, and are at the same spot from which we left. Here the Emperor has rejoined the Corps of Marshal Davout. We are marching to Smolensk, where we hope that the Russians will be waiting for us. If so we could celebrate [the Emperor's birthday on] 15 August with a battle. The weather has not been favourable up until now; it has rained heavily for three days." Surely the Russians would be found in Smolensk - and to find them was to crush them!

During a night march to Smolensk a part of the Regiment's column fell asleep in the saddle, and so gradually drifted to a standstill. The troops following them also stopped, thinking that a halt had been ordered; but these lancers quickly realised that something abnormal was happening and started shouting to know what was going on. The head of the column had marched on without noticing that the rest of the Regiment was not following. It was a shambles; the officers at the rear, in the absence of guides, did not know which road to take. They decided to wait for daylight before pressing on to catch up with the Regiment, which in the event they managed easily. Due to overcrowding the road to Smolensk was getting more and more difficult.

The entire Grande Armée was marching towards what they hoped would be a decisive battle at Smolensk with the combined forces of Barclay de Tolly and Bagration. Although the region through which they were advancing provided plentiful forage for the horses the troop's rations were insufficient. They had left Vitebsk with a fortnight's food in the wagon train, but this inevitably became delayed on the rudimentary and overcrowded Russian roads; in its absence the men had to get by on the thinnest of rations. From that time on almost the whole army would march as one body until the end of the campaign - maximising both its strength for battle, but also its ever-increasing logistic difficulties.

The Regiment crossed the Dnieper on one of the bridges built below the village of Rasasna, and set up its bivouacs on the left bank in fields covered with barley and hemp. From 14 August onwards the Red Lancers would form with the Polish Lancers a brigade commanded by General Colbert, and would henceforward operate independently of the rest of the Guard cavalry. On 15 August the Regiment continued its march on Smolensk, moving through the fields in order to avoid the overcrowded roads. All of a sudden Napoleon himself galloped past accompanied by his staff. The Red Lancers caught up with him a little further on, dismounted, riding whip in hand, standing by the road with Prince Poniatowski at his side. Moving forward, the brigade halted near a small village lying on the left of the road before Koritnya, close to the Imperial suite and the other Guard regiments. This village, called Oufimie, was on the right of a rather broad stream which flowed into the Dnieper. Here they found barracks abandoned by the Russians, which they cleaned up before installing themselves.

That night, wishing to celebrate Napoleon's birthday, the Light Horse Lancers decorated trees with inscriptions and lanterns bearing the monograms of the Emperor and Empress. These original ornaments were the work of a sergeant of the Polish Lancers, an educated young soldier named Skalski. When the lanterns were lit they were greeted with loud and repeated cheers from both regiments. Anyone who had a small store of spirits shared it with his comrades, and the Emperor's health was drunk with enthusiasm. By about 10p.m. everything had calmed down, and the camp was quiet.

A field canteen - a box covered with gold-tooled red leather and lined with green velvet containing a silver cup and cutlery - used by Colonel-Major Dubois of the Red Lancers on campaign in Russia, 1812. (Private collection, England)

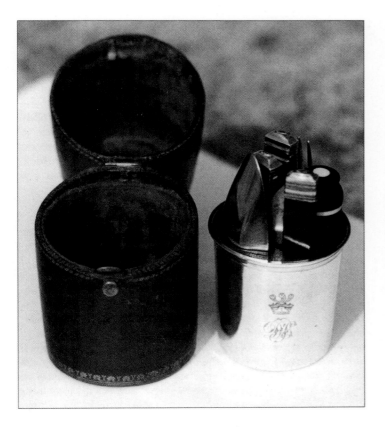

The next morning the assembled brigade were informed by one of Bessières' staff officers that Cossacks had been reported to the left of the line of march. They found traces of a recent bivouac, and followed the tracks of horsemen to the bank of the Dnieper; the Cossacks had swum their horses across towards Katyn. They remained on the riverbank on observation until General Mourier's brigade - from Marshal Ney's III Corps cavalry - came up to replace them. The generals considered the town of Katyn important enough for a reconnaissance, and ordered some dismounted soldiers to swim across the river with their sabres between their teeth.

Leaving Mourier's brigade the Regiment marched on, passing packed columns of troops. Among Mourier's cavalry they were surprised and pleased to meet their former comrades of the Dutch 2nd Hussars, now absorbed with a Belgian element into the French 11th Hussars; van der Netten, Pijman, Hoynck van Papendrecht and Sloet were among the Hussar officers who left the column to greet them.

The Red Lancers were dogged by ill luck with the Cossacks, who seemed insultingly eager to come to blows (perhaps as a result of their easy victory in the fight at Babinovitz). Sometimes when Cossacks saw a patrol of the Regiment they would make a rush at them, shouting *"A red one! Catch him!"*, and often forced them to flee. It is said that, on occasion, the more experienced Polish Lancers would exchange their sombre blue and crimson uniform for the Dutch scarlet, causing considerable surprise to overconfident Cossacks and encouraging a warier approach in future.

On the late evening of 16 August the Lancer brigade arrived before Smolensk, where the opposing armies were already in contact. On the 17th de Watteville wrote: *"We are sniping and cannonading each other while the Emperor is making his dispositions. The whole army is arriving. Everyone hopes that this engagement will be decisive."*

Once more, everyone would be disappointed. Napoleon's attempt to turn Smolensk from the south failed due to the stout resistance and fighting retreat of General Neverovsky's command at Krasnyi on 14/15 August. His subsequent costly frontal assault on the city was held back by General Raevsky's Corps during the 16th and 17th, giving Barclay and Bagration time to prepare an orderly withdrawal. Despite 20,000 French and allied casualties the battle of Smolensk ended with the ever-retreating Russian armies still a serious fighting force, and the main French army reduced to about 160,000 men.

During this battle the Regiment was held in reserve to the south of the city, as were most of the Imperial Guard. From there they tried to follow the progress of the fighting, which went on throughout the night of the 16th, setting Smolensk ablaze. The enemy rearguard were still fighting in the lower town on the east bank of the Dnieper the next morning, until driven out at bayonet point, and over the next 24 hours even they managed to avoid Napoleon's attempt to annihilate them.

Although held in reserve the Red Lancers often came under the fire of the Russian artillery. Two troops were deployed forward in a screen to watch for any unexpected attack from the nearest suburbs. Here they were exposed to the fire of Russian snipers, and after a while General Colbert ordered them back, their usefulness at that point not justifying their exposure. That night Lieutenant Jacob de Bellefroid of the Lancers ran into his brother, who was serving in the Grande Armée's Westphalian contingent in the rank of captain.

The Red Lancers passed through the smouldering, corpse-strewn streets of Smolensk on 19 August; as soon as the vanguard of the army had crossed the Dnieper the Guard followed. The Regiment pitched camp near a mill north of the town in the neighbourhood of Pasova village, and remained there until 24 August in broiling weather. As at Vitebsk, their task was to provide outposts covering the approaches to the town. The Regiment's field strength was recorded as 48 officers with 145 horses, and 638 lancers with 603 horses. The command of the 1st Squadron was vacant; the 2nd was led by Marie Michel de Tiecken, the 3rd by Jean François Coti, the 4th by Albert de Watteville and the 5th by Auguste Colin de Verdière.

Ordered to march without delay in the direction of Moscow at daybreak on the 24th, the Regiment had to leave behind a 150-strong foraging party under Captain Post (accompanied by five Polish Lancers), which came in that evening to find that their comrades had left Pasova for Dorogobuj. During that day the Regiment found themselves riding over the battlefield of Valoutina, where Ney, Murat and Junot had tried unsuccessfully to trap Barclay de Tolly's retreating rearguard on 19 August. The road was covered with the dead, corpses lay heaped and strewn throughout the woods along the roadsides, and in the sultry summer heat the stench of decomposition was ghastly.

Having set off first, the Red Lancers were considered as the vanguard of the Imperial Guard; Bessières instructed that an officer attend his headquarters every night to receive orders for the next day, and Adjutant Hubert de Stuers was selected for this duty.

The heat was undiminished on the 25th; men and horses alike suffered terribly from the choking, blinding dust and the lack of water. Some years later the former Lieutenant van Omphal, then a general in the Dutch army, remembered with admiration the thoroughness of the retreating Russian army's methods. Nothing useful that could be carried with them was abandoned; anything that could not be carried was burned. Although it is generally conceded that the great majority of the Russian officer corps was uneducated, ill-trained and professionally incompetent by Western standards, regimental officers did suceed in inspiring great loyalty and obedience among their brutalised but loyal serf-soldiers. Only an army with real discipline - however achieved - could have conducted such a retreat.

On 26 August the Regiment passed through Dorogobuj, one of the only towns which they found left comparatively intact even though it had been ransacked by the retreating enemy. There Colonel-Major Dubois fell ill just as the Lancers took the road for Viazma. Out in the vanguard they were being confronted more frequently by evasive bands of Cossacks, and occasionally by elements of the Russian rearguard covering the army's withdrawal. Once again a feeling of tension, of imminent action was spreading through the ranks of the frustrated French. From 29 to 30 August the Lancers remained in bivouac at Viazma, once a lovely town but now in ruins. The killing heat had been replaced by torrential rain. All ranks were conscious that they were, as van Hasselt wrote, "within fifty hours of Moscow".

To make up the losses suffered by the Grande Armée fresh troops formed in "marching regiments" - provisional, *ad hoc* units grouping available manpower for rapid deployment to the front - were crossing Europe to join the units in Russia. On 1 September one of these regiments, formed in Hanover and including ten Red Lancers, set off; they reached Berlin ten days later, and arrived at Vilna - now with only eight Red Lancers - on 27 October. Another Régiment de Marche formed in Berlin left on 3 September, with just four Red Lancers; they would reach Smolensk on 1 November.

Although marching as the vanguard of the army and the Imperial Guard was a demanding duty it also had some advantages. They sometimes entered villages which had not yet been plundered, and got first pick of any available food and forage - the army's main body normally found nothing but empty houses, looted or burned.

Between 1 and 4 September the Regiment rested in good weather with the other regiments of the Guard at Gjat. At that date the total "paper" strength of the Regiment numbered 1,406 troopers. The establishment of the five sabre squadrons was 1,212 troopers. The apparent surplus of 194 troopers was due to the drafts of 512 men made on the 34 Line cavalry regiments by the decree of 11 March 1812, and the incorporation of the Hussar

2nd Lieutenant Adriaan P. Paats van Wijchel (1787-1813), for some reason depicted wearing the uniform of a trooper. Wounded and captured at Babinovitz on 27 July 1812, he would die in Russian captivity the following year. (Photo © Musée Napléonien d'Art et d'Histoire, Fontainebleau)

squadron of the Dutch Royal Guard from Spain during the month of March.

In terms of fighting strength present with the Regiment in Russia the picture was rather different. Despite their limited exposure to combat the losses in men and horses had been heavy, and almost entirely due to sickness, injury and exhaustion; of the 1,200 men who had left Versailles only about 700 were still present. They were therefore happy to see a reinforcement of 40 lancers arrive on 3 September. Apart from the men taken at Babinovitz the great bulk of those absent from the ranks were not dead or missing in action, but had been left behind spread in handfuls along the Regiment's whole route, in hospitals and temporary depots from Magdeburg to Stettin, Elbing, Vilna and Smolensk. From Gjat, Chef d'escadron de Watteville wrote to his parents:

"Before Smolensk I had already noticed a slight pain in my right thigh, as if I had given myself a knock, but I could not see any blue bruising. During the five days that we stayed in Smolensk after the battle the pain increased, preventing me from walking about. The doctor prescribed rubbing with melted butter and camphor, and later with oil and alkali. This brought me no relief. The swelling was increasing and becoming hard, the function of the muscles was impeded more and more, and it was always painful. I kept up with the regiment in the saddle until we reached Dogorbni [Dorogobuj]. Then the pain became unendurable and, unable to sleep, I asked the general if I might ride in his carriage with him. In this manner I reached Viazma; I was not putting ointment on my thigh, since although the compresses gave relief the swelling got worse - this had now reached my knee, though it softened from time to time.

The doctor diagnosed an abcess.

"Since we were in bivouac during the day and he had not the means to treat me as the condition required, he wanted to await our arrival in Moscow. The pain was so great, however, that I begged him not to postpone the operation, and it was carried out in a barn near Viazma. The doctor cut the thigh open down to the bone; luckily he found the seat of the problem, and was very happy that he had proceeded with this intervention. He took out an enormous amount of very thick matter which had built up between the bone and the muscles, so much so that further delay could have endangered my life through bone decay and the loss of my leg. This was the reason for the unendurable pain. The operation was extremely painful, but since then I feel surprisingly relieved.

"What worries me is that the Emperor has announced that the general battle so long refused by the Russians [will take place at Borodino] tomorrow or the day after. I will not be able to take part in it, and thus will lose any professional advantage from this campaign - no one will be able to recommend me for favours, since everyone will have deserved them. My only hope is that the Guard will perhaps not be committed, since the Russians should number no more than 80,000 to 100,000 men while we have four united Army Corps. And then, they must be exhausted, having been harried along all the time by our divisions. In any case, this will see us in Moscow within a week. A few days' convalesence will be enough to stop suppuration and close the wound."

After his operation Albert de Watteville received from Napoleon the offer, confirmed by an order signed between Smolensk and Moscow, to stay in the rear or even to go back to France to continue his recovery. Predictably, the ambitious young squadron commander refused.

★ ★ ★

On 4 September the Lancers mounted at about 8a.m.; while the brigade was forming the duty officers checked the bivouacs, as usual, in order to extinguish any fires which might spread through loose straw to the houses of the village. All that day and the next the Regiment marched eastward. Since the French had left Dorogobuj every day had seen some part of the Grande Armée's outriding screen clash with the Russian rearguard; on 5 September it was to be the Netherlands troopers of the 11th Hussars, who made a brilliant charge though at heavy cost. The Red Lancers arrived before Borodino that evening; the whole Guard was brought together around the Emperor's tented headquarters, and remained there the next day.

Battle was imminent at last. Since 20 August Barclay's and Bagration's armies had been placed under the joint command of General Kutuzov - old, fat, half blinded; but shrewd, vastly experienced, and trusted by the soldiers. Arriving with the combined armies at Tsarevo on 29 August, he had ordered a further withdrawal to Borodino. Here he stood, forming his line on a slight ridge with a forward position at the village of Shevardino. His centre right was anchored on Borodino village, his centre on Semenovskaya, his left on Utitsa, and his line butressed by a number of strong earthwork redoubts contructed by his engineers. His army numbered perhaps 125,000, of which 30,000 were untrained recruits and peasant levies - the *opolchenie*, largely armed with pikes. The bulk of his forces were solid, however, and better rested than the French; his artillery was also stronger than Napoleon's by more than 50 guns.

Napoleon's 133,000-odd men came up before Borodino on 5 September; and that evening a preliminary engagement saw the Russian advanced position at Shevardino taken, recaptured, and finally abandoned. There was no real fighting on the 6th, as both armies readied themselves for battle. In every encampment of the Grande Armée soldiers looked to their gear, NCOs harassed their soldiers, and officers wasted their NCOs' time with unnecessary questions. A hundred thousand musket locks were cleaned, and swathed against the damp with scraps of oily rag; a hundred thousand new flints were snugly seated home in the jaws; from every side rose the sinister grinding of stones putting a murderous edge on cold steel. The crews of nearly 600 cannon scrubbed and greased and hammered and trued-up, while their sergeants

hovered muttering over the contents of trail boxes and caissons. Thirty thousand riders and drivers groomed and watered their thin, scabby, overworked horses, trying to ignore the obvious signs of poor condition. From every camp patrols and foraging parties fanned out across the plains. The weather had turned wet and chill; but the sun would shine briefly on the early morning of the 7th - the day of Borodino, which the French would call "the battle of the Moskowa".

On 7 September the blaring trumpets roused the Regiment at 3a.m., well before dawn. In full uniform they sat their saddles to hear the Emperor's address; then they moved off to take up their assigned position behind the centre right with the rest of the Guard reserve. And there, for most of the long day's fighting, they stayed.

Borodino/la Moskowa was an exercise in attrition which showed none of Napoleon's old flair for bold movements. Marshal Davout argued that since the French were far better trained in battlefield manoeuvering than the enemy, the plan of attack should hinge on a major flanking movement against the over-extended Russian left wing. For some reason Napoleon ignored this sound advice from his best Corps commander. Apart from a limited move against the Russian left at Utitsa by Poniatowski's Poles the whole day-long battle was simply a killing match, a competition in butchery and endurance. Foot, horse and guns tore into one another during a series of massive frontal attacks and counterattacks over the Russian fortifications. Advantage swayed back and forth for hours, until the Russian "Great Redoubt" finally fell and Napoleon pushed cavalry through the gap. Marshals Davout and Ney both pleaded with the Emperor that he should release the Guard to exploit the hard-won advantage; Bessières and Murat argued against it, and Napoleon, unwell and strangely listless, refused. The Russians fell back, but the French were too mauled and exhausted to turn the victory to decisive advantage. The Grande Armée suffered about 30,000 dead and wounded, Kutuzov's forces about 44,000 (including Bagration, mortally wounded) - perhaps 35 and 40 per cent of their totals.

At about noon General Colbert's Brigade of Lancers of the Guard was ordered to move across to the left of the French line. It was thought that they might have to move up in support of Prince Eugène's IV Corps, which appeared to be in difficulties in the face of an attack by some 8,000 of Kutuzov's cavalry. The Lancers crossed the Kolocha river and took up a position on the road to Borodino. After sitting a while under fire of the Russians the general sent Adjutant de Stuers to the Emperor to ask his instructions. Napoleon was watching events on foot accompanied by Marshall Berthier and many staff officers. De Stuers made his report to Berthier; the chief-of-staff repeated it to Napoleon, who replied: *"As soon as the village [Borodino] is occupied, Colbert will go and take position on its right, along the woods"*, pointing at the spot with his finger. Adjutant de Stuers relayed the order to Colbert; but after the Regiment had begun the movement the situation turned in favour of Eugène, and the Lancers returned to their start line.

With the other Guard regiments they were later moved forward to an area near the captured Semenovskoye redoubt where they stayed, surrounded by the dead and dying, until nearly six that evening. Wounded men were carried to any available surgeon in a never-ending stream; the Lancers' medical officers Mergell and Hennige worked without respite on the bloody field. The Regiment themselves suffered one notable loss - Lieutenant Georges Fallot was wounded, and would die in Moscow of a "brain fever" on 14 October. This was a sad personal blow for General Colbert, since Fallot was his favourite adjutant, sleeping at his commander's door each night and taking responsibility for his safety.

The Red Lancers spent the night after the battle in woods between Shevardino and the old road to Smolensk on the French right flank. This part of the field had been taken by the Polish troops of Prince Poniatowski's V Corps. The ground between the trees was so choked with dead men and horses that the Lancers had to lift scores of corpses out of their way before they could clear a space to make their bivouac. In the gathering darkness rain began to fall.

The next morning the Regiment received no marching orders; the Lancers used the respite to care for their horses and their uniforms, and to go out foraging. This was Colonel-Major van Hasselt's particular responsibility, and he organised forage and reconnaissance parties to ride out in all directions. After some time one of the foraging parties under the command of the younger Lieutenant Ziegler came riding into camp apparently panicstricken, claiming that they were being pursued by a strong force of Cossacks.

Shouts of *"To arms!"*, *"To horse!"*, and *"The Cossacks are coming!"* quickly spread throughout the bivouacs and horse lines of all the Guard cavalry regiments; trumpets began to shriek and drums rolled. Most of the horses were unsaddled and most of the officers and troopers in undress order. Some snatched up their carbines or lances to defend themselves on foot; those who could do so rode out, conducted by their officers, to buy time to allow their comrades to get into the saddle. Fortunately, the passing minutes soon proved that this was a false alarm.

Marshal Bessières, one of the first to get mounted, questioned young Pieter Ziegler closely; the lieutenant insisted that his party had been attacked by Cossacks who must have broken off the chase before reaching the encampment. To be on the safe side the marshal sent out a squadron; they soon returned without seeing any sign of Cossacks, and the troopers were able to get back to their camp chores - no doubt with a new subject for ribald humour.

Even the regimental jokers probably fell silent when, on the afternoon of the 8th, the Lancers were ordered to march to Mojaïsk and crossed the battlefield of Borodino diagonally to reach the main road to Moscow. The spectacle in all directions was like a picture of hell. Experienced veterans, some of whom had been campaigning for ten years and more, had never seen anything more horrible, or on such a scale. For nearly a mile the ground was thickly carpeted with dead men, wounded men in the last extremity of agony, torn-off limbs scattered among them,

dead and dying horses, and every kind of weapon and impedimenta smashed or discarded. Riding under a steady rain in column of fours, the Regiment could hardly pass over the field; the horses were constantly turning and stepping aside as they picked their way over the hideous harvest of battle, trying to avoid treading on the bodies. Taking a road through woodlands, it was night before they came out onto the cultivated plain before Mojaïsk, where they received the order to bivouac. The cold rain was falling in torrents.

On 9 September at seven in the morning the fighting started afresh. The Russians were withdrawing slowly and stubbornly, and were holding the town of Mojaïsk. Murat's Reserve Cavalry were attacked in strength; he ordered General Colbert's brigade to cover his right flank and to reconnoitre in that direction. During one of these reconnaissances several detachments were destroyed. At 11a.m. the enemy abandoned the town (nicknamed "Cabbageville"); and the Lancers later made their bivouacs in the village of Kadnirovo to the south.

★   ★   ★

At about four on the afternoon of the 10th Colbert's brigade were detached to act as raiders, cutting the road from Kaluga to Moscow and interrupting the enemy's communications with the Russian Army of Moldavia. After a number of halts while marching over a beautifully cultivated plain they reached a good-sized village named Gorki; here they set up their bivouac for the night, and found plenty of food for both men and horses.

On 11 September at about 11a.m. the brigade discovered a bivouac covered with hay where some oats and a few potatoes had been left. According to the peasants it had been occupied the previous night by Russian cavalry, who had retired upon the approach of a few hundred horses of the French army moving on the Mojaïsk road, and then went back by that same road. While the brigade was forming in the field the vanguard fired a few pistol shots and set off in puruit of some enemy horsemen, bringing two of them back as prisoners. From this point on the Lancers were marching through a mixture of woodland and frequent areas of attractive, well-cultivated terrain; the villages they passed through were deserted but less miserable than before,

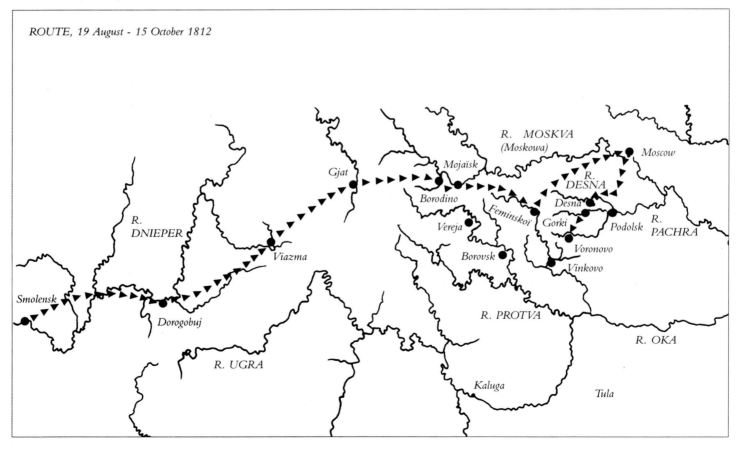

ROUTE, 19 August - 15 October 1812

and there were occasional estates with substantial country houses.

On 12 September the Lancers mounted before dawn as usual. The scouts returned with nothing to report; the horses were fed, and at about seven they left the village heading west. Probing ahead with very little information about what to expect, they passed by the village of Malkovo and reached Feminskoï, a small market town presided over by an attractive chateau belonging to one Prince Dolgorouki. On the 13th scouts were sent out for about six miles in every direction, but no troops were seen. Sometimes they captured peasants fleeing on small carts loaded with bad bread; and they came across large numbers of pikes, presumably intended for distribution to the serfs.

Every day General Colbert sent reports on the brigade's progress and situation to Marshal Bessières, carried by a lieutenant escorted by a dozen troopers. On another occasion Hubert de Stuers was sent to Marshal Murat to receive orders. To avoid drawing the attention of the Cossacks he took only one orderly with him. They passed by burnt-out villages, often turning aside or hiding to avoid parties of Cossacks; and after a seven-hour ride they came up with Murat's vanguard. Sumptuously uniformed as always, the King of Naples was riding at the head of his squadrons. Having collected his orders de Stuers took another road to rejoin his regiment. Not hearing the sound of guns to guide him or encountering any plundered or burnt-out villages, the adjutant lost his way. He and his orderly rode all night before falling in with a patrol of Red Lancers who could lead him back to the general.

On 15 September the Lancers, mounted at daybreak in front of their bivouacs, noticed a vedette who had ventured a little way from the woods in front of a position which men of the regiment were occupying to the east of the camp, on the left bank of the Nara river. The regimental outpost on the Moscow road received orders via an adjutant to send out a few men to seize the horseman. Meanwhile, passing through Feminskoï at a gallop, the general's aide-de-camp Lieutenant Brack was also making his way towards the enemy scout, and rapidly closed the distance between them. He fired a pistol shot, but then vanished into a ditch while chasing the Russian rider. Joined by troopers from the outpost and by a squadron which had spontaneously decided to join in, Fortuné Brack had the skirts of the woodland searched, but his quarry was nowhere to be seen.

Shortly afterwards a patrol of Red Lancers returned to the bivouac with an instructive tale. They had been following the Nara on its right bank; having noticed nothing suspicious they crossed the river after five miles and turned back again, riding rather too relaxed. At the rear Sergeant-Major Duyghuysen and one lancer halted; they had barely dismounted when several shots rang out. The trooper was killed outright, and a group of riders who looked like Cossacks dashed out from the cover of the nearby forest to drag away the unfortunate sergeant-major and both horses. When the officer leading the patrol turned back to assist his men he saw 80 to 100 horsemen breaking cover at the edge of the trees, apparently waiting for him to react in this way. The Red Lancers, who numbered only 30, decided to withdraw. From now on the brigade had to increase surveillance in the neighbourhood of their position, being without any quick means of communication with the army and ignorant of its movements.

On the 16th peasants brought back by the various patrols and foraging parties declared that many Cossacks had been seen in the locality, and that they were gradually closing into a circle around the brigade's area of operations. At about 10a.m. the outposts on the plateau to the south and on the open terrain within sight of Malkovo opened fire. As the brigade mounted a lancer rode in at full speed. He had been sent to General Colbert by the commander of the detachment, Chef d'escadron Coti, to inform him that a reconnaissance party had been taken by surprise by Cossacks in a wood on the road to Borovsk. This detachment consisted of 70 men drawn both from the Red Lancers and from the 7th Lancers of the Line (a unit raised from the former Vistula

Willem A. Verhellouw (1790-1815) entered the Dutch army in 1807, and after the annexation of Holland in 1810 was assigned to the French 11th Hussars. Promoted second-lieutenant on 2 June 1812, he served in Russia, where the Red Lancers had occasional contact with their fellow countrymen of the 11th. He survived the retreat, being promoted lieutenant on 2 August 1813 and fighting in the Saxon and French campaigns. After the first abdication he was one of many Dutch officers who joined the new army of the Netherlands; he would be killed fighting the French at Waterloo as a lieutenant in the 6th Hussars. (Collection of Dutch Royal Army Museum, Delft)

Lancers, veterans of Spain, who were attached to the Polish 1st Lancers of the Guard). The Cossacks had ambushed them from the front, the flank and the rear, throwing them into great confusion and putting them to flight.

At once the brigade made their best speed towards the detachment; but when they came up with them they found that the two outposts had already gone forward and helped the reconnaissance party to rally. The enemy, contained for the time being, had taken shelter among trees and undergrowth on flat ground to the south-east; they seemed to be about 200 strong. A squadron of the Polish Lancers charged and drove them off, supported by General Colbert with the rest of the brigade formed up 200 yards forward of the outposts, ready to move wherever needed.

The Lancers were angered by this skirmish; according to the Poles with the party it was a result of the recklessness of the reconnaissance leader. The men were furious at having seen Red Lancers put to flight by a gang of Cossacks, and they grieved for their dead: the Regiment had lost seven men, among them Trumpeter Grobé and Corporal Hamerslag.

The detachment from the 7th, commanded by Lieutenant Boguslawski, had lost five men wounded and taken prisoner. The Polish lieutenant was furious that these losses had been caused by the lack of experience of a superior officer; he challenged Lieutenant Deban de Laborde of the Red Lancers to a duel, which luckily did not prove fatal to either of them.

General Colbert was beginning to feel that his brigade had been completely forgotten. Each day they had to defend

Colonel-Major Charles M.J.Dubois (1772-1829), by Dubois-Drahonet; in this portrait he has had the artist paint him in the uniform of the Dutch Royal Guard Hussars, the fur-trimmed pelisse worn as a jacket. In 1787 at the age of fifteen he entered the Royal Dragoons, the regiment of his uncle Count de Villers, as a candidate for an officer's vacancy; two of his elder brothers were already serving in the regiment, one as an officer candidate and one as a captain. (Private collection)

themselves against groups of the enemy which seemed to surround him on all sides; and he could make little sense of the contradictory reports which were reaching him by more or less dubious routes. One night he was surprised to see on the horizon the glow of what was obviously a great fire whose source he could not make out. When local civilians told him that it was Moscow itself that was burning, he decided to go and search out for himself the orders which he had been awaiting in vain. By coincidence a staff officer arrived almost immediately from the castle of Petrowskoï, where the Emperor was installed, carrying orders for Colbert to bring his brigade to Moscow.

Moscow

On 18 September the scouts brought back some peasants they had caught at daybreak; these claimed that there were Cossacks at Borovsk, a lot of troops in Serpukhov, on the Oka, and on the road to Kaluga. They also said that they had been told that the entire Russian army was at Podolsk on the Pakhra.

Colbert's brigade, formed in column by platoons, left Feminskoï - untouched - at noon that day. Its outposts on the left bank of the Nara formed the vanguard, and its scouts and those on the right bank the rearguard. At a short distance from Feminskoï lay the road to Moscow. Like all the roads in open country, this was very wide; as the dirt surface was torn up by hooves and wheels those who followed automatically spread out onto firmer ground to either side. After passing through woodland the Lancers found themselves in sight of Bykassowa and its castle. At nightfall the brigade arrived in a large village occupied by French infantry where they made their encampment.

For the first time since they had left the main army eight days before they could sleep without fear of surprise attack.

The next day they set out again at eight in the morning for Moscow. After a few miles they began to make out the sun reflecting on the green and gold domes and spires of this enormous city, now partly concealed by vast curtains of smoke torn by whirlwinds of flame. Napoleon had sighted the capital on 14 September, by which time the civilian population was already being evacuated eastwards. The first French troops entered the city as the last Russian rearguard pulled out; nobody will ever know whether accident or deliberate arson started the fires which would reduce three-quarters of the city to ashes.

Before reaching the walls the brigade was guided off to its quarters on the left of the road - Troitskoï, a large and handsome village occupied by part of the cavalry and artillery of the Guard. With all its men, horses, wagons and impedimenta the brigade was spread over several smaller villages round about. Installed in their bivouacs that evening, the troopers had to endure a whole night of rain.

The Regiment were not allowed to enter the Holy City in strength, but small parties were sent in to collect fresh supplies. Inside they found wine, Russian "champagne" made from birch sap, tea, coffee, sugar, rice and tobacco. Flour was provided, and lancers were set to work producing fresh bread in a bakery established in the regimental quarters. These treats were not to be enjoyed at leisure, however. Rigorous inspections, ordered from the first morning rollcall in Moscow, confirmed that much of the Regiment's equipment was in urgent need of repair. Workshops were set up without delay. Farriers and veterinaries attended to the horses, which were now able to remain unsaddled night and day for the first time since the start of the campaign. It was while the Lancers were busying themselves in Moscow that Napoleon, noticing troopers going about their chores dressed in their sky blue stable jackets, said to General Colbert: *"Do you think that I put my Guard Lancers in red uniform just so that they could keep it for peacocking around the Palais Royal? Make them wear it."*

On 21 September Napoleon wrote to the Grande Armée's chief-of-staff, Marshal Berthier: "You will order the Duke of Istria [Bessières] to send out General Colbert today with the two Lancer regiments of the Guard to support General Girardin by moving forward on the road to Podolsk." It was the next day before the order to leave reached Colbert; he was to support Murat's troops sent in pursuit of the enemy, and was to take position as a reserve close to a village named Voronovo. Their brief rest was over, and the life of the outposts awaited them once more.

De Watteville was convalescing in Moscow when he heard that the Regiment had been ordered forward; keen to follow them but unable to ride, he succeeded in borrowing General Colbert's carriage. For four days he wandered lost on the steppe; his health growing worse, he was forced to return to Moscow where he was treated by Lherminier, Napoleon's doctor. He was accomodated in the palace of Princess Tsartoriska along with several of his comrades.

The Regiment set off with the Polish Lancers at 4p.m. on 22 September on the road south to Podolsk. Passing under the southern walls of Moscow they noticed handsome promenades, restaurants, taverns with dancehalls, attractive gardens and fine houses. This part of the city, inside as well as outside the walls, had not suffered badly from the fires. Arriving near the Serpukhov barrier they found themselves sharing the road with one or two cavalry divisions, an enormous convoy of baggage, and several very richly decorated carriages driven by soldiers. That evening they made camp in the rain at Molodtzi, where Marshal Bessières had his headquarters.

They had not long been on the road on the 23rd when the order was given to set up camp near a windmill and a hamlet of some ten houses. The squadrons made their bivouacs in rows, sheltered to some degree by gardens on the right and bushes on the left. Two guns were positioned near the mill, and half a battalion of infantry were in the nearby woods. The rain eased off after a while. On the 24th they mounted at about 9a.m. and passed through a fringe of forest before coming out onto the plain of Podolsk.

Contact with the Cossacks was now becoming an almost daily occurence. On 25 September a reconnaissance was organised under command of Chef d'escadron de Tiecken, composed of one squadron each from the Polish and Dutch Lancers led respectively by Captains Brocki and Calkoen. Their mission was to act as scouts and vanguard for the rest of the brigade, whose orders were to follow the main Tula road towards Podolsk, to make contact with the enemy, and to position themselves between the Corps of Murat and Bessières.

Nearing Bouïkhovo after nearly three hours' ride, Calkoen's squadron were advancing a few hundred yards ahead of the Poles when Lieutenant Doyen led his point troop up a hillock. They were immediately attacked from all sides by Cossacks. Lieutenant van Omphal's troop were at once sent to help them disengage, but were outflanked in their turn. The Red Lancers fell back towards the Polish squadron, who had halted and taken up battle formation. Under this cover the Dutch Lancers regrouped and charged the Cossacks again, and at that moment the brigade came up and the Cossacks fled.

A final charge by the Red Lancers allowed them to free some of the men captured by the enemy during this half-hour running fight, but almost the whole of Doyen's troop had been killed or taken prisoner. Lieutenant Nicolas Deban de Laborde had taken a lance thrust in his right arm. (At the end of the Empire in 1815 Deban de Laborde could say that he had lost six brothers on the field of honour: the eldest as colonel of the 8th Hussars at Wagram, two in the Navy and three in the Russian campaign.) Among the Poles, Captain Brocki had fallen into Cossack hands. Antonie van Omphal was furious at the outcome of the fight, feeling that the brigade had taken too long to come up in support. General Colbert calmed him down, praising his part in the engagement and opening one of two bottles of rum which had been found in a deserted country house.

Shortly after this Marshal Murat sent General Tyszkiewicz with his 4th Polish Mounted Chasseurs from the V Corps cavalry to reinforce the Lancers of the Guard. The Red Lancers' field strength was down to only 300 fit horses. (The general impatiently awaited the expected arrival on 5 November of the 4th Marching Regiment, which would leave Vilna for Moscow on 28 September with the rest of the Regiment's 5th Squadron under Captain Timmerman – 168 troopers and 172 horses.)

After the engagement near Bouïkhovo the brigade left the road to Podolsk, followed by the Poles, to head for the road leading to Kaluga. There they made camp on the evening of the 25th, six or seven hours' ride from Moscow. Suddenly a few Cossacks showed themselves not far away from the bivouacs. A troop from 6th Company led by Lieutenant de Wacker van Son, who was dining with Lieutenant van Omphal, were sent out to chase them off and reconnoitre. A quarter of an hour later the troop of 25 lancers rode into an ambush, and were slaughtered before any reinforcements could intervene. George de Wacker van Son was from Utrecht; at 26 years old, he had been in the Dutch army since joining the Waldeck infantry regiment as a cadet at seventeen. This was his first campaign.

That night the Regiment camped in the open as best they could, lashed by rain and a violent wind; they had no firewood, hardly any straw - and they had lost nearly 50 comrades in one day. At least the rain stopped next morning, and all ranks tried to dry their gear during a day mostly spent in scouting. That night they made camp at Rakitki where Marshal Bessières had his headquarters; in the event they stayed there until 29 September, and as before Lieutenant van Omphal acted as orderly officer to the marshal. During these three days a number of actions were taking place, but the Guard Lancer brigade were not involved. After having repaired the bridge at Rakitki, destroyed by the Russians, Bessières' column got on the road again; their aim was

Karel G.E.Mergell (1781-1851), the former surgeon-major of the Red Lancers, who rose to head the medical service of the Netherlands army and the hospital at Leiden. (Collection of Dutch Royal Army Museum, Delft)

to go to the support of Murat, who was pursuing the elusive enemy with units of his Reserve Cavalry.

On the afternoon of 30 September the brigade crossed the Desna to set up bivouacs at Gorki. From 1 to 4 October the lancers' only mission was to provide for the security of their own encampment. The weather was pleasant; the troopers used the opportunity to repair and clean their equipment, and also to build quite solid huts - their bivouac began to resemble a regular camp.

On the 4th General Lauriston, ADC to the Emperor and former ambassador to Russia, passed the French vanguard's camps in the afternoon on his way to the Russian headquarters for a parley. He had been instructed to discuss peace terms; according to the Emperor, "honour must be saved". Napoleon's situation was far from satisfactory. His army around Moscow had been reduced to about 95,000 men, but nevertheless the stripped capital did not offer enough in the way of supplies and usable resources to return it to full efficiency. Large numbers of men were scattered along his vulnerable lines of communication all the way back to the Niemen, and the strength and morale of many of the foreign contingents left much to be desired.

These rear lines were under increasingly frequent attack from Cossacks and by-passed groups of Russian regulars; they were cut, temporarily, as early as 24 September. Around Kaluga General Kutuzov was receiving recruits and volunteers fast enough to rebuild an army of between 110,000 and 120,000 men, now unified under his sole command; and a wave of Russian patriotism was expressed in rapidly increasing guerrilla activity at many points along the French corridor to Moscow.

While Napoleon awaited the Tsar's reply to his overtures a kind of armistice prevailed between the troops of the opposing armies - or at least between the regulars - and a brief period of peace settled over the Moscow region. On 5 October the Guard Lancer brigade received orders to move forward, and set off at 10a.m.; they crossed the Pakhra and headed for Mocza and

Voronovo, where they set up camp. Moscow's military governor, Rostopchin, owned a country house there, and in an apparent desire to prove that he too was willing to sacrifice all for the Motherland he had set fire to it before leaving. According to Dumonceau, he had left a message written on the walls: "I, Governor of Moscow, have burnt my chateau so that these French dogs cannot use it"; but Lieutenant van Omphal claimed that when he arrived the inscription referred simply to "the French", and that he noticed that somebody had added the word "dogs" only the following day. Van Omphal was happy to be able to rejoin the Regiment there due to the concentration of the Guard cavalry by Marshal Bessières during the armistice. It was on the 5th that Captain Calkoen found leisure to write to his father:

"We found Moscow absolutely deserted, not a single soul remaining. The government had ordered the inhabitants to leave their houses and evacuate the city. At four o'clock on the afternoon of 14 September the Emperor entered the city with the Guard, and by five o'clock fire had broken out in every quarter - another result of Russian brutality. They had released convicts on condition that, hidden all over the town, they would set it on fire at an agreed signal. When it became obvious that the flames were going to consume this beautiful city anyway, pillaging was allowed, and this lasted for three or four days. We have found a lot of objects of value in the cellars. Moscow is one of the most beautiful cities that I have ever seen, but it is almost completely burned down.

"We have been detached from the Guard and are involved daily with the Cossacks, who are doing us a lot of harm. Alerts are frequent. The Cossacks are not brave but they are very skilled at skirmishing, and they always outnumber us when they allow themselves be approached. They are strong because they know the tricks of laying ambushes. They are armed with lances.

"I have no recent news of Piet, who has been sent back to the depot at Smolensk because his horse was spent. He was in good spirits. General Lauriston has just passed by our bivouac to meet the Russian general commanding the road to Kaluga (we are here on this road nine leagues from Moscow). We have absolutely no idea what will happen to us during this winter; we have been in bivouac constantly for three and a half months now. Luckily we are having magnificent weather (for the moment, at least); the rains which are usually abundant at this season seem to be sparing us.

"God protect France. This campaign is certainly the most terrible yet. I am longing to be able to talk about it as a past experience; but with two armies, one always withdrawing and the other always pursuing across the vast fields of Russia, peace is not very likely to be made. It seems that the Russians make war like madmen, at least judging by the evacuation of Moscow. If the people had stayed there complete discipline could have been maintained, but a town deserted and in flames is good for nothing but plundering. As a rule we have found the houses empty and the inhabitants chased away by the enemy in every town where we have been. It is the same in the villages; the peasants flee into the woods. The result is that we sometimes have some difficulty in finding supplies; we have not had to go hungry yet, but drink is another matter - most of the time we are compelled to drink water. Hope upholds us...Now we are to mount again, to follow the road to Kaluga."

Marshal Bessières spent the night of 6 October at Voronovo. The weather was dry and very pleasant; the nights, too, were beautiful, though the morning cold was biting. As the strange calm persisted the Regiment stayed in its bivouacs. On the 10th they were ordered to head for Moscow to take some days' rest, and at once broke camp at Voronovo to recross the Pakhra and reoccupy their bivouac at Gorki, where most of their huts still stood waiting.

Colonel-Major van Hasselt took time to write a letter to his brother and sister; he had just received terrible news, and in the cruellest way.

During their stay at Voronovo he had been invited to the quarters of General Colbert, who informed him that he had just heard that van Hasselt's wife had died at Versailles on 2 September - yet just four days beforehand Jan van Hasselt had received a letter telling him that she had just born him their sixth child and that all was well. The general suggested that he return to Versailles at once to care for his children and make any necessary arrangements, but he refused; even if he had left immediately it would have taken him about three months to reach home. The pain of bereavement was given an additional twist by the loss of his last precious souvenirs of his family: a thief in the night had stolen from his packhorse not only his irreplaceable full dress uniform, but also the portmanteau containing his letters and a lock of his wife's hair.

The Regiment left Gorki the next day at eight in the morning, crossing the Desna at the village of the same name and riding via Rakitki, Sosenki and Teplyie-Stany to reach Serghievskoe in the afternoon. This village about seven miles from Moscow was not too badly damaged and was still inhabited; General Colbert moved into the chateau.

The Regiment in the field now numbered 48 officers with 145 horses, 508 troopers with 348 horses, and nine draught horses. A total of one officer with two horses and 242 lancers with 158 horses were detached to the various small depots at Danzig, Königsberg, Vilna and Smolensk; one officer and 56 lancers were in hospital. Three officers and 91 lancers were listed as having been taken prisoner. The Regiment's depot for the dismounted troopers and sick or lame horses was located in the village of Troiskaganenitscheva a couple of miles outside Moscow, on the left of the main road as one left the city. Large and small parties of reinforcements had until now been arriving continuously. On 13 October a marching squadron composed of 122 troopers and 152 horses drawn from the Mounted Chasseurs, Mounted Grenadiers and Lancers of the Guard set off from Minsk. They arrived at Smolensk on 25 October, but were ordered to proceed no further; since 14 October the Emperor had ordered that all reinforcements for Moscow should cease.

On the night of the 14th orders reached the Regiment to leave the next day and return to their hutted camp at Gorki; they got on the road at seven on the morning of the 15th. Although hostilities between the regular troops remained suspended it was noticeable that the Cossacks and partisans were becoming more and more active. On 17 October a Cuirassiers supply convoy was attacked and ten wagons captured; alerted, the Red Lancers attacked the Cossacks in their turn and managed to recapture some of the vehicles.

At Vinkovo on 18 October the armistice was brought to a brutal end. While he waited in frustration for the Tsar to agree to negotiate terms, Napoleon - who was under no illusions about wintering in ruined Moscow - had been planning to lead his army back to Smolensk. He was confident that Kutuzov did not have the means to prevent him; but at Vinkovo the one-eyed old general disabused him of that notion. There he took Murat's cavalry by surprise, inflicting a heavy defeat and driving him back towards Voronovo with the loss of 2,500 dead and wounded and 2,000 prisoners.

That night Lieutenant van Omphal was sent to the Emperor in Moscow with despatches from Murat, arriving at seven on the morning of the 19th. Brought before Napoleon, Antonie van Omphal delivered his report during a quarter of an hour. When he had passed on all the information he had the Emperor told him, *"All right, go and get some rest. I will meet the King of Naples during the day - I am leaving in one hour."*

Thus began the Grande Armée's retreat from Moscow.

CHAPTER III

1812: The Retreat from Moscow

On that day, 19 October 1812, the Red Lancers saw troops passing by their encampment down the road from Moscow; and on questioning them they were told that the evacuation of the capital had been ordered.

The next morning they watched the largely Italian and Spanish soldiers of Prince Eugène's IV Corps march by, to form the vanguard of the army on its march back to Smolensk. Shortly afterwards the Guard Lancer brigade were ordered to Desna to take up a rearguard position guarding the bridge crossing the river of the same name. After ensuring that no troops or baggage belonging to the army had been left behind they were to burn the bridge down.

The lancers marched at one o'clock in the afternoon of the 20th. Passing through Batukinka they found a number of wagons whose teams were already too exhausted by hunger to pull them any further. On reaching Desna village they crossed the bridge and established their bivouacs on the left bank near some barns close to the road from Moscow. This was packed solid with bodies of troops marching and riding, gun teams and vehicles; at this stage spirits seemed to be high, and the soldiers were marching with great confidence. The Grande Armée still numbered about 90,000 men with 500 cannon, vast numbers of wagons and carts of every description loaded with every kind of baggage and loot, and thousands of camp-followers. These latter included the lost and the opportunistic: the odds and ends of straggling soldiery of a dozen nationalities; the women and children who had risked all to accompany their men to war; the civilian servants, drivers and grooms who were in those days hired in large numbers for the duration of a campaign; the traders in every kind of goods and services, the thieves, whores, and other male and female hangers-on who always attached themselves to a marching army of that period.

On 21 October the Emperor wrote to his chief-of-staff Marshal Berthier:

"Instruct General Colbert to send at least 200 horse towards Moscow until they meet up with Colonel Deschamps' cavalry, and make certain that the officer who is carrying important orders gets to the Kremlin before nine o'clock in the evening. He will inform the Duke of Treviso [Marshal Mortier, military governor of Moscow] that he will await his answer and that he needs to have it before midnight. The Duke of Treviso will send his answer by one of his officers, who will return accompanied by the 200 lancers.

"P.S. The party which General Colbert sends out is to return to Desna, from where he will have a fresh officer bring the Duke of Treviso's answer to the Emperor's headquarters, via Gorki and on the right of the road to Fominskiya. General Colbert will make use of his detachment to clear the road from Moscow, picking up stragglers and burning all vehicles left behind. He will make certain that tomorrow, the 22nd, by seven in the morning, there will nothing left between Desna and Moscow."

The weather was still pleasant and comparatively mild. A little rain fell during the evening, but it did not last long.

On the evening of the 21st the brigade crossed the Desna again and took up position on the right bank in the gardens of the village, facing the bridge. A detachment composed of 50 men from each of the regiments and led by a chef d'escadron of the Red Lancers occupied Rakitki and reconnoitred the road on the far side of Sosenki. They saw no enemy, but came up with a number of vivandières' [sutler-women's] carts, and little parties of soldiers and civilians - dressed in a weird variety of clothing found in Moscow, loaded with supplies and loot, and straggling along in a long, chaotic column. The lancer patrol urged them to catch up with the army without further delay, and warned them that they would burn their vehicles if they found them the next day still too far behind the rearguard to profit from its protection.

On 22 October the brigade was reinforced at Desna with an infantry battalion from General Morand's division of Davout's I Corps (which at this stage was providing the main rearguard formation for the army). General Colbert was ordered to pull out that afternoon; in fact he decided to wait another four or five hours before finally destroying the bridge. His decision saved from certain death or captivity some 12,000 military and civilian stragglers of both sexes and all ages, who had put off leaving Moscow until the last minute and who crossed the bridge to follow the army during those next few hours.

When the flow dwindled away that evening, and Colbert's last patrols up the Moscow road found no one else, he had the bridge set on fire by Russian peasants gathered at the spot for that purpose. The orders of the Emperor were executed with care; everything that the lancers could not take with them was smashed or burned. The bulk of the Regiment set off towards Gorki, which they reached at about 9.30 in the evening, though Captain Post only rode in at midnight with the brigade's rearguard. The Guard Lancers occupied their comfortable former bivouacs for

Captain Everhardus H.Heshusius (1773-1822), in a contemporary painting showing him in the uniform of an officer of the Dutch Dragoons in 1815. As a lieutenant in the Red Lancers he distinguished himself in the action in a village near Borovsk on 25 October 1812. (Photo © Stichting Iconographisch Bureau, The Hague)

the last time. Before they left the players of the Théâtre Français, who had travelled on the same road, performed for the general and his officers in the barn where they had taken shelter. The next day the Red Lancers left Gorki forever.

An outpost of Line cavalry at Voronovo passed the word for the brigade to turn right onto the old road from Moscow to Kaluga via Feminskoï and Borovsk. The lancers were the last formed unit of the army along this route; they found the road deserted apart from a few stragglers here and there. The Regiment halted from time to time to gather them up and give them the chance to march in front of the lancers.

The Regiment crossed the Nara at four on the morning of 24 October heading for Borovsk, which they reached at about 10.30a.m. General Colbert - who had just received orders to keep contact with the rearguard while the Emperor fought a Russian blocking force which Kutuzov had thrown across his path at Malojaroslavetz - ordered the Red Lancers to establish a bivouac behind the village of Oevarofskoie, along the main road and surrounded by woods. It was also on the 24th that the Russian General Platov ordered General Koeteinikof to take his four Cossack regiments through the forest to attack the rearguard of the Grande Armée, while its vanguard, Eugène's IV Corps, were trying to fight their way into Malojaroslavetz - a fierce 18-hour battle which would last into the next day. On the evening of the 24th the first Cossacks appeared in the fringes of the forest.

At 6a.m. on 25 October their numbers were seen to have grown, and they continued to mass under the very eyes of the French convoys moving along the main road. A Cossack officer rode close enough to the Guard Lancers to shout, in fluent French, "Come on then, come on, dandies of Paris!" The nearest were rapidly driven back by 50 Polish Lancers, who covered the passage along the road of General Morand's division from Davout's rearguard.

General Colbert, very conscious of the danger of getting his brigade sucked into an encirclement by far superior forces, quickly recalled the lancers who had made this charge; but the Cossacks, whose numbers were still growing, charged forward on the right of the French. They numbered between 3,000 and 4,000 men; Colbert, who had only 1,000 lancers at his disposal, deployed them so as to have his right flank in front of the houses of Oevarofskoie. Here he intended to lay an ambush with 300 to 400 soldiers of all arms under the orders of Lieutenant Heshusius of the Red Lancers. The Polish Lancers took position behind the Red Lancers, with the baggage horses behind them; Colbert hoped that this visible thickening-up of his line would give the impression of a reserve held in hand.

Captain Schneither was sent with some 48 Red Lancers on observation at some distance forward of the Regiment; Lieutenant Verhaegen deployed his troop in skirmishing order and opened a harassing fire on the enemy. This situation lasted until 2p.m., when the Cossacks made a threatening move towards these skirmishers. At once General Colbert ordered a retreat in echelon towards the bivouac, and this manoeuvre was executed with such precision that Major Dautancourt of the Polish Lancers compared it to an exercise at the Chantilly depot. Suddenly 400 or 500 Cossacks charged Captain Schneither's isolated squadron, and within a few moments they had surrounded it. The lancers defended themselves vigorously, hoping to cut their way through the enemy, but in vain - the Cossacks were too numerous. General Colbert at once ordered Colonel-Major Dubois to lead his 2nd Squadron in a charge to drive a path through the enemy. Dubois' men reached Schneither's party, but then they in turn were encircled.

Colbert then charged with the last two squadrons of the

A striking impression of the Red Lancers during the retreat from Moscow. On 28 October the Regiment passed by the field of Borodino; nearly two months after the battle it presented a ghastly sight. (Collection of Belgian Royal Army Museum, Brussels)

Regiment, and finally succeeded in driving the Cossacks back. He gave the order "Left about turn by fours!" in a voice which soared above the din of fighting like that of an operatic tenor, and took his Regiment back with him to their first positions. The Russians pursued them closely for a quarter of an hour, until the moment when they reached the village of Oevarofskoie; here the fire of the ambush party put an end to the Cossack charges. Later on, Lieutenant van Omphal would remember the Polish Lancers shouting "Bravo, Dutchmen!", and waving their *czapskas* on the heads of their lances.

The Regiment had successfully resisted forces outnumbering them by three or four to one, but at severe cost: four officers wounded, 24 lancers and 30 horses killed or lost, not counting the vélites. (Lieutenant Hubert de Stuers would spend the whole of the coming night searching the field for his brother Leopold, a vélite-corporal - but in vain.) The Polish Lancers came forward to give the Red Lancers the chance to reform. Some of their wounded, plundered and left where they lay by the Cossacks, were rescued and put in carts. At 4p.m. on the 25th the Cossacks were seen to be withdrawing into the woods, but they still kept trying to cut off communications with Malojaroslavetz. General Colbert knew that he would not be able to resist such numbers if they turned on him again, and drew back to Borovsk where Marshal Ney's III Corps was stationed. There were repeated small engagements throughout the march.

* * *

On the 26th at 5p.m. the Regiment was ordered to join the rest of the Guard and to move on with them on the road to Vereja on the morning of the 27th. Marching as vanguard of the Imperial Guard they left Borovsk and crossed the Protva to reach Vereja. They were beginning to feel the cold; and on 27 October, when they mounted at daybreak, everything was covered with a thick blanket of snow. On the 28th they left at 7a.m., passing by Vereja, not far from the sinister field of Borodino; seven weeks after the battle this presented a nightmare spectacle. They established their bivouac near the abbey of Kolotskoï, a former field hospital which was still overcrowded with wounded men. On the 29th they were at Gjat, and on the 31st they reached Viazma where they stayed for two days. General Colbert was allowed to go foraging with his brigade; but on their return he was informed that the Emperor had already left, leaving orders for them to follow, which they did after a halt of about half an hour.

The Grande Armée's retreat was becoming harder by the day: their old enemies the Cossacks were following ever closer on their heels, and real hunger was starting to weaken men and horses - very little food could be found by foraging. Only in towns such as Gjat and Viazma were there small remaining depots, where distribution began in an orderly fashion but often ended in outright pillaging. Ironically, the weather was glorious - three or four degrees of frost under a brilliant sun. The first serious snowfall came on 3 November; the winter was upon them, although in daytime the sun's warmth still disguised its icy mask. It was on that day that the duty of guarding the rear of the retreating army passed from Davout to Michel Ney; in the weeks to come "the redhead" would show his finest qualities, but his Corps had already dwindled from some 10,000 to about 3,000 men.

By 4 November the Guard Lancers were only two hours' march to the right of the little town of Dorogobuj, and at 10a.m. the order was given to halt there. In order to gather forage for the day and to verify the brigade's position scouting detachments were sent out to the north and east, and - for once - returned laden with feed. It was a beautiful day, and the snow was melting a little in the unbroken sunshine. For a moment one might even have believed that the temperature was rising; but towards evening the cold set in again harder than ever. The Red Lancers were ordered to stand by to move off after midnight. At two in the morning they left their bivouacs to await the arrival of the Emperor and his Guard.

On 6 November they crossed the Dnieper and halted in a village on the right bank. On the 7th they stopped in a village which was only some six hours' march from Smolensk - the "promised land", where many hoped that they would be able to sit out the winter in relative comfort and plenty. After the milder weather of the last few days the snow was now drifting badly and the road had become almost impassable, especially at night.

On the 9th the brigade received the order to join the Emperor at Smolensk. The bridge over the Stabna was half destroyed and the Red Lancers, who were at the head of the column, had to cross it in single file.

They reached Smolensk at last, with its promise of shelter and food. The Regiment stayed for three days at the village of Prudiszi, where food and forage could still be found thanks to a Polish cavalry regiment stationed there since the first occupation of Smolensk - they had had time to assemble a stockpile which they now shared with the famished and exhausted lancers. The Red Lancers now mustered just 330 men and only 130 horses; 200 of them had made the last stages of the retreat on foot. At Smolensk they were reinforced by a detachment of 130 men, almost all from the 5th Squadron and the provisional depots, under the command of Captain Timmerman and Lieutenants le Sueur, de Jongh and Fischer. Here, too, each officer of the Imperial Guard was presented with a bottle of wine brought from France by the General Headquarters - since it was impossible to carry this back it was decided to distribute it.

On 8 November Prince Eugène wrote of his Corps: *"Three days of suffering have so dispirited the men that at this moment I believe them incapable of any serious effort. Numbers have died of hunger or cold, and many more in their despair have permitted themselves to be taken by the enemy."* The Grande Armée had left Moscow some 95,000 strong; by the time it reached Smolensk it was down to less than 42,000. The vanguard formations would strip the depots and magazines bare, leaving nothing for those who came in later. Eugène tried to reach the stores dumps at Vitebsk, but was driven back to Smolensk by Platov's Cossacks. There was now no possibility of the Grande Armée wintering safely in that city; news had reached Napoleon that the Russian flanking armies -

25,000 men under General Wittgenstein from the north, and 30,000 under General Tschitchagov from the south - had beaten or outmanoeuvred his own outlying Corps and were moving inwards to co-operate with Kutuzov's pursuing 80,000 by forming a pincer.

At Smolensk his comrades had news at last of Chef d'escadron Albert de Watteville, whom we left in Moscow under the care of Dr.L'herminier and resting in the house of the Princess Tsartoriska. De Watteville was helped by his friends de Briqueville and des Boulayes; they procured a carriage for him and his servant Baptiste Royer, stocked it with fur rugs and food supplies, and saw him off on the first leg of the retreat in the baggage train of Marshal Mortier's column. When the weather turned intensely cold in early November he suffered severely. Reaching Smolensk, he was placed in a hut outside the city - convoys were forbidden to enter it. Given the state of his health it was clear that de Watteville could not stay in this icy, primitive hovel; his servant took him on his shoulders and carried him into the city to the quarters of the recently arrived Captain de Briqueville. So much had his sufferings marked him that his old friend hardly recognised him. When they took his boots off they were distressed to find that his legs were frostbitten as black as coal. Marshal Berthier's doctor examined him, and declared that de Watteville had only two days to live. But they had to leave Smolensk, and his friends could not bear to leave him alone there.

Finally they found a Polish lady who was willing to lend them her coach. The younger officers harnessed the last horses they could find, and took him on the road with them. A few miles out of Smolensk he asked for something to drink; and while de Briqueville was melting some ice for water Albert de Watteville died in the arms of des Boulayes.

On 15 November 1815 his servant Baptiste Royer would describe how he had kept the body for three days, hoping for an opportunity to give it a decent burial once they reached Orcha. But on the way they were attacked by Cossacks; Royer was taken prisoner, the coach plundered, and de Watteville's body tipped out onto the road and stripped of its clothes. After two days Royer managed to escape and returned to the place where the coach had been left. He found the body of his unfortunate master, but was quite unable to bury him in the iron-hard earth; forced to abandon the corpse, he could only take with him some documents which the pillagers had left scattered around him. Baptiste Royer made his way to Orcha, where General Colbert gave him clothing and made him a servant to one of his aides, Fortuné Brack, whom he would serve throughout the Leipzig campaign the following year.

★   ★   ★

Instead of months, the Red Lancers' stay in winter quarters was to last only a few days before they left for Krasnoï on a scouting mission. The Regiment followed the main road from Smolensk to Orcha, which was curiously deserted even of stragglers. Joining up with the rest of the Imperial Guard the Regiment took up once more its role as flank guard, marching in the fields.

On 13 November Davout's I Corps were cut off at Viazma by the leading elements of Kutuzov's pursuit. By the time they were hacked free they had lost 6,000 dead and wounded and 2,500 captured, and the Corps - until now the best in the army - was shattered. On 15 November, preceded by the Red Lancers, the Guard reached Krasnoï. Here the Emperor halted to rally what was left of his army, which was dangerously strung out; and here Kutusov struck again, sending General Tormasov to cut off their retreat. The army was cut in half, with the Corps of Eugène, Davout and Ney apparently trapped. Eugène's IV Corps managed to fight their way through; the Emperor turned back to rescue Davout's I Corps, and in this action General Tindal's Dutch 3rd Foot Grenadiers of the Guard were almost wiped out. Tindal's 500-odd Grenadiers, supported by the cavalry of the Guard with a Red Lancers squadron in the second line, deployed in skirmishing order towards the village of Ouvarova. In the fighting which followed the Grenadiers fired away their last cartridges; when Tindal withdrew his regiment - which Napoleon had not long before called "Holland's Glory" - the survivors numbered some 36 men (among them, another brother of Lieutenant de Stuers). The gap they left in the line was filled by Marshal Mortier's Young Guard units. The battle at Krasnoï cost Napoleon about 6,000 dead, 20,000 captured, and 116 cannon. The Emperor and his Imperial Guard pressed ahead towards Orcha, leaving IV and I Corps to follow; the Red Lancers marched a short distance away on the left flank of the Guard. On 20 November they crossed the Dnieper at Orcha, where they would halt for two days.

As for Marshal Ney's III Corps: on 17 November they left Smolensk, reinforced to a strength of about 6,000 men with twelve cannon and a cavalry squadron. Napoleon, whipping his exhausted army along to ensure that they reached the Beresina crossings before the enemy, had lost touch with his rearguard. On the 18th Ney was cut off by Russian forces under General Miloradovitch; refusing an offer of surrender, he had many bivouac fires lit and and managed to extricate some of his troops under cover of night. On reconnaissance near Orcha one of the Red Lancers' patrols stumbled upon the survivors of Ney's rearguard, who had been given up for dead - "the redhead" had just 900 men left when he joined Napoleon at Orcha on the evening of the 21st. General Colbert himself brought the good news to the Emperor, who reacted with incredulous joy; it was on this occasion that he called Ney "the bravest of the brave".

★   ★   ★

At 8.30a.m. on 22 November the Guard Lancer brigade formed above Orcha on the right side of the road to Borisov, where they awaited the other Guard regiments. Once they had been brought together the chief-of-staff handed over Marshal Bessières' general orders dated the day before to the commanders of the cavalry regiments:

"Colonel-Major Dautancourt will take command of all depots of the mounted Guard; these depots will be brought together tomorrow morning at Kokhanov and will follow the movement of VIII Corps [Marshal Junot's Westphalians]. Tonight each cavalry regiment of the Guard will

Chef de bataillon Lambert J.C.A. de Stuers (1784-1866) of the 3rd Guard Grenadiers, elder brother of the Red Lancers staff officer Hubert J.J.L. de Stuers. Unlike their younger brother Leopold, Lambert survived the Russian campaign, although wounded at Krasnoï. An officer in the Guard Grenadiers from August 1810, he transferred in February 1813 into the Fusiliers-Chasseurs of the Middle Guard, fighting in the Saxon and French campaigns. He passed into the Chasseurs Royaux under the First Restoration (when this miniature was painted), but rallied to Napoleon in 1815 and served in the Foot Chasseurs of the Guard during the Hundred Days. (Photo © Stichting Iconographisch Bureau, The Hague)

OPPOSITE *The 3rd (Dutch) Grenadiers of the Imperial Guard at Krasnoï, 15 November 1812, where the regiment was almost entirely destroyed. In a famous passage from later in the retreat the memoirist Bourgogne of the Guard Fusiliers mentions the survivors supposedly travelling in a single large sledge, though this was not literally true. In 1813 surviving members of the unit were dispersed into the 1st and 2nd Grenadiers of the Old Guard. (Painting by Hoyck van Papendrecht, 1858-1933; collection of Dutch Royal Army Museum, Delft)*

send a chef d'escadron to Kokhanov to take command of that regiment's depot. Each regimental commander will give the necessary instructions to the chef d'escadron whom he sends. The first task of the chefs d'escadron commanding the depots will be to form companies of one hundred men; the colonels will provide the necessary numbers of officers and NCOs. Each regiment will form a battalion armed with muskets or carbines and provided with ammunition.

"The mounted units of the Guard must set an example to the rest of the army. The marshal [Bessières] is commanded by the Emperor to tell his regimental commanders that devotion shown to him while in Paris means nothing: the Emperor is counting on receiving it in these difficult circumstances, and each invididual of the mounted Guard must give him proof of it.

"Tomorrow during the day the regimental commanders will send the officers needed to organise their depots. Colonel-Major Dautancourt will report to the marshal on the measures he has taken, and is responsible for the good order of his depot."

In accordance with these orders the Red Lancers formed a dismounted battalion under the command of Colonel-Major van Hasselt; it numbered nine officers and 70 lancers, with 44 sick horses, and some Russian horses. The assembly of the battalions of dismounted troopers created quite a large column, still able to show fight; most of the men still had their firearms.

General Frédéric H. Count Walther (1761-1813); colonel of the Mounted Grenadiers of the Guard, he commanded a Guard cavalry division in Russia and later in Saxony. (Robert Lefèvre, 1755-1830; photo © Réunion des Musées Nationaux, Paris)

On 23 November at eight in the morning the still-mounted remnant of the Guard Lancer brigade marched off towards Bobr, where they organised their bivouac. The dismounted battalions of the brigade, joined by those of the Mounted Chasseurs, camped at the village of Plissa. Having passed Kokhanov the Regiment came upon half a dozen dismounted officers on the road to Toloczin; these proved to be Dutch survivors of the 11th Hussars, and their fellow countrymen shared with them such scant food as the Red Lancers still possessed. A gun was heard in the distance; and they were told that General Tschitchagov's Russians had taken possession of the Beresina river crossing at Borisov.

Napoleon immediately sent for General Colbert and enquired about the Beresina ford which the general had crossed with his lancers on the night of 13 July during their advance (Thiers' *History of the Consulate and Empire* was thus mistaken in attributing to General Corbineau the almost miraculous discovery of this vital ford). It was by this crossing at Vesselovo near Studianka that the Emperor decided to extricate the survivors of his army, and at his order work began the next day on building two bridges. The weather, alternating between freezing and milder spells, had left the ice over the Beresina too thin for passage; this was completely unexpected - the army's pontoon train had been burned at Orcha - and until practical bridges could be built the French were trapped on the east bank.

The Regiment made a halt before reaching Toloczin, where they stayed for two days. On the 24th the brigade marched off at 8a.m., halting near Lochnitza after a day of struggling through

heavy snowfalls; the snow stopped before a lethally beautiful night fell, the stars glittering above an icy wind. On the 25th the brigade camped at Niematitza; the few houses of this village were already packed with soldiers, and most of the Lancers spent the night in the snow. The next day at dawn they marched on towards Borisov, later branching off north-west on the road to Studianka in company with Napoleon and his staff. The Red Lancers spent that night at Zaboloty, a village still inhabited by peasants - and by some cattle, quickly butchered to provide the Lancers with a meal such as they had not enjoyed for weeks.

On that night of 26 November the temperature fell below -20°C, and on the following night below -30°C; each night spent in the open in such temperatures killed soldiers and horses by the hundreds. No accurate figure could be recorded for the effective strength of the Grande Armée by this date. Marshal Berthier, Napoleon's chief-of-staff, considered that perhaps only 25 per cent of the actual survivors were still in formed units under command, the rest having straggled off. The mounted branch of the army had only a tiny fraction of its old strength; this was the period when so-called "sacred squadrons" were formed entirely from officers who still had horses but no mounted troopers to command.

On 27 November Colonel-Major van Hasselt's dismounted battalion was under arms from 5a.m. standing guard south-east of Zaboloty village, returning there at 8a.m.; an hour later all the mounted elements were ordered to make for the plateau near the village of Trostianitsi. Here Marshal Bessières and General Walther inspected them and expressed their satisfaction. After the inspection the Regiment set off to cross the bridges over the Beresina.

This episode would pass into legend as one of the emblematic horrors of the retreat. The improvised bridges were flimsy, and thousands of soldiers pressed forward to cross them in scenes of panic, some resorting to the use of weapons to force their way through this living sea. Both Kutuzov's and Tschitshagov's Russian forces had come up and were attacking the area of the crossings from both banks, bringing fire to bear on the bridges and the desperate crowds; one bridge would collapse under artillery fire, and countless men would drown or die of cold in the icy water. Fierce fighting was necessary to hold the crossings; Napoleon had brought up Marshal Victor's reserve IX Corps to help cover the retreat, and at Studianka on the east bank they held the Russians off at hand-to-hand range with artillery support from guns on the west bank.

The Emperor and his staff passed across the bridge immediately followed by the Red Lancers; the first troop to follow Napoleon's entourage was commanded by Lieutenant van Omphal. Once on the west bank they met the 14th Cuirassiers led by Colonel Trip van Zoudtland, which had suffered greatly during the most recent fighting; this Netherlands regiment was serving with Doumerc's 3rd Heavy Cavalry Division and attached to Oudinot's II Corps. One of the Dutch cuirassiers brought up a riderless horse whose Red Lancers officer's shabraque was covered with blood. That night they made their bivouacs in woodland between the river and the road to Zembin.

The comradeship between fellow countrymen, and certainly between Belgian and Dutch troopers, became closer during those dark hours. Working up to their armpits in icy water, Dutch pioneers had been struggling to strengthen the bridges with materials taken from the houses of Studianka when the Red Lancers crossed. Recognising their compatriots, they had helped them across by throwing a broken carriage, some dead horses and other debris from the bridge into the water.

Vélite Auguste Mathieu le Maire noticed an officer of the 5th Hussars lying in the snow. Moved by some kind of presentiment, he dismounted; when he wiped the snow from the officer's face he found that he was still breathing, and recognised his compatriot Count du Val de Beaulieu, whose life he saved by putting him on his packhorse.

The crossing of the Beresina, 26-28 November 1812. The Grande Armée recrossed the river at the same spot where the Red Lancers had crossed during the advance on Moscow that July. (Hoyck van Papendrecht; collection of Dutch Royal Army Museum, Delft)

On Saturday 28 November, during the continuing battle of the Beresina, the dismounted detachment of the Regiment were ordered to escort the wagons containing the army's treasure and trophies. They endured a night of cold, wind and snow in a village right of the road near the forest edge. The mounted remnant of the Regiment returned to the bridges over the Beresina to act as a reserve and rearguard for Oudinot's II Corps. The 3,000 Russian prisoners taken during the battle were escorted to the rear and handed over to another unit by a Red Lancer detachment commanded by Lieutenant van Omphal. It was early on the 28th that the French engineers destroyed the Beresina bridges; perhaps 10,000 stragglers were abandoned on the east bank.

Colonel-Major van Hasselt was wounded during the battle at the Beresina, as were Chef d'escadron Colin de Verdière, who took a lance thrust in the left leg, Captain Adjutant-Major Courbe, Lieutenants Sterke and van Heiden, and 2nd Lieutenant Antoon Das, who would die of his wounds on 16 December.

On the 29th the dismounted lancers made their way to Plechnitsi and spent the night in a handful of huts named Moldesch in the forest on the left of the road. At one point they were awakened by fugitives shouting that the Russians had cut off the road; in the confusion a hut full of officers and soldiers caught fire, but luckily they all escaped. The next day the foot battalions gathered at 10a.m. at Plechnitsi and marched through the woods towards Ilia in temperatures of -30°C. Colonel-Major van Hasselt led his dismounted Lancers and Chasseurs of the Guard towards a small village with a mansion (probably Zalefs Kaïa) where they obtained a large amount of fodder for their few remaining horses. Here they passed another beautiful starlit night in killing cold.

During the march of 1 December Jan van Hasselt's men suffered severely; unaccustomed to prolonged marches on foot, the troopers only made headway through the snow with great difficulty, and the column had to halt several times to wait for stragglers to catch up. During these halts soldiers at the head of the column would sit down to rest; weakened by cold and starvation, many never got up again. During one of these halts the Emperor passed by the column, and Major Dautancourt drew up his troops to present arms - an increasingly rare happening by this stage in the retreat. At 3p.m. the exhausted column reached Ilia; this proved to be a Jewish village with plentiful goods to sell, though some complained at the prices. The bivouacs were set up around the village; during another cold night one of the barns was accidentally set alight by the large fires which the men built, and some sleeping Red Lancers were burnt alive before they could escape. The mounted element of the Regiment, still following Napoleon and the General Headquarters, halted at Staiki.

The 2nd was an exhausting day, though it proved the discipline and hardiness of the surviving lancers. The dismounted battalions set off at sunrise and reached Molodetschno in the evening - only to be ordered by Prince Eugène to continue towards Minsk to cover the camp of the headquarters staff. They marched several more miles over the fields before reaching bivouacs in the village of Zamok-Roegli. Before falling out to rest they lined up in battle order, searched the village, placed sentries and gathered in their stragglers. They had covered 27 miles that day, some on ice-covered roads, some over snow-covered fields; the state of some troopers' feet was pitiable. Even when they were finally at liberty to rest they still had to be on the alert for Cossacks.

Throughout the retreat the lurking packs of Cossacks were ever-present, haunting the flanks of French columns within menacingly short range, always watching for opportunities to sweep in. It was under the eyes of the Cossacks that the dismounted battalions marched back to Molodetschno on 3 December. There they were assigned the task of escorting nine more of the Emperor's wagons and 82 vehicles carrying senior officers and wounded men; these were followed by hundreds of frozen, filthy and disease-ridden fugitives, all begging for their protection. The Cossacks charged them without success and they managed to reach the village of Benitsa. This was a desperate day for both the Regiment's detachments, dismounted and mounted alike losing many men.

On 5 December at Smorgoni, one of the previously established staging posts, the Regiment passed a quiet night. There were some remaining stores, but the Regiment were not allowed to enter the town. The duty adjutant being occupied, Lieutenant van Omphal took a few lancers and managed to return with supplies loaded on an ox-drawn sledge.

It was on the 5th that Napoleon decided that he would be of more use in Paris than remaining with the Grande Armée, and left for France with a small, fast-moving entourage to begin the huge task of raising a new army in the aftermath of this disastrous campaign. Command of the army passed to Marshal Murat (who would himself leave after six weeks, command during the final stage being exercised by the capable Prince Eugène de Beauharnais). The mounted element of the Red Lancers was ordered to provide an escort for the first stage of Napoleon's journey, under the orders of Captain Jan Post. They were placed between Smorgoni and Ochmiana on the road to Vilna which the Emperor would follow in his sledge. Many of this 50-man detachment simply froze on the spot; and when Post reached Vilna on 9 December he had just four lancers left.

On 6 December the dismounted Guard cavalry battalions had only half of their original strength left, but were reinforced with 300 fit Würtemberg soldiers at Ochmiana. They passed that night at the small hamlet of Rafnopolia, where the temperature fell below -28°C. The next day the cold was worse than ever; corpses were strewn thickly along the road to their next bivouac at Miedniki. On the 8th and 9th the army - with perhaps 10,000 men still capable of fighting, though totalling several times that many - finally reached Vilna, where they hoped to find supplies, safety and rest. The temperature fell to -35°C.

On 9 December Major Dautancourt reported to Marshal Bessières early in the morning to brief him on the state of the dismounted Guard cavalry. Each battalion had been reduced to less than a third of its strength on 23 November. Certainly, not all of the missing had perished; many of them had fallen behind and been captured, and others had simply disappeared into the straggling mass of disarmed soldiers. Bessières disbanded the dismounted column and allowed the survivors to return to their regiments; Colonel-Major van Hasselt and his footsore troopers joined the mounted remnant of Red Lancers, who were then under command of Lieutenant Verhaegen.

Only the Würtemberg soldiers of the dismounted escort entered Vilna with the convoy, the Lancers spending the night in a suburb outside the town. Antonie van Omphal, who was on ground familiar to him since his period as an orderly officer to Marshal Davout, took two of his comrades to the Four Nations hotel whose proprietress he knew. She put them up in a tiny room at the back of the hotel where she served them a delicious soup, sauerkraut and roast goose. They had just begun to address themselves to this mouthwatering feast when the alarm was given and cannon fire was heard. But van Omphal and his brother officers simply refused to abandon this delicious spread; they devoured it to the last scrap, and washed it down with two bottles of wine. When they finally left the inn to rejoin the Regiment they found that they were just in time. Their walk back led through streets erupting in panic: the Cossacks were reported to be at the gates, and anyone who could walk or had any other means to leave the town was crowding onto the road west to

Kovno. About 24,000 soldiers were either too sick and exhausted to continue, or simply decided to take their chances where they were; the stores had been broken open, and vast quantities of spirits were being drunk.

On 10 December Captain Karel van der Meulen of the 1st Squadron, who was suffering from frostbite, fell behind on the road to Kovno; it was on that day that the army had to abandon almost every remaining wagon and cannon. The 51-year-old Captain Jan Timmerman of the 5th Squadron, wounded, would also disappear on the road to Kovno. On the 12th Lancer Antoine Steenis, brother of the Regiment's assistant medical officer, would be one of many to fall behind the column. Before reaching Kovno the Red Lancers had to swing north from the impossibly overcrowded main road, finally crossing the Niemen out of Russia. However, their orders were to assemble at Kovno; joining the main road on the Polish side of the border, they circled back into Russia. They could hardly believe their eyes when they were led into Kovno at about noon on 12 December.

On 13 December the entire Guard was formally assembled on the Russian side of the border. The Red Lancers were the last unit of the Guard to cross it, with a mounted strength of 20 officers and 40 troopers.

On that same day Marshal Ney, who had kept the rearguard of the Grande Armée in being and still fighting by sheer courage and force of character, finally gave up the impossible struggle to keep Platov's Cossacks at bay. He fought for several hours at Kovno bridge, musket in hand among his last handful of soldiers; then he burned the bridge and fell back. Legend has it that he was the last Frenchman to leave Russian soil. At this point those elements of the once 450,000-strong Grande Armée still present and under command numbered perhaps 20,000 staggering fugitives, of whom only a small minority were still bearing arms.

*   *   *

The Regiment's next bivouac was situated at Vilkoviski, where Lieutenant van Omphal met up again with Captain Calkoen and his brother Piet, who was severely ill with frostbite. Van Omphal himself had frozen ears; he managed to save one by rubbing it with snow, but the other was partially lost. Captain Jan Post also suffered from frostbitten ears, and would lose the upper parts of them. Abraham Calkoen, who did not want to leave his brother behind, travelled on towards Gumbinnen on a sledge in company with Lieutenant van Omphal. Piet's condition was deteriorating, and his brother was obliged to leave him at the hospital there. On 15 December the wounded 2nd Lieutenant Frederik Fischer disappeared on the road to Tilsit.

On 17 December the Regiment was at Stallupîhnen. General Colbert ordered Colonel-Major van Hasselt, who was completely exhausted, to hand over his command to Captain Dumonceau and to make his way to Elbing, the concentration point for the Guard cavalry where the Regiment had a depot. On the 19th the Red Lancers were still in the rearguard, and still occasionally being pursued by their old enemies the Cossacks, although the bulk of Kutuzov's forces had not crossed the Niemen.

On 25 December Colonel-Major van Hasselt reached Elbing where he was quartered at the house of one Frau J.F.Schwarck. Sick, and worn out by his exertions and his grief, Jan van Hasselt died there on the night of 29 December; he was 36 years old. On 22 March 1813 Frau Schwarck replied to a letter she had received from the colonel-major's brother; for its perfect evocation of the spirit of those times, as much as for the information it contains, it is worth reproducing in full:

"It is extremely painful for me to find myself honoured by a letter from the van Hasselt family. As you wish it, I take the liberty of replying with the greatest attachment I can show.

"I had the honour of receiving at my house Colonel van Hasselt together with three captains on the first day after Christmas Eve, 25 December. I already had a French colonel and a captain in my house; for this reason Colonel van Hasselt asked that the three captains be provided

"*A white-haired NCO, Russian Campaign, 1812*". (Former JOB collection; photo © La Cour d'Or, Musées de Metz)

with other lodgings, and took for his own accomodation a large room on the street side, which seemed to give him great satisfaction.

"On the first day he was still taking his meals with us, but was already complaining of fever and diarrhoea. That evening he asked for rice soup to be served in his room. His doctor had not yet arrived; I therefore suggested consulting Dr. Housselle, a well-respected doctor in our town who lives nearby and could attend him often. I was happy when his regimental surgeon, Dr. Mergell, arrived; since his lodging was far away, and since I recognised from my own experience that there was a risk of [the colonel's] condition deteriorating, I asked Dr. Mergell to stay in my house the easier to observe and care for the colonel, for whose interests I felt a great concern. On the one hand he was distinguished by nobility of character, and on the other I had been so touched by the confidence he had shown in me during my first visit to his bedside that I would have made any sacrifice in order to save him for his young children. He had lamented

to me in these words:

"'A strong man should be able to bear his misfortunes and another half besides. Remember, Madame, that I have lost everything - my belongings, my friends, my horses. I lay in the snow for five nights running, and when I opened my eyes it was to see my friends lying dead around the campfire. If I had found such a good bed as this I would not have been taken ill. How happy I am to have come to your home - I had been dreaming of reaching Elbing for many days. In Russia I got the news that my wife had been safely delivered and that she had already been walking in the garden with the infant. In Moscow I received a second letter, telling me that she had died of fever and diarrhoea on 2 September. A strong, beautiful woman...and now I have six children at Versailles without a mother, cared for by servants.'"

"I comforted him as best I could, and begged him to think of nothing but his recovery, for it was his duty to his children. He confided to me no more of his family affairs, since he did not expect to die so soon. The day before his end he wished to rise and get dressed; I made him understand that his strength would not allow it. He had to write to his family, he told me vehemently - 'They will surely think that I have already died'. I wanted to give him a small writing pad to use in bed, but in the meantime some officers [including Captain Dumonceau] came to visit him; I left him, and the letter was never written. While I normally cared for him until midnight I stayed until 2a.m. that night, since his condition was getting steadily worse.

"The next morning I found him very changed, and remarked on this to his doctors. He was fully conscious and still talking, but was thick of speech. Just an hour before he died the paymaster brought him a little money which he had been asking for impatiently for some days. Both Drs. Housselle and Mergell were at his side, discussing his condition and reaching agreement about the measures to take the following day. Housselle returned to his home while Mergell and an old faithful sapper stayed at his bedside. I was bringing his drink for the night when a servant called me anxiously; I found, with indescribable pain, that a nervous commotion had brought his life to an end - gently and happily for him, but with great sadness for us and his relatives. This was at 10p.m. on 29 December 1812.

"After having vainly tried all possible means to revive him Monsieur Mergell called the paymaster, who was the legal representative of the regiment. This officer drew up a formal inventory of the belongings of the deceased, counted the money, and handed everything over to Monsieur Mergell. As far as I can remember these comprised...a few pieces of gold in his coat, a brand new colonel's uniform with the latest epaulettes, a sash, a shoulderbelt and pouch, all in good condition, several old trimmings and epaulettes, a watch, a pair of buckles, the Grand Cross of the Legion of Honour [sic - it was the Order of the Reunion], a valuable shirt pin, seven fine quality shirts, a red belt, and a few other clothes. All these things were packed in a small case which I gave to the doctor. The gentlemen told me that the valuables would be sent at once to the family and the uniform and equipment would be sold within the regiment on behalf of the family.

"As the regiment had to march the day after the colonel's death Monsieur Mergell was kind enough to stay with me until after the funeral. He helped me to arrange the burial, together with that old sapper whose name I have forgotten. As none of the Guard officers had stayed behind my parents were proud to accompany the colonel to his last resting place on 1 January 1813. Monsieur Mergell paid all Dr. Houselle's fees as well as for the funeral (as shown by the document enclosed), and for the death certificate, which he took with him.

"I ask nothing of the van Hasselt family, however, and have not kept the smallest thing; this would have seemed selfish, and his memory will always remain with me. I have taken the liberty of sharing with you a small piece of the ribbon with which I draped his coffin; I have kept the rest of it, and your invaluable letter will remain a precious remembrance.

"His mortal remains rest in St Marien's cemetery in the town. As instructed by Monsieur the Marshal through his officer I provided the colonel with a civil funeral; in wartime any display is forbidden in our town, but I nonetheless had the bells of the Marienkirche rung. If for any reason you need to have a death certificate before the return of Dr. Mergell I will have it sent to you upon your request."

Captain Jean F. Dumonceau (1790-1884), painted in the uniform of the Dutch 6th Hussars, 1823, by Dubois-Drahonet. Dumonceau took over command of the remnants of the Red Lancers from the exhausted Jan van Hasselt when they reached Elbing on 17 December 1812. (Collection of Dutch Royal Army Museum, Delft)

★ ★ ★

On 29 December General Heudelet arrived from Danzig with fresh troops, taking over the rearguard as soon as he arrived. The Regiment's last detachment under arms were finally able to enjoy some rest. During that day they arrived at Waldau, where most of them changed into clean shirts for the first time in many months. From Elbing they marched on to Marienberg, Marienwerder and Graudentz, where they crossed the Vistula towards Bromberg; on 31 December they were at Friedrichswalde.

It was time to reform the Red Lancers around their surviving cadres. Those who were still fit for service and still mounted would remain with the Regiment - two small troops commanded by the Eagle bearer, Lieutenant Jan Verhaegen, and composed of men who had served at the various depots during the campaign. For instance, at Danzig on 11 December these had numbered one sergeant, four corporals, one trumpeter and 53 lancers with 17 horses, and two lancers in the hospital.

In all 171 days had passed between the Regiment's first steps on Russian soil and their return to Prussia. The sabre squadrons had started out with 1,000 lancers and had received 401 reinforcements; their mounted strength on the evening of 13 December was 60 - the campaign had cost them 1,341 horses. On 13 January 1813, a date when few people in France yet knew the true cost of the campaign, Sergeant-Major Schreiber of the Administrative Council at Versailles wrote to Colonel van Hasselt's family:

"This morning we have received sad news from the Grande Armée... Of the 56 officers who left from here, 32 are fit for service. The others have been killed, made prisoner, are sick, or have frostbitten feet and hands. Of the 1,090 NCOs and lancers, 191 have been killed by the enemy, 595 died of cold or hardship; and as for the horses, of 1,122 only 24 remain fit for service. The officers have lost everything - horses, servants, baggage, etc..."

The peculiar status of the vélites as officer-candidates serving in the ranks sometimes makes it unclear whether they are included in various quoted totals. A muster roll finally certified by the paymaster Captain Dufour at Versailles on 28 October 1813 makes all too clear how hard a lesson the Regiment's first campaign had proved for these young trainees. In October 1812 there had been 171 vélites in the Red Lancers - 113 at the depot, and 58 with the Grande Armée. Of those 58, 47 would not return; a digest of Dufour's notes on those 47 is perhaps worth quoting here, for its cumulative effect:

Astrupp, Thierry	fell behind on foot, 28 November
Archambauls, Eugène J.J.	fell behind on foot, 11 August
Boursauls, Léon P.M.	captured, 27 November
Bonnet, Pierre Alexandre	missing, 1 December
Bernardon, Arsène	fell behind, 30 November
Cassaigne, Jean Baptiste	missing (frostbite), 20 November
Calkoen, Pierre C.N.	left in hospital, Gumbinnen, 18 December
Coupé, Pierre	missing (frostbite), 5 November
Coti, Jean Baptiste	fell behind on foot, 7 September
Carpentier, Gustave Alexandre	fell behind on foot, 7 December
de Stuers, Léopold A.E.C	fell behind, 2 November
Déage, Jacques	left in hospital, Moscow, 25 September
Deschamps, Maximilien François	fell behind, 26 July
Delagarde, Jean Joseph	fell behind, 26 October
Dufau, Jean Marie	fell behind, 26 October
Dansaert, Chrétien J.J.	captured, 25 September
Delalande, Valgence	fell behind on foot, 29 November
Desys, Balthazard B.F.	left in hospital, Moscow, 27 September
Etienne, Jacques Antoine	fell behind on foot, 11 November
Gasse, Achille	captured, 25 October
Geesteranus, Pierre G.A.	captured, 27 July
Grisart, Lambert Henry	captured, 27 July
Gallot, Auguste Nicolas.	missing, 12 September
Gaubert, Pierre	missing (frostbite), 8 October
Garin, André F.A	fell behind on foot, 26 October
Houzelot, Georges	fell behind, 15 October
Hubert, Achille J.E..	fell behind on foot, 23 November
Hallié, Brutus la Montagne	fell behind on foot, 10 October
Hurand, Edmé H.L.	missing (frostbite), 10 December
Le Marchand, Auguste	missing (frostbite), 20 December
Le Clerc, Claude F.A.	fell behind on foot, 11 December
Maguin, Paul C.J.	fell behind, 26 October
Mouret, Jacques	fell behind, 8 October
Mathieu, Louis J.T.	missing (frostbite), 19 October
Marteau, Louis Félix	left in hospital, Moscow, 1 October
Oger, Alphonse Auguste	missing (frostbite), 18 October
Paul, Jean F.A.	missing (frostbite), 26 November
Perraud, Jacques	fell behind, 17 November
Prévost, Honoré Sébastien	fell behind on foot, 10 December
Rocher, François	missing (frostbite), 28 November
Senauls, Jean C.F.	fell behind on foot, 23 November
Teisseyre, Jean L.A.	fell behind, 7 October
Texier, Pierre L.A.	left at Königsberg depot, 17 June
Taillepied, Denis J.V.	fell behind, 20 September
Viallanel, Pierre Joseph	fell behind, 6 September
Vallée, Noâl	fell behind on foot, 5 December
Wilquin, Pierre Paul	fell behind on foot, 29 November

CHAPTER IV

1813: The Dresden Campaign

The Regiment reborn

The Emperor Napoleon had arrived back in Paris on Friday 18 December 1812 to face a daunting task. The war continued - and the virtual annihilation of the Grande Armée would encourage France's enforced allies and client states to defect. The most important was Prussia; early in January 1813 the Prussian Corps under General York, which had formed part of the northern flank force of the Grande Armée on the Baltic, changed sides, and their country soon broke out in patriotic revolt against the French. Schwarzenberg's Austrian contingent on the southern flank also "made a separate peace", falling back into Bohemia but not taking up arms against France. A new alliance of Russia, Prussia, Sweden and Britain would form against Napoleon in March 1813.

The Emperor had to raise a new army in France as rapidly as possible while Eugène's 68,000 men - the effective remnant of the Russian expedition, stiffened by hastily provided reinforcements - faced the 100,000 enemies who were soon massing on his eastern borders. Eugène was on the Elbe with his base at Magdeburg, and strong garrisons at Danzig and Thorn (Torun) on the Vistula and Stettin, Kustryn and Frankfurt on the Oder. It was a tribute to the ruthless efficiency of Napoleon's system of conscription and mobilisation that by late April 1813 he would be leading some 200,000 new recruits back into Germany to join Eugène - though most of them were of nothing like the quality of his old armies.

The New Year's Day reception at the palace had a very different atmosphere from those of the previous two years, and many faces were missing. Although the cadres of the Imperial Guard regiments had not suffered too heavily in Russia most of these officers were still with their units, others were absent by reason of family bereavement, and some who attended wore mourning dress. It was around these men that Napoleon was to rebuild his élite regiments.

Meanwhile the remnants of the Red Lancers had reached Germany. General Colbert was back at Versailles on 1 February; and following an order of Marshal Bessières dated 13 March 1813 the cadre who would form the skeleton of the rebuilt Regiment left Fulda for Versailles on the 14th, arriving on various dates ten days to two weeks later. A muster roll of these 50 officers and NCOs of the sabre squadrons who had returned from Russia and were fit for service is as follows:

de Bellefroid, Lieutenant	le Sueur, Lieutenant
Böcher, Lieutenant	de Tiecken, Chef d'escadron
Brepoels, Lieutenant	Tulleken, Captain
Colbert, General	Vitry, Veterinary
Colin de Verdière, Chef d'escadron	Ziegler A.J., Lieutenant (father)
Coti, Chef d'escadron	Ziegler P.A., Lieutenant (son)
Deban de Laborde, Lieutenant	
Delaisement, Lieutenant	Brand, Sergeant
Dubois, Colonel-Major	Brand, Trumpeter
Dumonceau, Captain	Bruière, Farrier
Duranti, Lieutenant	Chefsky, Corporal
de la Fargue, Captain Adjutant-Major	Eschweiler, Sergeant-Major
Frank, Lieutenant	Fournier, Sergeant-Major
Hennige, Surgeon-Major	Gisser, Sergeant-Major
de Jongh, Lieutenant	Grobé, Sergeant
Leutner, Lieutenant	Groenhuizen, Sergeant
Mergell, Surgeon-Major	de Groot, Sergeant
van Omphal, Lieutenant	Helling, Corporal
Post, Captain	Kreysig, Sergeant
Royen, Captain Sub-Adjutant-Major	Lesieur, Corporal
Schneither, Captain	Magné, Sergeant
Spies J.W.C., Lieutenant	van der Putte, Sergeant
de Stuers, Captain Sub-Adjutant-Major	Retterich, Sergeant-Major
Stutterheim, Sub-Assistant Surgeon-Major	Ruysens, Sergeant
	Speltije, Sergeant-Major
	Strautmaker, Armourer
	Wagemans, Corporal

Sub-lieutenant Antonie P. Godart Rivocet (1795-?), one of twenty pupils of the St Germain cavalry school assigned to the 2nd Light Horse Lancers during the rebuilding of the Regiment in March 1813. (Study by Rousselot, 1900-1992; photo © Musée de l'Armée)

One of the more experienced officers assigned to the Red Lancers early in 1813 was the remarkable Chef d'escadron Nicolas Thurot (1773-1835), depicted here in the uniform of the 8th Hussars to which he was appointed colonel that October. Thurot was serving in Spain when assigned to the Regiment, and spent many weeks in the saddle travelling to join them in Germany. He took the first of his more than a dozen wounds as an infantry grenadier in 1792, his last at Leipzig in 1813, and distinguished himself at the head of the 12th Cuirassiers at Waterloo in 1815. (Pastel by Boos; private collection)

As other survivors straggled in they were sent to the Imperial Guard depots at Fulda and Gotha to be re-equipped; whenever a number of fit men had been assembled there they were sent to rejoin the army in the field, where they were attached to the Guard cavalry squadrons under the orders of Colonel-Major Lion of the Mounted Chasseurs. They were not very numerous; at the start of 1813 the Regiment's field force numbered just three officers and 31 lancers.

On 6 January the Red Lancers were short by 674 men; all documents had been lost during the retreat, and it was impossible to clarify the number of men who had definitely died, been killed or captured, gone missing, or been left behind in various hospitals. The search was put in the hands of Colonel-Major Dubois, and on 17 January he was sent to Warsaw to recover the depots of the two Lancer regiments of the Guard.

The Russian campaign had not only been a harsh lesson for the Regiment; it had changed its nature forever. Even if the officer corps of the Red Lancers had suffered relatively few fatalities most of them were now sick or exhausted. The Dutch troopers and NCOs of which the Regiment had been composed had been virtually wiped out, and rebuilding it could only be achieved by having recourse to all possible sources of manpower.

On 14 January 1813 Grand Marshal Duroc wrote from Paris:

"His Majesty has taken the decision to replace by Frenchmen [some of] the Dutchmen who are serving in the cadre of the 2nd Light Horse Lancers of the Guard. I have the honour of suggesting that [the following] pass into the Line with ranks superior to those which they now hold - Messieurs Werner, Captain; Mascheck, Lieutenant; van der Brugghen, 2nd Lieutenant; Willich, 2nd Lieutenant, who are due for such promotion considering their length of service. [I suggest] nominating to that same regiment the following: Maurin, Captain ADC, for captain; Alexandre, Lieutenant of Dragoons of the Guard, for captain; Lemaire, 2nd Lieutenant of Mounted Chasseurs of the Guard, for lieutenant; Nettancourt, 2nd Lieutenant of Mounted Grenadiers of the Guard, for lieutenant. I have the honour to enclose their service records. All these officers are being put forward by General Lefebvre-Desnoëttes..."

Levies of conscripts were providing men for the Young Guard and, to prove their loyalty to the Imperial dynasty, some cities made the patriotic gesture of promising to provide mounted and equipped troopers. On 18 January Napoleon wrote to Minister of War Clarke:

"The city of Paris has offered me 500 Chasseurs, which I have accepted. As a mark of my appreciation I intend to have these 500 form part of the 3rd [sic] Lancers of my Guard. Consequently, give orders to General Lefebvre commanding the Guard cavalry to meet the Prefect, and to have the men and horses sent immediately to the depot of the 2nd Lancers. The regiment will arm, uniform and equip them and the city of Paris will reimburse the expense to the regiment.... As for those who do not meet the required standards for admission into the Guard but who would still be suitable for other regiments, if the city of Paris cannot provide replacements for them then General Lefebvre should send them to the closest [Line] Lancer regiment, which in turn should provide selected men for the Lancers of the Guard".

Numbers alone were not, of course, enough: it was experienced soldiers that were urgently needed. These would have to come from the Line cavalry regiments, from recalled veterans, and from the armies serving in Spain. With Paris providing enough men for two squadrons the Emperor decreed an increase in the regimental establishment from five to eight squadrons:

Palace of the Tuileries, 18 January 1813
Napoleon, Emperor of the French, King of Italy, Protector of the Confederation of the Rhine, Mediator of the Swiss Confederation. We have decreed and we decree as follows:
Chapter 1
Article 1
The 2nd Regiment of Light Horse Lancers of our Guard will be increased to eight squadrons, of 250 men each at full strength, bringing the total strength of the regiment to 2,000 men.
Article 2
All Light Horsemen who are serving at present with this regiment, as well as the vélites in service or about to be incorporated, will receive the established scale of pay and will be referred to by the term 'first lancers'.
Article 3
The Lancers offered and recruited by the Departments will be referred to as 'second lancers'. They will only receive the pay of the Line cavalry, with the extra allowance granted to troops in garrison in Paris.
Article 4
All the men provided by the city of Paris and those of the 1st Military Division, the Guilds and the individuals of the same Division will be incorporated into our 2nd Light Horse Lancers.
Chapter 2
Article 5
Only men and horses will be provided. Our good city of Paris and those of the 1st Military Division and the Guilds will deposit with the regiment the sum needed for clothing, equipping and arming the men and harnessing the horses, according to the rate fixed by our Minister of War and of War Administration. The regiment will dress, equip and arm the men and harness the horses. [The sum that the Guilds had to deposit with the Regiment was 466.40 francs for outfitting a trooper and 200 francs for harnessing his horse.]

Chapter 3
Article 6
General Lefebvre, commander of the Guard cavalry, will send one officer and two NCOs to every Department of the 1st Military Division to inspect the men and horses offered; after confirming that these meet the required standards they will direct them to the regiment at Versailles where they will be clothed, armed and equipped.

On 20 January Napoleon instructed Marshal Berthier: *"Inform General Colbert that I have just increased the 2nd Lancers of my Guard to eight squadrons and 2,000 men, and that these men will be with the regiment, effective and mounted, before 20 February. For this recruitment I have taken all the mounted troopers voluntarily provided by the districts of the 1st Military Division.... I have already instructed you that [Marshal Bessières] is to send all the dismounted men of my Guard cavalry back to Mainz."* Mainz became the assembly point for the new troops of the Imperial Guard.

The formation of the new squadrons, coupled with the enormous losses of all types of material during the last campaign, forced the Administrative Council presided over by Chef d'escadron Hoevenaar to purchase enough new supplies to virtually re-equip the whole regiment: 2,500 pairs of short boots with spurs, the same number of gauntlets and calf-skins, thousands of meters of lace and blue and red cloth, 1,500 complete saddles, cartridge pouches, 1,500 handkerchiefs - even 58 trumpets. This would be one of Nicolas Hoevenaar's last services to the Regiment; his right arm had been amputated, and in two months he would be appointed as a commandant d'armes.

Re-equipping themselves after their ragged return from the steppes would cost the officers a great deal (some officers of the Red Lancers were still paying for their last change of uniform), and for this reason Napoleon wrote to Grand Marshal Duroc on 7 February:

"I intend to divide one million francs among the generals, colonels and officers of the Guard who took part in the campaign of the Grande Armée and lost their baggage. The million will be distributed among the various individuals now living who have to re-equip themselves for campaign service. You will supervise this distribution through a committee under your own chairmanship and composed of Generals Walther, Curial, Lefebvre-Desnoëttes, d'Ornano, Michel, Colbert and the General of Artillery. Units eligible for this distribution will be the 1st and 2nd Lancers, the Mounted Chasseurs and Grenadiers, the Dragoons, the Artillery and all the Grenadiers and Chasseurs of the Young and Old Guard."

On 20 January 1813 the state of the Regiment could be summarised thus. The squadron serving with the Army of the Elbe had three officers with 14 horses, and 31 lancers with 31 horses. Detached at various depots were 39 officers with 52 horses, and 158 lancers with only 17 horses; there were also 44 dismounted troopers at Warsaw. Total strength was therefore 42 officers with 66 horses, and 244 rankers with 48 horses. (This shortage of mounts was entirely typical; at this time it is reckoned that Napoleon's entire army had only 15,000 horses in all, of which only perhaps 3,000 were fit for cavalry service.)

Other members of the Regiment were now turning up individually at the various depots, and some found time for correspondence. From Posen on 20 January 1813 Abraham Calkoen wrote to his father with a heavy heart:

"We have again been given a new destination. Instead of staying at Elbing, as I informed you from Königsberg, we are going straight to Mainz and from there probably to Versailles. Write to me care of Mainz where I will collect your letters, since we are moving by forced marches and without stopping over anywhere. I was hoping to be able to give you some comforting news about Piet, but I have none. The Russians entered Gumbinnen the day after my departure and I was told that he had died. He cannot have suffered, for he was already exhausted and his hands and feet were frozen when I brought him to the hospital; he had not eaten for three days and was taken with dreadful diarrhoea. Our regiment has suffered terribly. Out of 800 men only 200 are left, and of those only 30 are fit for duty."

Lieutenant Pierre J. Soufflot de Magny et de Palotte (1793-1893), who would join the Red Lancers during the Hundred Days and who would live to be the doyen of the Legion of Honour. He is depicted wearing the officer's uniform of a Mounted Chasseur of the Line, with buttoned-back lapels. (Author's collection)

Generals and staff officers in Paris were meanwhile achieving miracles. Within six weeks they had succeeded in organising a first division of the Young Guard, and on 9 February Napoleon could write to Clarke:

"The 1st Division of the Young Guard will be commanded by General of Division Barrois. You will order him to take command tomorrow; it will be composed of two brigades.... Attached to this division will be a squadron of Mounted Grenadiers with 250 men, a squadron of Dragoons with 250 men, two squadrons of Mounted Chasseurs with 500 men, one squadron of Lancers of the 2nd Regiment with 250 men; these five squadrons will be commanded by Major Leclerc of the Guard.... 125 Grenadiers with 250 horses, 125 Dragoons with 250 horses, 250 Chasseurs with 500 horses, 125 Lancers with 250 horses of the 2nd Regiment, in total 625 men with 1,250 horses will set out from Paris with this division. These horses will be harnessed and equipped. They will be taken to Fulda, where 625 of the men now stationed there will be mounted to complete the 1,250 men required for this cavalry column."

On 15 February, after a review in the presence of the Emperor, General Barrois' division set off for Mainz, where it would complete its organisation and carry on training. (On 10 April General Barrois handed over the command to General Dumoustier and himself took command of the 2nd Division of the Guard.)

At the time when General Barrois was leaving Versailles General Colbert asked Colonel Dubois, who was already at Mainz, to order Captain Calkoen to Frankfurt-am-Main with Lieutenants Heshusius, Chomel and van Heiden; there he was to place orders for the manufacture of sets of saddlery - 150 to start with and the rest to be ready by 1 April. The local civil and military authorities must provide lodgings, carriages, horses, forage, etc. for the officers' transport. Captain Calkoen's mission was so important to the Regiment that he should correspond directly with General Colbert. A few days later the order was withdrawn; the general wrote to Calkoen telling him not to proceed and to report back to Paris, but his letter arrived too late.

Lost men were still arriving at the Regiment's depots many weeks after the Russian campaign ended, and numbers were still under care in military hospitals in Germany or France. For instance, during January 32 Red Lancers were under treatment in

"The spearhead of the vanguard" - an impression of a Red Lancer of the Young Guard. The five junior squadrons ranking as Young Guard were recognisable by kurtkas in reversed colours (i.e. dark blue faced with red), as depicted; and by an uncrowned N on the czapska, as illustrated on page 94. (Louis Vallet, 1856-?; collection of Belgian Royal Army Museum, Brussels)

Light Horse...in good order to the Dragoon regiment of our Guard.

On the same day Napoleon wrote to Duroc: *"I see from your most recent report that the full strength of the 2nd Light Horse is 2,016 men. On 1 February it numbered 1,141, so 875 were still needed; but it only expected to receive 539 men. The shortfall is no more than 336 men. By my decree of today's date I have just increased this regiment's establishment by 500 men, but the squadron of Paris which is incorporated brings with it 250 men. It still lacks, on the one hand, 250 men, and on the other, 336: total, 586 men.*

"As for horses, the establishment is 2,012; there are 1,276; the shortfall is thus 736. The regiment should receive 290 remounts and 413 offered by the Departments: total, 703 - the shortfall is thus only 33. By today's decree I have added 500 horses to the establishment; however, 250 will be provided by the squadron of Paris. The regiment thus lacks, on the one hand, 250 horses, and on the other, 33: total, 283 horses. To summarise, the deficit of the regiment is 586 men and 283 horses...

"... Would it not be possible to deduct from the surplus [of Mounted Chasseurs] the 586 men who are needed by the 2nd Light Horse? .... Thus we could give [from the horses of the Mounted Chasseurs] 283 to the 2nd Light Horse."

One can only stand in awe of the mind which concerned itself with this type of arithmetic while bearing sole responsibility for conducting the affairs of an empire then facing the threat of extinction at the hands of most of the powers of Europe in alliance.

In the middle of the reorganisation the Emperor decided, on 5 March, to concentrate the depots at Frankfurt; he did not wish his troops to be seen leading spare horses across Germany towards the depot of the dismounted cavalry at Fulda. On that same day 19 officers, 400 lancers and 400 horses of the Red Lancers left Versailles for Mainz, where they arrived on 14 March.

A large number of harnesses were now ready; but Captain Calkoen was induced to distribute them between General Lefebvre and Lieutenant-Colonel Chlapowski. On hearing this General Colbert wrote from Paris on 30 March: *"I ask you not to give any of the saddles to anyone, and to have the shabraques and all the rest of the harnesses made within the shortest possible time."* He also told Calkoen to take back the saddles he had just given to Lefebvre and Chlapowski.

On 6 March Abraham Calkoen had written to his father: *"I am completely deprived, I possess neither horses nor linen. If my former servant Peter calls on you, drive him out with a stick - he abandoned me shamefully while I went to find poor Piet. My other servant vanished with my two last horses near Königsberg. Since trading with Prussia has been resumed I have written to Gumbinnen in the hope of getting reliable information about Piet's fate.... My health is recovering, and I hope to get General Colbert's permission to take the waters at Aix during the season. In that case I will be able to come to see you - I need this more than you can imagine; dear father, you are my last remaining friend. They say that there are many promotions within the Guard, but I have heard nothing of this yet."*

The daily state at the Versailles depot on 11 March, signed by Colonel-Major Dubois as commandant, gives us the following:

Personnel	Available	Unavailable
Officers	10	-
Men	125	918
Total:	135	918
Horses		
Officers'	20	-
Troops'	125	1,274
Total:	145	1,274

Paris, including 20 vélites and two trumpeters; in February, 38 including 13 vélites, one corporal and three trumpeters; in March, 30 including five vélites. The accounts show that the Regiment covered their hospital costs - 786 francs for January, 1,238 francs for February and 892 francs for March. The Regiment also had to deposit funds against the services during March, at a rate of 50 francs per month, of five supernumerary surgeons and two pharmacists who had served as sub-assistants at the hospital of the Imperial Guard during the first trimester of 1813. If such treatment failed the Regiment also paid for the coffin and shroud - 7.50 francs in the case of the unfortunate Vélite Lemoine, deceased on 18 February 1813.

Given the untried quality of much of his new army, his shortage of cavalry, and the strategic value of the Guard's steadiness during the retreat from Russia, Napoleon presumably anticipated an important role for it during the coming months. At any event, by 23 February he had changed his mind again and decreed a further increase in the size of the Regiment to no less than ten squadrons, one of which was to be formed from the former Dragons de la Garde Municipale de Paris:

Napoleon, Emperor of the French, King of Italy, Protector of the Confederation of the Rhine, Mediator of the Swiss Confederation. We have decreed and we decree as follows:
Article 1
The 2nd Light Horse of our Guard is increased from eight to ten squadrons each of 250 men, totalling 2,500 men.
Article 2
The squadron of Dragoons of the Paris City Guard will be incorporated into this regiment.
Article 3
The horses, saddles, equipment, clothing and arms of this squadron will be handed over to the 2nd Light Horse of our Guard.
Article 4
All items enumerated in the preceding article which could be of service to Dragoons, such as saddles, helmets, etc. will be handed over by the 2nd

"Observations: The 125 men will be ready to pass review by H.M. on the 14th of this month and will be selected to leave for the army on the 15th, with full uniform, equipment, weapons and baggage. The 'unavailables' are men and horses who have still received neither clothing nor equipment. The craftsmen and suppliers have been working continuously to outfit men who have departed for the army on various dates, which is the reason why we have been unable to equip these others until now."

On 15 March three officers and 125 mounted lancers did indeed leave Versailles for Mainz. The squadrons were being formed little by little; this was the third draft to leave for the forward depot since 15 February, on which date four officers left with 150 lancers and 250 horses, to be followed by a second party on 5 March.

Simultaneously with the physical rebuilding of the Regiment came confirmation of its status within the Guard, in a letter of 17 March from Grand Marshal Duroc to General Colbert:

"...By the new decree signed by His Majesty today, the five original squadrons of your regiment will retain their former status as part of the Old Guard. The five new squadrons are part of the Young Guard, and consequently the members of these squadrons' cadres, including the superior officers, will have the rank of Line officers and will be treated as such, or as NCOs [sic - i.e. both officers and NCOs of the squadron cadres had Line status only].

"It is on this basis that you should make your proposals regarding appointments, and I urge you to postpone them no longer. The Minister of War has assigned 20 pupils of the St Germain school to be sub-lieutenants of your five new squadrons. You should arrange to appoint to the first five squadrons all remaining officers and sub-lieutenants who have Old Guard status."

Baron de Maupoint, commandant of the cavalry school, communicated the decision the next day. The young gentlemen named for commissions in the 2nd Light Horse Lancers of the Guard were:

Alexandre	sergeant
d'Assier	quartermaster
Barbier d'Aucourt	corporal
Bidault-Cornesse	pupil
Biot	corporal
Bourdeau	corporal
Cenas	corporal
Desfourniels	sergeant
Devaux	grenadier
de Gienauth	grenadier
Godart Rivocet	corporal
Granger	corporal
Mareilhac	corporal
Molerat de Garsault	pupil
Platelet Lagrange de la Tuillerie	sergeant

(Arthur Molerat de Garsault, admitted to St Germain on 2 July 1812 at the age of sixteen, was the son of Louis Charles, Colonel of the Constitutional Horse Guard of King Louis XVI in 1792. Present at the storming of the Tuileries on 10 August, he was severely wounded and dragged along the streets of Paris with a rope around his neck; he committed suicide shortly afterwards.)

Another document dated 17 March is a letter from Abraham Calkoen, still hoping to take the waters:

"...Our regiment is dispersed in various places.... Many generals who were supposed to be prisoners of war are appearing again, one after another, so it is possible that we shall have the happiness of seeing poor Piet again some day - but alas, in what condition? - he was already showing signs of gangrene on his feet and hands.

"I am busy having saddles made for the regiment which must be ready on 1 April; then my duty here will be over, and I await my next destination. I have urged General Colbert to allow me to take the waters at Aix-la-Chapelle, which I need badly. I am suffering from a skin disease with congested glands under the armpits which give me a lot of pain. If permission for this is granted I could come to see you, but [otherwise] you can understand that this is not the time to demand leave. I beg you to send me some money, as I am in need of absolutely everything...."

Three days later Calkoen wrote to his father again: *"...The Imperial Guard is gathering here, and the cavalry is in the neighbourhood of Hombourg. Every day battalions of the Cohorts [National Guard] pass by, and the roads of France are packed with artillery and ammunition convoys. I believe that a new campaign will soon begin if peace is not agreed. There is a lot of talk of peace, but I must confess that I cannot see much possibility of it."*

The Regiment's state on 25 March at Frankfurt included ten officers with 26 horses, 311 lancers with 230 horses (of which 27 were unavailable), two lancers not ready and 22 in hospital. A few days before at Delitzsch north of Leipzig a detachment was reported with two officers, 26 lancers with 26 horses, three lancers reported sick and five in hospital, and three more lancers expected. Two of the Red Lancers' Dutch officers, Captains Tulleken and Macare, were put on the retired list by decree of 18 March 1813.

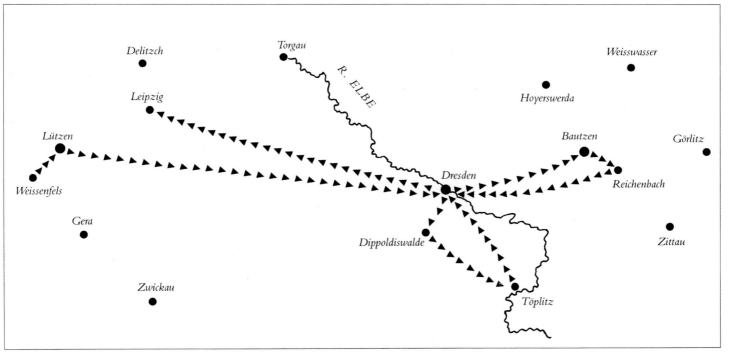

The 18th was also the date of Captain Calkoen's long-awaited promotion, to chef d'escadron in the Line cavalry, of which he was informed by a letter of 27 March from General Colbert in Paris. This briefly presented Calkoen with a dilemma, as he wrote:

"Finally, my dear father, I received a letter from General Colbert informing me that I am chef d'escadron in the Line, but that I must wait for my posting. It is possible that he wants to take me back into his regiment, where there are many places vacant - we shall see. My health is improving and I am feeling much better except on cold days; my feet still hurt. Troops are passing by each day and the town is packed with soldiers who are posted here."

Abraham Calkoen would soon receive his posting, as a squadron commander in the 3rd Line Lancers, and left the Regiment to join his new unit on 1 May 1813. This valuable and rather attractive correspondent now leaves the story of the Red Lancers; those who have followed him to Moscow and back may be glad to know that he survived the Napoleonic Wars.

All available men were now being sent to Mainz. On 28 March the Emperor asked Grand Marshal Duroc to appoint a replacement for General Colbert in the task of reorganising the regiment when the latter left Paris to join the field army. During the Russian campaign Colonel van Merlen had commanded the depot at Versailles; in January he was promoted to general of brigade and left the Regiment - as did the one-armed Chef d'escadron Hoevenaar. Colonel-Major Dubois was selected to take over the depot, and would see no further campaign service under the Empire.

New officers were coming into the Regiment to replace the old faces, some from far-away places. The indomitable Chef d'escadron Nicolas Thurot of the 1st Hussars was appointed in this rank to the Red Lancers on 29 December 1812. General d'Hautpoul had recommended him for a post in the Guard as long ago as 1805: *"...Very well educated, daring, showing initiative, devoted to the Emperor and eager to be admitted into the Guard. His bravery and good behaviour make him worthy of this honour."* His subsequent career had certainly confirmed his courage, if not his luck: he had already been wounded twelve times - by bullet, canister shot and sabre - and would be once again. Serving in Spain at the time of his appointment, Thurot halted on his journey on 21 February at Valladolid where Chef d'escadron de Vérigny of the 20th Mounted Chasseurs provided a luncheon in his honour; also present at table were Sub-lieutenant Jules Soufflot of the same regiment, who would enter the Red Lancers during the Hundred Days, and Captain Parquin of the 13th Mounted Chasseurs. By easy stages Thurot continued his journey, arriving at Versailles on

1 April 1813; he left for Germany on the 30th, and would join the field squadrons of the Regiment on 1 July.

Apart from Paris and some Military Divisions other departments were also contributing men for the Imperial Guard, witness a letter from the Minister of War to the Emperor dated 7 April:

"...The department of Maine-et-Loire has offered Your Majesty 133 men and 140 horses which have been directed to various regiments of the Line. The prefect of this department informs me that he has also selected ten men and thirteen horses for the Cavalry of the Guard. This department is not involved in the Military Divisions which have been called upon to send a tenth of their offered personnel to the Guard. However, the prefect has assured me that the men selected were in good health, experienced riders, that they could read and write, and that the horses had been specially chosen and were fit for service in the Lancers. [Therefore] I thought it right to direct this detachment without delay to Versailles to be admitted into the 2nd Light Horse Lancers of the Imperial Guard. I have the honour to ask Your Majesty to confirm this arrangement." In the margin is written *"Agreed, St Cloud 10 April 1813 - Napoleon".*

Days of promise

In April Napoleon moved to join Eugène's Army of the Elbe with his newly raised Army of the Main; his Russian and German enemies grew stronger every day, and he intended to move fast to defeat them separately in the old Austerlitz style. The Emperor ordered Marshal Bessières to leave for Frankfurt on 9 April with his staff and horses and to arrive by the 14th. There the whole Imperial Guard - including the cavalry under Colonel-Major Lion, and those stationed in Frankfurt - were gathered under Bessières' command. General Colbert also left Paris; he expected to reach the army on the 15th but was delayed, only arriving on 3 May - the day after the battle of Lützen - together with his ADCs Fortuné Brack and Daure.

The cavalry of the Guard marched for Eisenach to meet Marshal Marmont's VI Corps. It was composed of the Lancers of Berg, 530 Polish Lancers under the orders of Krasinski, about 700 Red Lancers led by Lefebvre-Desnoëttes, Guyot's 750 Mounted Chasseurs, Count d'Ornano and General Letort with 550 Dragoons, Generals Walther, Castex and Laferrière with 550 Mounted Grenadiers, and 50 Gendarmes under General Durosnel. From Eisenach they would march to Gotha to secure the communications between that town and Erfurt. On 10 April the Regiment recorded 26 officers with 121 horses and 664 lancers with 629 horses (31 lancers remaining in hospital). As

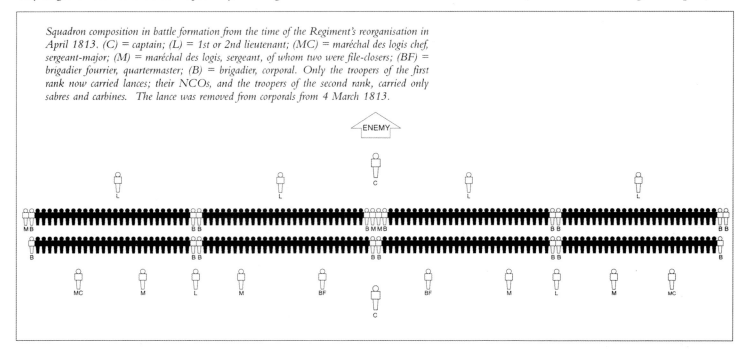

Squadron composition in battle formation from the time of the Regiment's reorganisation in April 1813. (C) = captain; (L) = 1st or 2nd lieutenant; (MC) = maréchal des logis chef, sergeant-major; (M) = maréchal des logis, sergeant, of whom two were file-closers; (BF) = brigadier fourrier, quartermaster; (B) = brigadier, corporal. Only the troopers of the first rank now carried lances; their NCOs, and the troopers of the second rank, carried only sabres and carbines. The lance was removed from corporals from 4 March 1813.

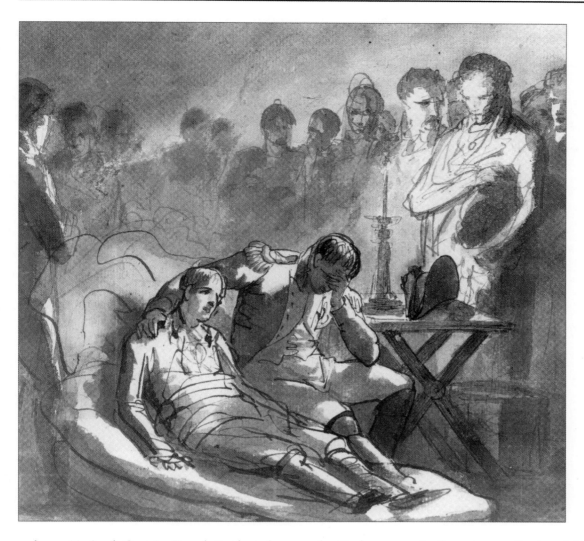

"His Majesty by the side of Grand Marshal Duroc, Duke of Friuli, mortally wounded in the battle of 22 May 1813". In the course of a few days Napoleon lost two of his most faithful servants, Duroc and Marshal Bessières. (Study by Matthieu van Brée, 1773-1839; photo © Historische Musea-Stedelijk Prentenkabinet, Antwerp)

early as 11 April Captain Evrard Berthaut became the Red Lancers' first officer casualty of the campaign, wounded by a bullet in his leg during a reconnaissance.

Two weeks later the Regiment fielded 706 lancers with 706 horses; another 138 with 140 horses were on detachment, and seven lancers were in hospital; in addition 727 lancers were on their way to Frankfurt with 721 horses. One feature of the regimental records for this campaign would be a constant flow of detachments and reinforcements from and to the Regiment in the field.

One of these reinforcements was commanded by Chef d'escadron Auguste Petiet, appointed to the Regiment by the decree of 18 March. Petiet, a well-born young former Hussar officer and marshal's ADC from Spain, was far from being merely a parade ground soldier, and had distinguished himself in several actions. His patience was to be strained after he set off on 15 April from the rear depot to join the Regiment in Germany with 300 lancers -

"...who could not exactly be called Red Lancers, since more than half of them were wearing blue kurtkas - there had been a shortage of red cloth a few days before their departure. I had seen them arriving in Versailles wearing cotton fatigue caps. [The depot] replaced these with czapskas, stuck lances in their hands, and believed that they had turned them into lancers. The problems which they caused me on the march were innumerable. During each day's stage I had to teach them - how to march in column, how to form in troops, how to double the ranks, etc.... Oh, the number who fell off when they had to trot! When we left overnight quarters each morning they were always forgetting bits of their kit in their rooms - even their weapons. The most strict supervision was needed to make sure that these men - mostly young lemonade-sellers or pastry cooks from Paris - took proper care of their horses.

"Guiding soldiers like these took a long time and was very demanding. To be fair to these conscripts, however, after they had crossed the bridge at Mainz and left their own countrymen behind they were more energetic; *they put more effort into their exercises, wanting to show that they were real soldiers and fit to tread in the footsteps of their predecessors."*

The composition of the squadrons was now rather different from that adopted in 1810-1811. Each still had two companies, and each company had four officers and a sergeant-major, but the number of NCOs per company was reduced - four sergeants instead of six, a quartermaster-corporal, and eight corporals instead of ten. The company establishment was slightly larger, at 108 troopers instead of 99 (including two farriers) plus three trumpeters.

The most obvious change, however, lay in their armament: all NCOs including corporals, and the troopers who formed the second rank when drawn up in line for battle, had abandoned the lance and were armed only with sabres and carbines, plus saddle holster pistols as available (pistols were in notoriously short supply). There had long been a school of thought which held that the lance was valuable for breaking into the enemy at first impact, but was a dangerous encumbrance in the resulting close-quarter mêlée against sabre-armed enemies. No doubt this argument was given force in 1813 by the sheer lack of time to train the Regiment's new recruits in the intricacies of handling the lance.

On 26 April the Imperial Guard was on its way to Weimar and from there to Auerstädt, where they arrived on the evening of the 28th. There the Emperor took personal command and led them towards Weissenfels. He crossed the Saale on 30 April, and on 1 May the army was moving towards Lützen and on to Leipzig. Neither the Allies nor the French had accurate intelligence about each others' locations or intentions.

Napoleon - weak in experienced cavalry to scout ahead - thought that the Allies were much further south-east than Leipzig, and intended to hook north through that city and around their right flank before attacking them from the rear. The Allies'

Cords from a czapska, and reverse side of trumpet banner, found near the body of Trumpet-Major Kauffman of the Red Lancers on the field of Reichenbach, 22 May 1813. Taken from the field to a museum at Görlitz, they were photographed by Jean Brunon in the 1930s. In 1997 the trumpet banner was offered for sale at Drouot's of Paris but remained unsold. A photograph of the obverse is reproduced on page 94. (© Collection of Musée de l'Empéri, Salon-de-Provence)

divided and confused multi-national high command were unaware of Napoleon's true strength and concentration. On 2 May they decided to launch Wittgenstein's 73,000 Russians and Prussians into the right flank of Napoleon's marching army south of Lützen to cut it in half. They did not realise that they would be attacking the strongest element of that army – Ney's III Corps; Ney, for his part, had failed to reconnoitre sufficiently and had no warning of the attack until it appeared. Both sides were surprised by their encounter; but while the Allies hesitated and fumbled, Napoleon came racing back from supervising Lauriston's V Corps (then driving other Allied forces out of Leipzig), and took decisive command. The battle of Lützen was over by 6p.m.; both sides lost between 15,000 and 20,000 men, but it was the Allies who retreated.

On the morning of 2 May the Guard cavalry had left their bivouacs just south of Lützen and followed the Emperor to Leipzig. They were grimly eager for battle: the previous day Marshal Jean-Baptiste Bessières - one of Napoleon's oldest friends - had been killed by a cannonball at Rippach. Although in mourning for his old commander Captain Hubert de Stuers had some reason for satisfaction that day, when he was decorated on the battlefield with the cross of the Legion of Honour awarded for his services during the Russian campaign. Led back to Lützen by the Emperor when the sound of cannonfire signalled the attack behind his right flank, the Guard was positioned between the villages of Kaja and Starsiedel in the centre of the French line. It was here that Napoleon broke the Allies with concentrated artillery fire; the Guard cavalry charged the enemy several times during that afternoon, and lost 54 men. After the battle Napoleon

marched his main force towards Dresden, while Ney was sent with nearly half the total on a wide swing to the north.

★　★　★

While the bulk of the Regiment were serving in Germany, back in Paris officers and lancers of the garrison continued to fulfill public duties at the Imperial court.

As part of the Imperial Guard the Red Lancers had to provide detachments to escort the Empress and the little King of Rome during the absence of the Emperor. The Empress was escorted whenever she went out on horseback or in a carriage; the officer commanding the escort was to keep her within close sight at all times, even when she was visiting friends or simply taking a walk in the fresh air. At night two beds were made up in a room immediately next to that of the Empress, one for the officer on duty (who was to remain dressed at all times) and the other for a page. The King of Rome required the same attentions, except that he was not often taken out, and that his duty officer was permitted to undress when he retired for the night. Meals were taken with the other officers of the escort and the pages at the table of an officer of the palace. In the evenings they attended the theatre, concerts or balls with the Empress. When the court was informed of the victory at Lützen it was celebrated by a *Te Deum* at the cathedral of Notre Dame and by a parade of the Imperial Guard in the city.

A few days after these ceremonies a detachment of Guard cavalry was ready to leave for the field army, the Red Lancers contingent being commanded by Lieutenant Antonie van Omphal. When they reached Dresden they found the Saxon capital in a state of armistice.

Death at Reichenbach
Napoleon captured Dresden a week after the battle of Lützen, and on the 11th Captain de Stuers - so often entrusted with high-level missions - was sent to Peterswalde with 150 lancers to escort King Frederick August of Saxony to his capital, where he arrived the next day. This unhappy monarch, originally an ally of Prussia, had been forced to collaborate with Napoleon since the disasters of

Jena and Auerstädt in 1806. Now half his country was occupied by the French and half by the Russians, and his attempts to detach himself from France by negotiations with Austria had come to nothing in the face of Napoleon's threats. On 16 May the army (now taking once more the title of Grande Armée) left Dresden to march eastwards towards Bautzen, where Wittgenstein had halted the retreat of his Russo-Prussian army in very strong positions behind the river Spree. The Red Lancers rode with the rest of the Guard cavalry (except, we find, for four lancers left in the hospital of the Arsenal suffering from fever, three from wounds, and two from venereal diseases...) In an advanced guard encounter the Regiment lost Vélite Auguste le Maire, a veteran of the Russian campaign, who was taken prisoner.

A letter to the Emperor from the Duke of Feltre dated 19 May underlines the practical difficulties of a multinational conscript army, the changed character of the Red Lancers - and also the astonishingly trivial matters on which the Minister of War felt he had to seek Napoleon's opinion in the middle of a critical campaign:

"On the 12th of last month Your Majesty ordered me to send six troopers of the 2nd Light Horse Lancers of the Guard to the 7th Light Horse Lancers of the Line to act as NCOs and to instruct the Dutch conscripts whom this corps have received. Colonel-Major Dubois, who is responsible for selecting these men, has informed me that the depot does not have any men capable of assuming this task. He proposes to detach two sergeants and one officer of his corps for this purpose for one month, after which they would return to their posts. This proposal seemed to me to partly fulfil Your Majesty's intentions, and I therefore thought best to accept it. I beg Your Majesty to inform me if he approves this measure.

"In case Your Majesty judges that this measure cannot entirely fulfil the object of his order of 12 April, I beg him to inform me if he would allow me to present him with three officers and an equal number of NCOs with knowledge of the Dutch language, selected from Line regiments, for assignment to the 7th Light Horse Lancers."

On Thursday 20 May, at Bautzen, Napoleon nearly achieved a victory to rank alongside the finest of his career; the opportunity was lost through a misunderstanding of his mission by Marshal Ney. Napoleon bridged the Spree and led the bulk of his army onto the east bank, drawing Wittgenstein into a frontal battle of attrition and deceiving him as to the French plan. This was that Ney's powerful detached command should swing down from the north behind the Allies' right flank, trapping them and assuring their destruction. But on the morning of the 21st Ney was remarkably slow to commit his Corps and misunderstood his objective; although the Allies were forced to retreat once more the balance of losses was in their favour, and Napoleon was denied the decisive victory he needed to fragment the enemy coalition.

General Colbert's brigade of Guard Lancers performed with distinction on the 20th, and on the 21st when fighting continued at Würschen. On 22 May the Emperor ordered General Walther to pursue the enemy and harass their retreat south-east across Silesia towards Schweidnitz:

"Leave with my cavalry, march steadily without halting until you have made contact with the enemy, then engage them. If need be, make an omelette of my Guard, and give me time to get there with the infantry."

The Guard cavalry quickly got on the road through Würschen heading for Reichenbach, situated in the foothills bordering the river Neisse. General Colbert's lancer brigade formed the vanguard of Lefebvre-Desnoëttes' light cavalry. After two hours' march they ran into Cossacks in the neighbourhood of Weissenberg where the bridge had been destroyed. The lancers crossed the Löbauerwasser on a raft ferry north of the town and drove the Cossacks back in a running fight.

A little further on their way was barred by a ravine which extended far to the right, and to the left up to the village of Reichenbach, where Russian artillery was emplaced and protected by other troops. Very soon the Cossacks were being supported by Russian Dragoons, and the position of Colbert's brigade became untenable. With hardly six squadrons at his disposal the general

ordered his Red Lancers to attack the Russian cavalry while the other squadrons of the brigade formed a second line. Counterattacked by much greater numbers, the first squadrons were forced to withdraw; the intervention of the second line bought them time to rally. Repeated clashes followed, and each time the Russians withdrew under the protection of the battery of twelve guns placed on the heights of the village. This engagement at Reichenbach lasted a full two hours before reinforcements appeared; the Mamelukes and Mounted Chasseurs of the Guard, at first spectators to this unequal duel, were sent up in support by General Walther, followed later by the Line cavalry of General Latour-Maubourg's Corps accompanied by Saxon cavalry. By the time they were relieved the Red Lancers were exhausted, and General Walther's "omelette" had cost them dearly. According to Captain Adjutant-Major de Stuers the Regiment lost that day four officers, 197 lancers and 199 horses. Captain Nicolas Alexandre, only two months' arrived from the Empress' Dragoons, would die of his wounds at Dresden on 30 May, followed on 6 June by Sub-lieutenant Jean Reyntjes. The wounded Captain Jean Baptiste Lemaire became separated from the Regiment, and died at Torgau on 23 November. Captain Louis François Jouet, a 46-year-old ex-ranker of the King's army who had come into the Red Lancers with the Dragoons of the Paris Municipal Guard, was wounded; as also, by two lance thrusts, was Sub-lieutenant François de Groot. Captain Alphonse Pierre Salvetat, who took three lance thrusts, was made prisoner of war. Sergeant August Bisiaux was wounded several times, though he would survive to return to duty; so too was Lieutenant Bartels Sijstes Böcher, another old soldier, whose exact movements in May 1813 seem to be shrouded in some mystery. Trumpet-Major Kauffman's body was later found on the battlefield.

At the end of the last charge Captain de Stuers himself had the narrowest of escapes. Followed by his squadron, he broke through the Russian lines but lost his way; for some time the rest of the Regiment believed him killed or taken. In fact his men were riding for their lives across the rear of the Russian lines, and in the process running into an infantry square which cost them more casualties before de Stuers could find his way back to the Regiment.

Lieutenant Amédée Paulin Benoit de Tarlé (1790-1877) in the uniform of an officer of Hussars. He joined the Red Lancers from the 4th Hussars in March 1813, and was promoted captain in the 5th that September. A Bonapartist during the Hundred Days, he would find employment as a cavalry instructor in Egypt in the 1820s. (Author's collection)

After Bautzen the Allied armies were in full retreat towards the Oder. The Red Lancers were with the vanguard of the army; and at 11p.m. on the night of 31 May, Chef d'escadron de Tiecken made his report on a typical reconnaissance to Marshal Soult, who had taken over command of the Imperial Guard:

"I have the honour to report you that with the detachment under my command I have made a reconnaissance to Kostenblut by way of Dietzdorf, Buchwaldchen, Ziesenvitz, Pirschen and Harthau. Nearly all the information which I gathered in all these places agreed that 300 to 400 Cossacks had passed through two to three hours ahead of us. Finally, after having searched Harthau and taken up battle position in front of Kostenblut, through which my advanced guard had already passed, I noticed infantry skirmishers supported by a few troops of horse between Harthau and Kostenblut, apparently coming from Raschütz.

"I sent out Captain Jobaart and Lieutenant Resing of the Lancers of Berg to scout this force; they reported to me that they were, effectively, Cossacks. As night was falling and since I formed the impression that they were going to try to flank me through the woods, I anticipated this manoeuvre by falling back and to the right; darkness masked this move. I have my bivouac placed a little rearwards at the right of Pirschen between two windmills. Tomorrow, Monseigneur, I will carry on my march with the same necessary caution in order to join my division."

On 1 June de Tiecken was able to report to the Marshal from Harthau:

"Monseigneur, the Cossacks still number 300 and have their bivouacs beyond Kostenblut. I have the honour to send you these peasants who have delivered oxen to the fortress of Silberberg, and who will be able to give you information about the enemy. I am on my way to Polkendorf to join my division, having fulfilled the mission with which I was entrusted.

"P.S. A few Cossacks were spotted at Scharndorf at about five o'clock this morning."

The Armistice

The Allies may have been on the defensive in front of the Grande Armée, and hampered by their sheer numbers and dispersal, but in strategic terms they were growing stronger. In the north Napoleon's former Marshal Bernadotte, now Crown Prince of Sweden, was leading 120,000 Prussians and Swedes on Berlin. Wittgenstein had been replaced at the head of the main Russo-Prussian army in Silesia by the bellicose old Blücher, who was pulling it into shape while holding off Napoleon's further advance. Austria, posing as a mediator, would soon be ready to strike openly, and Schwarzenberg had some 120,000 men in Bohemia. Negotiations had been proceeding behind the scenes for months; now both sides were happy to agree to an armistice, ostensibly as a prelude to peace talks but actually in order to strengthen their armies.

When the armistice was signed on 4 June the Red Lancers were at Neumark; when the Emperor moved back to Dresden his Guard followed, taking up quarters around the city. The regimental staff and the main bulk of the troops were accommodated in Neustadt, the quarter north of the Elbe, with a few detachments in Hohnstein and other villages in the same area.

On 20 June 1813 the regimental state was as follows. With the Regiment were 42 officers with 72 horses, and 726 lancers with 522 horses. Nine officers with two horses and 307 lancers with 29 horses were on detachment; two officers were posted away as ADCs; 89 lancers were in hospital. At other locations, there were 93 troop horses at Frankfurt; 15 lancers at Erfurt; an officer and 18 lancers at Wittenberg; ten lancers with ten horses at Glogau; and two lancers and seven horses "in the rear". Two officers and 124 lancers were listed as prisoners of war.

The daily state of 26 June allows us to follow the Regiment's progress in making good the losses of Reichenbach. Listed were 50 officers with 143 horses, and 1,058 lancers with 982 horses; an officer and 35 lancers with 47 horses were on detachment; two officers were serving as ADCs; 53 lancers were in hospital; and three lancers were on trial. The Regiment also numbered three

medical officers; three drivers for the packhorses; in the regimental train, four soldiers, four draught horses and two field forges. Elsewhere there were 11 officers with 38 horses and 403 lancers with 359 horses at Frankfurt; ten lancers with 11 horses at Glogau; and two lancers with two horses were still "in the rear". The number of prisoners of war was now listed as three officers and 78 lancers.

The normal irritations continued to take up the staff officers' time. On 10 July the mayor of Dorheim and an employee at the salt works of Nauheim, Monsieur Theure, complained about three officers of the Red Lancers. A detachment under the orders of Colin de Verdière had arrived there on 30 June and would leave on 4 July to join the army; one of the accused was Sub-lieutenant Jean Mareilhac.

On 18 July two new officers were appointed by decree: Captain Bernard and Major de Briqueville; the first, however, was also appointed with effect from the 16th as chef d'escadron in the 11th Hussars, and preferred to enjoy his new rank in the Line. De Briqueville, one of poor Albert de Watteville's companions on his last journey, was the son of a Royalist officer executed by Republicans during the savage war of the Vendée, and the stepson of an influential politician. Before the Russian campaign he had spent much of his previous service in relative comfort as ADC to General Lebrun, and owed his epaulettes more to his staff and court connections than to swordsmanship in battle. (Extracts from his correspondence will bring to the later pages of this account a gushing style which makes even de Watteville read like a brutalised warrior; but these were the manners of another age of the world, and Armand de Briqueville would show his mettle in action on more than one occasion.)

Having received all available reinforcements General Colbert wrote from Neustadt to General Count Lobau, Commander-in-Chief of the Imperial Guard, on 22 July:

"More and more convinced of the need for a 3rd Major, I am making this request to His Majesty. Feeling also the heavy burden of a cavalry regiment of 2,000 troopers when one has only a small number of officers at his disposal, I hasten to send you the attached request for replacements and my nominations. I beg you to bring them to the attention of HM and to support them.

"I am proposing Mr Curély, chef d'escadron in the 20th Mounted Chasseurs, for 3rd Major, firstly because HM has told me that he wanted to provide me with a 3rd Major, and secondly because this officer is indispensable to me.

"To replace Captain Alexandre, who has been killed, I propose Mr Brack, captain and ADC; this is a personal favour which I ask of His Majesty, which if granted will be entirely to the benefit of his service. This officer is a pupil of Fontainebleau; he has served seven years under my orders; he has the talents of a good engineer, the bravery of a hussar and the education of a good captain. He has served in six campaigns, and deserves that his short time in the rank of captain be no obstacle to his admission to the Guard.

"I request the retirement of Captain Jouet, an old soldier who was severely wounded on 22 May, and to replace him I propose Mr Potier, a captain in the 8th Hussars and an officer who bears an excellent character. I request Mr Hulot, lieutenant or captain in the 7th Chasseurs, for captain in the Young Guard to replace Captain Salvetat, who has been taken prisoner. This officer is as brave as his brother and has always served in the Line.

"Mr d'Hautpoul, adjutant-major, for whom I request the position of first lieutenant in the Old Guard in place of Lieutenant Böcher, taken prisoner on the 18th, is in the same situation.

"Be good enough, General, to support me in these various requests, which matter to the wellbeing of my regiment. This regiment is, as you well know, a child in need of protectors: it can barely walk, but will soon have to mount and charge in line."

On 29 July 1813 General Nansouty was placed at the head of the Guard cavalry, which was organised in three divisions. The first, commanded by Count d'Ornano, consisted of the Lancers of Berg, the 2nd Lancers commanded by General Colbert, and the

Dragoons of the Young Guard commanded by Colonel Pinteville.

Between 1 and 5 August a medical officer arrived with the Regiment from France with two horses; one lancer returned from enemy captivity; and six horses died.

More substantial reinforcements were on their way. A detachment with 246 lancers and 266 horses left Schlutern for Fulda where they stayed for two days. On the 4th they were in Hunefeld, the nightly stops thereafter being at Vach, Eisenach, Gotha, Erfurt, Weimar, Jena, Gera, Altenburg, Rochlitz, Nossen and, on 15 August, in Dresden. Another detachment with 52 lancers and 56 horses also marched on 1 August from Gotha, following the same itinerary to arrive in Dresden on the 9th.

The daily state on 5 August recorded 66 officers with 190 horses, and 1,487 lancers with 1,399 horses; one officer and 24 lancers with 20 horses were on detachment; 37 lancers were in hospital, and nine on trial. There were five medical officers; four drivers; and in the regimental train, four soldiers with six horses and two field forges. Absent in Frankfurt were eight officers with 23 horses and 319 lancers with 206 horses. The Regiment was strong, handsome, enthusiastic, and ready to fight.

Back at the Versailles depot Colonel-Major Dubois had been performing prodigies; hundreds of newcomers were uniformed, equipped, armed, and sent on their way to join the Regiment. But Dubois' troubles were not over yet: in a short time he had seen 3,000 men pass through, and he was expecting a further 500 - but the Regiment only had resources for the 2,500 men specified in Napoleon's decree. What was worse, Dubois had a suspicion that the actual figure would reach nearer 4,000 within a few weeks - what was he to do? One step he could take was to tread quietly on a request for retirement by the Regiment's chief bootmaker, Monsieur Eysenbach. On 5 August Dubois wrote to General Baron Dériot begging him to forget until further notice a request previously made to General Count Caffarelli concerning Eysenbach's retirement and his replacement by one Monsieur

The parade of 10 August 1813 at Dresden was the last proud demonstration of strength and confidence to celebrate the Saint-Napoléon; the Emperor's birthday festivities were brought forward by five days that year, since the end of the armistice was expected to interfere with the actual date. This painting by Rudolf Thost (1868-1921) was lost in Dresden during the Second World War.

Gagnaison. (This was no time to disrupt such a vital department as the cobblers' shop....)

In 1813 the Emperor's birthday was celebrated on 10 August instead of the 15th; the armistice was due to end on the proper day, and it was expected that hostilities would break out again on 17 August. The festivities were magnificent. The King of Saxony and a glittering staff accompanied Napoleon to Friedrichstadt, where 15,000 men of the Imperial Guard were assembled for a huge parade. The Guard cavalry were drawn up at the Nordgründbruch bridge prior to taking part. The whole Regiment were present except for a few hundred who were guarding the Bohemian border.

"Today I will be admitted to the regiment", wrote the new Chef d'escadron Armand de Briqueville to his mother. The tone of soldierly pride was perhaps slightly spoiled when he continued: *"The major has got some tea for you - but mine is much better than his...."*

Days of defeat

On 12 August 1813 Austria formally declared war on France; and on the 16th Marshal Blücher's Russo-Prussian Army of Silesia began hostilities against the troops of Marshals Ney and Macdonald. Napoleon's main line of defence against the several separate Russian, Prussian, Austrian and Swedish armies now converging against him was between Dresden in the west and Leignitz in the east; the Elbe was not an absolute barrier, but as he held most of the main crossings the Allies could not

manoeuvre at will. Marshals Oudinot and Davout were detached with part of the army to move against Bernadotte's Prusso-Swedish Army of the North and to threaten Berlin.

On 15 August Napoleon had already left Dresden for Bautzen, Görlitz and Löwenberg to force the Army of Silesia back across the Katzbach. Blücher transferred a part of his army south to join Schwarzenberg's Russo-Austrian Army of Bohemia, and on the 23rd the Emperor was warned by Marshal Gouvion St Cyr at Dresden that this force was moving north to threaten the city. Leaving three Corps to watch Blücher in the east, Napoleon dashed southwards with his Guard to defend his main base. The Regiment reached Dresden and its former quarters in Neustadt on the night of 26 August, when battle had already been raging all day. On the morning of the 27th they crossed the Elbe to move towards the position termed No.4 Redoubt, where the *escadrons de service* and General d'Ornano's Division were gathered.

Dresden was a brilliant victory in the old Napoleonic style. The Emperor drew up his divisions in an arc across the southern approaches to the city, faced by twice as many Allied troops (at least 170,000) whose co-operation was hampered by rain, swollen streams, boggy ground, poor communications and late reinforcements. Murat led an enveloping attack on the right wing, turning the Allies' left and forcing it inwards. The solidly emplaced French centre stayed on the defensive, and Napoleon smashed Wittgenstein's right flank advance along the Elbe; total casualties were about 10,000 French to 38,000 Allied. The Red Lancers made an honourable contribution to this victory; led by Chef d'escadron de Tiecken, the Regiment successfully charged against the Austrian Corps of General Gyulai.

Between 14 and 27 August the Regiment had lost 200 horses

and a considerable number of lancers. Fortunately they were still receiving a steady stream of replacements; on 22 August General Baron Dériot wrote to inform the Minister of War that a detachment of the 2nd Lancers of the Guard, composed of two officers and 201 NCOs and unmounted soldiers, had joined the Grande Armée on the 21st.

By the night after the battle it had been raining for 36 hours. On the evening of the 27th the Regiment made its bivouacs in front of the city walls in thick mud; the rank and file of the lancers – who had not been in Russia – complained that this was their worst ever campground. Some officers installed themselves in a small house where, after clearing out a number of enemy corpses, they were able to get warm and to dry their clothes. Lieutenant van Omphal and Captain Brack (the former ADC to General Colbert, appointed to the Regiment since 10 August) climbed the city walls and removed from an adjacent house two doors, which they used as shelter from the rain and mud. Those who were less lucky or resourceful had no way to dry their soaking clothing and kit.

Very early on 28 August the Red Lancers got on the road in pursuit of the forces of Schwarzenberg and Barclay de Tolly which were falling back towards Bohemia with some difficulty. Their exact routes and intentions were hard to discern, and Napoleon missed the chance to cut them off and destroy them. The Red Lancers were sent in the direction of Dippoldiswalde, where they encountered units of Allied cavalry covering the retreat and exchanged some shots; Lieutenant Hanneman was slightly bruised by a bullet in the chest.

The Lancers remained in bivouacs for two nights before continuing their march; it was then that Antonie van Omphal made a wager with some brother-officers that in spite of their

The battle of Dresden, 27 August 1813: a painting by Friedrich A.Schneider (1799-1855), lost in Dresden during the Second World War.

Brugghen and the Marquis de Nettancourt.

By 15 September they were at Pirna; regimental strength was up to 76 officers with 191 horses, 1,101 lancers with 1,100 horses, and 12 draught horses; 12 officers with 32 horses and 823 lancers with 724 horses were at Frankfurt and Torgau; 72 lancers were in hospital.

On the 16th they fought at Nollendorf, and the next day at Töplitz. The Guard Lancer Brigade was with the vanguard during the march on Töplitz. A hundred-strong detachment of the Red Lancers led by Chef d'escadron Colin de Verdière fought three Russian battalions and captured a battery of six guns. The lancers had been taking advantage of the meandering course of a deep ravine to get close to the battery. At the last possible moment Colin de Verdière launched his charge; the battery opened fire with canister shot, and Russian hussars came forward to protect the guns, but the Red Lancers smashed through to capture the battery. (According to Lieutenant van Omphal, however, they actually captured only the limbers and not the guns themselves.) That day the Regiment lost 25 lancers and 46 horses killed. Four officers, 24 lancers and 24 horses were wounded, the former being the newly decorated 2nd Lieutenant Dejean (by two lance thrusts), Captain Pierre Landrieve (bruised by a cannonball), Sub-lieutenant Louis Paillard and Lieutenant Alphonse Seran.

A letter from Napoleon to General Lefebvre-Desnoëttes dated 18 September suggests that the Emperor realised that he would soon be forced to fall back before the growing Allied armies:

"Have all the depots of cavalry and the wounded make for Erfurt and Gotha, as well as everything from Leipzig that is not really necessary." To the Minister of Foreign Affairs he wrote: *"The Red Lancers of the Guard have captured five guns ..."*

That day Chef d'escadron de Briqueville wrote to his stepfather, the Prefect of the Department of the Lower Rhine, in terms which set him startlingly apart even in that age of accessible emotions - from *"in front of Naldorf near Culm [sic], 3 hours from Töplitz: My dear Papa - I have received a letter from Brechtel telling me that Mama has left for Normandy. I am writing to you so that she may receive more prompt news about me. Yesterday we had a hot day, beautiful for us but with only five guns as a result. We are in a peculiar position, but there is no need to worry. Write to me, and beg Mama to write to me; love me as much as I love you, this will not lessen your tender feelings for my mother. I kiss you, my dear Papa, for your lasting love, and love you from the bottom of my heart - Your Armand... Let them know in Haguenau that Colonel Tureau [Thurot] is well."*

The Guard cavalry depot was located at Torgau with a smaller station at Glogau. Reinforcements continued to arrive, and were gratefully received; the constant need for cavalry to reconnoitre the complex movements of the divided Allied armies revealed perhaps the Grande Armée's most serious weakness in this campaign. A detachment of 142 lancers with 144 horses left Fulda on 22 September to reach Erfurt on the 27th.

The Regiment returned to Dresden where it was quartered in the charming village of Tharandt. During their stay there the Lancers were sent out scouting for their old enemies the Russian Cossacks. These probing missions were not without risk; on the 28th Captain Pierre Auguste Dufour was shot and slightly wounded during a skirmish near Altenburg (this was an officer who had arrived from the 8th Chasseurs that spring, not the long-serving paymaster Captain Pierre Alexis Dufour.) On 1 October Captain Jean Jacques Maurin - an experienced old soldier who had spent four years in British captivity after being captured by Portuguese guerrillas - was wounded while visiting the outposts.

On that day the Regiment numbered 62 officers with 172 horses, 933 lancers with 953 horses, and nine draught horses; at Frankfurt and Torgau were another 11 officers with 26 horses and

recent success the French army would be forced to cross back to the west bank of the Rhine before the middle of November. In the first days of September they marched towards Peterswalde, crossing the plain of Külm where General Vandamme, surprised by von Kleist's Prussians while trying to block the Austrian retreat, had been badly defeated on 30 August. When the pursuit clearly became pointless the Regiment returned to Dresden, where they stayed for a few days.

Now began a confusing, exhausting and costly period of marching and counter-marching for the Grande Armée. Napoleon's success at Dresden had not been matched by his detached marshals. In the north Oudinot's move against Berlin had been frustrated by Bernadotte at Grossbeeren on 22 August, obliging Davout to fall back on Hamburg; in the east Blücher defeated Marshal Macdonald on the river Katzbach four days later. On 6 September the so-called Army of Berlin under Ney and Oudinot was badly beaten at Dennewitz by Bernadotte. Napoleon now seemed to lose his strategic focus as he reacted first to one threat, then to another.

At Dresden on 1 September 1813 the Regiment numbered 36 officers with 88 horses, 554 lancers with 564 horses and 10 draught horses; at Frankfurt and Torgau were an additional four officers with nine horses and 214 lancers with 203 horses; 43 soldiers were in hospital.

During these past months many of the Red Lancers had been rewarded for their bravery. On 14 September five members of the Regiment were decorated with the cross of the Legion of Honour: Sergeant Jacques Groenhuysen, and Lieutenants J.W.C.Spies, Pierre Dejean (a veteran ranker commissioned in from the Guard Chasseurs that January), George van der

899 lancers with 726 horses; three officers and 84 lancers were in hospital.

The Battle of the Nations

After a series of marches, countermarches and skirmishes the Regiment arrived in the neighbourhood of Leipzig on 14 October; here they captured a large Allied food convoy escorted by Cossacks and drawn by Ukrainian oxen. The next day, at Strassenhause, the daily state was 63 officers with 159 horses, 731 lancers with 722 horses, and nine draught horses; at the Versailles depot another 15 officers with 36 horses and 1,102 lancers with 899 horses were recorded; two officers and 84 lancers were in hospital.

In Leipzig the regiment was quartered in one of the suburbs, most of the officers being accommodated in the pleasant house of a distinguished-seeming gentleman. Conversation revealed him to be none other than the city executioner.... At the officers' request he showed them his arsenal of instruments, each one with its grisly anecdote. Very early the next morning, Saturday 16 October, the Regiment set off towards Liebertwolkwitz. It was the eve of what would go down in history as "the Battle of the Nations": nearly 290,000 Austrian, Russian, Prussian and Swedish troops of four Allied armies were converging on Leipzig from the north, south and east. South-east of the city Napoleon faced them with less than 158,000, and about 900 cannon to the Allies' 1,500.

The battle of Leipzig lasted from 16 to 19 October; it cost each side some 60,000 casualties and saw no dazzling tactical manoeuvres. The noose around the French position was doggedly tightened by Blücher's Army of Silesia from the north-west and Schwarzenberg's Army of Bohemia from the south, furiously resisted and – on the afternoon of the 16th – driven back by a major counterattack. The Regiment was drawn up in reserve with the rest of Nansouty's 4,000 Guard cavalry, at first behind the village of Probstheide but later, as the line contracted, a mile or so west behind Augerau's IX Corps. Although not committed to face-to-face fighting the Red Lancers lost many men to the continuous enemy artillery fire. On the evening of the 16th the firing had stopped and the Lancers had dismounted when a stray shell rolled into the middle of a group of officers and exploded. Second Lieutenant d'Assier lost his left leg; one of General Colbert's orderly officers lost both and had his horse killed under him.

Throughout the 17th the Regiment held its position under fire without the opportunity to get into action; Napoleon seems to have fallen into one of his strange spells of lassitude, and wasted a precious day during which Bernadotte's army made progress to join Blücher and Schwarzenberg from the north-east. On the 18th the Allies renewed their attacks; Bernadotte had finally come up to support them, and that night Napoleon's Saxon allies deserted him. He could see only one end to the battle; but he had preserved a large part of his army in good order south and east of the city, and planned a disciplined withdrawal on the 19th through Leipzig and west across the Elster river towards Lindenau and Weissenfels.

On the night of 18-19 October some squadrons of the Red Lancers were ordered to move back into the city and across the only bridge; they reached the west bank between 11p.m. and midnight, and after the continual cannonade they found the quiet which reigned there astonishing. It was only a short respite; the next day the fighting flared up more fiercely than ever as the evacuation of the Grande Armée, which had begun in orderly fashion, turned into bloody confusion under Allied pressure which carried the fighting into the streets of the city. At about 1p.m. a corporal of Engineers – supposedly, coming under fire from snipers at a moment when his officer was absent – set off the charges prematurely and blew up the bridge over the Elster while between 15,000 and 20,000 troops were still on the east bank. To this figure must be added some 15,000 wounded, 36 generals, 325 guns, 900 ammunition caissons, and 28 regimental Eagle standards.

Chef d'escadron Jan Post, who suffered a bullet wound, found himself and his squadron trapped in Leipzig. Like many others he was determined not to fall into enemy hands; with the men who were left to him he fought his way to the river bank and plunged in to try to swim his horse across. When he dragged himself out on the far bank he was accompanied by one sergeant and one lancer; they managed to rejoin the Regiment at Lützen, but Post never did find out what happened to the rest of his men. One of the Regiment's sergeants saved Marshal Macdonald's life by giving up his horse to take him across the river; Prince Poniatowski, wounded four times, was drowned in the attempt.

The Regiment's losses were heavy. Among the officers, Sub-lieutenant Philippe Barbier d'Aucourt was killed; Lieutenant Sub-Adjutant-Major Mathias Brepoels was wounded and taken prisoner; Captain Pierre Landrieve was captured, as was Lieutenant d'Assier, left behind in hospital.

★　　★　　★

The Red Lancers, as part of General d'Ornano's division, provided the vanguard during the subsequent retreat westwards. They headed for Weissenfels via Erfurt, where the army's major supply depots were located. For most of their journey they came across only a few advanced enemy cavalry detachments; but at Hanau on 28 October the Bavarian General de Wrede attempted to block the road to the Rhine with 40,000 Bavarian and Austrian troops.

The fighting had already begun when the Red Lancers arrived before Hanau on the 30th. The Regiment took up an awkward position in woodland along the Gelnhausen road; the ground was strewn with branches and treetrunks shattered by artillery fire, and the noise was deafening. To force the Bavarian lines the Emperor skilfully committed the Guard artillery protected by the Lancers and Dragoons; the battle ended with cavalry charges in which the Red Lancers played their part, driving back the enemy but without persuading them to evacuate Hanau. The next morning it was Captain Hubert de Stuers of the Red Lancers - that ever-reliable envoy - who was sent forward with a trumpeter to demand their surrender. The sounding of the trumpet was met with shots, and after a while de Stuers turned back; Marshal Marmont had the town bombarded and then assaulted by General Charrière's brigade.

Leaving the battlefield with the Emperor, the Regiment arrived in Frankfurt on the afternoon of 1 November 1813. By that time its field strength was down to 52 officers with 130 horses and 462 lancers with 464 horses. At the Versailles depot were another 28 officers with 50 horses, and 1,407 lancers - but with only 503 horses. Three officers and 250 lancers were listed as prisoners of war in the aftermath of Leipzig.

At Mainz the Red Lancers took up position with the rearguard to watch and protect the crossing of the Rhine by the rest of the Grande Armée. With the help of his adjutant-major, Captain de Stuers, General Colbert made a final effort at the Kastell Gate to gather up any stragglers from the Regiment who might be lost in the crowd. Among the wounded from the battle of Hanau was 2nd Lieutenant Johan Geubels, who would die in hospital at Mainz on 11 December.

The Regiment's own turn to cross the Rhine came on 5 November, and they arrived at Worms on the 8th. Lieutenant van Omphal had won his bet made at Dippoldiswalde. On 7 November, impatient as ever to see his mother and stepfather again, the faintly embarassing Count Armand de Briqueville wrote:

"We are leaving Groswentenheim to go to Zornheim, which is only a league from Oppenheim. This is certainly a promising direction, which I greatly hope will lead us to Strasbourg. I kiss you, my dear good Mama, and I shall make it up to you for all the times that our letters did not arrive by telling you every day that I love you and that I kiss you with

Red Lancer - a spirited study, although with anachronistic details including the combination of officer's shoulder ornaments with lance and slung carbine. (Collection of Belgian Royal Army Museum, Brussels)

Chef d'escadron Hubert J. J. L. de Stuers (1789-1861), the intelligent and energetic young regimental staff officer who was entrusted by General Colbert with a number of important missions as a courier. (Miniature after a portrait; photo © Stichting Iconographisch Bureau, The Hague)

all my heart. Kiss Papa for me with all my heart ..."

Two days later he wrote again: *"We are well on the road to Strasbourg, but did not arrive in time to prevent partisans collecting contributions from a village near Ortheim. We are quartered with many soldiers from the infantry.... We have outposts to keep watch on the Rhine. Yesterday I asked for five or six days' leave. The regiment really needs to send to Strasbourg to have several essential items manufactured there, but I was unable to get permission. I am in Osthofen, a small town one hour from Worms. It is too crowded with men and horses for us to stay here long; but that does not bring me any nearer to you...."*

The 1813 campaign, which had started with such promise, was coming to an end on the very borders of France. The Regiment had suffered 50 per cent casualties in two and a half months. General Colbert was ordered to return to Versailles to reorganise it once more. Appointed general of division by decree of 25 November 1813, he was named a count of the Empire.

From Worms the Regiment marched to Sarreguemines, and eventually to Metz. Once more the adjutants and quartermasters had to throw themselves into their frustrating paper battles.... On 10 November eight officers were in Metz, of whom six were "unavailable"; there were 17 officers' horses, but only six of these were available for service. The previous night a detachment had arrived composed of 300 men and 120 horses. Another 400 lancers were unavailable for lack of uniforms; 142 more were listed sick and 26 invalided out. Another 64 troop horses would become available within a month; 47 horses were written off the roll, and 142 horses were more or less fit for service.

Within ten days the Regiment would number 54 officers with 152 horses, and 514 lancers with 493 horses. There were 1,272 lancers at Metz but with only 110 horses; another 120 men with 120 horses were at Lautern. Ten mounted lancers were on detached service with Marshal Mortier.

On 12 November, still tantalisingly close to home, Chef d'escadron de Briqueville wrote from Osthofen on those concerns which seemed to preoccupy him to the exclusion of all regimental duties: *"I am desolated, dear Papa, not to be able to come and see you, but you know as well as I do where we are. It is most painful that I am unable to kiss you and hear your voice at a time like this. Neither your letters nor my mother's are reaching me. I have someone searching for one of yours sent to Groswentenheim, which I left on the 7th. I notice important preparations for an attack....I have written to the Duke of Plaisance [General Lebrun asking to be sent to] Strasbourg. Only he can understand and support me; the Emperor's departure for Metz has dashed my hopes. General Colbert does not wish to accept responsibility for granting a leave of even 48 hours.*

"I am still an hour away from Worms, so do not send the servant and the goods to Mainz as I asked you, but to Worms instead, addressed to the director of the postal service - I will write him instructions in case I should be sent away. Send me also a good map of the Rhine borders and, if you can find them, some of the region where the war might take place."

Four days later he wrote again to his stepfather: *"Dear Papa, how pleased I am to have had a letter, to read it, to kiss it, to turn it over and over again. How I wish I could embrace you. The general is so hard on himself and we are so much on the alert, without knowing why, that I dare not leave even this little patch of ground which we are observing. We could stand our reversal of fortune well enough, my poor Papa, if only we could share these miserable days....I await Mama's return impatiently...all I want is to get news from her often. I received none during this whole last campaign, and that made things so much worse.*

"How I would love to be huddled up with all our friends in a good strong castle where we should [only] have to feed and defend ourselves....But to fight against one's will for people who are not worth the trouble is mystifying - and to be defeated, on top of it all, is saddening. It is not a very encouraging thing to have only empty-handed skeletons with which to defend one's country..."

On 18 November - clearly unconvinced of the difference his presence was making to the safety of the Empire, and dreaming of the pleasant life he knew on General Lebrun's staff - de Briqueville took up his pen yet again:

"General Colbert has refused to let me go to Strasbourg... [even though] there is no reason to fear any enemy movement in this direction, and I believe they would rather advance on Switzerland than between two fortified towns, which are very close to Metz where they know all our troops are assembling. The infantry which are stationed with us are relieved by fresh troops every day, and all these garrison changes are wearing out the countryside horribly.

"This morning I received interesting news. My comrade Chef d'escadron Petiet has been appointed adjutant-commandant and has been ordered to report to the 5th Cavalry Corps at Nied Ulm on the road from Metz to Mainz. At the bottom of the order General Piré wrote: 'Bring de Briqueville with you, and we can arrange something suitable for him'. I have written to General Piré to inform him that I cannot absent myself, [but] that I was sending him my service record, that I would trust to his friendship to put it forward, and that I would be very happy to have one of the regiments in his division.

"This would be a godsend - with any other man than General Colbert the matter would be settled. But Thurot has left without his help, and Petiet too. Now he wants to place one or two of his friends and is himself on the lookout for a regiment for them. I am too far away from General Lebrun to get this promotion. Send me a letter for General Nansouty, who commands not only the cavalry of the Guard but also that of the whole army. Do not ask for anything specific, just recommend me to him."

Back in France, the army was being reorganised once again. The Allies had offered Napoleon peace terms, but he had refused. To defend the Empire he relied upon the Rhine barrier, bolstered by fortified centres in Holland and by Metz and Luxembourg. But a patriotic revolt had broken out in Holland in October, and Napoleon's German puppet Confederation of the Rhine had also collapsed. With the cordon of defence compromised Antwerp,

A portrait in middle age of Major Charles E. de Lalaing d'Audenarde (1779-1859), commander of the Young Guard squadrons of the Red Lancers in Belgium under General Maison in 1814. (Private collection)

On 1 December 1813 the regimental state was as follows:
Squadrons with the army:
54 officers, 664 lancers, 615 horses
At or on their way to Brussels:
11 officers, 225 lancers, 225 horses
At the Versailles depot:
18 officers, 154 lancers, 100 horses
On their way to Versailles:
3 officers
At the Metz depot:
17 officers, 978 lancers, 311 horses
In hospital at Metz:
203 lancers
Total: 103 officers, 2,204 lancers, 1,251 horses.

On 13 December a detachment of one sergeant, four corporals and 45 troopers set off from Metz for the army under the command of Sub-lieutenant Briot, with two officers' horses and 50 troop horses.

The reorganisation also involved senior officers. By decree of 26 December 1813 Napoleon appointed Colonel Leclerc, major of the Regiment, as general of brigade in the Line, and General of Brigade de Lalaing d'Audenarde as major in the Regiment; the latter was at once sent to Brussels to take command of the Young Guard squadrons. Passing by Mechelen, the lancers of the Young Guard reached Antwerp on 30 December at noon. The next day they left for Breda, but before doing so Chef d'escadron de Briqueville, who commanded one of the Young Guard squadrons, snatched the time to write to his mother of a happy encounter:

"I feel at home - to my great pleasure I have found my general [Lebrun] who is Governor of Antwerp. I spent part of the evening at the theatre. I do not believe, dear Mama, that we will be staying in this country for long. These movements make me miserable; we should be together to cheer each other up, now that the beginning of the end is upon us. We are going to Breda; Berckheim left yesterday morning for Flushing."

Thus ended 1813. At the beginning of the campaign in Saxony the Red Lancers had had 700 troopers. By the time of the Great Parade on 10 August the Regiment had been reinforced with 1,600 men; another 150 had arrived on 15 October; but of the original 700, just 450 were left.

where Allied intervention was expected, became the pivot of the next campaign. On 30 November 1813 the Emperor wrote to General Drouot:

"Between Antwerp and Brussels a reserve of the Guard will be placed, to be composed of...a squadron of 200 lancers of the 2nd Regiment, of whom 150 left a week ago and 50 are leaving today. Let me know if there are still Chasseurs, Gendarmes, Lancers, Dragoons, Grenadiers, etc...in Paris who could be mounted."

The officers and those few lancers of the Regiment who were Dutch by birth were reluctant to fight against their countrymen. In a unanimous delegation the officers presented themselves to General Colbert and begged not to be sent to fight their compatriots; nevertheless they wished to fight for the Emperor and show their loyalty to France, and asked the general to intercede for them with Napoleon. This he promised to do; and the Emperor, moved by their predicament, sent only the Young Guard squadrons of the Red Lancers to Antwerp and Brussels, holding back the Old Guard squadrons to which most of the Dutch officers and soldiers belonged. Most of the army's units of Dutch origin were being disarmed and sent to the south of France; only the Red Lancers were kept with the Emperor.

CHAPTER V

1814: The Campaign of France

Napoleon still had some 118,000 troops on the eastern borders of France; 50,000 locked up in German garrisons; about the same number facing the Austrians in Italy; and 100,000 in the south-west resisting the Duke of Wellington's British army advancing from the Pyrenees. On the Rhine the Emperor faced invasion by three foreign armies, all with their eyes fixed on Paris. On 21 December 1813 the largest of these, about 210,000 Austrians and Russians under Schwarzenberg, began crossing the Rhine at Basel heading for the Belfort Gap. On New Year's Eve the 75,000 men of Blücher's Russo-Prussian Army of Silesia began crossing at Mannheim, Kaub, and other points into Lorraine. In the north Bernadotte invaded Holstein, acquiring Denmark for his new Swedish throne by mid-January, and then led 60,000 Russians and Swedes towards the Netherlands.

As the Emperor displayed undiminished energy reorganising his army in Paris, French forces were retreating on all fronts with little resistance. Nevertheless, in his dazzling conduct of operations over the next three months Napoleon would show that at his best he was still the master of any other general in Europe - moving fast between slower and more cautious opponents, striking unexpectedly to knock them off balance, and usually victorious although always fighting outnumbered.

In Belgium General Maison, commander of I Corps, prepared to defend the northern gateways into the Empire as best he could; among his troops was a cavalry division of the Young Guard under General Lefebvre-Desnoëttes, including about 300 troopers of the Mounted Chasseurs and the Red Lancers. On 10-11 January 1814 the enemy advancing from Holland attacked Hoogstraten to the north of Antwerp, their superior forces driving General Roguet's division out of the village and back to Wijnegem. This withdrawal obliged the forces commanded by General Ambert to leave Brasschaat and Donck and to fall back on Merksem.

In his memoirs Captain Fortuné Brack of the Red Lancers, present at Hoogstraten, remembered having to deal with Prussian Uhlan lancers holding narrow roads with deep ditches running each side. Brack placed picked men armed with carbines at the head of his column, followed by the rest of his troopers with lances slung and sabres in hand. During the engagement at Hoogstraten 2nd Lieutenant Sourdis was wounded in the course of a charge under the orders of Chef d'escadron de Briqueville who, at the head of 18 lancers, captured a Prussian unit and a cannon (thus giving the lie to the apparent lack of enthusiasm for regimental soldiering betrayed in his relentlessly sentimental letters - and not for the last time). Early in the fighting 2nd Lieutenant Lethuillier took a bullet through the right shoulder.

On the morning of the 13th General Maison, fearing encirclement in the city, left Antwerp in favour of mobile operations in open country, darting from one threatened point to another. On that same day 2nd Lieutenant Henry Reckinger was wounded in an engagement at Merksem.

★　★　★

In France, General Nansouty still commanded the cavalry of the Imperial Guard. General Lefebvre-Desnoëttes, called back from Belgium by the Emperor, left Paris for Châlons on 17 January, taking with him 1,650 troopers of the Guard and General Rottembourg's division. Two days later, on the 19th at noon,

Chef d'escadron de Tiecken presented a detachment of 250 Red Lancers to the Emperor at the Tuileries. They were sent off to join the field army on the same day by General Dériot, together with 220 Polish Lancers and 100 Scouts of the 1st Regiment. That night they halted at Claye on the road to Meaux.

Although recruits were still getting through to the depots it was no easy task to dress and mount them. On 19 January Napoleon decreed that the Light Horse Lancer, Hussar and Mounted Chasseur regiments of the Line must provide the Red Lancers with 400 complete sets of harness. Bargains were struck and orders placed for 1,500 saddles, 900 meters of scarlet cloth, 2,677 meters of dark blue cloth, 6,090 meters of sky blue cloth, 824 lancer caps for the Old Guard squadrons, 80 for NCOs, 1,200 for the Young Guard, buttons, gauntlets... Everything had to be done over again - not forgetting 30 trumpets. The Regiment's account books were a disaster.

To reinforce the Guard Napoleon asked Minister of War Clarke to use the mail coach system, without delay and whatever the circumstances, to bring up 1,000 former troopers of the Army of Spain and another 1,000 from the cavalry depots stationed in the 1st Military Division. This decision allowed General Nansouty to send a report to the Emperor concerning the Red Lancers' depot:

"This depot numbers 43 officers, 1,004 men and 624 horses - but we have 618 men in hospital, 49 craftsmen, 33 proposed for discharge and 10 on sick leave. Thus only 294 men are left over to take care of the 624 horses. The colonel asks that 200 or 300 men of the Army of Spain be granted to him. He also requests a few NCOs from the Light Horse Guard of the King of Spain, of which the cadres are at Orleans. The regiment should receive 600 Guards of Honour; 140 should have arrived already but over the four days since they started coming in only 60 have arrived, some not at all suitable for service. I saw the detachment that showed up last Thursday for review; men and horses are well dressed and equipped. Their training is under way and one can see that it is working. We have saddles being made and we are taking care of the uniforms."

On 24 January the Emperor ordered General Colbert to march that same day with 1,300 troopers of the Guard and 900 cavalrymen from the Versailles depots to protect the bridges at Nogent-sur-Seine until relieved. From there they left for Vitry and Arcis with General Bordesoulle's cavalry. The squadrons of the Red Lancers were led on campaign by distinguished officers: de Tiecken commanded the 1st Squadron, and Coti, Post, de Briqueville, de Lastours, de Potier, Schneither and de Stuers the others.

In accordance with Napoleon's decision concerning the King of Spain's Guard (the now redundant bodyguard of Napoleon's

Chef d'escadron M.M.B. de Tiecken (1777-1848) in the uniform of the Dutch 10th Lancers, 1823 - the corps to which the former Colonel-Major Dubois summoned a number of other veteran officers of the Regiment in 1819. De Tiecken particularly distinguished himself when leading the Red Lancers at the battle of La Rothière on 1 February 1814. A family legend has it that when Napoleon was boarding HMS Bellerophon to be taken into his final exile in July 1815, de Tiecken tried to smuggle himself aboard disguised as an English sailor in order to accompany his Emperor. Recognised and put off the ship, he threw himself at Napoleon's feet; the Emperor helped him up, and gave him a gold snuffbox as a parting gift. (Collection of Belgian Royal Army Museum, Brussels)

The medals - cross of the Legion of Honour, St Helena medal and its miniature - of Vélite Woot de Trixhe of the Red Lancers, who was appointed to the Legion of Honour for gallantry at Montmirail on 10 February 1814. (Private collection, Belgium)

brother Joseph, thrown out of his Spanish kingdom the previous year), the first officers arrived with the Regiment on 1 February 1814, among them Colonel Brousse, Chefs d'escadron Pitel and Bosc and Captain Gauthier.

In the Low Countries General Maison was still trying to hold off the Allied advance. He sent out reconnaissance parties to Sint-Truiden and along the road to Liège, which was said to be occupied by the enemy following its evacuation by Marshal Macdonald's cavalry. General Castex, who had just replaced Lefebvre-Desnoëttes, was ordered to send out scouts to confirm whether the bridge at Liège had been cut and whether the enemy held the town; if not, they were to take position there with artillery support and to inform General Maison.

On 22 January General Castex received new instructions to occupy Liège and Hasselt, to destroy the bridge at Liège if it could not be barricaded, and to establish a reserve at Sint-Truiden. An engagement against larger enemy forces, superior particularly in cavalry and artillery, forced General Castex to withdraw towards Sint-Truiden, Tienen and Leuven after suffering losses, especially among his cavalry. Lieutenant Jacques Colignon was wounded before Liège and taken prisoner on the 27th; during one of a number of reconnaissances later that day 2nd Lieutenant Benoist Alexandre was also wounded.

Retiring to Brussels where General Maison had his headquarters, the Red Lancers occupied Etterbeek, observing the village of Audergem on the road to Wavre and pushing patrols up the road to Leuven as far as Nossegem. Fifty horse led by Captain Brack and 150 infantry also occupied Waterloo, with outposts at Mont St Jean at the junction of the roads to Nivelles and Namur. In Waterloo the troops behaved badly towards the inhabitants - particularly, it seems, towards the widow Joos Bodenghien. The villagers stayed up on the alert on the night of 31 January-1 February until 2a.m. or 3a.m., when the Lancers left for Tubeke to join the troops who were evacuating Brussels.

On 31 January the Young Guard squadrons, under the command of Chef d'escadron de Lastours, recorded:
Present under arms: 22 officers with 65 horses; 258 lancers with 258 horses; three draught horses.
On local detached service: 15 officers with 42 horses; 404 lancers with 426 horses.
Absent without pay: Five officers and 114 lancers in hospital; 22 lancers on leave; three officers and 77 lancers prisoners of war.

★ ★ ★

The Emperor left the Tuileries palace at six on the morning of 25 January to put himself at the head of his troops at Châlons-sur-Marne, to which town Marshal Macdonald had been forced back by the Allied advance over the lower Rhine. Napoleon left General d'Ornano in Paris as commander of the entire Guard, with orders to organise as rapidly as possible a "Cavalry of the Guard of Paris" which was to number 300 Red Lancers. The army which he found awaiting his hand was largely composed of green young conscripts, but it was not without fighting spirit - Napoleon's name still had magic, and boys who have never heard gunfire are notoriously as liable to take crazy risks as to run away. He was about to use them in a quicksilver campaign against two separate enemy armies, darting and weaving back and forth as he landed blows first on one, then on the other.

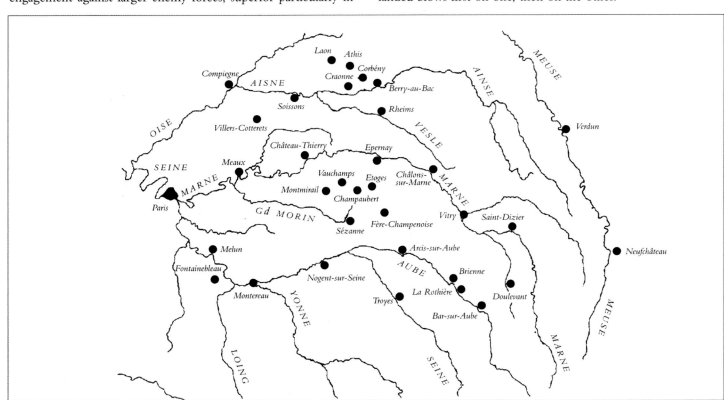

The situation was bad, nevertheless: the Prussians had already crossed Lorraine and had just occupied St Dizier, advancing diagonally along the Aube. Napoleon faced the choice of confronting either the Russians and Austrians under Schwarzenberg, or the Russians and Prussians led by Blücher. The nearest enemy would be paid the compliment of priority: he turned towards the Prussians. At daybreak on 27 January the French, after night marches, fell upon Blücher's vanguard between Vitry-le-François and St Dizier; part of the Regiment saw action during this victorious engagement. That evening the Emperor wrote to Marshal Mortier and to General Colbert:

"We have beaten the enemy at St Dizier.... We are on the enemy's lines, and the vanguard is moving towards Wassy.... Come closer, as Colbert will do, to the right flank of our army. Vitry is the pivot of all operations."

Blücher marched on Brienne where he concentrated his forces. He had to be stopped; and a few miles from Brienne, on the 29th at about noon, General Grouchy's 5th Cavalry Corps and the cavalry of the Guard overran General Pahlen's Russian cavalry in several brilliantly conducted charges which stripped away the flank guard of General Sacken's advance towards Brienne. At the end of the battle the bulk of Blücher's army, protected by their rearguard, withdrew in the direction of Bar-sur-Aube where they intended to link up with their advancing Austrian allies. On the 30th, in complete control of the Brienne position and with the

Prussians in full retreat, the Emperor called back everyone he could reach, including General Colbert (whose Scouts and Light Horse of the Guard were now termed the 1st Guard Cavalry Division). At 9.30p.m. on 30 January the Emperor ordered:

"It is certain that General Colbert has left for Châlons. The General-Major will send a courier to him at Sommesous as soon as possible to direct him at once to Brienne. The General-Major will also write to General Bordesoulle at Arcis-sur-Aube to have someone meet General Colbert to guide him to Brienne."

To this Colbert replied from Prameru at 2a.m. on the 31st: *"I have the honour of acknowledging receipt of the order Your Highness has sent me to head for Brienne. It was sent after me from Arcis, whence I had left to join General Gérard. Tomorrow at noon I will be at Brienne."*

On the day that General Colbert wrote these few lines Captain de Stuers arrived with the Regiment bringing a reinforcement of 200 lancers from Versailles - reinforcements which would soon be urgently needed to fill gaps in the ranks. The 31st also saw the appearance of the two Allied armies on the plain between Bar-sur-Aube and Brienne, and both sides spent that day in taking up their positions.

On 1 February gunfire broke out near La Rothière, the centre of the battlefield, where the Young Guard faced the elite of Blücher's forces. Old "Marshal Forwards" was on the offensive once more; and at 3.30p.m. enemy cavalry appeared in great strength, threatening the French artillery. The Red Lancers, led

Lazare Carnot (1753-1823) as governor of Antwerp in 1814, by Mathieu van Brée, 1773-1839.

by Chef d'escadron de Tiecken, slashed into their right flank together with the Polish Lancers of the Guard. Defeated and thrown into disorder, the enemy cavalry retreated behind the shelter of their own lines.

The army as a whole, however, was under threat of encirclement by the much stronger enemy, and on the left flank the battle took a turn for the worse. To cover the retreat of these units Napoleon threw Colbert's division forward, and General Nansouty led them into La Rothière. During repeated charges Chef d'escadron de Tiecken set an inspiring example of courage and dash, and the Red Lancers succeeded in recapturing the artillery lost by General Duhesme's division. During this action de Tiecken was wounded for the first time, by a canister shot which bruised his chest. That morning the Regiment had numbered 440 men; by nightfall 240 were left. Among the missing were Lieutenants Albert Frank and George van der Brugghen. The next day the French army marched toward Troyes. During rearguard engagements the Red Lancers lost another 55 men and 100 horses; Lieutenant Henri Ubaghs was among the wounded.

At the beginning of February a reinforcement of ten officers with 125 mounted lancers were ready to leave the depot. Only two officers with 24 lancers and 21 horses remained for duty in Paris.

On the morning of 4 February 1814 the entire Guard, Red Lancers included, assembled before Sancy (St Julien) to be reviewed by the Emperor; they greeted him with ringing cheers. After a few days' rest Napoleon decided to evacuate Troyes and move to Nogent. After the battle of La Rothière the Prussians had soon separated from the Austrian army to march on Paris down the Marne by the main Châlons road, driving in front of them Marshal Macdonald's Corps. Napoleon determined to launch a surprise attack into their flank. By 9 February he had most of his army at Sézanne, and that evening the patrols ran into enemy troopers on the banks of the Petit-Morin between Sézanne and Champaubert. On the 10th at Champaubert Napoleon inflicted the first of a bewildering series of reverses on Blücher, around whom he danced his army for five extraordinary days. The Army of Silesia was compelled to divide as it fell back, part towards Montmirail and part towards Etoges and Châlons.

Following York's Prussian and Sacken's Russian Corps, the French vanguard left Montmirail on the morning of the 11th; and that day Napoleon called up the cavalry of the Guard from a few leagues away to support a magnificent attack. (Lieutenant van Omphal, who was returning from patrol as the battle began, did not have a squadron appointment; without delay he led his detachment to support the Regiment's skirmishers.)

During this battle of Montmirail the Regiment was ordered to cover a twenty-gun battery of the Guard Artillery by taking position behind it. This was a focal point of the enemy's counter-battery fire, and the Red Lancers suffered severe losses from cannon fire passing over the gun line; they eventually moved to a position in front of the battery.

Thereafter the Regiment was detached by General Colbert to go to the support of the infantry of General Ricard's division which was defending the village of Pommessone against Sacken's Russians. Here de Tiecken led a charge which captured 600 or 700 prisoners. At the end of this glorious but bloody day the Red Lancers made bivouac at Epine-aux-Bois. They numbered 350 men, and received another 150 reinforcements. Among others, Vélite Louis Woot de Trixhe was appointed to the Legion of Honour for his admirable behaviour on this memorable day.

During the night of 11 February the enemy retreated towards Château-Thierry; although not closely pursued by the exhausted French they lost many vehicles along the muddy roads. The next day at 9a.m., after one brief encounter with the enemy, the Regiment pressed on down the road to Château-Thierry. For two

days their pursuit was stalled only 30 minutes' ride from the city, waiting for the repair of a bridge destroyed by the retreating Prussians. With the bridge finally serviceable the Red Lancers crossed the Marne at 3p.m. on 13 February.

They were now under the orders of Marshal Mortier, who was charged on the 13th with command of the 2nd Old Guard Division (the cavalry of Generals Colbert and Defrance, plus a sapper company and an engineer officer). Mortier followed the Corps of General York as far as Rocourt St Martin; the Emperor's instructions were explicit: *"With the cavalry division of General Colbert, the Duke of Treviso will start the pursuit of the enemy on the road to Soissons."* Napoleon intended to occupy himself with Blücher, whom he had left between Champaubert and Châlons. Between 10 and 14 February he had cost the enemy some 9,000 casualties for French losses of around 2,000 men.

On 15 February Colbert's 1st Guard Cavalry Division was at Oulchy-le-Château in the following strength:
Polish Lancers of the Line: Six officers, 149 troopers
2nd Scouts of the Guard: 12 officers, 241 troopers
2nd Light Horse Lancers: 15 officers, 247 troopers
Mounted Chasseurs & Mamelukes: 25 officers, 297 troopers
Total: 58 officers, 934 troopers.

The Red Lancers had lost 139 men and 174 horses either killed or wounded.

In the absence of the Emperor Marshal Mortier continued to pursue the Prussians to his front. On the 16th Colbert fought engagements with the enemy rearguard at Longpré and Chaudun. The Russian force commanded by General Winzingerode, hearing of Napoleon's latest defeat of Blücher at Vauchamps, evacuated Soissons on the 14th to withdraw to Rheims. For the time being Marshal Mortier sent Chef de batallion Cicéron with his 300 men and 150 of General Colbert's troopers to Soissons.

With the Prussian threat temporarily averted the Emperor quickly turned south towards Schwarzenberg's Austrians, defeating them (and with disproportionate loss, although he was outnumbered two to one) at Montereau on 18 February. He left most of the Red Lancers near Soissons at Villers-Cotterêts in the Forest of Retz. Blücher, informed that Napoleon was marching towards the Austrians, gathered his army to resume his march on Paris, forcing the Red Lancers to leave their bivouac. Among those members of the Regiment who went with the Emperor, 2nd Lieutenant Jean Charassin was wounded by a lance thrust in his right side at the battle of Montereau.

★ ★ ★

Meanwhile, far to the north, General Maison was doing his utmost to hold the Allied troops in check on the outskirts of Antwerp. On 1 February they launched an attack on the village of Deurne. After six hours' fighting, during which he had been repulsed three times, the Prussian General Thumen marched his men onto the Schijn bridge. General Aymard, obeying the orders of General Lebrun, the military governor of Antwerp, abandoned the blazing streets of Deurne and took up position in front of Borgerhout. The retreating French battalions were under attack by enemy skirmishers until Chef d'escadron de Briqueville made a well-timed charge at the head of a hundred Red Lancers which saved the situation. Deurne remained in French hands; and a grateful General Roguet recommended the young squadron leader for the officer's cross of the Legion of Honour. On 5 February Sub-lieutenant Louis Paillard of the Red Lancers was wounded near Antwerp.

A few days after this action General Lebrun was replaced as military governor of Antwerp by the legendary old Revolutionary minister Lazare Carnot, "the organiser of victory" in 1793-95. On 18 February news of the victories at Champaubert and Montmirail - perhaps a little exaggerated in the wording of the official reports - reached Antwerp from Lille; they were celebrated by a *Te Deum* at the cathedral followed by a banquet. The new governor was greeted with enthusiastic cheers when he visited the theatre, and the city was illuminated. In the morning Chef d'escadron de Briqueville was sent to parley with the commanders of the Allied besiegers. He told them that there was no need to worry if they heard gunfire during the meeting - this would only be the French artillery firing salutes to celebrate the Emperor's triumph over the Allies.

General Maison, with 6,000 men under command, hastened from one point to the next as he probed and harassed the enemy.

On 25 February 2nd Lieutenant François Cenas of the Red Lancers was killed during one of the reconnaissance patrols towards Antwerp. Late in the month Governor Carnot was informed that an Allied convoy was passing within reach of the city. On 27 February General Roguet sortied through the Red Gate of Antwerp at the head of the Red Lancers and several Guard battalions. He met the Allied force at Mortsel, and returned with prisoners as well as a Saxon army paychest.

General Maison, who was looking for a way to join up with Roguet's division, took the opportunity offered by an unsuccessful attack at Maubeuge to pass through the enemy lines towards Antwerp. Concentrating the 6,000 infantry of Generals Barrois and Solignac and General Castex's 1,600 horse, Maison left Lille. He overran the detachments occupying Kortrijk (Courtrai) on 5 March and made a feint of pursuing them towards Oudenaarde, only to turn off towards Ghent to meet Roguet, who had been kept informed of his intensions. General Penne, who was commanded to head for Ghent and to take it by surprise at daybreak, failed to do so, however; the city was heavily fortified, and after a brief bombardment General Maison returned to Kortrijk on 6 March, having lost only a dozen men during this audacious operation.

On 20 March the Red Lancers of the Young Guard squadrons under the orders of General Maison numbered:
Present under arms: 23 officers with 66 horses, 256 troopers with 256 horses.
Absent: 21 officers with 39 horses, 615 troopers with 426 horses.

Maison succeeded in taking Ghent on 26 March; there he was informed that Russian cavalry scouts were approaching Lokeren. He detached Colonel Vilatte with 50 Red Lancers and a company of light infantry with orders to reach Antwerp and carry despatches to General Carnot. By these he requested that the governor send him Roguet's division, some artillery, and all the Lancers and Chasseurs of the Guard - General Carnot should keep just one officer and 25 troopers of each arm. These reinforcements should be at Ghent or Dendermonde on 28 March.

On the 27th General Roguet's division of the Imperial Guard was assembled at Beveren; General Lebrun attached himself to the force, taking this opportunity to leave Antwerp. The division headed for Dendermonde and crossed the Scheldt pretending to march for Brussels; by this means they successfully joined up with General Maison at Ghent, bringing him a reinforcement of 4,000 soldiers, 250 horses and 14 guns. On 30 March the combined force left Ghent for Kortrijk.

At six o'clock that morning General Maison's Corps came under attack from a Saxon force, but the enemy were overrun and routed by General Roguet's division. General Count de Lalaing d'Audenarde, major of the Red Lancers, led the Mounted Chasseurs of the Guard into the flank of the Saxon Cuirassiers with bloody effect. Fighting continued until 2p.m., when the Saxons fled in all directions.

Back in Lille, General Maison was preparing to return to Belgium when he was informed of the latest events at government level.

★ ★ ★

Back on the rolling plains of Champagne the Regiment were still in the field with their Emperor. Having beaten Schwarzenberg at Montereau Napoleon now left Marshal Macdonald to watch them on the Aube while he dashed north again to foil Blücher's continued march on Paris - the Prussians were now within 25 miles of the capital. Macdonald would be beaten by Schwarzenberg at Bar-sur-Aube on 27 February and forced back

towards Paris in his turn. On 28 February Marshals Marmont and Mortier checked the advancing Army of Silesia at Gué-à-Tresmes. Chef d'escadron de Tiecken, commanding the Regiment, distinguished himself by throwing back enemy cavalry towards Etrépilly. (Two days earlier the Red Lancers' 2nd Lieutenant Doyen had lost his brother, Sergeant Lambert Doyen, appointed to that rank on 29 May 1813.)

On 29 February the Guard was reinforced with eight squadrons of fresh troops brought up by Baron Boulnois, commander of the Provisional Cavalry of the Guard. Among these replacements were 106 Red Lancers - mediocre material, badly dressed, but at least well mounted. The Regiment helped to throw back Prussian forces which - alarmed by the unexpected presence of Napoleon himself, and wrongly informed about the strength of the Corps of Marmont and Mortier - withdrew across the Marne in the direction of Soissons.

On the night of 2 March Napoleon's troops crossed the Marne, whose bridges had been destroyed by the retreating enemy. The Prussians faced two obstacles, the Aisne and Soissons; when General Moreau surrendered the latter he opened the way for them. The opportunity of trapping and defeating Blücher once again was lost, and the old marshal could now link up with the Corps of Generals Bülow, Winzingerode and Woronzow. The long, forced marches to catch up with the enemy had proved vain, but the Emperor could not abandon Paris.

Having crossed the Aisne, regrouped, and received 114,000 reinforcements, the enemy would certainly not refuse to fight the Emperor's 40,000 men. Before dawn on 5 March General Corbineau retook Rheims; and with his right flank now covered Napoleon crossed the Aisne at Berry-au-Bac. Nansouty's Guard cavalry took the bridges and dispersed the enemy covering them. The rest of the army followed and headed for Laon the next day. To give Blücher the time to rally around Laon the Corps of Winzingerode, Sacken and Woronzow occupied the heights of Craonne, which offered good protection against any frontal attack. At four on the morning of the 7th Napoleon wrote to his chief-of-staff Berthier:

"Order General Colbert and General Roussel to set off at daybreak and to come and take position behind Corbeny."

Fighting broke out at dawn and lasted most of the day. The Red Lancers' charge into the Russians' right flank from the Craonnelle road was decisive. For the third time Chef d'escadron de Tiecken had his horse killed under him. The Russians were slowly forced to give ground; at Ange-Gardien they stood for a few hours to give the Prussians time to evacuate Soissons and join them. The Regiment lost one officer - Lieutenant Johan Christiaan Spies, one of three confusingly-named brothers - and 50 lancers. Two sub-lieutenants were wounded: François de Groot lost his right eye to a bullet, and Jean Marie Duplan took three sabre cuts to the head, two lance thrusts in the back, and a bad bruise on his right thigh from a cannonball.

In pursuit of the Russians driven back from Etourelles the French army, with the Red Lancers in the van, reached the heights of Laon. During 9 March, for the fourth time, de Tiecken had a horse killed under him. By the evening the entire army was in the outskirts of Laon; but the Allies, fleeing before the Emperor for ten days, had simply become stronger for the concentration of the Corps of Bülow, Langeron, Sacken, Winzingerode, Kleist and York. Their position on the heights dominated the surrounding country, defying assault, and they outnumbered the French by three to one. Nevertheless, Napoleon attacked them.

It cost his army dearly - about 6,000 of 30,000 men, against some 3,000 of 100,000 Allies. The Emperor hoped for reinforcement by Marshal Marmont's Corps from Athies, but a surprise attack on the night of 9 March prevented Marmont coming up in support. Informed of this, Napoleon had to

Lancer of the Guard. (Collection of Belgian Royal Army Museum, Brussels)

Lieutenant Antonie F.J.F.J. van Omphal (1788-1863) - a miniature depicting him in the uniform of a general in the Netherlands army. (Photo c Stichting Iconographisch Bureau, The Hague)

abandon the idea of renewing his assault at Laon the next morning. On the 10th the Allies took the initiative, and Napoleon withdrew towards Soissons. Laon had been another bloody day for the Red Lancers. Sent out by General Colbert to charge an enemy square protected by a wide ditch, without scouting the ground first, the Regiment failed at heavy cost. General Colbert, not authorised to make such a charge, was severely reprimanded and threatened with dismissal from his command by the Emperor.

On 11 March Napoleon wrote to Berthier: *"... St Médard will be occupied by General Colbert's cavalry .... Only General Colbert is to stay at St Paul, occupy St Médard and push detachments on toward Bucy-le-Long."* That afternoon, safe at Soissons, he reorganised some commands within his army; Nansouty, who was ill, was to be replaced by General Sébastiani. The Regiment was with General Colbert at St Paul.

At five on the morning of 12 March Napoleon wrote to Berthier: *"Give the order to General Colbert to cross the bridge over the Aisne with all his artillery, cavalry and infantry today at seven in the morning. He is to cross the stone bridge and take position in the suburb of Rheims, informing us of his arrival there."* All the reserve parks received the same order, so as to reduce the overcrowding on the right bank of the river.

At six on the evening of the 12th the Emperor further ordered Berthier: *"Colbert's and Letort's divisions under the command of General Sébastiani will set off at once for Braisne with two batteries of horse artillery."*

During the night of 12-13 March it was reported that the Russian General St Priest had retaken Rheims for the Allies, thus restoring the lines of communication between the armies of

Schwarzenberg and Blücher. Napoleon at once marched on the city, boldly crossing the front of the Army of Silesia, and arrived at the gates of Rheims on the evening of the 13th. Fighting during that night, De Tiecken of the Red Lancers had his shoulder bruised by a bullet and 2nd Lieutenant Eugène Barras was either killed or captured while breaking through three enemy battalions defending one of the suburbs. At one in the morning Napoleon entered Rheims, whose recapture cost him about 700 casualties against 6,000 for the Allies. He stayed in the city until the 16th. For some this was a badly needed rest, but not for the Red Lancers; having just arrived at Neuvillette the Regiment were sent to Epernay on 14 March.

On 15 March Napoleon reorganised his Guard cavalry: *"The three cavalry divisions of the Guard will be organised as follows: 1st Division, General Colbert - the Poles of Pac, 600 men; the 2nd Lancers, 180 men; six guns of the Polish Light Artillery - total, 780 men. This division will be increased by 200 men of the 2nd Lancers and by 1,200 of Pac's Poles who are on their way...."*

On that date the Regiment at Epernay recorded totals of 28 officers, and 364 lancers and 307 horses; 16 officers, 822 lancers and 250 horses were not yet ready to join the Regiment in the field. (Between 9 and 20 March the Regiment would record the loss of 50 men.)

Stationed at Ay and short of every necessity, the Lancers had to cross to the far side of the Marne in order to find something to eat. Luckily the other bank was not occupied in strength, but encounters with the occasional Cossack patrol compelled the troopers to fight even for a few bottles of wine. Their stay there did not last for long. On 17 March Napoleon wrote to Berthier:

"Give the order to General Sébastiani to send General Colbert's division to Vertus tonight. Tomorrow at seven in the morning General Colbert is to leave Vertus for Fère-Champenoise and Semoine, to gather news from Sézanne and Arcis. For that purpose he must send intelligent peasants. Inform him that my headquarters will be at Semoine tomorrow."

On 20 March the Regiment were with their Emperor, facing Schwarzenberg's Army of Bohemia at Arcis-sur-Aube. This would be the last opportunity to divert the Austrians and Russians from their westwards march on Paris.

During the course of the fighting General Colbert, whose division was placed on the left wing, sent an adjutant to the Emperor to inform him that Colbert was faced by much stronger forces which he could not contain without artillery support.

Napoleon, ill-informed about the opposition which Colbert actually faced, angrily dismissed both the adjutant and his message. The division's situation became more and more dangerous; again Colbert sent word to the Emperor, this time by Lieutenant van Omphal. Anxious to avoid a rebuff, Antonie van Omphal reported first to Marshal Berthier, but the chief-of-staff immediately sent the Dutch officer to the Emperor. This time Napoleon, better informed about the situation, gave permission for van Omphal to take an artillery battery back with him.

A little later the division was relieved and joined the other cavalry regiments of the Guard in a series of charges which would last until nightfall. Outnumbered, they achieved little; the Lancers were often obliged to charge right through the enemy lines and circle round behind in order to avoid being trapped, rather than exploiting the impact of their attacks to best advantage. When darkness fell on the battlefield friend and foe could only be distinguished by their voices, and the Regiment encamped where they stood amid the corpses and the trash of battle.

At 2p.m. the next day the battle was raging again. Fighting at odds of one against three, Napoleon could not commit his troops without taking huge risks. On the evening of 21 March, under cover of darkness and protected by the Regiment, the French army began to withdraw. In the Emperor's camp it began to be acknowledged that it was no longer possible to stop the Allied advance before Paris. It was a curious war, General Colbert would later recall. During the retreat from Russia he had ordered his

General of Division Charles J. Count de Pully (1751-1832), painted early in 1814 by Dubois-Drahonet. The colonel of the 1st Regiment of Guards of Honour, he was a friend and billiards partner of Colonel-Major Dubois, who introduced him to the painter when the latter was serving as a vélite in the Red Lancers.

troopers to rescue stragglers exhausted by long marches, starvation and cold; here in France they were gathering up those same soldiers, but this time dead drunk.

Passing by Vitry-le-François, they reached St Dizier on 23 March; the next evening the Imperial headquarters were established at Doulevant-le-Château. The flanks of the army spread from Bar-sur-Aube towards St Dizier. Misled by the appearance of a Russian Corps marching on Vitry-le-François in the neighbourhood of St Dizier, Napoleon changed his plan to march on to Paris and turned back to St Dizier. Meanwhile, to the west, Schwarzenberg would drive back the last French troops between his army and Paris - the Corps of Marmont and Mortier - at La Fère Champenoise on 25 March.

At St Dizier on 26 March 1814 the Red Lancers fought with great distinction in their last battle of the campaign. Making one of their most splendid charges, they overran an 18-gun Russian battery and captured six guns, some 20 powder caissons, 400 horses and as many Russian Dragoons at the cost of only the lightest casualties (Lieutenant Buis was the only officer to be wounded that day). General Sébastiani reported to Napoleon that in twenty years' cavalry soldiering he had never seen a more brilliant charge. The defeated Russians fled from the battlefield over the bridges of Vitry and Bar-sur-Ornain.

Napoleon turned once more to his maps. Far out of reach of pursuit, Blücher's and Schwarzenberg's armies would link up before Paris on 28 March; Marmont and Mortier still stood in their path with about 22,000 men. Paris must not fall into enemy hands; whatever the maps told him, the Emperor would hasten back to his capital. But in his absence, panic was gripping his court.

The Abdication

At the Versailles depot of the Red Lancers all was quiet; Colonel-Major Dubois played billiards every day with General de Pully of the Guards of Honour. This peaceful routine was shattered on 29 March. That morning the carriages of the Empress' household were seen passing by, carrying Marie Louise herself, the little King of Rome, the Queen of Westphalia and Madame Mère in the direction of Chambord. Alarmed, Colonel-Major Dubois passed the word for all ranks to be ready to get mounted; he feared that the road from Paris to Versailles might be cut by the enemy during the night.

On the 30th Napoleon still had 35 leagues to cover, but the enemy had already reached the suburbs of Paris. At the Versailles depot they heard heavy gunfire from the direction of the capital. Marmont and Mortier, outnumbered five to one, were being driven back to Montmartre. Dubois sent out patrols. King Joseph Bonaparte and several ministers, as well as some marshals' wives, were met on the road from Paris; everyone who could was leaving in a panicky exodus before the dreaded Cossacks arrived. Versailles being in danger, orders were given to evacuate to Châteaudun, Tours and Angers.

It was now that some Dutch officers and lancers of the Regiment took the opportunity to leave, hoping to be admitted to the new Army of the Netherlands.

In Paris events were moving at precipitate speed. Convinced of the hopelessness of the situation, at 2a.m. on 31 March Marshal Marmont signed an instrument of armistice. Later that day Allied troops marched into Paris.

★ ★ ★

Informed of these developments, Napoleon arrived at Fontainebleau that same day. He installed his headquarters there and worked feverishly to save something from the ruin of his power. At one stage he planned to fight a last battle under the city walls of Paris.

News of the ceasefire spread quickly through the army; and many of the Red Lancers began to drift away, as had their

General Anne-Charles Lebrun (1775-1859), Count, later Duke of Plaisance; this former ADC to the Emperor was governor of Antwerp in 1814. He was the patron of Armand de Briqueville, who reported meeting him again with the delighted phrase, "Je suis en famille, j'ai retrouvé mon général..." (Author's collection)

comrades already on their way to Angers. Among the officers who departed were de Jongh, Hanneman, le Sueur, Royen, van Balveren, van der Linden and Veldhuys. Another was Nicolas van Geyn, twin brother of Herman van Geyn who had died in the hospital at Versailles on 5 May 1813. (The brothers, voluntarily enlisted in the Dutch Royal Guard, had passed into the Red Lancers at the same time, Nicolas to the 4th Company and Herman to the 1st Company.)

It was not only foreign-born company officers who were leaving the service of the Emperor. During the night of 4 April, under the eyes of the Red Lancers stationed at Ponthiers, Marshal Marmont - who had received Royalist envoys to discuss his future - defected with his entire Corps at Essonnes. Deserted by his politicians, his generals and his marshals, the Emperor Napoleon signed an act of abdication on 6 April in favour of his little son. The Allies refused to accept this; and on 11 April he abdicated unconditionally.

Until the very last days of the Empire the Regiment, now encamped before Melun, was still receiving reinforcements: an officer and 102 lancers of the Line, with 87 spare horses.

Before the collapse of the Empire, General Colbert asked for twelve nominations to the Legion of Honour and seven to the Order of the Reunion for his officers and warrant officers. Proposed for the Legion of Honour were Chef d'escadron Pitel, Captains Laserre, Lori, Chappe and Bertholet, and Lieutenants Viravaud, Lesage, Bourdeau, d'Ham, Bouchardon, Laborde and Lethuiller. For the Order of the Reunion he put forward Chef d'escadron Bosc, Captain de Stuers, Lieutenants van Omphal, de Bellefroid and Ubaghs, and Assistant Surgeons Stutterheim and Barth. All these nominations were granted; they received the insignia of their orders with official citations dated on 3 April 1814.

The First Empire was no more; France turned back to the Bourbons.

(Above) Red Lancers on parade, by Hoynck van Papendrecht (1858-1933). At the left is one of the company's three trumpeters uniformed in highy visible white faced with scarlet; since tactical commands in battle were passed by trumpet calls it was vital for an officer to be able to pick out his trumpeter easily at all times. The troopers in the front rank carry slung lances, those in the second rank carbines, in the manner prescribed from spring 1813. (Collection of Belgian Royal Army Museum, Brussels)

(Left) General of Division Edouard Colbert (1774-1853), depicted in front of Moscow in flames by Alexandre Jean Dubois-"Dubois-Drahonet" (1791-1834). At the head of the 7th Hussars he took part in the campaigns of 1805 and 1806; after the battles of Bergfried, Eylau, Friedland, Guttstadt and Heilsberg his men nicknamed him Eisenmann, "Iron Man". At least one of the wives of his Dutch officers of the 2nd Light Horse Lancers found him domineering and tactless. (Château d'Ainay-le-Vieil, France)

81

(Left) *Colonel-Major Charles Dubois (1772-1829). In June 1813 at Versailles the senior Dutch-born officer in the Red Lancers took the opportunity to sit for the painter Alexandre Dubois while the latter was serving with the Regiment. The portrait shows us a severe and confident man of war, his splendid uniform set off against menacing clouds. At 41 years old Charles Dubois, the son of a doctor, had achieved success; he had risen through the Batavian and Dutch armies to become second in command of a superb regiment of the Imperial Guard which, in June 1813, was being rebuilt stronger than ever after the losses suffered in Russia.*

A year later he asked the painter to add his newly-awarded decorations to the portrait, and the date on the canvas was subsequently altered to June 1814. In November 1814 he was promoted to maréchal de camp *under the restored monarchy, and returned to the studio once more; now the epaulettes, sash and embroidery had to be modified, and the Imperial insignia altered to those of the Bourbons.*

Despite the official character of the portrait it begs comparison with others of a more intimate nature. The painter includes a self-portrait in the right background. (Château d'Écaussines-Lalaing, Belgium)

(Above) *"Quartermaster of the Red Lancers" - an unsigned miniature. The resemblance to the self-portrait of Alexandre Jean Dubois in the background of the painting opposite, the rank of quartermaster and the uniform all confirm that we have here an earlier self-portrait of the soldier-artist. (Anne S.K. Brown Military Collection, Brown University Library)*

(Left) *Detail showing the self-portrait of the artist, Vélite-Sergeant Alexandre Dubois, later Dubois-Drahonet - see also page 121 for a detail of the identifying "IPSE F." inscription. An interesting item of this uniform is the aiguillette, which seems to be in mixed gold, blue and red for this rank.*

(Above) *Major Jan H.C. van Hasselt (1776-1812). Heartbroken by the news of his wife's death while he was serving with the Red Lancers in Moscow, he would command the dismounted debris of the Regiment during the retreat, only to die of exhaustion at Elbing in December 1812. (Private collection, South Africa)*

(Right) *Chef d'escadron Jan Post (1778-1841). At the crossing of the Beresina in November 1812 he saved one of his troopers by pulling him out of the water by his hair. Wounded at Leipzig in October 1813, he tried to lead the remnant of his squadron - trapped by the destruction of the only bridge - across the Elster to safety; only one sergeant and one trooper reached the far bank with him. (Portrait by Louis Moritz, 1773-1850; private collection, Holland)*

Lancer of the Imperial Guard. Uniform details are at odds with several other sources - black leather equipment; Hussar-style barrel sash; red-tipped plume; reversed pennon colours; blue portmanteau instead of red, topped with a second, rectangular-section dragoon type, etc.). Together with the artist's difficulty in capturing the square-crowned czapka convincingly, these suggest that this was not painted from life. (Watercolour by Jan A.Langendijk, 1780-1818; The Royal Collection © Her Majesty The Queen)

Officer of the Lancers of the Guard. For full dress parades officers did wear sashes, but not this Hussar barrel style; the Red Lancers wore one in gold silk net with blue stripes, terminating in blue and gold interwoven tassels. The epaulette and aiguillette are reversed here. Officers frequently wore buttoned covers over their expensively laced pouch belts when on campaign (Watercolour by Jan A.Langendijk, 1780-1818; The Royal Collection © Her Majesty The Queen)

(Above) *General Colbert at Gorki, Russia, September 1812. Leading his Guard Lancer brigade on detached duty and left without orders while surrounded by enemy forces, he took the decision to march to Moscow when peasants told him that the capital was burning. (Alphonse Lalauze, 1872-?; Château d'Ainay-le-Vieil, France)*

(Right) *Chef d'escadron Jean J.A.Schneither (1779-1849), painted in January 1814 by Alexandre J.Dubois. He was promoted to this rank in the Young Guard squadrons in March 1813, and was admitted to the Legion of Honour the following month; in June 1814 he was assigned to the 3rd Line Lancers. (Collection of Dutch Military Academy, Breda)*

(Above left) *Chef d'escadron Armand de Briqueville (1785-1844), painted in his uniform of an ADC to General Lebrun before assignment to the Red Lancers. At Moscow and during the retreat he attempted to care for his friend Albert de Watteville, and was with him when he died on 7 December 1812. De Briqueville's own service with the Red Lancers from July 1813, and as colonel of the 20th Dragoons in 1815, gives the lie to the strikingly sentimental tone of his correspondence. (Private collection, Switzerland)*

(Above) *Captain Fortuné P. Brack (1789-1850) - a miniature of 1815 by Nicolas Jacques (1780-1844). Although he did not join the Red Lancers until August 1813 he was a long-serving ADC to General Colbert, and so served with the Guard Lancer brigade in Russia. He left a vivid description of the Regiment's experience at Waterloo, extensively quoted in Chapter VII.*

(Left) *A Polish undress cap or confederatka worn by Chef d'escadron de Watteville, clearly copied from those of the officers of the 1st Light Horse Lancers for its comfort and handsome appearance - de Watteville was something of a dandy. (Photo © Musée d'Histoire de Berne, Switzerland)*

(Right) *Chef d'escadron Albert de Watteville (1787-1812); this officer's letters are an invaluable source of eye-witness impressions of the Red Lancers' travels before their arrival in Moscow. The portrait was commissioned by his close friend the Princesse de Gavre from François van Dorne (1776-1848) before the Regiment left Versailles in spring 1812; the second copy, retained by the princess, is now in a private collection in Paris. (Private collection, Switzerland)*

(Above) *An impression by Pierre Benigni of a trooper of the 2nd Light Horse Lancers of the Guard pursued by Cossacks during the advance on Moscow in autumn 1812. He wears full marching order: covered czapska, the red-collared light blue stable jacket which Napoleon remarked upon when the Regiment was in Moscow, rolled cloak, and dark blue riding overalls piped and striped red, with brass buttons up the outer leg opening. Note the mass of weaponry which the trooper has to manage: the lance, a carbine slung from his right side, a sabre on the left, and a bayonet worn with it from the Dragoon-style waist belt. A pair of saddle* pistols *were also supposed to be issued, but troopers were lucky to receive one. (Photo Musée de l'Empéri, Salon-de-Provence)*

(Right) *"Red Lancer at the crossing of the Beresina, 1812" - a striking impression by Jules Rigo (1810-1892). The decorated keg seems to identify the woman whom he is trying to save, together with her infant, as a cantinière, one of the huge train of semi-official camp followers who accompanied Napoleonic armies. (Private collection)*

(Above left) *Trumpeter of the Red Lancers in full dress. (J.B.Edouard Détaille, 1848-1912; collection of Belgian Royal Army Museum, Brussels)*

(Left) *Czapska of the five Young Guard squadrons of the Red Lancers. (Collection of Belgian Royal Army Museum, Brussels)*

(Above) *Both sides of the trumpet banner found by the body of Trumpet-Major Kauffman on the field of Reichenbach, May 1813. The ground was originally dark blue; note, incidentally, the lance pennons in white over red correctly shown in the lower corner motifs. (Author's photographs)*

(Opposite above) *General Colbert presents himself to Napoleon at the Tuileries, 24 March 1815; the few words he addressed to the Emperor would be enough to send him into exile after the Second Restoration. (Alphonse Lalauze; Château d'Ainay-le-Vieil, France)*

(Opposite below) *General Colbert at the head of the Red Lancers at Waterloo, 18 June 1815. (Alphonse Lalauze; Château d'Ainay-le-Vieil, France)*

(Overleaf) *The Red Lancers at Waterloo. (Alphonse Lalauze; photo Peter Newark's Military Pictures)*

CHAPTER VI

1814: The First Restoration

With the peace treaty signed, and the former Emperor preparing to leave for exile on the Mediterranean island of Elba with an army reduced to a token battalion and squadron of the Old Guard, the Regiment stayed for another few days in the neighbourhood of Melun before heading for Angers where the depot was now located.

In Belgium, General Maison too had just signed an armistice with the Allies, bringing to an end hostilities between the regular troops of each side - although the Cossacks continued to harass the French, as did some of the local civilians. In his memoirs Captain Brack of the Red Lancers remembered:

"At the end of the 1814 campaign the Cossacks - helped by the inhabitants, and although the armistice had been signed by General Maison - were still carrying out attacks against us. The general sent a hundred Lancers of the Guard with orders to put an end to this state of affairs, and to operate between Lille, Veurne, Nieuwpoort and Dunkirk. The detachment set off with covered czapskas and shabraques hooked up [the badged rear corners of the horse cloth could be hooked up to protect them from mud, showing the plain underside]. The rebels, seeing no eagles and misled by the red uniforms, welcomed them with shouts of 'Down with the French! Long live the English! Long live the Saxons!'

"The commanding officer, appreciating the delicacy of this situation, remained unflustered. He kept his new friends at a distance, and used as intermediaries lancers of Alsatian background who were told to say that they were in the service of England. In this way he obtained information which he turned to his advantage during his march and future operations."

The return of the monarchy meant the removal of the tricolour cockade worn on the headgear by all French soldiers since the Revolution. At Lille the order to replace it with the white cockade of the Bourbons was not universally appreciated; on the evening of 14 April some lancers of the Young Guard had to be confined to quarters when they refused.

Chef d'escadron Armand de Briqueville, who had accompanied "his General" Lebrun from Antwerp to Lille, was undisturbed by all this; next day he wrote to his mother in his usual osculatory frenzy:

"This is one letter which you will definitely receive, though it is the eighth that I have sent. I kiss you, dear Mama, I embrace you, dear Adrien - I would like to have some news from you, it is the only thing that interests me.... Generals Castex and Meuziau are in very good health. I have had the honour of meeting the latter the day before yesterday; he was going back to Douay, and we embraced as men who were destined to meet. All is quiet at the moment."

With rather less enthusiasm he wrote from Poperinge in Flanders on 23 April: *"So peace has been made in Paris, and [yet] here we are surrounded by enemies, with the Allies breaking and pillaging everything!"*

On 24 April - the day King Louis XVIII embarked at Dover to cross to Calais - the Regiment numbered 32 officers, 374 lancers and 424 horses under arms at Melun; one week later the figures were 32 officers, 352 lancers and 418 horses.

At Nemours, while on their way to Angers, the Regiment received orders to send all mounted men to Paris in order to escort the king from St Denis to Paris for his entry into the capital. On 3 May 1814, the day of the entry, the units of the Old Guard were assembled on the Place du Carrousel to march together towards St Denis where they were to await the king. Grudgingly obeying the order to wear white ribbons in their buttonholes, the Red Lancers met up with a detachment of the Regiment's Young Guard squadrons who had served under General Maison, and who had escorted the king from Calais. After the ceremonies street fights broke out between the Guard and Russian and Prussian troops; they stayed only a short time in Paris before being sent south to the Loire.

During this march the Regiment made an overnight halt about one league from Orleans. Corporal Christiaensen, a sergeant and six troopers were billeted in a house of which the ground floor was already occupied by infantrymen. During the night the Lancers were woken by fire and smoke coming from below; there was no escape by the staircase, and they began to leap from the window. The sergeant and two lancers perished in the flames - a miserably pointless way to die after surviving the dangers of battle.

Marching via Tours and Saumur the Regiment reached Angers, where it was paraded several times before the Duc de Berry.

The time had come to gather together the scattered detachments. On 12 May the Minister of War, Dupont, sent orders to General Maison at Lille:

"There is a detachment of about 200 mounted men of the 2nd Light Horse of the Guard in the 1st Army Corps. There is also a detachment of about 50 men with 113 horses at this regiment's depot at Douay. The intention of the king is to unite this regiment at Angers. Please order the detachment in the neighbourhood of Lille to go and join the one at Douay, and have them leave Douay together on 16 May to head for Angers, according to the attached marching order. Pray communicate the itinerary that this detachment will be following to your commissary so that he may take steps to ensure supplies and quarters along the road they will take. Inform me of its departure from Douay."

Dupont informed General Colbert of these orders on the same day, adding that the combined detachments should arrive at Angers on 5 June.

The Royal Corps of Light Horse Lancers of France

The returned Bourbon regime was ambivalent towards the former Emperor's army, and particularly towards his Imperial Guard. On the one hand, King Louis' government of vengeful returned emigrés and opportunist former Bonapartists were supported by the Allied forces, and many of them deeply distrusted the new officer class created by Napoleon. On the other hand, they could not afford to antagonise his scores of thousands of proud veterans too openly, or to behave like occupying conquerors. The Guard was to some extent purged; but it was neither wholly trusted nor disbanded.

On 12 May 1814 the Guard's titles were changed. The Red Lancers were rechristened as the "Royal Corps of Light Horse Lancers of France", with an establishment as follows:

Staff: One colonel (lieutenant-general), one major, two chefs d'escadron, two captains adjutant-major, one captain quartermaster, one standard bearer (2nd lieutenant), one surgeon-major, one sub-assistant surgeon-major, two adjutant NCOs, one veterinary 1st class, one veterinary 2nd class, one corporal trumpeter, four craftsmen.

Squadrons: Four squadrons each of two companies, totalling 42 officers and 601 NCOs and troopers.

The foreign-born officers and soldiers who were still serving in the Regiment were finally given royal permission to leave if they so wished. Some Frenchmen, too, chose to resign at this time; officers and men, foreign and French, took their leave of their comrades with mixed feelings and turned towards their homes. On 21 June 2nd Lieutenants Moretti and Mareilhac departed; on 15 July, 2nd Lieutenants Bazin and Bidault-Cornesse; and on 30 July, Bauman, Stutterheim, de Bellefroid, Spies J.W.C., van Omphal, de Groot, Leutner, Ziegler P.A., Gisser, Breitenbach and Eschweiler. Surgeon Steenis of the Young Guard squadrons, who had left for Holland on 11 May 1814 with the authorisation of General Maison, had already made his choice not to rejoin the Regiment.

Most of the Dutch officers chose to seek places in the army of the new Kingdom of the Netherlands, hoping that their experience and status as former officers of the Imperial Guard would earn them senior rank. General Colbert gave the departing Chef d'escadron Jan Post a letter of recommendation dated in Paris on 9 July 1814:

"I, the undersigned Lieutenant-General [and] Colonel commanding the Light Horse Lancers of France certify that Monsieur Post, Lieutenant-Colonel, has served with honour and distinction since his admission to the French Imperial Guard, that he has conducted himself remarkably during the campaigns of 1812 and 1813, and that he has earned the respect of all who know him."

It was not always easy for these former officers; sometimes questions of nationality caused problems, as in the cases of de Stuers and de Tiecken. Both applied for posts in the new army of the Netherlands; but one had been born at Roermond and the other at Tongeren. Roermond had been in Austrian territory, then annexed to France, and at this moment it was occupied by the Prussians; Tongeren, too, was in a disputed area over which the Allies had as yet made no decision. The matter would remain unresolved until Napoleon's return put it temporarily in abeyance; in the meantime, with Europe at peace for the first time in nearly twenty years, our two Lancer officers seemed to have no reason to worry about any agonising career choices.

On 2 July 1814 Marshal Ney was charged with organising the cavalry of the Royal Corps of France. At Angers on 2 August he presented a detailed report by the Inspector-General on the Royal Lancers of France. In the table which follows the abbreviations stand for present *(P'nt)*, full establishment *(Est)*, shortfall *(Short)* and surplus to establishment *(Spls)*:

Ranks	Officers				Total horses	
	P'nt	Est	Short	Spls	P'nt	Est
Colonel	1	1	-	-		
Major	2	1	-	1		
Chef d'escadron	3	3	-	-		
Quartermaster	2	2	-	-		
Standard bearer	1	1	-	-		
Surgeon	2	2	-	-		
Captains	6	10	4	-		
Lieutenants	2	10	8	-		
2nd Lieutenants	10	20	10	-		
Totals	29	50	22	1	48	82
Adjutant NCOs	2	2	-	-		
Veterinary Sgts	3	2	-	1		
Cpl trumpeter	1	1	-	-		
Craftsmen	4	4	-	-		
Sgt majors	7	8	1	-		
Sergeants	42	32	-	10		
Quartermasters	13	8	-	5		
Corporals	92	64	-	28		
Troopers	302	464	162	-		
Trumpeters	16	16	-	-		
Enfants de troupe	-	16	16	-		
Totals	482	617	179	44	409	597

Captain Jacques P.A. de Chastenet de Puységur (1790-1846), appointed to the Royal Corps of Light Horse Lancers of France in 1814, and to the Lancers of the Imperial Guard in April 1815. He chose not to follow the Emperor in the Hundred Days campaign; and is depicted in the later uniform of a lieutenant-colonel of Hussars. (Private collection, France)

The content of the following passages is quoted directly from the report, though rearranged here for clarity from partly tabular format into continuous text:

The regiment is composed of the 2nd Lancers of the Old Guard (leaving out of account the men who have left), and numbers 32 officers and 482 men. The Inspector-General has made the following count of the men who left the corps before its organisation: unfit for service, 17; proposed for retirement, one officer and one man; dismissed, none; total, one officer and 18 men.

Those now proposed for retirement must be posted as follows: six to the Royal Hôtel des Invalides; none to the Veterans; none to the Gendarmerie; total, six men. After their departure the strength will be reduced to 32 officers and 476 men.

The number of officers not included in the organisation and who have received another posting or who have been sent home is seven. These were surplus to establishment, without taking into account the supernumary officers. There are also one colonel and two majors with the Corps waiting for a decision to be taken on their postings.

The number of troop horses included in the organisation but which have been found unfit for service and therefore sold or slaughtered is 104.

Morale and training of the unit
Colonel Colbert is a general officer, skilled and distinguished in all disciplines.
Majors Dubois and Brousse: no notes have been provided on their behalf. Chefs d'escadron: De Tiecken adds experience to bravery; Coti has as much bravery as de Tiecken but less experience; de Briqueville is an excellent soldier in respect of both courage and intelligence.

Adjutant-majors: Delafargue has some knowledge of administration; de Stuers has outstanding ability; Chappe performs his duties with intelligence and precision.

Quartermasters: Dufour is a good bookkeeper; Seran, ditto.

Company officers: They are generally well spoken of, especially Messieurs de Potier, captain, and Doyen and Reckinger, second lieutenants. There is a good collective spirit.

NCOs and troopers: Their morale is as good as that of the officers.

Those vélites now serving with the unit who have considerable means desire a definitive discharge.

Theoretical training

Officers: The continuous state of war has caused this aspect to be neglected. The colonel is concentrating on its improvement in accordance with the regulations left by the inspector.

NCOs: Schools have been established according to the recommendations of the inspector in order to improve this aspect.

Practical training

Officers: Practical training needs to be improved; they are working on it.

NCOs: The regiment is working to improve this aspect. The NCOs are intelligent and capable of serving well.

Troopers: They need to be drilled from first principles, and the recommendations seek to achieve this.

Manoeuvres: Although executed well enough, they are being worked upon daily to achieve the greatest possible precision.

Riding school: The location used during bad weather to demonstrate the principles is unsuitable and unnecessarily delays the training.

Discipline: Good.

General impression of the troops: Mediocre. The effective strength of the unit is weak; the inspector recommends assigning to the regiment a certain number of returned prisoners of war.

Military establishments and supplies

Barracks: They are as badly located as they are ventilated. The prefect has promised to make them more salubrious.

Furniture: The rooms are not provided with all necessary items.

Stables: Insufficient.

Stores buildings: The inventory covers only those effects which are actually present. The main regimental stores are still at Versailles with the records and the accounts. The few manufactured items which are at Orleans are of little value.

Hospitals: The soldiers are being treated at the town hospital which is very well managed.

Cells: They are healthy, well kept and strictly guarded.

Disciplinary room: Ditto

Storekeeping: Distributions are made on a regular basis; the bread is of regulation weight and of good quality.

Fodder: Also of good quality, and the store is well provided.

Uniform, equipment, etc.

Uniforms: Shabby and irregular. Clothing needs much repair. It is moreover very incomplete and lacks all uniformity since the regiment has received soldiers from various units - the Guards of Honour, etc. - who have not been issued with full lancer uniforms.

Equipment: That of the troops also needs repairing and its amount is insufficient. The minor equipment is complete. That for the horses is, like the men's major equipment, insufficient.

Armament: The unit is short of 100 carbines, 269 pistols and 12 lances. The arms in use are in good condition.

Stores: There are no uniforms, nor materials for their manufacture, with the exception of some shakos. There is very little equipment, and the quantity of harness is also very low.

Horses: The standard of the horses is very poor; their number exceeds that of the lancers.

Finances

The accounts, records and all documents relating to the former bookkeeping of this regiment having been kept at Versailles by authorisation of HE the Minister of War, the Inspector-General cannot make any pronouncement on the finances and the bookkeeping. The funds in the regimental chest include the amount of 10,577.53 francs in gold and silver and the sum of 39,402.37 francs in credit notes. It is the responsibility of the Regimental Council to recover these debts, and they have been urged to

submit accounts as soon as possible.

Summary of the orders given by the Inspector-General:

He has ordered the establishment of:

(1) New accounts, and muster rolls of the men and horses, in accordance with the instructions of the Minister.

(2) Registers of companies and records of the NCOs and soldiers. It has also been recommended that careful attention be given to the details of administration; and that schools be established for the theoretical training of the officers as well as the NCOs, in order to achieve all necessary precision in the command and execution of manoeuvres.

Finally, orders have been given for enforcing the observance of all regulations with respect to the soldiers' health and wellbeing; for their instruction in their duties; for their submission to a strict but not a humiliating discipline; and for encouraging in them that obedience and loyalty which every Frenchman owes to the King.

The composition of the Regiment at this date must be understood. The original five squadrons, created from units of the Dutch Royal Guard, were decreed part of the Old Guard on 12 March 1813; nevertheless, in practice they never received the pay, allowances and other privileges of the Old Guard proper, and (to avoid confusion...) the unit was termed part of the "Middle Guard". These senior squadrons were composed of Dutchmen - many of whom had died or had now left the service - of vélites, and of men from the Guards of Honour incorporated in 1814. The elements around which General Colbert had now to rebuild the Regiment were the former squadrons of the Young Guard.

One early step was to try to obtain rewards for some of his officers, and on 5 May 1814 "his most humble and loyal servant, Ed.Colbert, lieutenant-general" wrote to the Duc de Berry:

"On my first presentation to Your Royal Highness of the officers of the corps that I command, I had the honour of soliciting your Highness's particular goodwill on behalf of Baron Dubois, colonel-major in my regiment; and Your Highness directed me to send him a written note. I consequently lose no time in carrying out a mission which is as pleasing to me as it is useful to Colonel-Major Dubois.

"This officer is especially to be recommended in respect of his background, his integrity and his military talents. He has completed 26 years of service in the cavalry without interruption; has participated in 15 campaigns; has been wounded twice; and was promoted captain on the field of battle. Three of his brothers have been killed in action. He has been a colonel for the last six years.

"I have nothing but the highest praise for the character, turn-out and discipline of the Hussars of the Guard of King Louis of Holland of which Monsieur Dubois was the commanding colonel, a regiment which he had

The decorations of Colonel-Major Charles Dubois: Legion of Honour, Order of the Reunion, Order of St.Louis, Order of the Lily. (Private collection, England)

Captain Hendrik Werner (1768-?), painted by Dubois-Drahonet in the uniform of the Royal Lancers of France during the First Restoration. This officer first enlisted as a twelve-year-old drummer in the Dutch Regiment van Bylandt in 1780; after service with the Hussars in Spain he was promoted captain in the Red Lancers in October 1810, and served in 1812 with the 8th Company, 4th Squadron. (Collection of Royal Dutch Army Museum, Delft)

formed [and which] passed into the Guard as a result of the union of that country with France. Everything testifies to the zeal and energy with which Colonel Dubois has served.

"Consequently, I venture to recommend him particularly to Your Royal Highness' powerful protection, for promotion to Maréchal de Camp while maintaining his status as a colonel or second-colonel in the Guard of His Majesty the King. The attached service records support what I have had the honour of mentioning to Your Royal Highness in Colonel Dubois' favour."

Within the new organisation we find the names of only 14 officers, NCOs and troopers who had been serving with the Regiment since its creation on 21 September 1810. These were the officers de la Fargue, de Tiecken, de Stuers, Dufour and Dubois; the NCOs Jean Alexandre, François Wettig, Toussaint Thibault and Henry van Otterloo, all sergeants; the lancers Guillaume Fréquin and Laurent la Haye (the latter a legless and decorated veteran, doubtless kept on the books in a non-combatant post); Joseph Wilmotte, master saddler, Nicolas Borsu, master tailor, and Pierre Vitry, who was a veterinary.

During the last months of the Empire 90 NCOs and troopers whose service could be traced back to 21 September 1810 had left the Regiment without permission to make their own way home. Of those former 3rd Hussars who returned from Spain in spring 1812 to join the Red Lancers, only four were left. During this period 56 men were officially dismissed from the Regiment as foreigners. Major de Lalaing d'Audenarde, Chef d'escadron de Lastours, Assistant Surgeon-Major Imbert and Lieutenants d'Hautpoul and de Nettancourt passed into the Royal Household in July 1814.

The officers, of whom some had been serving in the field for the past two or even three years without significant rest, were tired, and some were still suffering from their wounds. Chef d'escadron de Briqueville and Captain Salvetat, who remained with the Regiment, requested that they be put on half-pay for reasons of health. De Tiecken, who had led the Regiment during its last two campaigns, had been ill for a long time; Surgeon-Major Hennige asked that he be given the chance to recover his strength at a spa, and General Colbert seconded him with a request for three months' paid leave - if any officer deserved it, it was Chef d'escadron de Tiecken.

On 29 August the Regiment was ordered to march to Orleans, its new garrison town (the monarchy was not anxious to have such troops in Paris). Once the reorganisation had been completed General Colbert was appointed commander of the Lancers of France (the official date of 19 November merely confirmed the position he had actually filled since 24 August). On 3 September 1814 Colonel-Major Dubois was named maréchal de camp, remaining on the roll of the Regiment as second in command.

The Regiment looked superb, even if most of the officers were battered veterans of the Empire. If the government of the Bourbons had treated the army it inherited from Napoleon more diplomatically it could have asked much of them; but some emigrés who returned to positions of influence displayed a stupidly short-sighted vindictiveness towards soldiers who had every reason for pride in their record in the service of France. Tales of insult and ill-treatment became widespread throughout 1814. The economy was in crisis, and the army was cut by two-thirds in just seven months. Nearly 12,000 officers were dismissed on niggardly half-pay, which often never arrived, while commissions were reserved for returning Royalists who had never heard a shot fired in anger. Beyond the army, too, the new regime justified Talleyrand's remark that the Bourbons had learned nothing and forgotten nothing. Some of those who surrounded Louis XVIII set about dismantling Revolutionary liberties with foolish zeal; however nominal these had been under Napoleon's regime, they were valued by the population.

At the beginning of 1815 the Duchesse d'Angoulême visited Orleans, and even with the best of intentions she succeeded in making the entire officer corps feel uncomfortable. After being conducted before them and addressing a few words to two or three, she returned to the middle of a semicircle which the officers formed around her and said to Colbert in a lively tone: *"General, your officers are very handsome, but that is not enough - they must also be good."*

"Madam", replied Colbert, *"until today they have been everything that you could wish; and I dare assure you that they will always be just as they have been."*

Napoleon returns

On 1 March 1815, gambling on his ability to exploit the discontents of which his agents had kept him informed during eleven months in exile, Napoleon and his Elba army of barely a thousand men landed near Antibes. At the Tuileries the initial response was calm; but each time they sent troops to stop his steady progress towards Paris the soldiers joined him instead. On 7 March at Grenoble a battalion of the 5th Line Infantry disobeyed a direct order to fire upon Napoleon and, cheering, tore off their white cockades. At Auxerre it was Marshal Ney, and 6,000 troops with him. The advance became a triumphal progress as the sinews of the Bourbon regime melted away.

At the beginning of March 1815 the Royal Corps of Lancers of France were still in garrison at Orleans; their undemanding duties consisted of escorting public vehicles on the roads of the Department of the Loiret. To throw some light upon the events which followed we have the evidence of Maréchal de Camp Dubois to the commission of enquiry created by royal order on 12 October 1815:

"I was Maréchal de Camp Major at the Royal Lancers of France in garrison at Orleans. As a result of the departure of various generals I was appointed provisional commander of the Loiret department under the orders of Lieutenant-General Pajol.

"Fully occupied with all possible measures to ensure obedience to the King and the public peace, particularly in the city of Orleans, I soon formed the painful conviction that all my efforts were in vain. Hour by hour the spirit of sedition and revolt was showing itself in the various units of the garrison. HE Count Dupont, commanding the Reserve Army of

the Loire, was present in Orleans; I had the honour of communicating with him on many occasions, and kept him well informed of anything that could be of interest to him during these various meetings.

"Since some of the squadrons of the Royal Lancers of France had left for the Pithiviers region on 15 March, only a strong depot force of the regiment remained in Orleans together with the other units. This part [of the Regiment] behaved with moderation and even with a passive obedience, although a few malicious soldiers did venture to sell their fleurs-de-lys [badges]. I began by making an example of them, throwing them into the cells for three months and publishing their misconduct and its punishment in the orders of the day.

"As mutiny and confusion increasingly seized the minds of the troops, orders and counter-orders were given in which neither I nor the troops under my command took any part.

"Marshal Count Gouvion St Cyr arrived in Orleans. I had the honour to report to him and to render an account of the situation in which we found ourselves. I asked him if there was any Royal army to which he could direct me with my depot. I did not obtain any decision from him - desertion was soon spreading from one unit to another, and many regiments were leaving the garrison without orders to set off for Paris. The marshal's voice was ignored, and he himself was obliged to leave Orleans after having exhausted all means of imposing his authority.

"From that moment on my only concern was to maintain my depot, consisting of 300 men and horses. I had the satisfaction of seeing that not one let himself be swept away by the torrent of desertion; they took no part in the disturbances, and they consistently displayed obedience and firm discipline.

"Contact with Paris being restored, I was ordered to proceed with my troops to Versailles in order to reoccupy our former quarters. After my arrival in this town on 8 April I did not leave it throughout the reign of the usurper, nor did I take part in any festivities, nor was I with the army...."

Major Dubois also rescued from the flames the standard of the Lancers of France, and kept it until he was asked to hand it over to the General Headquarters in Paris.

Napoleon arrived at the Tuileries on 20 March 1815, and appointed Marshal Davout as Minister of War. On 21 March at three in the morning Davout asked General Colbert to take up the tricolour cockade once again; and later that day he sent orders to General Pajol at Orleans to direct the Dragoons and Lancers of the Guard to Paris. The bearer of these letters was Armand de Briqueville, who was placed under arrest by Marshal Gouvion St Cyr and General Dupont. Two days later Gouvion St Cyr received a letter from Davout ordering him to proclaim Napoleon as Emperor. He did not obey, and had the ADC who brought the letter arrested. During the night of 23 March the troops remaining in Orleans took up arms; helpless to put down the mutiny, Dupont and Gouvion St Cyr were compelled to leave the city - as described in Dubois' testimony.

The squadrons of the Regiment which had left Orleans on 15 March were now at Augerville, where on the 21st they received orders to set off for Versailles. They reached their old garrison on the 23rd; and the next day, together with the other units of the Guard, they paraded in front of their Emperor.

Preceding his regiment, General Colbert reached Paris on the same day. Napoleon, holding a review on the Place du Carrousel, noticed the general hastening towards him:

- *"Ahah! There you are, General Colbert; you are arriving quite late!"*

- *"Sire, I could come no sooner."*

- *"Come on,"* jeered the Emperor, taking hold of the general's moustache; *"You're late - what kept you?"*

At this Colbert retorted, *"Sire, not as late as Your Majesty - I have been waiting for you for a year."* Later these words - recorded by the newspaper *le Nain Jaune* - would nearly cost the general dear.

On 22 March 1815 the Emperor decreed that the Imperial Guard was to be restored to its former functions and privileges.

CHAPTER VII

1815: The Hundred Days

Within the reborn Guard there was to be a single regiment of lancers, under the old title of Light Horse Lancers of the Imperial Guard. Built around the Royal Corps of Lancers of France, its inclusion of an additional Polish squadron was detailed in a further Imperial decree of 22 April 1815:

Article 1
The Light Horse Lancers of Our Guard will be brought up to five squadrons organised according to our decree of the 8th of this month.
Article 2
The first squadron will be composed entirely of Poles. It will wear the uniform of the former Polish Lancers of Our Guard and will be recruited among Poles who have taken service in France.
Article 3
The Polish squadron will be commanded by Colonel Jermanowski, major in the cavalry of Our Guard. This squadron will be under the orders of the Lieutenant-General Colonel of the Light Horse Lancers of Our Guard; it will be treated and administered by the regimental Administrative Council like the other squadrons.

A few days later Napoleon reversed his decision and ordered that the Poles should be termed "the Polish Squadron" rather than the 1st, the former 2nd to 5th Squadrons becoming the 1st to 4th. The purchasing of necessary equipment commenced, in such a hurry and in such a mood of careless euphoria that orders were placed without even asking for competitive estimates. Time was short and the future was uncertain.

Within a week of the news of Napoleon's return reaching the other European powers they had unanimously declared unconditional support for Louis XVIII. Napoleon was characterised as a treaty-breaker and an outlaw, "the disturber of the repose of the world"; and Austria, Britain, Prussia and Russia each pledged to field an army of 150,000 men to crush his coup. The returned Emperor had only as much time as it would take for the powers to mobilise their forces and march them to France's borders. He would raise his new Army of the North with great speed, without formal conscription, and despite strong hostility – to the extent of armed rebellion – in the south and west of France. He did this largely by recalling men demobilised by the Bourbons; enthusiasm among the regimental officers and men was high, and in some senses this entirely French army was his best since Friedland. But few of his marshals would rally to the colours: of the greats, only Ney, Davout, Soult, Grouchy and Suchet (and at least four of these would be sadly misused).

On 27 April Minister of War Davout ordered Grand Marshal Bertrand to have a detachment of the Guard leave for Compiègne on the 30th under the command of Chef d'escadron Kirmann, among them a squadron of 120 Red Lancers.

On 30 May Napoleon wrote to Lieutenant-General Count Drouot, commanding the Imperial Guard: "We must prepare for the departure of the Guard on 5 June... The Red Lancers will form two regiments, each regiment of four squadrons. We will form a third regiment as soon as possible, which will give us twelve squadrons."

In practice the so-called "second regiment" then being

The Assembly on the Champ du Mai, 1 June 1815, by François J.Heim (1787-1865). (Photo © Réunion des Musées Nationaux, Paris)

Captain Claude N. B. Gauthier (1767-1815), by Dubois-Drahonet. This officer passed into the Young Guard squadrons of the Red Lancers from the former Spanish Royal Guard in February 1814. Serving with the duty squadron in attendance on Napoleon, he was wounded at Ligny on 16 June; two days later he was killed at Waterloo. (Private collection, Belgium)

organised as part of the Young Guard could count no more than 16 squads - hardly a single squadron strength; the first ten squads were commanded by Lieutenant Poupon, the other six by Lieutenant Bernet.

Before dealing with the enemies of France the régime had to make a gesture of confidence, celebrating the return of the Emperor on the Champ de Mai. On 1 June, on a radiant and baking hot day, electoral delegates, officials and a multitude of invited guests took their places in the semi-circular amphitheatre built by the architect Fontaine. Two hundred regimental Eagle-bearers and 87 officers of the National Guard paraded their standards; each regiment had sent a delegation of five officers and twelve NCOs and soldiers. The Imperial Guard, the Paris garrison and the twelve Legions of the National Guard - 45,000 men in all - were drawn up in formation.

At 11a.m. a salute of a hundred guns was fired by the battery on the Tuileries terrace and repeated by many other batteries all over the capital, announcing the start of the Imperial procession. After the *Te Deum* the Emperor distributed only three Eagles, for lack of time: those of the National Guard of the Seine, the 1st Line Infantry and the 1st Marine Corps. Escorted by the Eagle-bearers Napoleon then proceeded to the Champ de Mai, where he took his place on a stage surrounded by the regimental standards and delegations. There he presented Eagles to the Imperial Guard and the National Guard of Paris. He addressed the battalions in these words:

"I am entrusting you with the Eagle in the national colours. Swear to die defending it. Swear to recognize no other rallying sign. You, soldiers of the National Guard of Paris, swear that you will never allow a foreigner again to dishonour the capital of this great nation. I am committing it to

your bravery. And you, soldiers of the Imperial Guard, swear to surpass yourselves in the campaign that is about to begin, and to die rather than to suffer foreigners to dictate laws to your native country." His address was interrupted by cries of *"We swear it!"* and *"Vive l'Empereur!"*

The regimental daily state of the Red Lancers on 1 June 1815 was recorded as follows:

	Officers	Troops	Horses
Present & available	30	426	691
Unavailable	25	609	261
Detached at Compiègne	5	115	
In hospital	3	42	
On trial	1		
Totals	63	1,193	952

After ceremony and spectacle one must return to reality. The Allies had planned to invade France in late June. Wellington would lead a combined Anglo-Netherlands army of 95,000 from the north-east, and Blücher 124,000 Prussians from the east. It was planned that these forces would be supported by 200,000 Russians marching through the Saarland, by Schwarzenburg with 210,000 Austrians from Switzerland, and by 75,000 more Austrians and Sardinians crossing the Alps from Italy.

The timetable for this majestic plan was extremely optimistic, and by mid-June Wellington would have available only about 32,000 British and roughly similar numbers from both the Netherlands and various German states. The quality of these troops varied sharply, from a small core of excellent veteran battalions to poorly trained recruits and militia. Blücher's generally reliable Prussians had reached a strength of about 117,000 by mid-June. The Russians and Austrians were still far away; and Napoleon had no intention of waiting until they arrived. His only hope lay in attacking and defeating both Wellington and Blücher seperately, along one of three routes which each offered different opportunities to exploit the Allies' dispersal.

On 3 June Napoleon sent orders to General Drouot (employing the confusing terms of "1st and 2nd Regiments" for the two elements of the Light Horse Lancers of the Guard): *"... On Monday 5th you will also have the 1st Lancers, 4 squadrons strong and numbering at least 400 horses, leave for Soissons....On Tuesday 6th you will have the 2nd Regiment of Red Lancers leave.... These columns will reach Soissons in three days, in order to be there on the 8th and 9th. All the Guard detachments will take the road via Dammartin...."*

On 6 June the Regiment was reinforced with nine officers and 239 men, bringing the strength of the sabre squadrons for this campaign up to 47 officers and 823 men (833 by the time the fighting began). The Regiment's total paper strength by the middle of the month would be 67 officers and 1,303 lancers with 1,149 horses.

On the 9th, with the excuse of the imminent campaign, General Colbert proposed the promotion of Chef d'escadron de Tiecken to colonel, but his request remained unanswered.

From Soissons the Guard marched to Avesnes, reaching there on the 12th and staying the next day. Little by little, and with every attempt at concealment of his intentions, Napoleon was assembling his 124,000-strong army on the Belgian border; his headquarters were established at Beaumont on 14 June, and there his Guard joined him. The next day was the anniversary of Marengo, and of Friedland. In the darkness before dawn on 15 June 1815 Napoleon's last army crossed the frontier in three columns.

Quatre-Bras

Napoleon and his Guard marched with the centre column, to cross the Sambre at Charleroi; beyond that town lay the direct road to the Anglo-Netherlands headquarters, Brussels. Leading the column were General Pajol's troopers from the 1st Reserve Cavalry Corps; they were supposed to be followed by General Vandamme's III Corps, but this formation was late starting and the

Tablet commemorating the officers of the Dutch 6th Hussars killed at Waterloo including the names of General van Merlen and Captain van Heiden, both late of the Red Lancers. (Chapel Royal, Waterloo)

(Right) The last charge of the Red Lancers at Waterloo, 18 June 1815: "Bon Dieu! protège nos vieux débris..." (Lithograph by Raffet, 1804-1860; collection of Belgian Royal Army Museum, Brussels)

Guard overtook it. The Guard infantry were followed by the Guard light cavalry - Mounted Chasseurs and Lancers - under Lefebvre-Desnoëttes, and the heavy Dragoons and Mounted Grenadiers under General Guyot. The Guard was followed by III Corps and - eventually - VI Corps.

The advance was frustratingly slow; the bridge over the Sambre was only eight meters wide. At about 2p.m. on the afternoon of the 15th the Emperor was informed by Colonel Clary of the 1st Hussars that the Prussians were present in strength at Jumet and Gosselies. The Guard light cavalry were sent forward with their horse artillery batteries to support Clary's regiment.

At 3.30p.m. Marshal Ney reported to the Emperor in Charleroi, and received the detached command of the left wing of the Army of the North. Progress was still worrying; the scattered Prussian blocking forces encountered by the probing cavalry were making a skilful fighting retreat, and the mass of the French infantry which could have engulfed them were far behind schedule. Ney would command I and II Corps (Generals Reille and Drouet d'Erlon), the 3rd Reserve Cavalry Corps (General Kellermann), one of Pajol's light cavalry brigades, and the Light Cavalry Division of the Guard - *"However, do not make use of them"*, added Napoleon of his cherished Guard. The intention was that Ney should push his troops (once they were all finally on the north bank of the river) through Gosselies and Frasnes and on towards Quatre-Bras on the Brussels road.

Ney attacked the Prussians on the outskirts of Gosselies and forced them back, noticing that they were withdrawing east to Fleurus. He had them followed by Girard's division, while ordering the rest of his vanguard on up the main road to Frasnes.

At about 6.30p.m. a Nassau infantry brigade of the Netherlands 2nd Division, supported by a horse artillery battery and positioned on the road south of Frasnes, noticed movement to their front and left; first isolated riders, then patrols - wearing scarlet lancer uniform.

Growing more numerous, the French cavalry attacked the Nassauers, assisted by detachments of dismounted troopers. General Lefebvre-Desnoëttes decided that it was folly for cavalry alone to try to drive infantry out of a village, and called for infantry support. A battalion from General Bachelu's division would take until 9p.m. to reach the outskirts of Frasnes.

While his vanguard were at grips with the Nassau troops General Colbert led the Polish Squadron round the east of Frasnes and advanced, getting close to Quatre-Bras without encountering any resistance. The remainder of the Red Lancers were now nearing Frasnes, travelling parallel with the road from Charleroi. They came under fire from the Netherlands artillery battery, which dissuaded them from attempting a frontal attack while not preventing them from extending in the direction of Villers-Perwin.

The enemy retreated up the road in good order towards Gémioncourt farm and Bossu Wood. The Red Lancers pursued them by passing around Frasnes on the east, and got within short range before the Nassauers' fire forced them to break off the chase. On his return to Frasnes General Colbert reported to General Lefebvre-Desnoëttes. With night falling, still without infantry or artillery support, and uncertain of the enemy's strength and disposition, Lefebvre had no intention of venturing his tired troopers any further. At 9p.m. he sent a report to Marshal Ney at Gosselies:

"Arriving at Frasne [sic] according to your orders, we found it occupied by a regiment of Nassau infantry numbering about 1,500 men and eight guns. When they noticed that we were manoeuvring to turn them they left the village. There we had them, in effect, surrounded by our squadrons; General Colbert at least was within musket shot of Quatre-Bras on the main road. But the ground was difficult; the enemy had retreated into Bossu Wood and were delivering a very brisk fire with their eight guns, and it was impossible for us to overrun them. The troops that we found in Frasne did not take up that position this morning, nor were they those who fought at Gosselies. They are under the orders of Lord Wellington, and seem to wish to retreat towards Nivelles. They have lit a beacon at Quatre-Bras and have fired their cannon a great deal.

"None of the troops which were fighting this morning at Gosselies have passed by here; they have marched towards Fleurus. The peasants are unable to tell me of any large troop concentration in this

neighbourhood, only of an artillery park at Tubise composed of 100 caissons and 12 cannons. They say that the Belgian army is in the neighbourhood of Mons and that the headquarters of young Prince Frederick of Orange is located at Brenne-le-Comte [Braine-le-Comte].

"We have taken fifteen prisoners and have suffered the loss or injury of ten men.

"At daybreak tomorrow I will send a reconnaissance party to occupy Quatre-Bras if possible, for I believe that the Nassau troops have left. I have just received an infantry battalion which I have put in front of the village. Since my artillery did not join me I have sent orders for them to bivouac with Bachelu's division; they will join me tomorrow morning.

"I am not writing to the Emperor, having nothing more important to report to him than what I have told Your Excellency....

"I am sending you a sergeant who will receive Your Excellency's orders. I have the honour to point out to Your Excellency that the enemy have not yet shown us any cavalry, but that the artillery is light artillery."

At 11p.m. on the 15th Marshal Ney sent an ADC with the general's report to the Emperor's headquarters for his instructions.

That same day a frustrated Marie Michel de Tiecken wrote to Napoleon requesting a regiment. It was a reasonable request: he was the senior among the chefs d'escadron, he had led the Regiment at Dresden and in France, and many of his brother-officers had already received preferment. His timing was unfortunate; he would be appointed colonel only on 1 July.

On the evening of that first day of the campaign the Light Cavalry Division of the Guard encamped behind a battalion of the 2nd Light Infantry from General Bachelu's division. Mounted vedettes were posted on the higher ground north of Frasnes, and patrols were sent out as far as Thyle and Sart-Dames-Avelines.

On the morning of 16 June these mounted sentries and the

Regiment's patrols were attacked and driven in by Dutch cavalry. For the rest of that day the Red Lancers were held back in reserve as spectators to the fighting which raged around the crossroads of Quatre-Bras.

Both sides must have understood its importance in commanding the east-west highway between Wellington's and Blücher's armies; but for some reason Ney, probably believing that Napoleon was marching west to join him, delayed attacking the Allies until the afternoon. By then Wellington had managed to rush reinforcements down the Brussels road and construct an untidy, scrambled-together but successful defence against Ney's repeated attacks in the afternoon. This prevented Ney moving east to support Napoleon in his simultaneous battle against Blücher at Ligny. The Red Lancers' only taste of action was when they covered the withdrawal of General Kellermann's Cuirassiers after their admirable charge. Even so, General Colbert was wounded by a shot in his left arm. (Captain Gauthier and Lieutenant Cabard, both serving with the service squadron from the Regiment which attended the Emperor in person, were wounded that day at Ligny.)

On the 17th, having beaten Blücher's army but neither destroyed it nor forced it eastwards away from any possible junction with Wellington, Napoleon seems once more to have been attacked by that strange apathy which sometimes cost him dear; he delayed in giving orders to his marshals, and wasted the morning. He eventually marched ahead of his main force towards Quatre-Bras, expecting to find Ney either in possession of it or locked in battle for it. But Ney was awaiting both reinforcement and clarification of the Emperor's vaguely worded orders. He had allowed Wellington the respite he needed to withdraw his troops

The czapska worn at Waterloo by Captain Soufflot. The Imperial symbols were taken back into use during the Hundred Days, but for many there was no time to acquire them; Soufflot's cap plate bore no insignia. (La Sabretache)

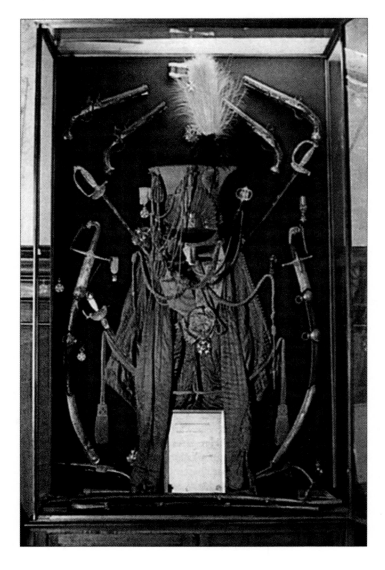

The czapska of General Edouard Colbert surrounded by other personal souvenirs of himself and his two brothers. (Château d'Ainay-le-Vieil, France; photo Souvenir Napoléonien)

gradually from the crossroads and north towards his long-chosen battlefield of Waterloo.

The Emperor's vedettes from Colonel Marbot's 7th Hussars ran into Allied troops a few miles from Quatre-Bras. Hoping to link up with Ney's troops, Napoleon sent a detachment of the 7th to Frasnes. Here they encountered first of all a detachment of the Red Lancers; surprised to see red uniforms and thinking these were British, they opened fire and wounded several Lancers.

Throughout the afternoon of the 17th the French chased the Anglo-Netherlands army north, but were unable either to outflank them or to engage them closely enough to slow them. A violent rainstorm broke out, turning the heavy soil of the fields to glutinous mud and limiting the pursuers' movements. The Red Lancers were to the fore in this pursuit, and clashed with the British light horse of Generals Vivian and Vandeleur near Thyle as they covered the Allied withdrawal in textbook fashion. The outcome of such skirmishes was more or less even; only when Lord Uxbridge unleashed his heavy cavalry of the 1st Life Guards were the pursuers driven back any distance.

That night both armies reached the shallow valley and gentle ridge of Mont St Jean south of the village of Waterloo, beyond which the Brussels road disappeared into the Forest of Soignes. The soldiers and horses of both sides, soaked to the skin, had to bivouac in the sodden rye fields - "like stepping into a bath". It continued raining throughout the night.

Waterloo
On Sunday 18 June the Emperor had to delay the start of his attack on the Allied position to give the softened ground, over which his artillery was unable to manoeuver, some time to harden under the sun. It was not until the afternoon that the Regiment went into action, but this time the Guard would not be held back. On this last great day of battle they would play a tragic but heroic part in the premature cavalry charges which helped decide the fate of the Empire.

For the Regiment the fighting of 18 June 1815 would have a special poignancy: many former brothers-in-arms, officers and men of the Army of the Netherlands, stood waiting for them over there in Wellington's battle line. Among them General van Merlen, at the head of the 5th Light Dragoons, would not see another sunrise; one of his ADCs was Lieutenant de Bellefroid. On the first page of this story we have seen that Captain van Omphal was serving on General Chassé's staff. Captain Heshusius was there; so was Surgeon-Major Mergell, leading the medical service of I Netherlands Corps. Captain van Heiden would die at Waterloo; Captain Charles Mascheck was already dead, killed defending Quatre-Bras at the head of his troopers of the 4th Light Dragoons. His cousin Joseph was an officer in the 3rd Carabiniers, which served that day in the 1st Netherlands Cavalry Brigade led by General Trip.

The story of the battle is too widely documented to repeat here except in so far as it involved the Red Lancers. After perhaps 3.30p.m., at a period when the distracted Napoleon had handed tactical control of the battle to Ney, a gigantic cavalry movement began to take place. Exact responsibility for this rash gamble has been endlessly argued but never settled. What is clear is that the French cavalry went on to smash themselves, repeatedly, on the rocks of Wellington's unbroken lines of infantry squares. For the purposes of this text we may limit ourselves to the eyewitness account of Captain Fortuné Brack of the Red Lancers, written in reply to a letter from General Pelet and dated 11 March 1835. (Note that his mention of the "Nivelles road" is deceptive; all sources agree that the Guard cavalry were drawn up behind the centre left of the army, just south-west of the road leading from the

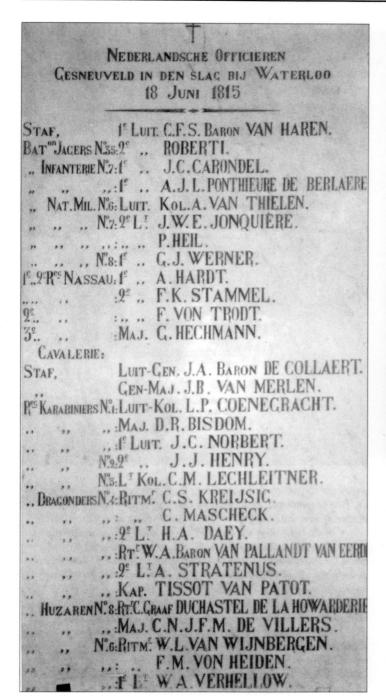

Naif but interesting drawing of Sergeant Théodore Wampach (1778-1841), apparently known simply as "the Lancer" in his later years. Although retired, he voluntarily returned to the Regiment as soon as he heard of Napoleon's return in 1815. The drawing shows careful detail of his marks of senior NCO rank: epaulette and aiguillette apparently of mixed blue and gold. (Collection of Belgian Royal Army Museum, Brussels)

(Left) *Tablet commemorating officers of the Dutch cavalry killed at Waterloo, including the names of the former Red Lancers van Merlen, Charles Maschek and van Heiden. (Chapel Royal, Waterloo)*

Rossome fork north-west towards Braine l'Alleud.):

"At Waterloo I was part of the Lancers of the Imperial Guard. It is true that General Domon had me request of the Emperor the command of the 9th Mounted Chasseurs, whose Colonel Baron du Kermont had deserted, so it was said, to the enemy; but this request was made too late.

"The four regiments of the Guard cavalry, forming a division under the orders of Marshal Ney, were not separated during the whole day. They stood beside their horses, quite close to the Nivelles road. They were stationary until the moment when the cavalry of General Ponsonby attacked. This attack [by the Union Brigade] was at first very surprising and vigorous, but was later powerfully repulsed. It caused the [Kellerman's] Cuirassier Division, which had been next to us for several hours, to move into the front line.

"Ponsonby's cavalry made three errors normal for any new cavalry - errors which our own would undoubtedly make tomorrow if they were to be led into battle by inexperienced senior officers:
(1) They did not make any preliminary reconnaissance of the ground in front of them before the charge.
(2) They started their charge from too far away.
(3) They were unable to stop the charge and rally in time.

"This impetuous charge went through our badly supported batteries and one of our younger regiments, the 44th I think, whose Eagle it captured [it was the 45th]. But due to the difficulty of the ground, the thoughtless dash of its officers, and arriving in too extended a formation at the point where it ran into strong, fresh opposition well aligned and well led, it squandered the advantage it had won. Under the sabres of our Cuirassiers and the thrusts of our 4th Lancers of the Line, commanded by Colonel Bro, they strewed the ground with their dead....This success thrilled our cavalry, who were now more impatient than ever to cross sabres.

"The Guard cavalry having been ordered to move forward, we marched towards the enemy in the direction of the fortified farm of La Haie-Sainte, from which we were separated by a slight undulation, a gentle slope and a small level area. The four regiments were on the same line, mounted on the main road, the Lancers on the right and then, to the left, the Mounted Chasseurs, the Dragoons and the Mounted Grenadiers.

"There now occured an incredible event, but I can swear to its all too real authenticity. It was one of those caprices of warfare which overturn all reasoned calculation and all prudence, and which have happened so often in our bloody history. Sometimes, when a genius grasps the implications of these fluke events at once and moves to exploit them, they can bring victory.

"I said that the cavalry of the Guard was in a single line and that a fold in the ground separated them from the plain on which they were going

A plate decorated with gilt Imperial motifs with a view of the palace of St Cloud, showing (see detail) a Red Lancer at the gate, 1815. Painted by Jean-Baptiste Langlacé, porcelain manufactury of Sèvres. (Photos © Réunion des Musées Nationaux, Paris)

to have to fight hand-to-hand. This undulation was not continuous along our battle line, and only completely masked the first four squadrons of our regiment which, standing on the right, happened to be those on which the division dressed its line.

"General Curély had been, like me, an aide to General Colbert, our former colonel; he and I loved one another like brothers. Without a command on that day, he was following the General Headquarters while waiting to have a command entrusted to his courage. He noticed the regiment from a distance and came over to see me. I welcomed him, and while we were chatting we climbed to the top of the fold in the ground a few yards from the extreme right of the regiment.

"No sooner had I reached this spot than I recognised the field that lay in front of me. In January 1814, while under the orders of General Maison, I had occupied for a few days a position at the junction of two roads with a squadron and a battalion, to cover the headquarters of the Army of the North which was then in Brussels.

"Impassioned by our recent success against Ponsonby, and by the forward movement that I noticed being executed by the Cuirassiers to our right, I exclaimed, 'The English are lost! The position on which they have been thrown back makes it clear.... They can only retreat by one narrow road confined between impassable woods. One broken stone on this road and their entire army will be ours! Either their general is the most ignorant of officers or he has lost his head! ...The English realise their situation - there - look - they have uncoupled their guns!' I was ignorant of the fact that the English batteries usually fought uncoupled.

"I spoke loudly, and my words were overheard. From the front of our regiment a few officers pushed forward to join our group. The right hand files [of our regimental line] followed them; the movement was copied in the squadrons [to the left] to restore the alignment; and then by the Mounted Chasseurs of the Guard. This movement, of only a few paces at the right, became more marked [as it passed to] the left. The brigade of the Dragoons and Mounted Grenadiers, who were awaiting the order to charge at any moment, believed this had been [given].... They set off - and we followed! That is how the charge of the Imperial Guard cavalry took place, over the reason for which so many writers have argued so variously.

"From that moment, lining up to the left, we crossed the road diagonally so as to have the whole Guard cavalry on the left side of this road;

we crossed the flat ground, climbed up the slope of the plateau upon which the English army was drawn up, and attacked together. The order in which that army was drawn up, or the part exposed to our view, was as follows:

"To its right were the Scots Foot [Guards?], close to undergrowth which extended down to the bottom of the slope; this infantry delivered heavy and well-directed fire. Then came the squares of Line infantry, ordered in a chequerboard pattern; then similar squares of the Hanoverian Light Infantry; then the fortified farm. Between the squares were uncoupled batteries, whose gunners were firing and [then] hiding under their guns; behind them, some infantry and some cavalry.

"We were nearly level with this farm, between which and us our Cuirassiers were charging. We rode through the batteries, which we were unable to drag back with us. We turned back and threatened the squares, which put up a most honourable resistance. Some of them had such coolness that they were still firing ordered volleys by rank. It has been said that the Dragoons and Mounted Grenadiers to our left broke several squares; personally I did not see it - and I can state that we Lancers did not have the same luck, and that we crossed our lances with the English bayonets in vain. Many of our troopers threw their weapons like spears into the front ranks to try to open up the squares.

"The expenditure of ammunition by the English first line and the compact pattern of the squares which composed it meant that the firing was at point-blank range; but it was the harm which the artillery and the squares in the second line were doing to us, in the absence of infantry and artillery to support our attack, which determined our retreat.

"We moved slowly, and faced front again in our position at the bottom of the slope, so that we could just make out the first English line. It was then that Marshal Ney, alone, without a single one of his staff accompanying him, rode along our front and harangued us, calling out to the officers he knew by their names. His face was distracted, and he cried out again and again: 'Frenchmen, let us stand firm! It is here that the keys to our freedom are lying!' I quote him word for word.

"Five times we repeated the charge; but since the conditions remained unchanged, we returned to our position at the rear five times. There, at 150 paces from the enemy infantry, we were exposed to the most murderous fire. Our men began to lose heart: they were being hit at the same time by bullets from the front and by cannonballs from the flank, and by new projectiles (small shells) which exploded above their heads and fell [these were Shrapnel shells, invented by an officer of that name, which the Red Lancers had not encountered since they had never before fought the British Royal Artillery].

"At last a battery of the Guard was sent over to support us; but instead of the Light Artillery it belonged to the Foot Artillery Reserve of twelve-pounders. It had the utmost difficulty in moving forward through the mud and only took up position behind us after endless delay. Its first shots were so badly aimed that they blew away a complete troop of our own regiment.

"A movement to the rear was ordered. We carried this out at ordinary pace and formed up again behind the battery. The Mounted Chasseurs, Dragoons and Grenadiers of the Guard extended their movement further than us, and took position in echelon a short distance behind and to the left of the Lancers. The English cavalry advanced on and off to follow us, but as soon as they came up with our line they stopped, respecting our Lancers above all - the long lances intimidated them. They were limited to firing their pistols at us before retiring behind their infantry line, which made no move. Between us and the infantry they left a few squadrons of Light Dragoons to form a line of skirmishers, supported by the Scots Foot.

"Then a voluntary truce, so to speak, was reached between the combatants due to the complete exhaustion of the troops. Half of our squadrons dismounted inside musket range. The Intendant-General, d'Aure, can testify to this fact for, with his usual bravery, he came to visit us during this peculiar episode. This suspension of arms lasted about three-quarters of an hour, during which we were hoping that the Emperor's genius would change the face of the battle, forming a general, supported and decisive attack... But nothing! Absolutely nothing! ...

"It was then that we changed from participants into spectators of an incomprehensible drama of which the terrible absurdity was soon recognised, and roundly condemned, by even the least of our simple troopers. The small plain which we bordered on one side was, as it were, a great circus whose boxes were occupied by the English. Into this bloody arena descended, one after another, poor men destined for death, whose sacrifice was all the easier and quicker since the English, without danger to themselves, were waiting for them at point-blank range.

"At first a few battalions came past our left and presented themselves in column to the English right and its fearless Scots under cover in a wood.

"When these had been stretched on the ground it was the turn of our Carabinier Brigade. This emerged on our right at a gentle trot, crossed the arena alone in column of troops, and rode along all the enemy batteries to attack the English right. Then Wellington's musketry and batteries awoke together, aiming at the same point, and [despite] the thunder of their fire [we heard] three butcher's cheers. Within a few seconds the Carabiniers had vanished, in death or flight.

"To make our grief complete, rumours were running through our ranks: 'Our right was routed...Grouchy had sold himself to the enemy...Bourmont, Clouet, du Barail and many other officers had deserted. A senior officer of the infantry column that had just attacked the Scots had fallen hit by a case-shot, and 200 white cockades had spilled from his shako... When the English retired from their first position they had left proclamations on the field signed by Louis XVIII which promised pardon, amnesty, retention of rank and post'.

"When there were no more victims to offer for the great sacrifice, when the circus games had come to an end, our attention was drawn to a new spectacle which worthily crowned that day. On the plateau to our right appeared black lines; they came forward, preceded by their guns. They were the Prussians, who had escaped Grouchy!... Ah! How can I describe to you the consternation among the Guard cavalry? They cried out for the Emperor, whom they not seen since their commitment to battle - and they wouldn't see him yet!

"The order to retreat was given. How ominous was that retreat - a funeral procession.... Our light cavalry brigade, reduced to two and a half squadrons and commanded by Generals Lefebvre-Desnoëttes, Lallemand and Colbert (wounded), retreated slowly and extended its line in order to form a curtain which somewhat concealed our routed army from English observation. So we marched, until we met again on our left what remained of the Old Guard infantry which, with us, formed the extreme rearguard. They were formed in square on the road and on the southern side of a

A poignant souvenir: a self-portrait of General Colbert in prison at l'Abbaye during the "white terror" of 1815 - the Bourbon purge of those who had rallied to Napoleon during the Hundred Days. In the event Colbert was neither imprisoned nor exiled for long. In this painting the figure wears a dark blue coat, grey trousers, and the Red Lancer officer's old pattern bonnet de police with scarlet top, blue band and gold lace. (Château d'Ainay-le-Vieil, France)

slope whose crest served as protection against the English cannonballs. They were facing to the rear; we halted level with them and turned about too. We numbered at that time 100 to 150 officers and troopers of the Lancers and Mounted Chasseurs, exhausted and wretched. We were about 500 paces to the left of the above-mentioned infantry, separated from them by a low meadow and some undergrowth. The sun had almost disappeared over the horizon, and it was nearly dark.

"Our three generals came together in front [of our line] and some officers joined them - I was a member of this group. A powerful assault column of the enemy was marching on the road and was heading for the Foot Guards' square. As far as the twilight allowed me to make it out this column was composed of infantry in battalions, flanked by a double column of artillery and by cavalry in divisions; it marched with order and confidence. Its head had barely appeared on the crest behind which the Foot Guard were standing when the latter opened fire. This shooting was well enough co-ordinated, but was perhaps premature; and it seemed to me that it would have produced more effect if it had been delivered from closer to the crest and thus as plunging fire. This firing was answered by a rather poor salvo from the enemy; this was followed by a mêlée which was concealed from me by the night and the distance.

"General Lefebre-Desnoëttes cried out in the greatest excitement that 'It is here that we must all die; that no Frenchman could outlive such a horrible day; that we must look for death among this mass of English facing us...'. We tried to calm him down. A discussion began in which we all took part and, strangely enough, the man who maintained his sang-

"*Recognising troops still under discipline, the Emperor came towards us. Never has such a bright moon lit a more horrible night. The moonlight fell full on the face of the Emperor as he stood in front of our ranks. Never, even during the retreat from Moscow, had I seen a more confused and unhappy expression on that majestic face.*
    - *'Who are you?', asked His Majesty.*
    - *'The Lancers of the Guard.'*
    - *'Ah, yes! The Lancers of the Guard! And where is Piré?' [General Piré commanded the cavalry of II Corps, including the 5th and 6th Lancers of the Line.]*
    - *'Sire, we know nothing of him.'*
    - *'What, and the 6th Lancers?'*
    - *'Sire, we do not know, he was not with us.'*
    - *'That's right... but Piré?'*
    - *'We have no idea', replied General Colbert.*
    - *'But who are you?'*
    - *'Sire, I am Colbert, and here are the Lancers of your Guard.'*
    - *'Ah, yes... and the 6th Lancers?... and Piré? Piré?'*
    "*I report these words with religious accuracy. He spoke a few phrases which I did not catch; and then, at the sound of a shot from back down the road, one of the generals with him dragged him away, and he disappeared into the night. Our grief knew no bounds.*"

The euphoria of his return from Elba and the first promising results of the campaign had rebuilt Napoleon's confidence: nothing could stand between the French army and a brilliant, decisive victory. The defeat at Waterloo was thus all the more shattering. Brack's description paints a picture of a completely demoralised Napoleon, conscious of the dreadful consequences he faced as a result of this defeat.

★   ★   ★

As Captain Brack described, the Regiment had advanced east of Hougoumont roughly towards Maitland's brigade, in support of the Cuirassiers of Generals Dubois and Farine of Milhaud's division. The artillery batteries of Webber, Smith, Bean and Sandham received them with heavy fire. During the afternoon the Red Lancers also attacked the batteries of Peter Grey and Ramsay, whose gunners defended themselves with the sabre; and the squares of Maitland and the Brunswickers. When Allied light horse came forward between the squares the Lancers found themselves under attack by the 1st Light Dragoons of the King's German Legion (from Dörnberg's 3rd Brigade). Noticing the numerical inferiority of the enemy cavalry, General Colbert rallied two squadrons and drove the Hanoverian troopers back; however, this pursuit carried the Lancers into the fire of Bolton's battery and they suffered heavy casualties.

Better conducted than the Cuirassiers, the Red Lancers returned to the charge several times against the British squares, but on each occasion were thrown back without succeeding in breaking open any of these formations. Repeated interventions by the Allied light horse of van Merlen, de Ghigny, d'Arentschildt and Dörnberg finally forced the Red Lancers to give up their attacks.

froid - who still thought we had a tomorrow to look forward to, who talked about making a useful retreat all the way to Paris - was the one man who would instantly lose his life if the Bourbons laid hands on him: General Lallemand. He ignored his own interests in order to consider the general situation, discussing matters coolly and with authority. That night I formed the highest opinion of the soundness of his character and his spirit.

    "*I strongly supported General Lallemand and suggested that we wait in the nearest defensible town, which was Maubeuge. There we should rally all the scattered men we could find and then, in a few days, reappear behind the enemy to start guerrilla warfare. If our numbers grew and we had some luck in our first attacks we could create a large and useful diversion. This view gained majority support; but it was agreed that first of all we should march to Quatre-Bras where we would probably get news.*

    "*General Lefebvre-Desnoëttes repeated his desperate proposal; but we were just a handful of exhausted men on horses which could barely carry us. A shell fell at our feet, and several English squadrons were heading our way; we began our retreat at walking pace. Thus it was that we were the last to leave the field. We followed paths running parallel to the road, and our isolation was such that we did not hear the slightest sound of war. During this silent march stragglers of all arms joined us. We found Colonel Gobert of the Cuirassiers, who was said to have been killed.*

    "*After several hours we began to make out a muffled noise to our left. This grew louder, and soon we broke out [onto the road] at Quatre-Bras. Here we came upon the most crowded, breathless and disordered retreat that I ever saw. We lined up in battle formation facing to the rear, our right being close to the Charleroi road. This movement was barely completed when one of our officers said, 'There is the Emperor!' At once all eyes turned in the direction of the road and there, among a mass of infantry, vehicles, cavalry and wounded, we saw the Emperor riding, accompanied by two officers wearing greatcoats just like him and followed by four or five Gendarmes d'élite (this was, I believe, at one o'clock in the morning).*

110

The price of their bravery and determination was high. Among the wounded were Lieutenants Billard, Reiautey and Bisiaux - the last by shrapnel in his right arm. Lieutenant Boudgout took a bullet in the forehead, but survived; 2nd Lieutenant Fonnade and Lieutenant Lethuiller were both wounded in the right hand by bullets, the latter while leading his squadron. Lieutenant Gutschenreiter was wounded and taken prisoner; so was Lieutenant Enjubeault (also known as Laroche), wounded here for the fifth time. The former Mameluke Captain Renno was wounded in the right arm by shrapnel; Captain Gauthier, already wounded at Ligny, was killed. Sergeant Theodore Wampach, a former sergeant in the Spanish Royal Guard and member of the Legion of Honour, was wounded by a sabre cut; he had returned to his native Germany in 1814, but had not hesitated to offer his services to the Emperor once again.

Retreating through Charleroi, the Emperor crossed the bridge over the Sambre at about 2a.m. on the 19th, accompanied by Generals Bertrand and Drouot and escorted by a detachment of Red Lancers. When they reached Philippeville Marshal Soult ordered the General Headquarters to move to Laon and the entire Imperial Guard to Soissons. Back at Beaumont, General Colbert was working hard to regroup and reorganise his Regiment; and the Red Lancers formed up on the glacis at Avesnes on 20 June at about seven in the morning.

(It was on that day that Chef d'escadron Jean Coti, who had been taking the waters at Bourbonne spa in an attempt to cure himself of the effects of his long campaigns with the Red Lancers, finally died there of exhaustion.)

On 23 June the sabre squadrons of the Regiment mustered 30 officers and 507 lancers; two days later the number of rank and file had increased to 525, with 529 horses. It would be a few days before General Colbert learned that Napoleon had signed an instrument of abdication on 21 June.

The cavalry of the Guard marched to Laon under the orders of General Lefebvre-Desnoëttes, taking the Soissons road and stopping at Clichy. Here it was recorded that the Regiment still had nine officers and 240 lancers available in Paris and 11 officers with 230 lancers unready for service; 33 lancers were in hospital.

On 29 June Napoleon left Malmaison, where he had retired for a few days after the abdication. He had been guarded by 300 "Grumblers" of the Old Guard infantry quartered at Rueil, 50 Dragoons of the Guard, and 25 Red Lancers commanded by Captain Brack.

On 2 July 1815 the reassembled Regiment was still quartered in the village of Clichy; it now numbered 41 officers and 738 lancers. In the course of that month the Guard cavalry was ordered to head for the Loire once more. The Red Lancers travelled by Montrouge, Longjumeau, Etampes, Pithiviers and Loury to reach Orleans on the 10th. There they met up with the rest of the Guard, and were quartered at St Mesmin. Colonel Dubois, still at Versailles with the regimental depot, left to join the Regiment during its march to the Loire in order to prevent the depot's resources falling into enemy hands.

The disbandment of the Red Lancers

After the Waterloo campaign and the second restoration of King Louis XVIII there was to be no mercy for the Guard; the progressive disbandment of its regiments began on 3 August.

Relieved of his command, General Colbert was not forgotten. The Regiment's officers and NCOs expressed their feelings to him in two letters of farewell. That from the officers was dated 18 August at Châtellerault:

"General - The officers of your regiment have read your farewell: the affection [it expresses] is equalled by the fondness they extend to you.

Grave of Fortuné Prosper (de) Brack (1789-1850) in the cemetery of Fontainbleau. Although retired for fifteen years after Waterloo he was rehabilitated in 1830, and his manual on light cavalry tactics became a standard work. (Alain Chappet collection)

The chapel where Edouard Colbert (1774-1853) lies buried at Balancourt. He would suffer the last of his eight wounds in July 1835, from a fanatic's bomb; and was present at the capture of Constantine, Algeria, in 1836. (Alain Chappet collection)

You have been their exemplar, their father and their friend. Who can console them? If the regiment has done well it is through you and by you; its glory was yours. What will be left to it if you are leaving? For the two years since the death of Auguste Colbert the Hussars of the 3rd Regiment have worn a black flame [flash or ribbon] on their shakos. On your departure your officers will show their mourning in your [sic] heart; and it will only end with your return amongst them. Let them hope that your absence will not last too long; that those whom you have declared yourself happy to command will not have to suffer too long - for you alone can lighten the grief which overcomes them. They no longer have Colbert to help them bear it...."

The letter from the NCOs expressed the same respect, in slightly more soldierly terms:

"We felt too honoured to be serving under your command not to be affected by the loss we have suffered through your removal from the unit. The assurance that you give us of your continuing interest lessens our sorrow but does not console us. The non-commissioned officers of your regiment beg you to believe in their gratitude and their devotion.

"If in this time of disaster the regiment has deserved any praise, it is because your presence supported it and your spirit animated it. In bad times as well as in victory they had your example to follow and to imitate. They cannot believe you must leave them; if obliged to believe it, they would be inconsolable. Give them hope that they may see you leading them again soon, and their happiness will equal the affection and the deep respect with which they sign themselves, General, your devoted subordinates."

For rallying to the returned Napoleon during the Hundred Days, Colbert was arrested on 20 November 1815 following the

second restoration of the Bourbon monarchy and government. He was sent into exile for more than six months. The letter which he sent on the day after his arrest suggests that in Edouard Colbert the confidence proper to an officer of light horse remained unshaken:

"I have been under arrest for 24 hours as a suspect, held in solitary confinement like a criminal. This, when I am doing my duty as a citizen with uncommon energy, when my exemplary behaviour should earn me the benevolence and the protection of the government ..."

General Colbert was kept in captivity at l'Abbaye for two months, and was only authorised to return to Paris in June 1816.

On 12 September 1815 the Eagle and banner of the Regiment were handed over to be destroyed. Soon afterwards the process of disbandment began; this would last until December, as the squadrons were dispersed and disbanded one by one.

On 9 November 1815 the Sub-Inspector of Reviews, Jean François Lignac, and the Maréchal de Camp, Count de Castries, presided over the disbanding of the 3rd Squadron at Castelsarrazin in the department of Tarn-et-Garonne. Present were six officers: Lieutenant Limbourg and 2nd Lieutenants Billard, Arnaud, Blandin, Larouvière and Duplan. Among the 86 rank and file were three sergeant-majors, six sergeants, three quartermasters, 18 corporals, four trumpeters, three farriers and 49 lancers.

On 16 November it was the turn of the 4th Squadron, disbanded at Grenade in the Haute-Garonne. At that time the squadron numbered five officers - Captain Salvetat and Lieutenants Rollin, Alliment, Arnaud and Lhotte - and 95 lancers.

Helmet worn by Colonel Armand de Briqueville (1785-1844) when he led the 20th Dragoons at the battle of Rocquencourt on 1 July 1815. (Private collection, France)

On 25 November the regimental staff and the 1st Squadron were drawn up in battle order on the Grandplace of Gignac, wearing their full dress uniforms for the last time. Like their comrades before them, they were informed of their disbandment with effect from 16 December. The inspectors worked meticulously and their reports are very detailed. The result of the preliminary review of the staff and 1st Squadron dated 20 November 1815 shows the following:

Officers - Staff	Present	Absent	Total
Colonel (Lt.General)		1	1
Major (Maréchal de camp)		1	1
Lieutenant-Colonel	1		1
Adjutant-Major	1		1
Sub-Adj.-Major	2		2
Quartermaster	1		1
Officier d'habillement	1		1
Lt.Quartermaster	1		1
St'd. bearer (2nd Lt)	1		1
Surgeon-Major	1		1
Assist.Surgeon-Major	1		1
Sub–Assist.S–M	1		1
Chef d'escadron	1	3★	4
Captain (1st Lt.)	2		2
2nd Lieutenant	3	2	5
Total	*17*	*7*	*24*

(★ Chef d'escadron de la Fargue was absent but rejoined the Regiment for its disbandment on 16 December.)

Troops - Staff	Present	Absent	Total
Sergeant-Major	1		1
Veterinary 1st Class	1	1	2
Veterinary 2nd Class	1		1
Trumpeter corporal	2		2
Master farrier	1		1
Master saddlemaker		1	1
Master armourer	1		1
Master tailor		1	1
Master bootmaker	1		1

Companies			
Sergeant-Major	5		5
Sergeant	11	1	12
Quartermaster	3		3
Corporal	16	1	17
Trumpeter	4		4
Farrier	3		3
Lancer	52	9	61
Enfants de troupe	2		2
Total	*104*	*14*	*118*

We read that the regimental non-commissioned staff - *Petit Etat-Major* - had three horses available, the two companies 83, and four troop horses were absent; officers' horses, being their private property, were not mentioned.

Of the 24 officers, twelve remained available for service, five were to be retired, one passed into the Gendarmerie, and six were absent.

From the total of 118 NCOs and troopers, 16 remained available for service, 15 passing into the Hussars of the Royal Guard and one into the Gendarmerie. Nine were to be retired, one was certified disabled and two were discharged as unfit; the rest were simply sent home. Since 18 June, 185 men had gone absent.

Grave of Hubert de Stuers (1789-1861) at Maastricht, Holland. This very able officer survived long service in the Dutch Indies after Waterloo, retiring as major-general and commander-in-chief. (Author's collection)

Grave of Captain Henricus Royen (1788-1859) at Naarden, Holland; a veteran of Russia, Saxony and the French campaign, he chose a career in the new Dutch army in March 1814. (Author's collection)

Whatever the feelings of ruined emperors sailing into exile and limping heroes turned off to beg, the bureaucrats had inventories to check and books to get signed off.... The regimental stores had 69 lancer caps, of which 41 were unusable; 67 cap covers (55 unusable); 69 lancer jackets (53 unusable); 67 epaulettes and aiguillettes (47 unusable); 54 riding cloaks (18 unusable); 66 pairs riding overalls (61 unusable); 40 pairs stable trousers (35 unusable); 52 stable jackets (all unusable), and 62 fatigue caps (58 unusable).

The usable surplus of all these items, together with the equipment and the saddlery, was to be distributed among the Hussars of the Royal Guard, the Gendarmerie and the Invalids or transferred to the military stores at Montpellier.

On 20 December 1815 the last existing squadron, the 2nd, was disbanded at Agen in the prefecture of Lot-et-Garonne; it then numbered seven officers and 117 rank and file.

On 1 October 1815 the Polish Squadron passed into Russian service, like their brothers-in-arms in 1814. The last trace of the Light Horse Lancers of the Imperial Guard had vanished from the army of France.

★　★　★

Paper lasts longer than regiments or empires, however; and the soldiers who fought with pen and ledger would be working for years on the battlefield of the regimental account books.

On 1 September 1817 Chef d'escadron Quartermaster Dufour, delegate of the Administrative Council of the Light Horse Lancers of the Former Guard, calculated that some former officers had still to receive back-pay for the time they had spent in Spain, viz:

Timmerman, Captain	420.39 fr.
Hannemann, 1st Lt.	807.96 fr.
le Sueur, 2nd Lt.	1,093.29 fr.
Thurot, Chef d'escadron	4,246.31 fr.

The tireless Dufour also calculated that 15 officers were entitled

(Opposite) Former Chef d'escadron de Tiecken (1777-1848) depicted wearing the uniform of a general officer of the new Belgian army, 1830. The sundering of Holland and Belgium into two independent monarchies separated his later career from that of his former comrades of the Red Lancers. (Private collection)

to an allowance of one month's pay awarded to the unit on the Emperor's birthday on 15 August 1812, received by the regimental council but never passed on to the officers, the funds having been used for general regimental expenses:

de Watteville, Chef d'escadron	500.00 fr.
Fallot, Sub-Adjutant Major	225.00 fr.
Steenis, Sub-Asst. A-M	133.33 fr.
van der Meulen, Captain	333.33 fr.
Timmerman, Captain	333.33 fr.
Sterke, Captain	333.33 fr.
Heshusius, 1st Lt.	225.00 fr.
Böcher, 1st Lt.	225.00 fr.
Mascheck [J.] H., 1st Lt.	225.00 fr.
Geubels, 2nd Lt.	200.00 fr.
van Doorn, 2nd Lt.	200.00 fr.
van Son, 2nd Lt.	200.00 fr.
Das, 2nd Lt.	200.00 fr.
van der Brugghen, 2nd Lt.	200.00 fr.
Fischer, 2nd Lt.	200.00 fr.

However, Dufour also calculated the debts which many of the officers had left outstanding at their tailors and other suppliers when leaving the country; and various unjustified expenses claims which others had been paid.... In fact, the Ministry of War was looking for ways not to pay the former officers, and even went so far as to try to reclaim money from former foreign officers, some of whom had died on the battlefield years before. Thus finally ended, with the closing of the books in 1820, the saga of the Red Lancers of Napoleon's Imperial Guard: in the manipulation of the account books by Chef d'escadron Dufour.

What became of them?

As we have seen, many officers of the Regiment were members of aristocratic families, and some of these families continued to play prominent roles in public affairs during the first half of the 19th century. Some of the veterans of the Red Lancers died young; others lived in gentlemanly obscurity; but many pursued careers in politics, in the army, or even in the arts. (The notes in Appendix III give fuller details.)

Charles Eugène de Lalaing d'Audenarde entered the Gardes du Corps under the First Restoration. He remained loyal when Napoleon returned, accompanying King Louis XVIII to Ghent in 1815. He would continue in a military career, and also became a Peer of France in 1837 and a Senator in 1852 under Napoleon III.

Guillaume Duranti, former page of King Louis of Holland, became a farmer and would preside over the agricultural committee of Aubigny. As mayor of Blancafort for twenty years he was appointed as deputy for the Cher department on 26 December 1852.

Nicolas Thurot, probably the most wounded member of the Regiment, would be mayor of Haguenau between 1820 and 1830.

Jean Guillaume Colins de Ham was present at the battle of Rocquencourt in July 1815. He took refuge in America, like many officers of the Empire, and reached the Bonapartist colony at Champ d'Asile, but did not stay for long. King Joseph, brother of Napoleon and former King of Spain, sent him to Vienna in an attempt to see the Duke of Reichstadt - the former King of Rome, Napoleon's son, who was being brought up by his maternal grandfather at the Austrian court; in the event the visit was forbidden. A socialist philispher, Colins de Ham wrote several works of which the first was entitled *On the Social Compact and Political Liberty Considered as a Moral Complement to Mankind*.

Among those who were retained in the army, Fortuné Prosper Brack became colonel of the 13th Mounted Chasseurs in 1830, and was later the commander of the Eure department. His name would be kept alive for generations by his manual on *Light Cavalry Outposts*.

Pierre David (Edouard) Colbert was forgiven after a few

Under the Second Empire a number of surviving veterans of the Imperial Guard were sought out for photography, posed in reconstructed uniforms of their old corps, some of which betrayed a more recent cut. Above, Veteran Dreux; right, Veteran Verlinde. (Photos Anne S.K.Brown Military Collection, Brown University Library, USA)

years, like many heroes of the Empire; he became ADC to the Duke of Nemours, and a Peer of France in 1832. He was wounded at the side of Marshal Mortier when the latter was killed by the assassin Fiechi's "infernal machine" in 1835.

Auguste Ambroise Colin de Verdière ended his career as commander of the Doubs department.

Ange François de Sourdis was killed as a colonel on 23 August 1823 near Granada in Spain, during France's intervention in the first of two Spanish civil wars fought before 1840.

Armand de Briqueville became colonel of the 20th Dragoons in 1815; on 1 July he fought at the head of his regiment at Rocquencourt, the last battle of the war, where he took three sabre cuts to the head (see photos on page 113). After a brief period in disgrace he re-entered public life, and was deputy for Cherbourg from 1827 to 1834.

Hubert de Stuers passed into the military service of the Netherlands after Waterloo; he ended his career as a major-general and commander of the Army of the Indies. He had been writing his memoirs, but his notes were lost in Russia; after the 1812 campaign he started recreating them. His son Victor de

Pierre J. Soufflot de Magny et de Palotte (1793-1893). Briefly a lieutenant in the Red Lancers in the 1815 campaign, he survived to be the senior living member of the Legion of Honour in 1893, his hundredth year. (Photo Bibliothèque Nationale de France, Paris)

Stuers consulted his father and his uncle, a former officer in the Guard infantry, when rewriting the memoirs, which remain unpublished.

Marie Michel de Tiecken became Baron de Tiecken de Terhove in 1847. After Belgium's independence he was appointed ADC to King Leopold I, and commanded the Army of the Scheldt during the Ten Days' Campaign against Holland in 1831.

Charles Marie Joseph Dubois – who was the brother-in-law of Colonel Achille de Deban de Laborde of the 8th Hussars killed at Wagram in 1809 – passed into the service of the Netherlands after the Hundred Days. He organised the 10th Lancers at Mechelen in 1819 as a copy of the Red Lancers (though with dark green and orange uniforms). He selected experienced officers from among the veterans of the Red Lancers, including de Tiecken, Royen, Eschweiler and de Bellefroid.

Jean François Dumonceau became a lieutenant-general in the Army of the Netherlands and would write his memoirs.

Karel Mergell, surgeon-major of the Regiment, became Inspector-General of the Health Service in the Army of the Netherlands in 1815; we have seen that he was present at Waterloo as head of the medical staff for I Mobile Corps. He became director of Leiden hospital in 1819.

Jan Post became a major-general in the Army of the Netherlands and commanded the 1st Cavalry Brigade from 1830. Henricus Royen also ended his career as a Netherlands major-general.

Walraven van Balveren became lieutenant-colonel of the

Netherlands 10th Lancers and colonel of the 6th Hussars. He had his head split by a sabre cut on 7 August 1830. He too became a major-general before his retirement.

Antonie van Omphal, also a Netherlands army major-general, was appointed adjutant to King William I. He wrote his memoirs, which have never been published. Arnaud van Zuylen van Nyevelt returned from captivity in Russia, and entered the service of the Netherlands. Posted to the Dutch Indies, he died there in 1821.

One veteran, Adjutant-NCO Friedrich Schroeder, became president of one of the societies of German veterans of the First Empire, at Oppenheim. Lancer Doublet, from Ghent, would have his name inscribed on the veterans' monument erected in the graveyard of St Amand. Corporal Christiaensen, a member of the Prévoyance (a society of Napoleonic veterans at Antwerp), wrote his memoirs and dedicated them to his fellow members.

The decades passed, and the Red Lancers disappeared one by one. Pierre Jules Soufflot, senior surviving member of Napoleon's Legion of Honour, died in June 1893 six months short of his hundredth birthday. Légionnaire Baptiste François Blondinot was still alive in 1895 at La-Mothe-St Héray; a veteran of Russia, Saxony, France and Waterloo, he was perhaps the last survivor. After that date no trace of him has been found.

Lancer motifs on the gravestone at Vienne, France, of Captain Marie-Charles Naudet, an officer of the Young Guard squadrons in 1813-1814. (Alain Chappet collection)

Grave of Vélite Woot de Trixhe, decorated for gallantry at Montmirail. Shortly before publication of this book the remains were removed to the chapel where members of the Woot de Jannée family are buried. (Author's collection)

From 23 April to 27 June 1827 a committee sat to consider a new model of weapon for issue to the lancer regiments which the British had formed shortly after the Napoleonic Wars as a result of their experience of facing the Emperor's cavalry. One example considered was that brought back from the field of Waterloo by Cavalié Mercer, the memoirist who commanded a Royal Horse Artillery battery in June 1815. He had given some comfort to a wounded Red Lancer, Clement of the 7th Company, who had given him his lance as a gesture of gratitude. This was the pattern approved by the committee on 24 February 1829.

BIBLIOGRAPHY

1. Archives:

NATIONAL ARCHIVES OF HOLLAND, The Hague: files Calkoen, Dumonceau, de la Fargue, and the Contrôles Nominatifs de la Garde Royale de la Royaume de Hollande.

ARCHIVES OF THE MUSÉE DE L'EMPÉRI, Collections Brunon, Salon-de-Provence, France

ARCHIVES OF THE ARMY HISTORICAL SERVICE, Vincennes, France

Files:

C2

167, Etats des pertes, Grande Armée de 1813

290, Correspondance de Davout du 28 avril au 5 octobre 1812

350, Relevé chronologique des mouvements de troupes du 3 janvier 1810 au 23 avril 1813

351, idem

352, idem

523, Grande Armée, organisation générale, feuilles d'appel, Garde Impériale 1812

525, Premier Corps, Davout, et troupes sous son commandement en 1812

533, Grande Armée, détachements de marche, dépôts, dépôt général de cavalerie 1812

534, idem

537, Organisation Garde Impériale de 1813

554, Organisation Garde Impériale de 1814

721, Registre de correspondance, commadant du dépôt de Hanovre 1813

C12

1, Itinéraires et emplacements des Q.G. et des troupes de 1805 - 1814

2, idem

3, idem

4, idem

5, idem

C15

34, Situation de la Garde Impériale en 1815

C17

189, Grande Armée, Ordres du jour du 10 avril au 8 décembre 1813

193, Décrets Impérials, correspondance du ministre, major-général 1815

20 Y c

Garde Impériale de an VII à 1815, état nominatif des troupes

161, 21 septembre 1810 à 7 mars 1813 (1 à 2004)

162, 9 mars 1813 à 21 juin 1814 (2005 à 2642)

163, Vélites, 21 août 1811 à 29 mars 1814 (1 à 545)

164, Escadrons de Lanciers, 26 janvier 1813 à 3 juillet 1814 (1 à 2421)

165, Corps Royal des Chevau-légers Lanciers de France du 21 juin 1814 au 20 mars 1815 (1 à 735)

166, Garde Impériale 1815, 8 avril 1815 au 22 décembre 1815 (1 Ö 1608)

2 Y b

Garde Impériale, état nominatif des officiers

86, Cavalerie de la Garde Hollandaise devenue Garde Impériale

87, 2e régiment de Chevau-légers Lanciers de la Garde Impériale

88, idem

X ab

42, 2e régiment de Chevau-légers Lanciers de la Garde Impériale

73, idem 1815

LIBRARY OF THE BELGIAN ROYAL ARMY MUSEUM, Brussels:
Fonds Jordens

LIBRARY OF THE DUTCH ROYAL ARMY MUSEUM, Delft:
Fonds de Wilde

LIBRARY OF THE DUTCH ARMY HISTORICAL SERVICE:
Memoirs of General van Omphal

2. Printed texts:

BERNAERT (F.), *Fastes Militaires des Belges au service de la France 1789-1815*, Bruxelles 1898

BOWDEN (Scott), *Napoleon's Grande Armée of 1813*, Chicago 1990

CALMON-MAISON (Marquis), *Le général Maison et le 1er Corps de la Grande Armée*

CHAPPET, MARTIN, PIGEARD, ROBE, *Répertoire mondial des Souvenirs Napoléoniens*, Paris 1993

FALLOU, *Histoire de la Garde Impériale*

GARROS (Louis), *Quel roman que ma vie*, Paris 1947

HOUSSAYE (Henri), *1814*

HOUSSAYE (Henri), *1815*

LACHOUQUE (Henry), *La Garde Impériale*, Paris 1956

LACHOUQUE (Henry), *Napoléon en 1814*, Paris 1959

LACHOUQUE (Henry), *Napoléon à Waterloo*, Paris 1965

LEMONCHOIS (Ed.), *Dictionnaire des Officiers du Consulat et de l'Empire, originaires du département de la Manche*

LENIENT (E.), *La solution des énigmes de Waterloo*, Paris 1915

MARTINIEN (Aristide), *Tableaux des officiers tués et blessés par corps et par batailles pendant les guerres de l'Empire (1805-1815)*, Paris 1984

NAFZIGER (George F.), *Napoleon's Invasion of Russia*, Novato, USA 1988

NAFZIGER (George F.), *Lutzen & Bautzen*, Chicago 1992

QUENNEVAT (Jean-Claude), *Atlas de la Grande Armée*, Bruxelles 1966

REMBOWSKI (Alex), *Sources documentaires concernant l'histoire des Chevau-légers Lanciers de la Garde de Napoléon*

RÉVÉREND (Vte A.), *Armorial du Premier Empire*, Paris 1974

SABRETACHE, Carnets de la, Paris, depuis 1893

SAVANT (Jean), *Les Mamelouks de Napoléon*, Paris

SCHUTTE (Otto), *De orde van de Unie*, The Hague 1985

SIX (Georges), *Dictionnaire biographique des généraux et amiraux français de la Révolution et de l'Empire (1792-1815)*, 2 vols., Paris 1934

SOCIÉTÉ BELGE D'ÉTUDES NAPOLÉONIENNES, Revue de la, Brussels, since 1951

SOUVENIR NAPOLÉONIEN (Le), Bulletin et revue, Nice & Paris, since 1948

TRANIÉ (J.) & CARMIGNIANI (J.-C.), *Les polonais de Napoléon*, Paris 1982

TRANIÉ (J.) & CARMIGNIANI (J.-C.), *La campagne de 1812*, Paris 1981

TULARD (Jean), *Dictionnaire Napoléon*, Paris 1989

VERHAEGEN (Paul), *La Belgique sous la Domination Française 1792-1814*, 5 vols., Brussels 1929

3. Biographies:

ALVILLE, *Un Suisse officier d'ordonnance de Napoléon, Albert de Watteville (1789-1812)*, Lausanne 1951

IMBAULT (Gaston), *Le général Nicolas Thurot (1773-1835)*, Moulins 1965

LAGRANGE (E.), *Les frères Laurillard-Fallot, souvenirs de deux officiers du temps de l'Empire*, Brussels 1904

THOUMAS, "Les Trois Colbert", *Revue de Cavalerie*, 3rd Year, vol. VI, Paris

WEITZEL (A.W.P.), "De generaal-majoor Jhr. Hubert ridder de Stuers", *De Militaire Spectator*, derde serie, zevende deel, Breda, 1862

4. Memoirs:

CHRISTIAENSEN, *De Lotgevallen van een Krijgsman*, Antwerp

PURAYE (Jean), *Mémoires du général comte François Dumonceau (1790-1830)*, 3 vols., Brussels 1958-1963

JOURQUIN (Jacques), *Souvenirs du commandant Parquin (1803-1814)*, Paris 1979

5. Catalogues:

GÉRICAULT, Musée des Beaux-Arts de Rouen, Rouen 1982

MUSÉE NATIONAL DU CHÂTEAU DE VERSAILLES, Les Peintures, 3 vols., 1995

NAPOLÉON, Grand Palais, Paris 1969

NAPOLÉON ET LA LÉGION D'HONNEUR, Paris 1968

SOUVENIR NAPOLÉONIEN À CHARLEROI (Le), Charleroi 1966

PORTRAITS FOR A KING, The British Military Paintings of A. J. Dubois-Brahonet (1791-1834), Spencer-Smith (Jenny), London 1990

APPENDIX I

A SOLDIER-PAINTER

On 30 August 1834 the painter Alexandre-Jean Dubois-Drahonet died at Versailles, not far from the old barracks of the regiment with which he had served under the Empire. This talented pupil of Jean-Baptiste Régnault (1754–1829) was born Alexandre-Jean Dubois in Paris on 23 December 1790; it was after his marriage to Caroline Drahonet that he began to sign his work with their joined names (he was certainly using this style by 1821 when he exhibited at the Salon de Bruxelles). By the time of his early death the painter was widely known for his portraits, both official commissions and more intimate studies. His work was distinguished by a mastery of light effects, by his taste for curves and counter-curves, and by a monumental style based on purity of line. Apart from portraits he also left architectural drawings, a few interior scenes of domestic life, and a large number of military subjects.

Alexandre-Jean Dubois entered the 2nd Light Horse Lancers of the Imperial Guard as a vélite – an officer candidate who paid for his place, and served as a ranker while fitting himself for an eventual commission. This must have been during the rapid rebuilding of the Regiment following its virtual destruction in Russia in 1812; and we know that the 22-year-old Dubois was promoted sergeant as early as 1 March 1813. One may wonder whether he owed this rapid promotion more to his prowess with a paintbrush than to his mastery of the sabre exercise: as early as 1812 he had shown his work in the Salon de Paris, and would continue to do so regularly until his death.

It is clear that his talent was noticed by the regimental officers of the 2nd Light Horse Lancers and by others in garrison at Versailles, where the sergeant of vélites had already set up a studio. Among the officers of the Red Lancers who commissioned him to paint their portraits we notice General Colbert himself, Chef d'escadron Schneither (in January 1814), and the ill-fated Captain Gauthier. Indeed, while the 1814 French campaign was raging and the Allied armies were converging on the capital, there was a constant traffic of senior officers to the studio of Maréchal des logis Dubois. After the completion of his own portrait General de Pully of the Guards of Honour took the painter with him to Paris.

It was while officially "on convalescence" in the capital after the First Restoration that Dubois was removed from the regimental muster roll of the Corps Royal de Chevau-légers Lanciers de France on 2 August 1814. Before his departure he painted Chef d'escadron Werner and Colonel-Major Baron Charles Dubois; the latter had commissioned a full-length portrait, and at his side we can recognize the second known self-portrait of the painter, wearing his vélite uniform and holding the colonel-major's horse (see page 82).

Enjoying a good reputation as a portrait painter in military circles, Dubois continued to receive a steady flow of commissions

Portait by Dubois-Drahonet of General Trip van Zoudtland (1776-1835) in the uniform of a general in the Dutch army. Colonel of the French 14th Cuirassiers 1810-1814, he fought in Russia - where he took a bullet in the head at the Beresina crossings - Saxony and France; but at Waterloo he commanded a Dutch cuirassier brigade of the Allied army. (Photo © Stichting Iconographisch Bureau, The Hague)

Dubois-Drahonet's full length portrait of General of Brigade Baron Gaspar Gourgaud (1783-1852), premier officier d'ordonnance to Napoleon in 1815. He followed the Emperor into exile and helped him write his memoirs; in this 1833 portrait he wears the uniform he wore on St Helena, and an impression of Longwood House can be seen in the background. (Photo © Réunion des Musées Nationaux, Paris)

after the Second Restoration. In 1816 he painted Surgeon-Major Guillaume Gervais Millet of the 2nd Cuirassiers of the Royal Guard; and in 1817 he immortalised the young Baron Laborde, wreathing the bust of his father killed at Wagram. It was not long before he was invited to go to the Netherlands to execute a number of official paintings. We do not know, but may presume that Dutch former regimental officers assisted him; it was during this period that he painted the portraits of François Dumonceau, former captain in the Red Lancers, and of Trip van Zoudtland, former colonel of the 14th Cuirassiers. After returning to France Dubois received his first Royal commissions; he painted the Duchesse de Berry in 1827, the Duc de Bordeaux in 1828, the Duc de Penthièvre and the Prince de Joinville.

In 1831 he received an important commission from King William IV of England, to paint a large series of studies of the uniforms of the British army reflecting the changes introduced after William's accession to the throne the previous year. This fascinating series of works (of which 97 are known, 92 of them in the Royal Collection) are not merely meticulous fashion plates, but attractive individual portraits of the officers, non-commissioned officers and private soldiers sent to model for him in his London studio. At a fee of seven guineas each, they occupied the painter until 1834. After returning to Versailles once more he was awarded a similar commission by King Louis-Philippe to record French uniforms; but he had only completed sixteen paintings by the time of his death later that same year.

Detail from Dubois-Drahonet's self-portrait in the background of the full length portrait of Colonel-Major Dubois (see page 82); on the pouch he has added IPSE F., "made by himself". (Château d'Ecaussines-Lalaing, Belgium)

APPENDIX II

LOSSES AMONG DUTCH PERSONNEL IN RUSSIA, 1812

A total of 1,086 Dutch Hussars were incorporated in the 2nd Light Horse Lancers of the Imperial Guard created in 1810. Subtracting those who left the regiment before 1812 by retirement, final leave or transfer to other regiments, 742 of these men were with the Regiment when it set out for Russia.

In addition to these, 102 men had been transferred from the Dutch 3rd Hussars in Spain when the 5th Squadron was created in spring 1812. Of these, 65 actually joined the 5th Squadron, the remainder being posted to various other regiments. In total, then, 807 Dutch Lancers took part in the Russian campaign. Of these, 514 would be killed or listed as missing, and 119 would be captured on Russian soil. The regiment's Dutch personnel thus suffered 633 casualties out of 807; only 174 managed to make their way back from Russia more or less fit - just over 21 per cent.

During the first two months of the campaign - July and August - losses were limited, with the exception of the detachment captured at Babinovitz. They increased during September when, on the march towards Feminskoï, the Regiment came into almost daily contact with the Cossacks. After they reached Moscow in mid-September the Lancers' casualties decreased significantly for the short duration of the *de facto* truce. Once the Grande Armée began its retreat in mid-October skirmishes with the Cossacks became frequent; and after the onset of snow, with temperatures eventually dropping below -30°C, the Lancers perished at an appalling rate during November and early December. After crossing the Russian-Prussian border in mid-December the survivors suffered only 15 further losses in two weeks; but by then, of course, total losses of more than 78 per cent had already effectively destroyed the Regiment.

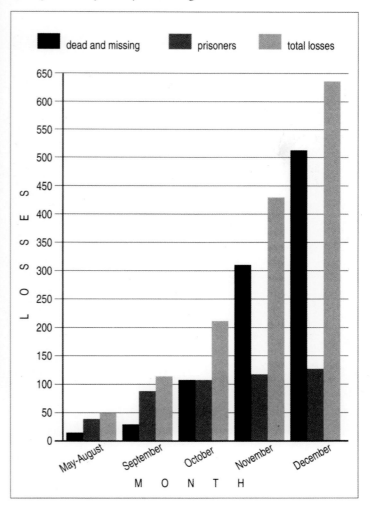

APPENDIX III

Muster Roll of the Officers of the
2nd Light Horse Lancers of the Imperial Guard
from 1810 until 1815

Garde Impériale.

2ᵐᵉ Régiment des Chevau-Légers-Lanciers.

ED. COLBERT, *Général de Brigade, Baron de l'Empire, Commandant de la Légion-d'Honneur, et de l'Ordre Militaire de Bavière, Colonel-Commandant le 2ᵉ Régiment des Chevau-Légers-Lanciers de la Garde Impériale.*

J'ai l'honneur de vous saluer

E. d. Colbert

Names are listed in alphabetical order; where the honorifics "de" and "van" occur the name is listed under the initial of the final surname; e.g. de Gienauth under G, d'Ham under H, de la Villasse d'Audibert under V, van der Linden under L, etc. Where the sources give Christian names in the archaic Latin form these are reproduced here.

Names printed in *italic CAPITALS* indicate those officers who were promoted into the corps but never actually took up their appointments. Comments on individuals' qualities or acts of bravery, printed in italics, are those recorded by commanding officers.

Dates are abbreviated in the European manner, e.g. 1/3/1814 = 1st March 1814; dates given simply as e.g. 11/1812 indicate e.g. "during month of November 1812". Where dates are illegible or conflicting dates are given in different sources they are given as e.g. 10?-20?/5/1812.

The information recorded in the Muster Roll is neither comprehensive nor always presented in a consistent fashion. The following abbreviations are used in this Appendix:

[b]	born
[s]	son of
[d]	died or killed
[p]	prisoner of war
[m]	missing
[a]	assigned to or appointed
[e]	entered or enlisted in (note that appointment and actual entry dates to units, military schools etc. often differed)
[e/v]	entered as volunteer
[pm]	promoted
[t>]	transferred to or passed into
[ds]	dismissed from service
[r]	retired

Ranks & appointments:
For clarity most of these are given in English translation.

Cpl	Corporal
QM	Quartermaster (*fourrier*, a corporal's appointment, unless officer rank indicated)
Sgt	Sergeant
SM	Sergeant-Major
S-M	Surgeon-Major
Adj-NCO	Adjutant (non-commissioned rank)

SLt	Sub-lieutenant
2nd Lt	Second lieutenant
(1st) Lt	Lieutenant
Lt-Capt	Lieutenant ranking as captain
Capt	Captain
Adj-M	Adjutant-Major (S-Adj-M = Sub-)
ADC	Aide-de-camp
Asst	Assistant (in title of staff appointment, e.g. sub-assistant surgeon-major, S-Asst S-M)
Cd'E	Chef d'escadron (squadron commander)
Maj	Major
Col-M	Colonel-Major
LtCol	Lieutenant-Colonel
Col	Colonel
Gen	General

Units & sub-units:
Most units are given here in their French form, e.g. "Chasseurs à cheval" rather than "Mounted Chasseurs" as in the narrative text. Specific abbreviations used here are as follows:

2e CLGI	2e Régiment de Chevau-légers Lanciers de la Garde Impériale (the Red Lancers)
CRCLF	Corps Royal de Chevau-légers Lanciers de France (Guard Lancers under First Restoration)
LGI	Lanciers de la Garde Impériale (composite Dutch & Polish Guard Lancer regiment during the Hundred Days, 1815)
Lanciers de Ligne	The corps of numbered Line Lancer regiments created in 1811 were not individually titled e.g. "3e Régiment de Chevau-légers Lanciers de Ligne", but we use the term here for clarity of distinction from the Guard Lancers.
Bn	Battalion
Cie, Co	Company
DB	Demi-brigade (infantry regiment - Revolutionary period term used in both French and Batavian armies)
Esc, Sqn	Squadron
Regt	Regiment

A

ALEXANDRE, Benoist Paul
[b] Charleville (Ardennes), 13/3/1794; [s] Thomas Camille A. & Jeanne Benoist Pierquet.
[a] St Germain Military School, by decree 23/4/1812, [e] 1/6/1812; [a] as SLt to 2e CLGI, 18/3/1813; [a] Lanciers de Ligne, 9/6/1814.
Wounds Wounded in skirmish near Liège, 27/1/1814.
Campaigns 1813, Saxony; 1814, France.

ALEXANDRE, Nicolas
[b] Hautteville (Manche), 9/7/1776; [s] Jean François A. & Cathérine Buhot; [d] of wounds, Dresden, 30/5/1813.
[e] Ecole de Mars, 1/6/1794; [a] secretary to Gen Mignotte, 5/11/1794. [a] Artillerie de la Marine, 21/6/1799; [pm] QM, 20/7/1800. [a] Grenadiers de la Marine de l'Armée d'Italie, 21/11/1800. SLt in 8e Dragons, 24/12/1800; [p] Wischau, 28/11/1802; returned to France, 1/1/1806. SLt in Grenadiers à cheval de la Garde Impériale, 1/1/1806. Lt S-Adj-M in Dragons de la Garde Impériale, 13/9/1806; [a] as Capt to 2e CLGI, 14/1/1813; reported to regt, 26/3/1813.
Wounds Mortally wounded at battle of Reichenbach, 22/5/1813.
Campaigns 1795-99, in the West; 1800, Italy; 1801, Armée d'Observation du Midi; 1805, Austria; 1808, Spain; 1809, Austria; 1810-12, Spain; 1813, Saxony.
Awards Legionnaire, Legion of Honour, 26/5/1808.

ALLIMANT, Antoine

[b] St Hippolyte (Haut-Rhin), 13/6/1773?-1774?; [s] George A. &
Catherine Kintzeule.

[e] 7e Chasseurs à cheval, 26/7/1792; [t>] Chasseurs à cheval de la Garde
Impériale, 28/3/1801; [pm] Cpl, 18/12/1805; Sgt, 1/2/1808; SLt,
6/12/1811; Lt, 27/2/1813. [t>] CRCLF, 5/8/1814; [a] LGI by decree,
14/4/1815. Proposed for retirement after Hundred Days; [ds]
16/11/1815.

*"On 21/2/1814 Allimant was on a reconnaissance between Arcis-sur-Aube and
Montereau with 17 Chasseurs à cheval of the Guard, where he took 64 prisoners of
whom two were officers; he also took 13 pontoons, two supply wagons, a caisson and
98 horses. Napoleon awarded him the Officer's Cross of the Legion of Honour."*

Wounds Bayonet wound to knee in the Vendée; bayonet wound to hip
when serving in Armée de l'Ouest; sabre cut to left hand at Austerlitz,
2/12/1805.

Campaigns 1792, Rhine; 1793, Armée d'Ouest; 1795-96, Sambre &
Meuse and Switzerland; 1797-98, Italy; 1799, Holland; 1803-04,
Boulogne; 1805, Austria; 1806-07, Prussia & Poland; 1808, Spain; 1809,
Austria; 1812, Russia; 1813, Saxony; 1814, France; 1815, Armée du
Nord.

ARNAUD, Bernard-Benoist

[b] Paris, 13/10/1777.

[e] 23e Chasseurs à cheval, 10/2/1799 to 21/1/1803. [t>] Dragons de
Paris, 27/7/1803; [pm] Cpl, 30/7/1806; Sgt, 1/12/1809; SM, 8/2/1811;
SLt, 1/7/1812. [a] as SLt to 2e CLGI, Young Guard, by decree
18/3/1813; [t>] CRCLF, 2/8/1814; [a] LGI, by decree 14/4/1815.
Proposed for retirement after Hundred Days; [ds] 9/11/1815.

Campaigns 1798-99, Rhine; 1805, Armée du Nord; 1813, Saxony;
1814, served under Gen Maison; 1815, Armée du Nord.

Awards Legionnaire, Legion of Honour, 29/11/1813.

ARNAUD, Pierre

[b] Pouilly-le-Monial (Rhône), 31/10/1771; [s] Mathieu A., vinegrower,
& Antoinette Demathieu.

[e] 8e Régiment de Cavalerie, 29/1/1794; [t>] Garde des Consuls,
29/11/1799; Grenadier à cheval de la Garde des Consuls, 3/1/1800; [pm]
Cpl, 25/11/1802. [t>] Dragons de la Garde Impériale, 26/7/1806; Sgt,
13/7/1807; SLt, by decree 18/1/1813. [a] CRCLF, 2/8/1814; [a] LGI, by
decree 14/4/1815. Proposed for retirement, 16/11/1815; [r] 23/3/1816.

Campaigns 1793-1804, Coasts; 1805-07, Prussia & Poland; 1808, Spain;
1809, Austria; 1813, Saxony; 1814, served under Gen Maison.

Awards Legionnaire, Legion of Honour, 1/5/1806.

ARNOULD, Adrien Cyprien

[b] Paris, 30/12/1786. Studied at Fontainebleu Military School; [a] as SLt
to 17e Dragons, 10/10/1806. Lt, 20/9/1809; Capt, 27/4/1811; Cd'E in
the Line and Capt in 2e CLGI, by decree 18/3/1813; being at Danzig, he
was unable to join his regiment.

*"He distinguished himself in Spain on 23/3/1811: while on a reconnaissance in
front of Coluin he killed a captain and two troopers, and for this action he was
promoted captain."*

Campaigns 1807, Grande Armée; 1808-12, Spain; 1813, Saxony.

D'ASBONNE, Abdallah

[b] Bethlehem (Syria), 26/10/1776; [d] Melun (Seine-et-Marne), 22/11/
1859. Scout and translator to General Staff of Armée d'Orient, 2/8/1798;
[t>] Corps des Janissaires Syriens, 25/3/1800. SLt, Mamelukes de la
Garde des Consuls, 15/4/1802; 2nd Lt, 18/12/1805; Cd'E, Capt-
instructor, 27/2/1811. [t>] as Cd'E into CRCLF, 5/8/1814; [a] LGI by
decree 14/4/1815. Returned with other Mamelukes to Chasseurs à cheval
de la Garde Impériale; on sick leave, Paris, 1/7/1815; removed from
muster roll, 22/12/1815; [r] 10/1828.

Returned to active service, [a] as orderly officer to Gen Boyer,

19/10/1831; commander of Place d'Arzew, Algeria, 9/9/1833;
commander of a native corps, 19/1/1834; French consul, Mascara,
23/3/1834; recalled by Gen Frésel, 24/6/1835; commander of Arzew
until 27/8/1835; [r] 24/9/1836.

"He saved the life of Col Kirmann on 28/9/1813 at the battle of Altenburg".

Wounds etc. Bullet in belly at Heliopolis, where his horse was killed;
broken arm at Eylau when horse killed; seven sabre cuts and horse killed,
Golymin, 25/12/1806; horse killed, Dresden, 23/8/1813; bruised by
cannonball which killed his horse, 28/9/1813; lance wound to chest,
Altenburg; lance wound, Weimar, 28/10/1813; bullet wound and horse
killed, Hanau; horse killed, Brienne, 1814. In Algeria, kept prisoner for a
day, 26/6/1835; wounded in shoulder, Macta, 28/6/1835.

Awards Legionnaire, Legion of Honour, 14/6/1804; Knight, Order of
the Reunion, 27/2/1814; Knight, Military Order of St Louis, 27/2/1815;
Officer, Legion of Honour, 9/8/1832.

D'ASSIER, Jean Joseph

[b] St Victor-sur-Loire (Loire), 3/10/1793; [s] Pierre Christophe d'A. &
Catherine Henriette de Larochette.

[a] St Germain Military School, by decree 23/6/1812, [e] 2/7/1812; [a] as
SLt to 2e CLGI, by decree 18/3/1813. Left for the army, 30/4/1813;
crossed Rhine, 4/5/1813; [p] 18/10/1813. Resigned and returned to his
home, 30/9/1814.

Wounds Lost left leg at battle of Leipzig, 16/10/1813.

Campaigns 1813, Saxony.

Awards Legionnaire, Legion of Honour, 24/11/1814.

B

BALINSKI, ?

Polish Lancer of Imperial Guard; member of Napoleon's Elba squadron,
1814-15; [pm] Cd'E in LGI, by decree 14/4/1815. [e] Russian Army,
1/10/1815.

VAN BALVEREN, Walraven Elias Johan, Baron, Lord of Echteld and Leur

[b] Leur, 17/11/1784; [s] Christiaan Hendrik Wilhelm Ernst v B., Lord
of Leur, & Wilhelmina Johanna Lubina, Baroness of Friedach; [d] Echteld,
12/8/1865.

[e] Dutch Army Engineers as apprentice, 1/9/1800; [t>] as cadet into 2nd
Dragoons, 29/9/1803; [pm] 2nd Lt in Dragons de la Garde du Grand
Pensionnaire, 28/6/1805; Lt, Horse Grenadiers of Royal Guard,
11/12/1806; Capt-instructor, Cuirassiers, 1/5/1807 (regt became
Régiment des Gardes à cheval, 1808, & Régiment Garde Cavalerie,
1809); [t>] 2e CLGI, 30/10/1810. Took part, at his request, in Russian
campaign, 1812; left regt without permission, 31/3/1814; resignation
accepted, [t>] Dutch Army, 1814.

Titular Maj, Dutch 6th Hussars, 30/4/1814; present at Waterloo,
1815; LtCol, 10th Lancers, 19/2/1819; [t>] 8th Hussars, 22/2/1820;
adjutant to King of Holland, 8/9/1820 to 1826; Col, 6th Hussars,
20/12/1826; served under Prince Frederick in 1830 as commander of
Hussars of Boreel; wounded at battle of Krempt, 7/8/1830; MajGen,
13/2/1840.

"A very good officer, serving with distinction, who knows his job very well."

Campaigns 1805, Germany; 1806, Prussia; 1812, Russia; 1813, Saxony;
1814, France.

Awards Legionnaire, Legion of Honour, 5/4/1814; Knight, Order of the
Union, 25/11/1807; Knight, Order of the Reunion, 7/3/1812; Knight,
Military Order of William, 4th Class, 24/11/1816; 3rd Class, 31/8/1831;
Knight, Order of the Netherlands Lion, 29/7/1831.

BARBIER D'AUCOURT, Philippe Armand

[b] Amiens (Somme), 14/11/1794; [s] François B d'A., Référendaire près
du sceau des titres, & Adélaâde Marie Victoire Berthe; [d] in battle,
Leipzig, 18/10/1813.

[a] from Amiens Lyceum to St Germain Military School, by decree 11/11/1811, [e] 15/12/1811; [a] as SLt to 2e CLGI, by decree 18/3/1813.

Cd'E Petiet said of him: *"This officer serves badly; the only thing he has learned is the grotesque manners of the soldier's life. He loves to sleep, always walks around in slippers when on outpost duty, is drunk most of the time, and beats the peasants."*

Campaigns 1813, Saxony.

BARNIER, Daniel
[b] Poyols (Drome), 12/11/1769.
Capt in Spanish Royal Guard, 13/6/1809; [t>] Young Guard squadrons of 2e CLGI, 1/2/1814; left for Angers, 30/3/1814; [a] 3e Lanciers de Ligne, 9/6/1814.
Campaigns 1814, France.
Awards Legionnaire, Legion of Honour, 3/4/1814.

BARRAS, Eugène
[b] Mons (Jemmapes), 4/3/1779; [s] Eugène B. & Marie Thérèse Garoise; [d] 14/3/1814.
[a] from Spanish Royal Guard as 2nd Lt to 2e CLGI, 1/2/1814; killed while escorting Russian prisoners, 14/3/1814 (confirmed, 20/1/1836).
Campaigns 1814, France.

BARTH, ?
Asst S-M in military hospitals of the Grande Armée; S-Asst S-M in 2e CLGI, Old Guard, by decree 26/5/1813; reported to army, 1/9/1813; left regt without permission, 31/3/1814.
Campaigns 1813, Saxony; 1814, France.
Awards Knight, Order of the Reunion, 3/4/1814.

BAUMAN, Franciscus
[b] Amsterdam, 2 /3/1779; [s] François B. & Marie Waltz.
[e] Batavian Hussars, 11/9/1801; [t>] Dutch Royal Guard, 15/7/1805; [pm] Cpl, 15/2/1807; QM, 9/9/1809. [a] as Sgt to 2e CLGI, 21/9/1810; Lt, 18/3/1813. Passed after Napoleon's first abdication into Dutch Hussars, 21/1/1815; [r] 8/3/1816.
Campaigns 1806-07, Prussia; 1809, Brabant; 1812, Russia; 1813, Saxony; 1814, France.
Awards Order of the Lily, 4/5/1814.

BAZIN, Denis François Hypolite
[b] Fontenay-aux-Roses (Seine), 2/1/1793; [s] Louis François Barthelemi B. & Magdelaine Grivot.
[a] as Vélite to 2e CLGI, 21/4/1812; QM; [pm] 2nd Lt, by decree 6/1/1814; [a] 6e Lanciers de Ligne, 6/6/1814.
Campaigns 1813, Saxony; 1814, France.

DE BELLEFROID, Jacobus Philippus
[b] Goor, 4/2/1788?-90?; [s] Philippus Jacobus de B., retired Capt, & Isabelle Elisabeth Joanna, Baroness of Westerholt; [d] 16/1/1817.
[e] Dutch Navy as cadet, 3/2/1804; [t>] as cadet-NCO into Grenadiers of the Dutch Royal Guard, 29/1/1807; [pm] Sgt, 13/8/1807; [pm] as SLt into 2nd Hussars, 3/7/1808; [t>] with rank into cavalry of Dutch Royal Guard, 6/10/1809; [t>] as Lt into 2e CLGI, 30/10/1810. Lt S-Adj-M in Old Guard, 18/3/1813; left for Holland, 16/6/1814; resignation accepted, 30/7/1814. [e] Dutch Army as Capt of Hussars, 18/9/1814; ADC to Gen van Merlen at Waterloo.
"A good officer, still young."
Campaigns 1809, Brabant; 1812, Russia; 1813, Saxony; 1814, France.
Awards Legionnaire, Legion of Honour, 14/4/1813; Knight, Order of the Reunion, 3/4/1814; Knight, Military Order of William, 4th Class, 18/6/1815.

BERNARD, François
SLt in 8e Hussards, 30/12/1802; [a] 4e Hussards, 11/3/1803; [pm] Lt, 24/1/1807; [a] ADC to Gen Soult, 12/1/1808; Capt, 15/8/1811; [a] ADC to Gen Dumas, 12/3/1812; [pm] Capt into 2e CLGI, 18/7/1813, but also [pm] Cd'E in 11e Hussards, 16/7/1813 - preferred to join latter.

BERNET, Thomas
[b] St Flour (Cantal), 23/5/1787.
[e/v] 11e Hussards (later became 29e Dragons, finally 6e Lanciers de Ligne), 4/5/1802; [pm] Cpl, 24/7/1806; QM, 1/4/1807; SM, 23/5/1809; SLt, 2/9/1812; Lt, 28/9/1813. [a] with rank into LGI, 19/5/1815; commanded company of Young Guard squadron, 22/5/1815.
Campaigns 1805-06 & 1809, Italy & Naples; 1812, Russia; 1813, Saxony; 1814, France.
Awards Legionnaire, Legion of Honour, 28/9/1813.

BERTHAUT, Evrard Henri (Jacques Eugène)
[b] Rocroi (Ardennes), 27/1/1783; [s] Jacques B., Knight, Military Order of St Louis, & Philippine Renard.
[e] 1er Chasseurs à cheval, 1/3/1800; [pm] QM, 9/4/1802; Sgt, 28/5/1803; SM, 22/11/1806; SLt, 21/3/1807; Lt, 7/4/1809; Adj-M, 12/8/1809; Capt, 12/2/1811; [pm] Capt into 2e CLGI, Young Guard, by decree 18/3/1813; [a] 4e Lanciers de Ligne, 10/6/1814.
Wounds Bullet wound during a reconnaissance, 11/4/1813.
Campaigns 1799-1800; 1803-05; 1806-07, 1809; 1813, Saxony; 1814, France.
Awards Legionnaire, Legion of Honour, 1/10/1807.

BERTHOLET, Léopold
[b] Paris, 14/2/1776.
[a] from Spanish Royal Guard as Capt into 2e CLGI, Young Guard, 1/2/1814. Left for Angers, 3/1814; [a] 5e Lanciers de Ligne, 6/6/1814.
Campaigns 1814, France.
Awards Legionnaire, Legion of Honour, 3/4/1814.

BIDAULT-CORNESSE, Jean Baptiste
[b] Laval (Mayenne), 15/1/1793; [s] Jean Nicolas B-C. & Renée Amboise Duchemin Morinière.
[a] St Germain Military School, by decree 9/9/1811, [e] 24/10/1811; [a] as SLt to 2e CLGI, by decree 18/3/1813. Left for Angers, 3/1814; [a] 4e Lanciers de Ligne, 10/6/1814.
Campaigns 1813, Saxony; 1814, France.

BILLARD, Jean Pierre
[b] St Pierre-de-Cormeilles (Eure), 30/8/1766; [s] Jean B. & Catherine Lefèvre.
[e] 11e Régiment de Cavalerie, 17/12/1786; [t>] Chasseurs à cheval de la Garde des Consuls, 17/11/1800; [pm] Cpl, 15/10/1802; Sgt of Vélites, 18/12/1805; 2nd Lt, 27/2/1813. [a] CRCLF, 5/8/1814; [a] LGI, by decree 14/4/1815; [ds] 9/11/1815.
Wounds Two sabre cuts to arm, Kikeback, 1793; bullet wound to left leg, Wissembourg, 1794; wounded at Waterloo, 18/6/1815.
Campaigns 1792, Rhine; 1793, Moselle; 1794-96, Rhine; 1797-98, Italy; 1800, Naples; 1803-04, Coasts; 1805, Austria; 1806, Prussia; 1807, Poland; 1808, Spain; 1809, Austria; 1812, Russia; 1813, Saxony; 1814, France; 1815, Armée du Nord.
Awards Legionnaire, Legion of Honour, 14/3/1806.

BISIAUX, Auguste
[b] Valenciennes (Nord), 14/7/1790; [s] Augustin B. & Marie Anne Caniet.
[e] 5e Dragons, 26/7/1809; [pm] Cpl, 2/8/1810; QM, 15/12/1810; [a] 2e CLGI, 12/3/1812. [t>] Grenadiers à cheval de la Garde Impériale, 2/4/1812; Cpl, 20/7/1812; Sgt into 2e CLGI, 20/1/1813; SM,

12/2/1813. Adj-NCO, with rank of SLt, in CRCLF, 2/8/1814; 2nd Lt, 10/2/1815. [a] Supernumerary 2nd Lt in LGI, by decree 14/4/1815; Lt, S-Adj-M by decree, 22/5/1815; [ds] 16/12/1815.
Wounds Wounded several times at Reichenbach, 22/5/1813; slight bullet wound to right foot, 1814; wound to right arm, Waterloo, 18/6/1815.
Campaigns 1809, Nord; 1813, Saxony; 1814, France; 1815, Armée du Nord.
Awards Legionnaire, Legion of Honour, 16/8/1813.

BLANDIN, Jacques
[b] Ledèvre (Côte-d'Or), 2/2/1773; [s] Cir B. & Jeannette Ragait.
[e] 10e Chasseurs à cheval, 24/8/1792; [a] Chasseurs à cheval de la Garde des Consuls, 31/3/1800; [pm] Cpl, 15/10/1802; Sgt, 18/12/1805; [t>] Vélites, 1/8/1806; SM instructor on regimental staff, 21/8/1809; 2nd Lt, 25/1/1813; [t>] CRCLF, 5/8/1814. [a] LGI, by decree 14/4/1815; proposed for retirement after Hundred Days; [ds] 9/11/1815.
Wounds Sabre cut to left arm, Lautensburg, 1794; canister shot wound to right arm, Eylau, 8/2/1807.
Campaigns 1793-95, Rhine; 1796-99, Italy; 1803-04, Austria; 1806, Prussia; 1807, Poland; 1808, Spain; 1809, Austria; 1812, Russia; 1813, Saxony; 1814, France; 1815, Armée du Nord.
Awards Legionnaire, Legion of Honour, 31/8/1805.

BÖCHER, Bartel Sijtses
[b] Bergen-op-Zoom, 16/9/1778; [s] Johannes B. & Anna Stimrica; [d] 16/4/1819.
[e] Dutch 1st Cavalry Regt as cadet, 18/2/1796; [pm] 2nd Lt, 19/8/1802; [t>] Cuirassiers of Dutch Royal Guard, 26/10/1806; Lt, 3/9/1809; [a] 2e CLGI, 30/10/1810. Left Fulda 14/2/1813, arrived Versailles 24/2/1813. Fell behind on 18/5/1813; claimed to have returned to regt - on 1/6/1813 he was believed killed or taken prisoner, but on 1/7/1813 he was recorded as *"in the army without mutation"*. Resigned, 29/9/1814; Capt in Dutch Army, 2/9/1815; with Army of the Indies, 31/12/1816.
"An old soldier who knows the routine of military life."
Wounds Wounded at Reichenbach, 22/5/1813.
Campaigns 1799, Holland; 1800-06, Germany; 1812, Russia; 1813, Saxony.
Awards Legionnaire, Legion of Honour, 14/4/1813.

BOCKENHEIM, Nicolas
[b] Bambiderstroff (Moselle), 19/5/1774.
Famous in the Chasseurs à cheval de la Garde Impériale, this surgeon-major served first in the Légion Maltaise, then with the Dromadaires, and was medical officer in the Mameluke squadron. S-M in CRCLF, 16/2/1815; S-M in LGI, by decree 14/4/1815; [ds] 16/12/1815.
Awards Legionnaire, Legion of Honour, 1806.

BONTEMPS, Louis
[b] Berville (Seine-et-Oise), 24/12/1775.
[e] 22e Régiment de Cavalerie, 1/12/1793; [t>] 24e Dragons, 24/1/1794; [pm] Cpl, 16/1/1799; Sgt, 5/11/1800; [a] Dragons de la Garde de Paris, 23/7/1806; [pm] Cpl, 13/7/1807; Sgt, 22/10/1808; Lt into 11e Cuirassiers, 8/2/1813. [a] Lt in 2e CLGI, by decree 18/3/1813; [a] 4e Lanciers de Ligne, 10/6/1814.
Campaigns 1793-1800; 1805, Austria; 1806, Prussia; 1807, Poland; 1808, Spain; 1809, Austria; 1813, Saxony; 1814, France.

BOSC, François Joseph Alexandre
[b] Nîmes (Gard), 2/3/1772; [d] 1/2/1819.
[e] Army, 30/1/1790; married Marie Joséphine Paschale Lapeyre, 21/1/1803, when Lt in 25e Chasseurs à cheval; Maj in Line cavalry, by decree 19/3/1813; [a] from Spanish Royal Guard as Cd'E to 2e CLGI, Young Guard, 1/2/1814. [t>] as Maj into CRCLF; [a] 4e Lanciers de Ligne, 10/6/1814; [r] 28/7/1814.

Campaigns 1814, France.
Awards Knight, Order of the Reunion, 3/4/1814.

BOUCHARDON, Etienne
[b] Montaigut (Puy-de-Dôme), 16/10/1781.
[e] 25e Chasseurs à cheval, 23/4/1801; [pm] Cpl, 2/10/1802; [a] Light Horse of Royal Guard of King of Naples (later became King of Spain), 1/8/1806; Sgt, 29/3/1808; SM, 1/11/1809; SLt, 1/7/1813; [t>] as 2nd Lt into 2e CLGI, 1/2/1814; [a] 4e Lanciers de Ligne, 10/6/1814.
Campaigns 1800-04, Italy; 1805-07, Naples; 1808-13, Spain; 1814, France.
Awards Legionnaire, Legion of Honour, 3/4/1814.

BOUDGOUT, Jacques (Jean) Marie
[b] Vitry-sur-Seine (Seine), 10/5/1776.
[a] as Sgt to 5e Bataillon du Panthéon français, 19/2/1793; [a] 11e Chasseurs à cheval, 9/3/1797; [pm] Cpl, 4/3/1801; Sgt, 22/12/1802; [a] Light Horse of Royal Guard of King of Naples, 1/8/1806; SLt, 10/7/1810; [a] from Spanish Royal Guard to 2e CLGI, 1/2/1814. At Angers, 6/7/1814; in military hospital, 9/7/1814; [a] CRCLF, 2/8/1814; [a] LGI, by decree 14/4/1815; proposed for retirement after Hundred Days; [ds] 16/12/1815.
Wounds Three separate wounds to left leg; bullet wound to belly, Manheim, 1795; bruised by bullet, Mondovi, 1798; bullet wound to right leg at crossing of the Tagliamento, 1802; bullet wound, Waterloo, 18/6/1815.
Campaigns 1793-95, Rhine; 1796, eastern Italy; 1797-1806, Naples; 1808-13, Spain; 1814, France; 1815, Armée du Nord.
Awards Legionnaire, Legion of Honour, 3/4/1814; Knight, Royal Order of Spain, 21/1/1809.

BOURDEAU, Martial Camille
[b] Limoges (Haute-Vienne), 26/12/1793; [s] Joseph B. & Joséphine Rossignon.
[a] St Germain Military School, by decree 11/5/1812, [e] 15/6/1812; [a] as SLt to 2e CLGI, by decree 18/3/1813; [a] 4e Lanciers de Ligne, 10/6/1814.
Campaigns 1813, Saxony; 1814, France.

DE BOUTECHOUX DE CHAVANNES, Count Albert Jérôme Joseph
[b] Montreuil-sur-Mer (Pas-de-Calais), 16/10/1793; [s] Count Guillaume Marguerite de B. de C., Seigneur de Villette de Montigny-les-Arsures, & Marie Louise Charlotte Croeser.
[a] St Germain Military School, by decree 23/6/1812, [e] 27/12/1813; [a] as SLt to 2e CLGI, by decree 19/2/1814. [a] 2e Lanciers de Ligne, 24/6/1814; [r] from military service, 1822, with rank of Adj-M in 1er Cuirassiers de la Garde Royale.
Campaigns 1814, France.

BRACK, Fortuné Prosper
[b] Paris (Eure), 8/4/1789; [s] of Directeur des douanes at Genua under the Empire, & Laure Coquet de Trayzèle; [d] Evreux, 21/1/1850.
[e] Prytanée de Paris, later Imperial Lyceum, 1802; [e] Fontainebleu Special Military School as cadet, 30/12/1806; left as one of the most promising pupils, 4/3/1807, [a] at Col Colbert's request to 7e Hussards. [pm] SLt, 9/4/1807; Lt, ADC to Gen Colbert, 29/4/1809; Capt, ADC, 3/3/1813; [a] 2e CLGI, by decree 10/8/1813. [t>] CRCLF, 2/8/1814; [a] LGI, by decree 14/4/1815. On leave from 1/11/1815; [ds] 16/11/1815.
  Col, 13e Chasseurs à cheval, 11/9/1830; Col, 4e Hussards, 5/1/1832; Maréchal de camp, 24/8/1838; commandant, Military Cavalry School, 2/9/1838; left after suffering stroke, 19/11/1840; commanded Department of Eure, 28/11/1840; [r] 8/6/1848.

Campaigns 1807, Poland; 1809, Austria; 1812, Russia; 1813, Saxony; 1814, France.
Awards Legionnaire, Legion of Honour, 21/9/1809; Officer, 24/11/1814; Knight, Military Order of St Louis, 27/2/1815.

BREEDENBACH, Reinhart
[b] Friedberg, near Frankfurt, 27/11/1780; [s] Gaspar Diederich B., merchant, & Maria Catharina Snold.
[e] Batavian Dragoons, 23/10/1799; [pm] Cpl, 20/5/1801; Sgt, 14/12/1803; SM, 26/8/1806; Lt, 26/2/1807; [a] as 2nd Lt into 2e CLGI, 30/10/1810. Left for Russia, 10/2/1812; crossed Rhine, 12/3/1812. Left for Angers, 3/1814; left for Holland, 26/6/1814; resignation accepted, 30/7/1814.
Campaigns 1801 & 1805-06, Germany; 1808, Coasts; 1812, Russia; 1813, Saxony; 1814, France.

BREPOELS, Matthias Jacobus
[b] Breda, baptised 5/11/1786; [s] Wynandus B., LtCol in Dutch Royal Guard, who died Madrid 29/1/1810, & Johanna Maria Cornelissen; [d] in captivity 1813.
[e] Dutch 1st Cavalry Regt as cadet, 17/5/1799; [r] 20/12/1804; returned to Army, [a] 2nd Hussars, 1/12/1805; [pm] QM, 6/1/1807; Sgt, 14/3/1807; Lt Adj, 4/6/1808; [t>] with rank into cavalry of Dutch Royal Guard, 6/10/1809. [a] as 2nd Lt to 2e CLGI, 30/10/1810; Lt, S-Adj-M in Old Guard, 18/3/1813.
"The colonel recommends this officer for the post of adjutant to replace Lt Spies [qv], who is not equal to this job although a good officer at company level."
Wounds Wounded and captured at battle of Leipzig, 18/10/1813.
Campaigns 1807, Germany; 1809, Brabant; 1812, Russia; 1813, Saxony.
Awards Legionnaire, Legion of Honour, 14/4/1813.

BRIOT, François Félix
[b] L'Isle-sur-le-Doubs (Doubs), 25/6/1792; [s] Hugeus François B. & Jeanne Françoise Félix Didelot.
[a] St Germain Military School, by decree 12/12/1811, [e] 1/2/1812; [a] as SLt to 2e CLGI, by decree 18/3/1813; [a] 4e Lanciers de Ligne, 10/6/1814.
Campaigns 1813, Saxony; 1814, France.

DE BRIQUEVILLE, Armand François Bon Claude, Count
[b] Bretteville (Manche), 23/1/1785; [s] François Claude Marie de B., former Royalist officer executed by Republicans, & Françoise Renée Carbonnel de Canisy (his mother remarried Adrien de Lézai-Marnézia, Prefect of the Bas-Rhin Department); [d] Paris, 19/3/1844.
[e] Fontainebleu Military School, 21/7/1804. Lt, ADC to Gen Lebrun, 12/3/1807 (& later to the Emperor). Capt-Asst with General Staff of Armée du Portugal, 24/4/1810; Capt, ADC to Gen Lebrun, 25/2/1812; Chef de bataillon, 3/10/1812; LtCol, 20/6/1813; [a] 2e CLGI, 18/7/1813. On sick leave from 31/5/1814 with permission of Minister of War; [t>] CRCLF, 2/8/1814; Col, 20e Dragons, 2/4/1815; placed on inactive list without pay, 12/1815. Deputy for Cherbourg, 1827-34; Col, 2e Hussards, 13/11/1830.
Wounds Bullet wound, Sarpi (Golf of Policarto), where mentiond for good conduct; bullet wound at Krasnoï during retreat from Russia under Marshal Ney; several sabre cuts to head, arm, hand and waist at Rocquencourt, 1/7/1815.
Campaigns 1805-06, Armies of Italy, Naples & Calabria; 1807, Armée de Naples, Prussia & Poland; 1808-11, Spain & Portugal; 1812, Russia; 1813, Saxony; 1814, served under Gen Maison.
Awards Annuity of 2,000 francs drawn on Trasimène, 15/8/1809; Legionnaire, Legion of Honour, 6/4/1811; Officer, 27/4/1814; Commander, Legion of Honour.

BROUSSE, Jean Baptiste
[b] Nîmes (Gard), 7/5/1768; [s] Mathieu B., Capt of town guard, & Louise Pélegrin; [d] Blois (Loire-et-Cher), 4/6/1834.
Dragoon in Chartres-Dragons (from 1791, 14e Dragons) on 24/11/1785; QM, 4/2/1789. Capt, 2e Bataillon de Volontaires du Gard, 25/9/1793; Cpl, Guides des Pyrénées Orientales, 10/1/1794; QM, 11/12/1794; SLt, Corps des Hussards des Alpes, 31/1/1795; Lt QM, 20/3/1795 (from 1/9/1795, this regt became 13e Hussards). [t>] 7e bis Hussards, 16/5/1796; Capt, 27/6/1798; [pm] temporary Cd'E by C-in-C Armée de Naples, 30/6/1799 (confirmed 2/1/1801). 28e Dragons formed from 7e bis Hussards, 24/9/1803; authorised to pass into service of King of Naples, as Maj of Light Horse of Royal Guard, 30/9/1806; followed king to Spain, 1808; Col, Light Horse of Spanish Royal Guard, 19/11/1810; authorised to remain in service of Spain, 1/3/1813; [t>] French Army as supernumerary Col, 2e CLGI, 1/2/1814. Left for Angers, 30/3/1814; placed on inactive list, 22/12/1814; [a] Corps Royal des Cuirassiers de France, 5/1/1815; remained at depot during Hundred Days; [ds] with Armée of the Loire, [r] 1/1/1818. Became director of stud farm at Blois.
Wounds Bullet wound to right leg during trench fighting, Villelongue, 2/11/1793; wounded by explosion at battle of La Trebbie, 19/6/1799.
Campaigns 1793, Armée des Pyrénées Orientales; 1796-99, Italy & Naples; 1805, Italy; 1806, Naples; 1808-13, Spain; 1814, France.
Awards Legionnaire, Legion of Honour, 14/6/1804; Officer, 1/9/1814; Knight, Military Order of St Louis, 14/11/1814; Knight, Royal Order of the Two Sicilies, 8/5/1808; Commander, 19/6/1808; Knight, Royal Order of Spain, 25/10/1809.

VAN DER BRUGGHEN, George Tammo Theodoor Adriaan
[b] Utrecht, 1/12/1784; [s] Joan Carel Gideon v d B. & Margaretha Geertruida Falck; missing in battle, 1/1/1814.
[e] Dutch Army as orderly officer to King Louis, 29/10/1806; Lt, 20/12/1806; [t>] from Royal Guard Hussars as SLt into 2e CLGI, 8/4/1812. Left for Russia, 14/4/1812; crossed Rhine, 8/5/1812; missing at Brienne during battle of la Rothiére, 1/2/1814.
Campaigns 1808, Coasts; 1809, Spain; 1812, Russia; 1813, Saxony; 1814, France.
Awards Legionnaire, Legion of Honour, 14/9/1813.

BRUNEAU DE BEAUMETZ, Adolphe Félix Maurice, Count
[b] Douai (Nord), 3/8/1786; [s] Bon-Albert-Brios, Count d B., *Député de la Noblesse aux Etats Généraux.*
Former cadet at Fontainebleu Military School, [e] service 9/6/1803; SLt, 3e Hussards, 20/2/1804; Lt, 14/2/1807; Adj-M, 19/12/1808, ranked as Capt, 19/6/1810; Capt, 31/7/1811; Lt, Chasseurs à cheval de la Garde Impériale, 25/1/1813; [t>] as Capt into 2e CLGI, Old Guard, by decree 18/3/1813, reported to regt 1/4/1813. ADC to Marshal Mortier, 1/9/1813; Cd'E, ADC to Marshal Mortier, 1/2/1814; [a] 4e Lanciers de Ligne, 10/6/1814; [r] 1823 as LtCol of Hussars.
Wounds Bullet wound, battle of Tudela, 23/11/1808.
Campaigns All campaigns from 1803.
Awards Legionnaire, Legion of Honour.

BUIS or BUYS, Gerard Jean
[b] Nijmegen, 22/1/1788; [s] Philippe B. & Hélène Gansling.
[e] Batavian Dragoons, 2/5/1804; Cpl in Dutch Royal Guard, 20/10/1806; SM, 8/9/1809; [t>] as Sgt into 2e CLGI, 21/9/1810. Lt, Young Guard, 18/3/1813; [a] 5e Lanciers de Ligne, 6/6/1815.
Wounds Wounded at battle of St Dizier, 26/3/1814.
Campaigns 1806, Prussia; 1809, Brabant; 1812, Russia; 1813, Saxony; 1814, France.
Awards Legionnaire, Legion of Honour, 5/4/1814.

C

CABARD, Jean Baptiste
[b] Narbonne (Aude), 11/2/1766; [s] Jean Paul C. & Antoinette Vigier.
[e] 3e Bataillon de l'Aude; [a] Guides du Général Bonaparte, 11/10/1796;
[t>] Chasseurs à cheval de la Garde des Consuls, 3/1/1800; [pm] Cpl,
15/10/1802; Sgt, 18/12/1805; 2nd Lt, 3/4/1809; Lt, 27/2/1813. [a]
Corps des Chasseurs à cheval de France, 30/7/1814; [t>] CRCLF,
5/8/1814.
[a] LGI, by decree 14/4/1815; removed from muster roll, 9/11/1815.
Wounds Bullet wound to elbow, Benavente, 29/12/1808; wounded at
battle of Ligny, 16/6/1815.
Awards Presented with *carabine d'honneur*, 20/10/1802; Legionnaire,
Legion of Honour, 24/9/1803; Knight, Order of the Reunion,
27/2/1814.

CALKOEN, Abraham, Lord of Kortenhoef
[b] Amsterdam, 6/4/1780; [s] Nicolaas C., Lord of Kortenhoef, & Sara
Maria van Loon; [d] Arnhem, 2/10/1830.
[e/v] Danish service in 1800; [pm] Lt, Chasseurs of Danish Royal Guard,
1802; resigned 1804, [t>] Dutch service. 2nd Lt, 28/6/1805; Lt,
Grenadiers of Royal Guard, 23/9/1806; Capt, Dutch 2nd Hussars,
6/1808; [t>] Cuirassiers of Royal Guard, 12/1808; 1st Schildknaap,
ranking as Capt, in Gardes du Corps à cheval, 27/9/1809; [t>] 2e CLGI,
30/10/1810. Left for Russia, 10/2/1812; crossed Rhine, 12/3/1812.
Cd'E in 3e Lanciers de Ligne, 18/3/1813. Left Imperial Guard,
1/5/1813. [e] Dutch Army as commander, 1st & 2nd Mounted Volunteer
Companies, 1814; Maj, 15/6/1815; LtCol, 2/9/1815; Col, 17/8/1823,
commander 1st Cuirassiers.
"Knows his job but serves with nonchalance."
Campaigns 1801, Copenhagen; 1806, Germany; 1809, Brabant; 1812,
Russia; 1813, Saxony; 1814, France.
Awards Legionnaire, Legion of Honour, 5/9/1813.

CENAS, François
[b] New Orleans, 27/10/1792; [s] Pierre C. & Marie Joseph Reine; [d] in
battle, 25/2/1814.
[a] St Germain Military School, by decree 26/10/1811, [e] 9/11/1811; [a]
as SLt to 2e CLGI, by decree 18/3/1813. Killed during reconnaissance
near Antwerp, 25/2/1814.
Campaigns 1813, Saxony; 1814, France.

CHAPPE, Maurice
[b] Annecy (Mont-Blanc), 15/7/1779; [s] Gabriel C. & Jeanne Sonnerac.
[e] 25e Chasseurs à cheval, 1/12/1797; [pm] Cpl, 19/10/1800; Sgt,
30/7/1802; SM, Light Horse of Royal Guard of King of Naples,
1/8/1806; Adj-NCO, 1/7/1808; SLt S-Adj-M, 29/3/1809; Lt,
10/6/1810; Adj-M, 11/7/1812; Capt Adj-M in Spanish Royal Guard,
6/1/1813; [t>] 2e CLGI, 1/2/1814. [a] CRCLF, 2/8/1814; [a] LGI, by
decree 14/4/1815; Lt, 1/5/1815. Recalled as Capt Adj-M to the Line,
1/9/1815; [ds] 16/12/1815.
Campaigns 1798, Naples; 1800-01, Spain; 1802, on observation,
Gironde area; 1803, Coasts; 1805, Italy; 1806-07, Naples; 1808-13, Spain;
1814, France.
Awards Legionnaire, Legion of Honour, 3/4/1814; Knight, Royal Order
of Spain, 21/1/1809.

CHARASSIN, Jean Philibert
[b] Dijon (Côte-d'Or), 22/8/1786.
[e] Chasseurs à cheval de la Garde Impériale as Vélite, 12/1/1806;
SLt, 21e Chasseurs à cheval, 1/2/1808; [a] as 2nd Lt to 2e CLGI, by
decree 18/3/1813. Left for the Army, 30/4/1813; crossed Rhine,
24/5/1813. [a] CRCLF, 2/8/1814; removed from muster roll for long
absence, 1/5/1815 - on sick leave since 8/7/1814.

*"A very brave officer, mentioned more than once in Army despatches; he took a
standard from a British regiment in Spain."*
Wounds Bruise to left leg, Eylau, 8/2/1807; while in advance guard
towards Gebora, 19/2/1811, three sabre cuts to head and bullet wound to
right leg; lance wound at battle of Albuhera, 16/5/1811; wound to left
foot by explosion at battle of Kulm; lance wound to right side at battle of
Montereau, 18/2/1814.
Campaigns 1806, Prussia; 1807, Poland; 1808-12, Spain; 1813, Saxony;
1814, France.
Awards Legionnaire, Legion of Honour, 27/2/1814.

**DE CHASTENET DE PUYSEGUR, Jacques Paul Alexandre,
Marquis de Puységur, Viscount of Buzancy**
[b] Strasbourg, 27/2/1790; [s] Armand Marc Jacques d C. d P., Marquis
de Puységur, Viscount of Buzancy, Count of Guerchy, Col of Régiment
d'Artillerie de Strasbourg, LtGen in 1814, & Marguerite Baudard de St
James; [d] Paris, 6/5/1846, buried at Buzancy (Aisne).
Sgt in 27e Chasseurs à cheval, 29/10/1806; SLt, 6/12/1806; Lt,
6/4/1812; Capt-Asst with staff of 1st Cavalry Corps, 26/5/1813; [a] ADC
to Gen de Latour Maubourg, 15/6/1813; Capt, 2e Gardes d'Honneur,
7/11/1813; [pm] Cd'E, 7/8/1814. Capt in CRCLF, 13/2/1815; [pm]
supernumerary in LGI, by decree 14/4/1815; left regt without
permission, 1/6/1815; followed the Duc de Berry, 1/6/ to 7/7/1815.
Cd'E in Lanciers de la Garde Royale, 12/10/1815; LtCol, 7/8/1818;
[t>] with rank into Hussars du Jura, 9/10/1822; LtCol, Hussars du Nord
(4e), 23/10/1822; on paid leave, 9/8/1830; [r], 3/2/1838.
Campaigns 1807-08, Prussia & Denmark; 1809-12, Spain; 1813,
Germany;
1814, France; 1823, Spain.
Awards Legionnaire, Legion of Honour, 3/11/1813; Knight, Military
Order of St Louis, 25/4/1821.

CHOMEL, Fréderic Guillaume
[b] Amsterdam, 10/7/1785; [s] Pierre C., commercial adviser and consul
of King of Prussia, & Madelaine le Normant; [d] Leiden, 12/9/1851.
[e] Dutch Army as cadet-NCO, 26/3/1807; SLt, ADC to Gen Travers,
6/9/1808; Lt, 2nd Cuirassiers, 9/11/1808; [t>] as Lt to Dutch Royal
Guard, 18/8/1809; Lt, 2e CLGI, 25/11/1811. Left for Russia,
10/2/1812; crossed Rhine, 12/3/1812. Capt, 1er Hussards, by decree
18/3/1813; left regt, 25/5/1814; [a] 7e Hussards, 1/9/1814; [r]
1/10/1815. Returned with rank to Dutch Army, 7/12/1815; [a] Capt,
Adj to Gen Travers, 23/12/1816; [a] as supernumerary to 5th Light
Dragoons; [t>] 4th Light Dragoons; [pm] commander Compagnie
Maréchaussée of the Province of Antwerp, ranking as Capt, 21/7/1828;
Maj, 10/4/1837; LtCol, 17/11/1840; Col on [r] 4/1/1844; commander,
Gouda Militia.
"A very good officer, intelligent, active and educated."
Campaigns 1809-10, Zeeland; 1812, Russia; 1813-14, Italy.
Awards Legionnaire, Legion of Honour, 5/3/1814; Knight, Military
Order of William, 4th Class, 31/8/1831; Knight, Order of Netherlands
Lion, 28/11/1840.

COLBERT DE CHABANAIS, Pierre David (Edouard), Baron
[b] Paris, 18/10/1774; [s] Louis-Henry-François, Count C., Col of
infantry, & Marie Jeanne David; [d] Paris, 28/12/1853.
[e/v] 7e Bataillon de Paris, "Bataillon de Guillaume Tell", 1793; served in
Armée du Haute-Rhin, then in Vendée. SLt in 11e Hussars with Armée
de l'Ouest, 28/9/1795; suspended by Gen Hoche, 25/1/1796, on
suspicion of royalist sympathies. Temporary Commissioner of War in
Armée de l'Orient, 20/5/1798; Commissioner 1st Class, 18/8/1799.
Temporary supernumerary Capt, 3e Dragons, 1/12/1799; [a] ADC to
Gen Damas, 9/12/1799; Capt Adj-M, Mamelukes de la Garde des
Consuls, 15/4/1802.
ADC to Gen Junot, 6/11/1803; ADC to Marshal Berthier,

21/9/1805; with Grande Armée, Austria, 1805; Cd'E, 15e Chasseurs à cheval, 1/3/1806; served in Italy, 1806, then with Grande Armée 1806-07; Col, 7e Hussards, 30/12/1806. Served at Eylau 8/2/1807, at Heilsberg 10/6/1807, and at Friedland 14/6/1807; with cavalry brigade of Gen Pajol in Armée d'Allemagne, 1808. Gen of Brigade, 9/3/1809; served with Armée du Rhin and in Germany, 1809; commander, light cavalry brigade, 2nd Army Corps under Marshal Lannes, 30/3/1809; present at battle of Amstetten, 5/5/1809, and at Raab, 14/6/1809; commander, 7th Light Cavalry Brigade, 2nd Army Corps under Marshal Oudinot, 21/7/1809. With Corps d'Observation de la Hollande, 1810; unattached, 19/7/1810; commanded cavalry of Corps d'Observation, 5/8/1810; commander, light cavalry brigade, Armée d'Allemagne, 25/12/1810. [a] Col, 2e CLGI, 6/3/1811.

Commanded search for deserters and conscientious objectors, 22nd Military Division, 18/3/1811. Led the Red Lancers in Russia, 1812; returned to Versailles, 1/2/1813. Served in Saxony, 1813; distinguished himself at battle of Bautzen, 21/5/1813; commander of dragoon brigade, division of Gen L'Héritier, 5/10/1813; Gen of Division, 25/11/1813. Present with Red Lancers in Champagne, 1814; at La Rothière 1/2/1814, Château-Thierry 12/2/1814, Nangis 18/2/1814, Craonne 7/3/1814, Rheims 12-13/3/1814, took Epernay 14/3/1813, at Arcis-sur-Aube 20/3/1814. Colonel of CRCLF, Orléans, 24/8/1814; and retained at head of LGI, by decree 14/4/1815; served with Armée du Nord in Belgium, 6/1815.

Imprisoned during Second Restoration, 1815-16; unattached, 22/12/1815; reinstated to General Staff, 30/12/1818. Inspector Gen of Cavalry, 17/5/1826; commander, 2nd Cavalry Division, Lunéville Military Camp, 1827; member, Special Committee for Cavalry, 3/1/1830; General Staff, 7/2/1831; ADC to Duc de Nemours, 12/6/1834; followed Duc de Nemours on expedition against Constantine, Algeria, 1836.

Wounds Bullet wound to arm, Upper Egypt, 1799; bullet wound to thigh, Austerlitz, 2/12/1805; three lance wounds, Prussia, 17/7/1807; bullet wound to head, Wagram, 6/7/1809; bullet wound to left arm, Quatre-Bras, 16/6/1815; wounded by Fieschi's "infernal machine", 28/7/1835.

Awards Annuity of 14,000 francs drawn on Westphalia, 17/3/1808; Baron of the Empire, 28/5/1809; annuity drawn on Illyria, 1/1/1812; Knight, Military Order of St Louis, 24/8/1814; Grand Officer, Legion of Honour, 29/10/1828; Peer of France, 11/10/1832; Grand Cross, Legion of Honour, 30/5/1837.

COLESSON, Jacques Philippe
[b] St Dié (Vosges), 18/8/1772; [d] of wounds, 20/5/1813.
[e] 3e Hussards, 5/10/1798; [pm] Sgt, 20/6/1800; [t>] as Lt into 6e Hussards, 17/2/1803; Lt, 25/1/1807; [a] ADC to Gen Pajol, 4/5/1807; Lt in 4e Hussards, 5/7/1807; Capt, 17/8/1809; Cd'E, 6/8/1811; [a] Cd'E in 2e CLGI, by decree 18/3/1813; died before taking up appointment.
"On 30 October, near Laventosa, kingdom of Valencia, at the head of 60 hussars, he surprised and routed an enemy wagon park consisting of six guns, six ammunition caissons and wagons."
Wounds Bayonet wound to right thigh and bullet wound to left arm, 1798; three lance wounds in an action before Taragona, 24/6/1811; wounded near Daroca, Aragon, 15/11/1811; wounded at Yecla, 13/4/1813, from which he died the following month.
Campaigns 1798-1800, Germany; 1802-04, Holland; 1805-07, Grande Armée; 1808-13, Spain.
Awards Legionnaire, Legion of Honour, 29/12/1809.

COLIGNON, Jacques
[b] Paris, 10/1/1773; [s] Antoine Alexandre C. & Michelle Jacqueline Saladon.
[e] Régiment de Quercy, 26/9/1787; [t>] 2e Chasseurs à cheval, 9/5/1788;

[dst] 1/2/1790, [t>] the same day to 13e Infanterie Légère; [t>] 26e? or 36e? Division, Gendarmes à pied, 26 /1/1793. [e/v] Dragons de la Garde de Paris, 22/6/1803; [pm] Cpl, 6/7/1806; Sgt, 10/10/1809; Adj-NCO, 1/7/1812; [a] as Lt into 2e CLGI, by decree 18/3/1813. [p] 27/1/1814; returned to France, 25/3/1814; [a] 5e Lanciers de Ligne, 6/6/1814.
Wounds Near Liège, 24/1/1814; at battle of Ligny, 16/6/1815.
Campaigns 1813, Saxony; 1814, France.

COLIN DE VERDIERE, Auguste Amboise
[b] Paris, 5/7/1780; [s] Jean Christophe C. d V., stablemaster-instructor to Gardes du Corps de Monsieur, Gen of Division during Revolution and Empire, & Henriette Marie Louise Piot; [d] Besançon, 28/3/1840.
[e/v] 10e Hussards, 26/1/1796; [pm] SLt into 21e Chasseurs à cheval, 12/9/1797; [a] ADC to his father, 14/9/1797; [pm] Lt, 14/9/1798; [a] ADC to Gen Rochambeau, 30/10/1801; Capt, 21/10/1802; [a] ADC to Gen Junot, 15/12/1803; Capt in 8e Chasseurs à cheval, 9/11/1805; Cd'E, 7/8/1809; [a] to 2e CLGI, 8/1/1812; arrived Versailles 25/2/1812. [pm] Col in the Line, 28/11/1813, at age of 33 and with 17 years' military service. Col, 7e Chasseurs à cheval, 16/12/1813; left the Red Lancers, 31/12/1813. Under First Restoration retained command of his regt, reformed as Chasseurs d'Orléans, 8/10/1814; retained command during Hundred Days, assigned to Armée du Rhin. Placed on inactive list, 13/11/1815.

Recalled as Col, Hussards du Jura (1er), 26/11/1817. Served in Spanish campaign with Armée des Pyrénées, 1823; Maréchal de camp, 29/6/1823; C-in-C Burgos, later Madrid, 9/8/1823. [a] Inspector Gen of Cavalry, 16th Military Division, 29/6/1825; unattached, 1/1/1826; commander, 4th Military Sub-Division, 27/12/1826; of 5th Sub-Division, 18th Military Division, 6/6/1827; unattached, 17/12/1828; commander, 2nd Sub-Division, 6th Military Division, 3/5/1829. Retained command of the Jura after July Revolution, 6/12/1830; General Staff, 22/3/1831; commander, Department of the Doubs, 16/12/1832. *"Distinguished himself at the battle of Sacile, 16/4/1809...At the battle of Töplitz on 17/9/1813, at the head of two squadrons, he routed three Russian battalions and took a battery of six guns."*
Wounds Wounded at battle of la Crête at Pierrot, Santo-Domingo; lance thrust to left leg at battle of the Beresina, 28/11/1812.
Campaigns 1798, Holland; 1800-01, Armée du Rhin; 1802-03, Santo-Domingo; 1805, Grande Armée; 1809, Austria; 1812, Russia; 1813, Saxony; 1814, France; 1815, Armée du Rhin; 1823, Spain.
Awards Legionnaire, Legion of Honour, 31/10/1809; Officer, 16/8/1813; Commander, 26/6/1831; Knight, Military Order of St Louis, 1/9/1814; Knight, Royal and Military Order of St Ferdinand, 4th Class.

COLINS DE HAM, Jean Guillaume César Hippolyte, Baron
[b] Brussels, 24/12/1783; [s] Jean-Guillaume C. d H., officer and chamberlain at the Austrian court at Brussels, & Anne Joseph de Ricot; [d] Paris, 12/11/1859.
[e/v] 8e Hussards, 24/11/1803; [pm] Cpl, 11/10/1804; QM, 10/1/1806; Sgt, 5/3/1807; Adj-NCO, 1/4/1807; 2nd Lt, by decree 26/4/1809; Lt, 11/9/1809; [a] Imperial Veterinary School, Alfort, 1810; [a] as 2nd Lt to 2e CLGI, Old Guard, by decree 18/3/1813. [t>] CRCLF, 2/8/1814; [pm] Lt, ranking as Capt in Line, and placed on half pay, on 24/12/1814. [a] LGI, 20/3/1815, as ADC to Gen Exelmans. Commanded, as ADC, cavalry charge at battle of Fleurus, 16/6/1815; [pm] Cd'E on battlefield of Vélizy and Rocquencourt near Versailles, 1/7/1815.
Campaigns 1803-04, Coasts; 1805, Austria; 1806, Prussia; 1807, Poland; 1809, Austria; 1813, Saxony; 1814, France; 1815, Armée du Nord.
Awards Legionnaire, Legion of Honour, 28/11/1813; Knight, Order of the Reunion, 1/4/1814.

COTI, Jean François
[b] Zevaco, Liamone, Corsica, 15/7/1777; [d] Bourbonne Spa,
12/6/1815.
[e] French Army as Lt, 17e Demi-Brigade, 30/12/1793; Lt, 104e DB,
1/8/1795; Lt, 83e DB, 10/1/1796; Lt, Gendarmerie départmentale,
Liamone, 26/11/1796. Adj-M with General Staff, Alexandria, Egypt,
6/7/1798. Lt, Gendarmerie départmentale, Roâr, 16/5/1802 to
22/12/1804. [e] Dutch Army; Capt-Asst with General Staff, 1/5/1807;
[t>] as Capt to Gendarmerie, 12/10/1807; LtCol, Hussars of Dutch
Royal Guard, 2/3/1810; Cd'E in 2e CLGI, 30/10/1810. Left for Russia,
10/2/1812; crossed Rhine, 12/3/1812. [t>] CRCLF, 2/8/1814; [a] with
rank into LGI, by decree 14/4/1815.
Campaigns 1793-98, Italy; 1799-1801, Armée d'Orient; 1805-07,
Grande Armée.
Awards Legionnaire, Legion of Honour, 18/4/1813; Knight, Order of
the Union, 15/11/1807; Knight, Order of the Reunion, 7/3/1812.

COURBE, Jean Joseph Bénigne
[b] Salins (Jura), 8/7/1777; [d] of wounds, 26/12/1812.
[e] as Cpl, 14e Bataillon du Jura, 8/7?-9?/1793; [t>] 5e Bataillon du
Doubs, 17/1/1795; trooper, 12e Régiment de Cavalerie, 23/10/1798;
[t>] Guides de l'Armée du Rhin, 28/10/1799; [a] 6e Hussards,
14/7/1800. [pm] SLt, 29/5/1802; Lt by seniority, 1/6/1807; Capt,
10/7/1810; [a] as Capt Adj-M to 2e CLGI, 22/6/1811.
Wounds Wounded at battle of the Beresina, 28/11/1812; died Elbing,
26/12/1812.
Campaigns Present on all campaigns of the Republic & Empire -
Rhine, Danube, Germany, 1803-1806 in Holland, later in Grande Armée,
Italy and Russia.
Awards Legionnaire, Legion of Honour.

D

DAS, Antoon Mathias
[b] Breda, 29/3/1777; [s] Henricus D., former soldier, & Joanna Wens;
[d] Russia, 16/12/1812.
[e] Dutch Cavalry Regt van der Duyn, 4/1/1794; [pm] Cpl, 2/3/1794;
QM, 5/3/1797; SM, 6/1/1800; Lt in 2nd Cuirassiers, 21/10/1806; [t>]
Dutch Royal Guard, 25/8/1809; [a] as 2nd Lt to 2e CLGI, 30/10/1810.
Left for Russia, 21/1/1812, with 3e Esc, 7e Cie; crossed Rhine,
11/2/1812; died a victim of the Russian winter, 16/12/1815.
"A good officer."
Wounds Wounded at battle of the Beresina, 28/11/1812.
Campaigns 1796, Germany; 1797, embarked at Texel; 1799, Holland;
1800-09, Germany; 1812, Russia.

DEBAN DE LABORDE, Nicolas Joseph
[b] Paris, 13/4/1780; [s] Jean D. d L., Sgt in Gardes Françaises,
& Marie Thérèse Josèphe de Mouy.
[e] 19e Chasseurs à cheval, 1/4/1799; [pm] Cpl, 30/4/1801; [a] Chasseurs
à cheval de la Garde des Consuls, 12/7/1801; QM, 12/7/1803. SLt in 8e
Dragons, 29/8/1805; Lt, 2/1810; supernumerary Lt in 2e CLGI, by
decree 8/1/1812. Left for Russia, 14/4/1812; crossed Rhine, 8/5/1812.
Left from Fulda 14/2/1813, arrived Versailles 20/2/1813; Capt, Young
Guard, 18/3/1813. [t>] CRCLF, 2/8/1814; Cd'E, ranking as Capt,
24/11/1814; [a] as Capt d'habillement to LGI, by decree 14/4/1815; [ds]
22/12/1815; placed on half pay & [r], 10/5/1829.
Wounds Lance wound to right arm, before Moscow, 25/9/1812.
Campaigns 1798-1805, Grande Armée; 1806-07, Prussia & Poland;
1808-11, Spain & Portugal; 1812, Russia; 1813, Saxony; 1814, France.
Awards Legionnaire, Legion of Honour, 14/4/1813.

DEFONTENAY, Auguste Félix
[b] Rouen (Seine-Inférieure), 26/8/1792; [s] Pierre Nicolas D. & Marie
Elisabeth Ricard.

[a] St Germain Military School, by decree 10/9/1812, [e] 27/12/1813; [a]
as SLt to 2e CLGI, by decree 19/2/1814; [a] 3e Lanciers de Ligne,
9/6/1814.
Campaigns 1814, France.

DEHAMM, Louis Bernard Pierre Marie
[b] Munster, 8/5/1793; [s] Germain Ignace D. & Marie Claire Gertrude
Wotte. Cadet at St Germain Military School, 27/12/1813; [a] as SLt to 2e
CLGI; [t>] to infantry, 7/1/1814.

DEJEAN, Pierre
[b] Castres (Tarn), 13/4/1778.
[e] Bataillon du Tarn, "le Vengeur", 1/1/1794; [e] Ecole de Mars,
29/6/1795; unattached, 30/6/1796 to 23/10/1798; [e] 4e Chasseurs à
cheval, 24/10/1798 (became 24e Chasseurs à cheval, 12/2/1799); [pm]
Cpl, 22/3/1800; QM, 4/2/1801; Sgt, 10/2/1803; SM, 24/7/1809; [a]
Chasseurs à cheval de la Garde Impériale, 1/11/1809. [pm] Cpl,
10/7/1810; QM, 5/10/1810; Sgt, 12/4/1812; SM, 15/1/1813; [a] as
2nd Lt to 2e CLGI, Old Guard, by decree 25/1/1813; left for the
army, 5/3/1813. [t>] CRCLF, 2/8/1814; placed on half pay & inactive
list, 12/1814; [a] as 2nd Lt to LGI, by decree 22/5/1815. Proposed for
retirement, 16/11/1815; [ds] 16/12/1815.
Wounds Two lance wounds at battle of Töplitz, 17/9/1813.
Campaigns 1793, Toulon; 1798-99, Italy; 1800-01, Spain; 1802-06-09,
Italy & Germany; 1812, Russia; 1813, Saxony; 1814, France.
Awards Legionnaire, Legion of Honour, 14/9/1813.

DELABORDE, Augustin Charles
[b] Paris, 2/11/1793; [s] Jean Baptiste D. & Anne Françoise Le Crosnier.
[a] St Germain Military School, by decree 12/2/1812, [e] 19/3/1812;
[a] as SLt to 2e CLGI, Young Guard, by decree 18/3/1813. [t>] CRCLF,
2/8/1814. Left for Martinique in former 26e Régiment d'Infanterie de
Ligne; Lt, 4/9/1814; Adj-M, 2/2/1815; returned to France, 12/5/1815;
[p] of British, 23/6/1815; returned, 9/8/1815.
Campaigns 1813, Saxony; 1814, France.
Awards Legionnaire, Legion of Honour, 3/4/1814.

DELAIZEMENT, François Henri
[b] Neuilly-sur-Seine (Seine), 15/3/1771; [s] Nicolas Jean D. & "Jetje"
Sellier.
[e] 5e Dragons, 21/6/1789; [pm] QM, 15/10/1793; Sgt, 27/4/1796;
SM, 5/1/1797; Lt, 26/5/1797; resigned, 27/5/1798. [e] Dutch Army as
Lt, Cavalry of Royal Guard, 11/12/1806; [a] as 2nd Lt to 2e CLGI,
30/10/1810. Lt S-Adj-M in Old Guard, 18/3/1813; [t>] CRCLF,
2/8/1814; placed on half pay, 25/8/1814; left regt, 10/12/1814.
"A good officer."
Wounds Sabre cut to right hand, Alla, 7/9/1796.
Campaigns 1792-1798, Armée du Nord; 1809, Brabant; 1812, Russia;
1813, Saxony; 1814, France.
Awards Legionnaire, Legion of Honour, 15/3/1813.

DELRUE, Pierre
[b] Boulogne-sur-Mer (Pas-de-Calais), 7/3/1795; [s] an innkeeper and
shipowner.
S-Asst S-M in civil and military hospital at Boulogne; received
commission at his request, 30/5/1813; [pm] S-Asst S-M in 2e CLGI,
Young Guard, by decree 26/5/1813; [a] 5e Lanciers de Ligne,
6/6/1814.
Campaigns 1813, Saxony; 1814, France.

DESELVE, François Joseph
[e] Fontainebleu Special Military School as cadet, 5/12/1805;
[a] as supernumerary SLt to 12e Dragons, 24/12/1806; SLt, 4/4/1807;
Lt, 29/1/1810; 2nd Lt, Dragons de la Garde Impériale, 9/7/1812; Lt,

28/11/1813; [t>] 2e CLGI, 1?-5?/4/1814; [a] 5e Lanciers de Ligne, 6/6/1814; placed on half pay, 1/9/1815.
Wounds Wound to right arm, Hanau, 30/10/1813.
Awards Legionnaire, Legion of Honour, 22/12/1809.

DESFOURNIELS, Jacques Isidore
[b] Bordeaux (Gironde), 10/11/1795; [s] Jacques Antoine Verdelhan D., Lord of des Fourniels, & Jeanne Marie Adélaïde Daudier.
[a] St Germain Military School, by decree 23/4/1812, [e] 14/6/1812; [a] as SLt to 2e CLGI, by decree 18/3/1813; [a] 4e Lanciers de Ligne, 10/6/1814; resigned, 20/9/1814.
Campaigns 1813, Saxony; 1814, France.
Awards Legionnaire, Legion of Honour, 5/4/1814.

DIACON, Jean François
[b] Versailles, 7/6/1773; [s] Pierre D. & Marie Anne Benard.
Lt in 2e Cie, Dragons de la Garde de Paris, 29/6/1810; [a] as Lt to 2e CLGI, 27/2/1813; [a] 1er Chasseurs à cheval, 1/5/1813.

DINI, François
[b] Jiosella, Trasimène, 10/6/1793; [s] Louis D. & Estelle Pieraubiani.
[e] St Germain Military School, 27/5/1812; [a] as SLt to 2e CLGI, by decree 18/3/1813; [a] 4e Lanciers de Ligne, 10/6/1814.
Campaigns 1813, Saxony; 1814, France.

DOMERGUE, Eugène
[b] St Hippolyte (Gard), 17/9/1788.
[e] Gendarmerie d'ordonnance, 9/10/1806; [pm] Cpl, 25/10/1806; Sgt, 22/1/1807. Lt in 21e Dragons, 16/7/1807; Capt, 4/9/1812; [a] as Capt to 2e CLGI, Young Guard, by decree 18/3/1813; [a] 3e Lanciers de Ligne, 9/6/1814.
Campaigns 1806-07, Grande Armée; 1808-11, Spain; 1813, Saxony; 1814, France.
Awards Legionnaire, Legion of Honour, 29/11/1813.

VAN DOORN, Johan
[b] Gorinchem (Gorkum), 23/1/1784; [s] Anthonie Johannes v D. & Agatha Maria van Velsen; [d] 5/2/1816.
[e] Batavian Dragoons as cadet, 4/12/1794; Lt, 28/6/1805; [t>] from Dutch 3rd Hussars in Spain as 2nd Lt into 2e CLGI, 30/10/1810. Left for Russia, 1812, with 1er Esc, 5e Cie; left regt without permission, 20/8/1813. [e] Dutch Army as Capt, 2/9/1815.
Campaigns 1800-01, Germany; 1805, embarked at Texel; 1806-07, Germany; 1808-09, Spain; 1812, Russia; 1813, Saxony.

DOYEN, Johannes
[b] Gronsveld (Meuse Inférieure), 29/6/1774; [s] Lambertus D., carpenter, & Maria Anna van der Boorne.
[e] Bylandt Dragoons, 22/12/1792; [pm] Cpl, 30/11/1795; Sgt, 23/1/1803; SM, 4/2/1807; 2nd Lt, 26/2/1807; [t>] from Dutch 3rd Hussars in Spain to 2e CLGI, 8/4/1812. Left for Russia, 14/4/1812; crossed Rhine, 8/5/1812. Left for Angers, 3/1814; [t>] CRCLF, 2/8/1814; [t>] as 2nd Lt into LGI, by decree 14/4/1815; Lt, by decree 22/5/1815; resigned, 1/7/1815.
Campaigns 1793, Brabant; 1799, Holland; 1800, Germany; 1808-11, Spain; 1812, Russia; 1813, Saxony; 1814, France; 1815, Belgium.
Awards Legionnaire, Legion of Honour, 27/2/1814.

DUBOIS, Charles Marie Joseph, Baron
[b] Hilversum, 22/10/1772; [s] François Reignier D., surgeon, & Françoise Marie Joséphine le Comte de Bus; [d] Mechelen, 4/7/1829.
Supernumerary SLt in Dragoon Regt de Prade, Dutch Army, 12/7/1787; fled to France, 1787; [e/v] French Royal Dragoons, 20/4/1788; [pm] Lt in Dragons de Flandre, 1789; resigned after 1792-95 campaigns. Returned

to Dutch Army, [a] as 2nd Lt to 2nd Cavalry Regt, 9/7/1795; Lt, 27/2/1798; [pm] Capt on battlefield of Castrum, 20/10/1799; [t>] as Capt into Grenadiers de la Garde du Grand Pensionnaire, 15/7/1805; [pm] Capt, Dutch Royal Guard, 5/6/1806; LtCol, Cuirassiers (later Hussars) of Dutch Royal Guard, 5/10/1806; Col, 5/8/1809; [a] Col-M of 2e CLGI, 30/10/1810.

Left for Russia, 10/2/1812; crossed Rhine, 12/3/1812; distinguished himself at battles of Malojaroslavetz and Borovsk. Left Fulda 14/2/1813, arrived Versailles 25/2/1813. Left with the regimental depot for Angers, 30/3/1814. [a] as Maj to CRCLF, 2/8/1814; Maréchal de camp, 24/11/1814; retained rank of Maj in LGI, by decree 14/4/1815; commanded Versailles depot during Waterloo campaign. On leave from 18/7/1815; resigned, 3/12/1815; [ds] 22/12/1815.

Applied to rejoin Dutch Army, 1/11/1815; commander, Dutch 10th Lancers, 19/2/1819; [r] as MajGen, 28/7/1822.
"Promoted captain on the battlefield of Castrum by General-in-Chief Brune for having rallied retreating troops, which resulted in the capture of two enemy guns."
"A very distinguished officer, fit to be promoted for his fine service and for his capability."
Wounds Sabre cut to head, Landau; bullet wound to thigh at Felle, before Mont Verte.
Campaigns 1792-95, France & Rhine; 1796-97, Armée du Rhin; 1799, Holland; 1803, Hanover; 1806, Prussia; 1809, Brabant; 1812, Russia; 1813, Saxony; 1814, France.
Awards Legionnaire, Legion of Honour, 14/4/1813; Baron of the Empire, effective 24/1/1814, and annuity of 4,500 francs, by decree 26/11/1813; Officer, Legion of Honour, 24/10/1814; Knight, Order of the Union, 20/6/1806; Knight, Order of the Reunion, 7/3/1812; Knight, Military Order of St Louis, 15/2/1815; Order of the Lily, 2/5/1814.

DUCLOS, ?
[e] Army, 31/6/1794; [pm] Cpl, 28/7/1802; Sgt, 23/12/1802; [a] as SLt to 13e Chasseurs à cheval, 7/4/1809; [pm] Lt into 20e Chasseurs à cheval, 9/2/1813; [pm] Lt S-Adj-M into 2e CLGI, by decree 18/3/1813. In fact retained in Chasseurs à cheval, [pm] Capt in the Line, by decree 9/10/1813.

DUFOUR, Pierre Alexis
[b] Evreux (Eure), 29/6/1770.
[e/v] 1er Bataillon de l'Eure, 20/6/1791; Grenadier, 18/6/1792; [pm] QM, 17/7/1792; trooper, 5e Chasseurs à cheval, 15/3/1793; [pm] QM, 1/7/1793; Sgt, 20/7/1796; SM, 19/5/1797; SLt, 29/5/1797; Lt QM, 20/7/1801; Capt QM, 10/7/1809; [a] as Lt QM to 2e CLGI, 30/10/1810; Capt QM in 1811. [t>] CRCLF, 2/8/1814; [a] LGI, by decree 14/4/1815; proposed for retirement; [ds] 22/12/1815.
Wounds Wound to waist by mine explosion at siege of Valenciennes, 20/7/1793.
Campaigns 1792-93, Armée du Nord; 1793-95, Sambre & Meuse; 1795-96, Armée du Nord; 1797-99, Germany; 1813, Saxony.
Awards Legionnaire, Legion of Honour, 5/4/1814.

DUFOUR, Pierre Auguste
[b] Evreux (Eure), 29/10?-30/11?/1771; [s] Jean D. & Marie Anne Bélissent.
[e] 6e Chasseurs à cheval, 11/3/1793; SLt, 13/5/1797; Lt, 1/3/1803; Capt in 8e Chasseurs à cheval, 24/1/1810; [a] 2e CLGI, 18/3/1813. [t>] CRCLF, 2/8/1814; [a] LGI, by decree 14/4/1815; served in Escadron de service, Waterloo, 18/6/1815; [ds] 21/12/1815.
Wounds Bullet wound to belly in Russia, 1812; bruised by bullet at Altenbourg, 28/9/1813.
Campaigns 1793, Armée du Nord; 1793-95, Sambre & Meuse; 1796, Armée du Nord & du Rhin; 1797-98, Germany & Switzerland; 1799-1800, Rhine; 1802, Switzerland; 1804-07, Italy; 1809, Italy & Germany;

1812, Russia; 1813, Saxony; 1814, France; 1815, Armée du Nord.
Awards Legionnaire, Legion of Honour, 17/7/1809; Knight, Military Order of St Louis, 12/1814.

DUMONCEAU, Jean François, Count
[b] Brussels, 1/3/1790; [s] Johannes Baptista D., Gen & Count of the Empire, Count of Bergendael, & Anna Maria Apollonia Colinet; [d] The Hague, 1/3/1884.
[e] Army in 1799; 2nd Lt, 28/6/1805; Lt, 1/5/1807; [a] as Lt to 2e CLGI, 30/10/1810. Capt, 22/6/1811. Left for Russia with 2e Esc, 6e Cie, 10/2/1812; crossed Rhine, 12/3/1812. Left Fulda 14/2/1813, arrived Versailles 22/2/1813. [pm] Cd'E in 5e Chasseurs à cheval, 18/3/1813. [e] Dutch Army after Hundred Days; Maj, 19/2/1819; LtCol, 16/4/1830; Col, 22/10/1836; MajGen, 26/3/1841; LtGen, 8/9/1852; [r] 9/9/1854.
"A good officer, serving well; the son of a general."
Awards Legionnaire, Legion of Honour, 12/3/1814; Knight, Military Order of St Louis, 27/12/1814; Knight, Military Order of William, 4th Class, 31/8/1831; 3rd Class, 28/11/1840; Knight, Order of the Netherlands Lion, 29/7/1831; Commander, 6/12/1844; Grand Cross, 9/9/1854.

DUPLAN, Jean Marie
[b] Toulouse (Haute-Garonne), 29/5/1781?-4/11/1780?
[e] 12e Hussards, 3/6/1798; [pm] Cpl, 22/11/1799; Sgt, 8/6/1806; [a] Light Horse of Royal Guard of Naples, 1/8/1806; SM, 7/2/1808; SLt, 1/9/1809; [a] from Spanish Royal Guard to 2e CLGI, 1/2/1814. [t>] CRCLF, 2/8/1814; [a] as supernumerary 2nd Lt to LGI, by decree 14/4/1815; proposed for Gendarmerie; [ds] 9/11/1815.
Wounds Bullet wound to right foot; at battle of Craonne, 7/3/1814, suffered three sabre cuts to head, two lance wounds to back and bullet bruise to right thigh.
Campaigns 1799-1801, Italy; 1805-06, Naples; 1807-13, Spain; 1814, France.
Awards Legionnaire, Legion of Honour, 3/4/1814.

DUPUIS, ?
[a] from Spanish Royal Guard as Capt Adj-M to 2e CLGI, 1/2/1814; left regt without permission; removed from muster roll, 1/3/1814.

DURANTI, Guillaume Antonie François, Count of Concressault
[b] Paris, 17/3/1791; [s] François Marie D. & Jeanne Marie Charlotte Boissonnière; [d] in his castle of Blancafort (Cher), 3/11/1856.
[e] service of King of Holland as page, 1/7/1807; [a] as Lt to Dutch 3rd Hussars, 1/2/1808; [t>] 2e CLGI, 8/4/1812; [pm] Lt S-Adj-M, 18/3/1813. [t>] CRCLF, 2/8/1814; Cd'E ranking as Capt, 24/11/1814; [a] as Capt to LGI, by decree 14/4/1815; present at Waterloo, 18/6/1815; [ds] 21/12/1815; elected Deputy for Cher Department, 1852.
Campaigns 1808-1811, Spain; 1812, Russia; 1813, Saxony; 1814, France; 1815, Armée du Nord.
Awards Legionnaire, Legion of Honour,14/4/1814; Officer, Legion of Honour.

E

ESCHWEILER, Johannes Baptist Michael
[b] Bois-le-Duc? 's Hertogenbosch?, 25/2/1783; [s] Johannes Bernardus E. & Hendrica Maassen; [d] Oirschot, 30/1/1833.
[e] 1st Batavian Cavalry, 26/1/1799; [pm] Cpl, 10/6/1802; QM, 15/9/1802; [a] Garde du Grand Pensionnaire, 30/7/1805; [t>] Horse Grenadiers of Dutch Royal Guard, 1/8/1806; Sgt, 26/9/1806; SM, 1/11/1806; [a] Cuirassiers of Royal Guard, 1/1/1808 (reformed as Royal Guard Hussars, 1/1/1810); [t>] as Sgt to 2e CLGI, 21/9?-30/10?/1810. [pm] Lt, Young Guard, 18/3/1813; resignation accepted, 30/7/1814. [e]

Dutch Army, 2/8/1814; [a] as Lt-Adj to 1st Dragoons, 9/1814; Capt, 2/9/1815; [t>] 10th Lancers, 19/2/1819; Maj, 5th Light Dragoons, 19/3/1831.
Campaigns 1799, Holland; 1800-01, Germany; 1803, Coasts; 1804-05, Coast of Zeeland; 1806, Prussia; 1809, Brabant; 1812, Russia; 1813, Saxony; 1814, France.
Awards Knight, Military Order of William, 4th Class, 16/11/1830.

D'ESCOUBLEAU DE SOURDIS, Ange François Théophile, Count
[b] Paris, 23/10/1789; [s] Antoine René d'E. d S., Maréchal de camp, & Augustine Olympe Sophie de Besiade; [d] Grenada, Spain, 23/8/1823.
[e] Gendarmerie d'ordonnance, 24/3/1807; [a] Chasseurs à cheval de la Garde Impériale, 6/12/1807; SLt in 9e Chasseurs à cheval, 3/6/1809; Lt, 9/8/1812; [t>] as 2nd Lt into 2e CLGI, by decree 18/3/1813; [pm] Capt in 1er Lanciers de Ligne, 10/5/1814; Cd'E, 19/6/1814. [a] Gardes du Corps du Roi, 19/7/1814; Col, 12/11/1814; Col, Chasseurs du Var, 27/9/1815; killed in Spain, 1823.
Wounds Bullet to right arm, Carasal, 2/5/1807; lance wound to left arm, 23/4/1812; wounded 11/1/1814 while serving in advance guard near Hoogsträten.
Campaigns 1807, Poland; 1808-11, Spain; 1812, Russia; 1813, Saxony; 1814, served under Gen Maison.
Awards Legionnaire, Legion of Honour, 6/9/1811; Officer, 28/8/1814; Knight, Military Order of St Louis, 9/8/1814.

F

DE LA FARGUE (VAN NIEUWLAND), Jan Willem David Emanuel
[b] The Hague, 11/4/1771?-1778?; [s] Isaac Louis v N. & Diderika Dorothea Piekmans.
[e] as Grenadier, Regt Orange Gelderland, 23/2/1793; [pm] Cpl, 23/4/1793; Sgt, 23/6/1793; standard bearer, 4/5/1794; cadet in Dutch 1st Cavalry Regt, 27/1/1796; Lt in 7/1796; Lt, 2nd Dragoons, 1/7/1805; [t>] 3rd Hussars, 7/10/1807; [a] as Lt to 2e CLGI, 30/10/1810. Paymaster; Capt Adj-M, 22/6/1811; served in Russia, 1812. Left Fulda 14/2/1813, arrived Versailles 25/2/1813. [t>] CRCLF, 2/8/1814; [a] LGI, 1/6/1815; returned to his squadron after Hundred Days, when it was disbanded 16/12/1815.
Campaigns 1793-94, Brabant; 1796, Germany; 1797, embarked at Texel; 1799, Holland; 1800, Hanover; 1801-03, Coasts; 1806, Prussia; 1812, Russia.
Awards Legionnaire, Legion of Honour, 5/4/1814; Knight, Order for Military Merit, 27/2/1815.

FINTOWSKI, ?
Polish Lancer of Napoleon's Elba squadron; [t>] as Lt into LGI, 25/4/1815; [pm] Capt, 22/5/1815. [e] Russian Army, 1/10/1815.

FISCHER, André
[b] Rocroi (Ardennes), 21/9/1781; [s] Michel F., trooper in (3e) Hussards (de Esterhazy), & Jeanne Marie Devouge; [d] 11/2/1823.
[e] 8e Hussards, 15/12/1796; [t>] as Cpl into Chevau-légers de Berg, 1/7/1807; Sgt, 21/10/1808; [a] with rank to Chasseurs à cheval de la Garde Impériale, 11/1/1809; Sgt, 26/12/1811; 2nd Lt, 27/2/1813; [a] CRCLF, 5/8/1814. [a] LGI, by decree 14/4/1815; placed on half pay, 20/12/1815; [ds] the next day.
Wounds Bullet wound to left leg, Zürich, 1799.
Campaigns 1796, Rhine; 1797-98, Switzerland; 1799-1800, Rhine; 1803-04, Coasts; 1805 Austria; 1806-07, Prussia & Poland; 1808, Spain; 1809, Austria; 1811-12, Spain; 1813, Saxony; 1814, France; 1815, Armée du Nord.
Awards Legionnaire, Legion of Honour.

FISCHER, Frederik
[b] Utrecht, 8/5/1786; [s] Jan Justus F., retired LtCol, & Francisca Maas;
[d] of wounds, Russia, 12/1812.
[e] Dutch 1st Dragoons, 6/2/1799; Lt, 28/6/1805; [t>] from Dutch 3rd
Hussars in Spain as 2nd Lt into 2e CLGI, 8/4/1812. Left for Russia,
14/4/1812; crossed Rhine, 8/5/1812. Wounded and disappeared on road
to Tilsit, 15/12/1812.
Campaigns 1805, embarked at Texel; 1805-07, Germany; 1808, Coasts;
1809-11, Spain; 1812, Russia.

FOBLANT, Charles Antoine
[b] Dieuze (Meurthe), 5/2/1796; [s] Jean Etienne F. & Anne Louise
Constance Benoist Lamothe.
[a] St Germain Military School, by decree 12/2/1812, [e] 18/3/1812;
[a] as SLt to 2e CLGI, by decree 18/3/1813; [a] 3e Lanciers de Ligne,
9/6/1814.
Campaigns 1813, Saxony; 1814, France.

FONNADE, Jean François
[b] Beauchalot (Haute Garonne), 24/5/1772?-7/3/1774?; [s] Louis F. &
Bertrand Baris; [d] Paris, 14/2/1827.
[e] 15e Dragons, 24/6/1790; [a] Guides du Gen Bonaparte, 22/9/1796;
[a] Chasseurs à cheval de la Garde des Consuls, 3/1/1800; [pm] Cpl,
11/11/1800; Sgt, 15/10/1802; 2nd Lt, standard bearer of Mamelukes de
la Garde, 6/12/1811 to 5/8/1814; [a] CRCLF, 5/8/1814. [a] LGI, by
decree 14/4/1815; [ds] 16/12/1815; [r] 23/3/1816.
Wounds Two sabre cuts to head, Spain, 19/5/1793; bullet wound to
right hand, Waterloo, 18/6/1815.
Campaigns 1792, Piedmont; 1793, Toulon; 1793-94, Pyrénées
Orientales; 1795, Italy; 1796-98, Spain; 1799, Italy & Egypt; 1803-04,
Coasts; 1805, Austria; 1806, Prussia; 1807, Poland; 1808, Spain; 1809,
Austria; 1812, Russia; 1813, Saxony; 1814, France; 1815, Armée du
Nord.
Awards Presented with *sabre d'honneur* at Aboukir in 7/1799;
Legionnaire, Legion of Honour, 8/2/1801?

LE FORESTIER, Charles
[b] Chaumont-en-Vexin (Oise), 15/4/1775.
[e/v] Artillerie de la Marine, 5/11/1797; Adj-NCO ranking as SM in 2e
Demi-Brigade, 28/4/1799; [t>] 79e DB, 19/1/1801; [t>] Guides à cheval
du Gen Bernadotte, 1801; SLt, 30/12/1801; Lt, ADC to a Gen of
Brigade, 7/10/1806; ADC to Gen Richard, 11/2/1807; Capt, 9/8/1809,
ADC to Gen Daultane; [t>] 2e CLGI, Old Guard, by decree 18/3/1813.
Left for the army, 15/4/1813; crossed Rhine, 13/5/1813; recrossed
Rhine, 3 or 9/11/1813. [t>] CRCLF, 2/8/1814; [r] and placed on half
pay, 12/1814.
Wounds Bullet wound and two sabre cuts to left thigh.
Campaigns 1797-1801, Armée d'Ouest; 1802-04, Coasts; 1805, Grande
Armée; 1806-07, Prussia & Poland; 1808-09, Spain & Portugal; 1810-12,
Andalusia & Aragon, Spain; 1813, Saxony; 1814, France.
Awards Legionnaire, Legion of Honour.

FOURE, François de Sales Benjamin
[b] Nantes (Loire-Inférieure), 24/1/1785; [s] Mathieu F., cotton mill
owner, & Margueritte Lecocq. [e] 7e bis Hussards, 18/10/1802; [pm]
QM, 23/12/1803; Sgt, 12/1/1805; SLt, 11/8/1810; Lt, 21/3?-
10/4?/1813; [t>] as 2nd Lt into Grenadiers à cheval de la Garde
Impériale, 15/5/1813. [a] CRCLF, 1/11/1814; [a] supernumerary 2nd Lt
in LGI, by decree 14/4/1815; [m] 6/7/1815. Placed on inactive list,
1/9/1815; [r] with pension of 450 francs, 20/10/1819.
   [a] temporary commander, with rank of Capt, Compagnie de
Gendarmerie du Vendée, 3/9/1830; rank confirmed, 10/1/1831; Cd'E,
Compagnie des Basse Pyrénées, 25/4/1835; [a] with rank to Compagnie
des Deux Sèvres, 9/5/1835; [a] Compagnie de la Maine et Loire,

5/3/1839; [r] 10/2/1846.
Wounds Left hip injured by fall from horse in 1805; sabre cut to right
knee, battle of the Piave, 9/5/1809; bullet wound to left leg at the
Moskowa, 7/9/1812.
Campaigns 1803-04, Coasts; 1805, Italy; 1806-08, Naples; 1809,
Austria; 1812, Russia; 1813, Saxony; 1814, France.
Awards Legionnaire, Legion of Honour, 17/7/1809; Officer, 20/4/1839.

FRANK, Albert
[b] Bokkenheim, Duchy of Frankfurt, 26/12/1776; [s] Johannes F.,
administrator of sovereign of Anholt, & Antoinette Carolina
Schmetzguislin.
[e] Army as hussar, 26/1/1801; Cpl, 10/2/1803; Sgt, 20/12/1804;
[t>] Dutch Royal Guard, 29/8/1806; Lt, 15/10/1806; [a] as 2nd Lt
to 2e CLGI, 30/10/1810. Lt, Old Guard, 18/3/1813; [r] accepted by
Minister of War, 9/11/1814 - absent since 1/2/1814.
"A good officer."
Campaigns 1805, embarked at Texel, Germany; 1806, Westphalia;
1809, Brabant; 1812, Russia; 1813, Saxony; 1814, France.
Awards Legionnaire, Legion of Honour, 14/4/1813.

G

GAUTHIER, Claude Nicolas Benoit
[b] Faucogney-et-la-Mer (Haute-Saône), 21/3/1767; [d] in battle,
Waterloo, 18/6/1815.
[e] 4e Chasseurs à cheval, 23/3/1784; [pm] Cpl, 21/3?-6?/1792;
Sgt, 8/7/1793; SLt, 7/4/1803; [a] Light Horse, Royal Guard of King of
Naples, 1/8?-30/9?/1806; Lt, 1/11/1808; Capt, 18/10/1809; [t>] from
Spanish Royal Guard as Capt into 2e CLGI, Young Guard, 1/2/1814.
[t>] CRCLF, 2/8/1814; [a] LGI, by decree 14/4/1815.
Wounds Bayonet wounds to right leg and thigh, and sabre cuts to left
arm; wounded at Ligny, 16/6/1815; killed at Waterloo, 18/6/1815.
Campaigns 1792, Savoy; 1793-98, Rhine; 1799-1800, Batavian
Republic; 1805, Austria; 1806-07, Naples; 1808-13, Spain; 1814, France;
1815, Armée du Nord.
Awards Presented with *sabre d'honneur*, 15/9/1802; Legionnaire, Legion
of Honour, 15/9/1802; Knight, Royal Order of the Two Sicilies,
18/5/1806; Knight, Royal Order of Spain, 22/10/1810.

GAUTHIER (LECLERC), Jean Pierre, Baron
[b] Septmoncel (Jura), 23/2/1765; [d] Ville-d'Avray (Seine-et-Oise),
14/6/1821.
[e] Régiment du Roi (became 18e Dragons), 15/4/1783; [pm] Cpl,
16/1/1788; Sgt, 8/7/1791; SM, 1/1/1793; SLt, 1/4/1793; Lt,
21/3/1794; Capt, 20/4/1794; Cd'E, 8/9/1799; Maj in 9e Dragons,
19/6/1806; 2nd Col commanding 11e Régiment Provisoire de Dragons,
Orléans, 31/3/1809;
Col, 9e Régiment Provisoire de Dragons, 15/3/1810; unattached when
regt disbanded, 29/5/1810; [a] to Headquarters, then Col, 25e Dragons,
23/8/1811; [a] as Maj to 2e CLGI, by decree 12/1/1813. Col-M, 2e
Éclaireurs de la Garde Impériale, at organisation of regt; Gen of Brigade,
26/12/1813; left the regt, 1/1/1814. Served in division of Gen St
Germain, 11/2/1814; with 6th Heavy Cavalry Division of Gen Roussel
d'Hurbal, under Marshal Mortier, 28/3/1814; commander, Department
of Vaucluse, 23/6/1814; with Duc d'Angoulême at Avignon, 4/1815;
resigned, 18/4/1815. Recalled to command 2nd Brigade, 6th Division de
Réserve des Gardes Nationales (Gen Pannetier) in Armée des Alpes under
Marshal Suchet, 5/6/1815; [r] 6/10/1815.
*"He distinguished himself at the landing of British troops at Aboukir
on 8/3/1801."*
Wounds Wounded at Austerlitz, 2/12/1805.
Campaigns 1793-95, Armée des Pyrénées Occidentales; 1796-98, Italy;
1798-1801, Egypt; 1803-05, Coasts; 1805-06, Grande Armée; 1809-12,
Spain; 1813, Saxony; 1814, France; 1815, France.

Awards Presented with *sabre d'honneur*, 9/5/1801; Officer, Legion of Honour, 14/6/1804; annuity of 4,000 francs drawn on Rome, 15/8/1809; Baron of the Empire, 25/3/1810.

GEUBELS, Johan

[b] Zutphen, 6/5/1781; [s] Johannis G., retired Sgt, & Aaltje Brouwens; [d] Mainz, 11/12/1813.
[e] Dutch 2nd Cavalry Regt, 6/5/1796; [a] Cape Dragoons, 4/5/1802; [pm] Cpl, 4/6/1805; [t>] Cavalry of Dutch Royal Guard, 4/6/1806; Sgt, 6/10/1806; SM, 11/10/1807; Lt, 7/9/1809; [t>] as 2nd Lt into 2e CLGI, 30/10/1810. Left for Russia, 10/2/1812; crossed Rhine, 12/3/1812; Lt, Old Guard, 18/3/1813; [e] military hospital, Mainz, 8/12/1813, where he died three days later.
"A good officer."
Campaigns 1797, embarked at Texel; 1799, Holland; 1802, embarked for Cape of Good Hope; 1806, Prussia; 1809, Brabant; 1812, Russia; 1813, Saxony.
Awards Legionnaire, Legion of Honour, 14/4/1813.

DE GIENAUTH, Charles

[b] Reims (Marne), 31/12/1794; [s] François Daniel d G. & Marie Anne Lucile Bruyère.
[a] St Germain Military School, by decree 9/4/1812, [e] 7/5/1812; [a] as SLt to 2e CLGI, by decree 18/3/1813; [a] 3e Lanciers de Ligne, 9/6/1814.
Campaigns 1813, Saxony; 1814, France.

GISSER, Jacques

[b] The Hague, 28/11/1779; [s] Jacob G. & Marie Bernard; [d] 14/5/1866.
[e] 2nd Batavian Foot Artillery Bn, 6/1/1796; [pm] Cpl, 20/6/1799; [t>] Cape Dragoons, 2/5/1802; QM, 14/5/1803; [t>] Batavian Dragoons, 20/6/1805; SM, 1/2/1807; [a] Dutch Royal Guard, 16/4/1807; [pm] 2nd Lt in 2e CLGI, 21/9/1810. Lt, Young Guard, 18/3/1813; [r] 30/7/1814. [e] Dutch Army and [a] Dutch Indies Cavalry, 3/10/1815; Capt, 17/7/1818; Maj, 1823; LtCol, 10/7/1826; [r] 26/12/1832.
Campaigns 1796, Cleves; 1797, embarked at Texel; 1799, Holland; 1802, Cape of Good Hope; 1806, Prussia; 1809, Brabant; 1812, Russia; 1813, Saxony; 1814, France.
Awards Legionnaire, Legion of Honour, 3/4/1814.

GODART RIVOCET, Antonie Paul

[b] Soissons (Aisne), 28/5/1795; [s] Louis Christophe G. & Anne Elisabeth Adélaïde Warel-Beauvoir.
[a] from Imperial Lyceum to St Germain Military School, by decree 9/10/1811, [e] 17/11/1811; [a] as SLt to 2e CLGI, by decree 18/3/1813; [a] 2e Lanciers de Ligne, 24/6/1814.
Campaigns 1813, Saxony; 1814, France.

GONDRE, Joseph

[b] Dieppe (Seine-Inférieure), 12/10/1778.
[e] École de Mars, 29/6/1795; [a] 2e Chasseurs à cheval, 19/11/1795; [t>] 7e Dragoons, 27/6/1801; [pm] Cpl, 5/4/1802; Sgt, 11/3/1804; [a] as Grenadier to Grenadiers à cheval de la Garde Impériale, 19/6/1806; [t>] Gendarmerie de la Seine-Inférieure, 10/4/1811; [pm] Sgt in 2e CLGI, by decree 1/4/1813. Adj-NCO in CRCLF, 2/8/1814; 2nd Lt, 10/2/1815; [a] as supernumerary 2nd Lt to LGI, by decree 14/4/1815; [ds] 16/12/1815; [e] Gendarmerie.
Campaigns 1795-96, Germany; 1797-98, Bretagne; 1799-1800, Italy; 1801-05, Naples & Calabria; 1806-07, Prussia & Poland; 1809, Austria; 1813, Saxony; 1814, served under Gen Maison; 1815, Armée du Nord.
Awards Legionnaire, Legion of Honour, 24/11/1814.

GOUREL, Jean Baptiste

[b] Barr (Bas-Rhin), 10/10/1774.
[e] 10e Chasseurs à cheval, 14/4/1792; [pm] QM, 20/4/1794; Sgt, 8/9/1798; SM, 8/8/1799; SLt, 25/7/1802 to 17/8/1803. [a] Dragons de la Garde de Paris, 23/12/1803; Cpl, 19/7/1804; Sgt, 8/2/1806; SM, 30/7/1806; SLt, 15/10/1809; [a] as 2nd Lt to 2e CLGI, by decree 18/3/1813. [t>] CRCLF, 2/8/1814; placed on half pay, 25/8/1814; [r] 22/12/1814; recalled as 2nd Lt to LGI during Hundred Days.
Wounds Sabre cut at battle of Hohenlinden, 3/12/1800.
Campaigns 1792-93, Rhine; 1793-95, Vendée; 1796, Italy; 1797-98, Switzerland; 1799, Germany; 1813, Saxony; 1814, France.

GRABOWSKI, ?

Polish Lancer of the Guard, member of Napoleon's Elba squadron; [a] LGI, 25/4/1815; [pm] by decree, 22 /5/1815, Capt at Polish Lancers depot; on mission in Paris. [e] Russian Army, 1/10/1815.

GRANGER, Achilles Claude

[b] Paris, 19/1/1793; [s] Louis G. & Cathérine Eléonore Nicolle.
[e] St Germain Military School, 15/1/1812; [a] as SLt to 2e CLGI, by decree 18/3/1813; [a] 5e Lanciers de Ligne, 6/6/1814.
Campaigns 1813, Saxony; 1814, France.

DE GROOT, François

[b] Ordingen, Roër, 7/7/1785; [s] Guillaume d G. & Gertrude Gisse.
[e] Batavian Hussars, 25/9/1801; [t>] Dutch Royal Guard, 14/8/1806; [pm] Cpl, 21/9/1809; SM, 21/9/1810; [t>] 2e CLGI, 21/9/1810. SLt S-Adj-M, Young Guard, 2/4/1813; left for Holland, 15/6/1814; resignation accepted, 30/7/1814.
Wounds Two lance wounds, battle of Reichenbach, 22/5/1813; lost right eye from bullet wound, battle of Craonne, 7/3/1814.
Campaigns 1805, embarked at Texel; 1806, Prussia; 1809, Brabant; 1812, Russia; 1813, Saxony; 1814, France.
Awards Legionnaire, Legion of Honour, 27/2/1814.

GUTSCHENREITER, Jean Baptiste

[b] Wattwiller (Haut-Rhin), 13/1/1782; [s] Charles G. & Cathérine Jux; [d] Rouffach (Haut-Rhin), 21/6/1859. [e] 6e Dragons, 19/9/1802; [pm] Cpl, 25/6/1806; [t>] Chevau-légers de Berg, 27/5/1807; Sgt, 15/7/1807; [a] Chasseurs à cheval de la Garde Impériale, 11/1/1809; SM, 21/8/1809; 2nd Lt, 6/12/1811; Lt, 27/2/1813; S-Adj-M, 21/12/1813. [a] as Lt to CRCLF, 5/8/1814; [pm] S-Adj-M in LGI, by decree 14/4/1815; [p] Waterloo, 18/6/1815; returned to France, 9/1/1816; placed on inactive list after regt disbanded.
"Took a Russian standard at the battle of Wiechouw."
Wounds Bayonet wound, Wiechouw, 1805; sabre cuts to head and left hand, Hanau, 29/10/1813; wounded at Waterloo, 18/6/1815.
Campaigns 1803-04, Coasts; 1805, Austria; 1806-07, Prussia & Poland; 1808, Spain; 1809, Austria; 1812, Russia; 1813, Saxony; 1814, France; 1815, Armée du Nord.
Awards Legionnaire, Legion of Honour, 14/4/1813.

H

VAN HAERSOLTE, Gerard Godart Antonie Zwier, Baron

[b] Harderwijk, 13/2/1790; [s] Baron Anthony Frederik Robbert Evert v H., Lord of Staverden, & Catharina Jacoba Johanna Taets van Amerongen; [d] Arnhem, 7/9/1819.
[e] Dutch 2nd Dragoons, 1805; 2nd Lt in Dutch Royal Guard, 25/3/1807; [pm] Lt into 2e CLGI, 10/1810. Left for Russia, 10/2/1812, with 4e Esc, 4e Cie; crossed Rhine, 12/3/1812; believed lost during retreat from Moscow, but succeeded in returning to regt at Elbing, 17/12/1812. Under First Restoration [e] Dutch Army, 1814; [pm] Capt in Dutch Hussars.

D'HAM, Hugues Jean
[b] Cologne, Röer, 1/11/1774.
[e] Dutch 12th Hussars, 22/8/1798; [pm] Cpl, 20/7/1803; [a] to service
of King of Naples; Sgt, 1/10/1806; [t>] Spanish Royal Guard; SM,
1/11/1809; SLt, 11/3/1812; [t>] as 2nd Lt into 2e CLGI, 1/2/1814. [a]
CRCLF, 2/8/1814; [a] LGI, by decree 14/4/1815; [ds] 21/12/1815.
Wounds Sabre cuts to head and to shoulder, battle of Montebello,
9/6/1800; bullet wound at siege of Gaäte, 8/6/1806.
Campaigns 1798-1801, Italy; 1805-07, Naples; 1808-13, Spain; 1814,
France.
Awards Legionnaire, Legion of Honour, 3/4/1814; Knight, Royal Order
of Spain, 9/9/1809.

HANNEMAN, Johan Christiaan Frederik
[b] Wesel, Lippe, 2/5/1788; [s] Casper Christophe H., Lt of Artillery in
Prussian service, & Maria Margaretha Huymers.
[e] 1st Hussars, 29/10/1800; [pm] 2nd Lt, 1806; Lt, 1809; [a] from Dutch
3rd Hussars in Spain to 2e CLGI, 8/4/1812. Left for Russia, 7/5/1812;
left army without permission, 31/3/1814.
Campaigns 1800, Germany; 1805, Coasts; 1808-11, Spain; 1812,
Russia; 1813, Saxony; 1814, France.
Awards Legionnaire, Legion of Honour, 14/4/1813.

VAN HASSELT, Jan Hendrik Cornelis
[b] Zutphen, 27/3/1776; [s] Johan v H., Mayor of Zutphen, & Susanna
Françoise van Sonsbeeck; [d] of wounds, Elbing, 30/12/1812.
[e] Vanderhoop Regt as cadet, 1789 (nephew of Gen Vanderhoop);
standard bearer, 13/12/1793; 2nd Lt in Dutch 1st Cavalry Regt,
15/8/1795; Lt in 1st Co, 27/12/1795; Lt-Asst ranking as Capt in Garde
du Grand Pensionnaire, 15/11/1805; [t>] Dutch Royal Guard, 4/7/1806;
LtCol, Line Hussars, 5/10/1806; LtCol, Royal Guard Hussars, 1/1807;
[t>] with rank to the Line, 10/10/1807; returned to Royal Guard,
5/3/1808; Maj, 2nd Hussars to replace Maj Weerts, 3/7/1808; Col,
ranking as Capt, Gardes du Corps à cheval, 25?-27?/9/1809; Col-M
ranking as Col, Gardes à cheval, 5/5/1810; Maj, 2e CLGI, 30/10/1810.
Left for Russia, 10/2/1812; crossed Rhine, 12/3/1812. At Orscha,
20/11/1812, took command of dismounted detachment.
"A very good officer, serves with distinction, knows his job very well."
Wounds Bullet wound to left leg, 1799, in action against the British;
wounded at the Beresina, 28/11/1812.
Campaigns 1793-94, Brabant; 1795, siege of Breda; 1796, Armée du
Nord; 1799, Holland; 1800, Germany; 1806, Westphalia; 1812, Russia.
Awards Knight, Order of the Union, 1/1/1807; annuity of 2,000 francs,
1/1/1812; Knight, Order of the Reunion, 7/3/1812.

D'HAUTPOUL, Richard Olivier Hyppolite, Count
[b] Hautpoul Félines (Hérault), 11/2/1782; [s] Jean Marie Alexandre
d'H., Marquis d'H F, Knight of Malta, & Angélique Le Noir.
[e] 18e Dragons, 29/9/1803; [pm] Cpl, 30/1/1804; QM, 15/5/1804; Sgt,
18/10/1804; Adj-NCO, 1/1/1806; SLt, 20e Dragons, 4/11/1806; Lt,
11/12/1808; [p] Eylau, 8/2/1807; Adj-M, 8/5/1812; Capt, 19/6/1813;
[a] Lt in 2e CLGI, by decree 10/8/1813; reported to regt, 15/10/1813.
   [t>] as SLt into Gardes du Corps de Monsieur, 20/7/1814; Maj,
3/9/1814. [t>] as LtCol into Royal Guard Hussars, 12/10/1815; Col,
30/10/1818; Col, Chasseurs de la Dordogne, 17/12/1818; on leave,
1/10/1830; [r] 28/2/1834.
"He distinguished himself at Merksem, near Antwerp, in 1814."
Campaigns 1803-04, Coasts; 1805, Austria; 1806, Prussia; 1807, Poland;
1808-12, Spain; 1813, Saxony; 1814, served under Gen Maison in
Flanders.
Awards Legionnaire, Legion of Honour, 24/11/1814; Officer,
25/4/1821; Commander, 23/7/1823; Knight, Military Order of St Louis,
24/8/1814; Knight, Order of St Ferdinand, 2nd Class, 23/11/1823.

HAYOT, Jean Philippe
[b] Paris, 21/2/1778?-2/12/1777?.
[e] 25e Dragons, 4/5/1798; [pm] Cpl, 21/4/1801; QM, 12/5/1802;
Sgt, 24/10/ 1803; Adj, 15/2/1805; SLt, 21/11/1806; Lt, 11/7/1810;
[a] as Lt to 2e CLGI, by decree 18/1/1813; reported to regt, 1/2/1813.
[t>] CRCLF, 2/8/1814; [a] LGI by decree 14/4/1815;
[ds] 22/12/1815.
Campaigns 1799-1800, Armée du Rhine; 1805-06-07, Grande Armée;
1809-11, Spain & Portugal; 1812, Spain; 1813, Saxony; 1814, France.
Awards Legionnaire, Legion of Honour, 14/3/1806.

VAN HEIDEN, Frederik Maurits
[b] The Hague, 22/9/1775; [s] Sigismund Pieter Alexander, Count v H.
of Entinge and Reinestein, Chamberlain to Princess of Nassau-Oranien
and Great Chamberlain to Prince William V, & Maria Frederica Baroness
van Reede; [d] in battle, Waterloo, 18/6/1815.
[e] Corps des Mineurs as cadet, 1/3/1787; 2nd Lt, 1/7/1790; Lt,
17/3/1794; resigned 1795. Served briefly in Brunswick Dragoons, 1807;
returned to Dutch Army as Lt, Corps de Gendarmerie, 26/2/1807; [t>]
Royal Guard Cavalry, 6/10/1809; [a] as Lt to 2e CLGI, 30/10/1810. [t>]
as Capt to 17e Dragons, 18/3/1813. After First Abdication returned to
Dutch Army as Capt, 1/1/1815; killed in Dutch service at Waterloo.
Wounds Wounded at the Beresina, 28/11/1812.
Campaigns 1793-94, Brabant & Flanders; 1812, Russia; 1813, Saxony;
1814, France.

HENNIGE, Frederik Augustus
[b] Coennern (Coennen), Saale, 26/5/1770; [d] Leiden, 3/6/1834.
Chirurgien-élève in Régiment Suisse, also known as "de Gumoens",
31/8/1787; company surgeon, 1/1/1794; S-Asst S-M, Dutch Swiss
military hospital, 28/4/1796; Asst S-M, military hospitals of Batavian
Republic, 23/8/1799; Asst S-M, 2nd Batavian Cavalry Regt, 1/11/1802;
2nd S-M, Dutch Royal Horse Guards, 26/9/1806; [t>] French Imperial
Guard, 9/7/1810; [a] as S-M to 2e CLGI, 1/10/1810. Left Fulda
14/2/1813, arrived Versailles 26/2/1813. [t>] CRCLF, 2/8/1814;
resigned, 11/2/1815; [e] Dutch Army.
Campaigns 1793-94, Flanders; 1799, Holland; 1803-05, Flanders -
embarked at Texel; 1805, Germany; 1808, Coasts; 1809, Brabant; 1812,
Russia; 1813, Saxony; 1814, France.
Awards Legionnaire, Legion of Honour, 5/4/1814; Knight, Order of the
Reunion, 16/8/1813.

HERVAL, Adolphe
[b] Vasouy (Calvados), 29/1/1794; [s] Jean Philippe Antoine H. & Reine
Elisabeth Hubert.
[a] St Germain Military School, by decree 9/1/1812, [e] 18/2/1812; [a] as
SLt to 2e CLGI, by decree 18/3/1813; [a] 5e Lanciers de Ligne,
6/6/1814; [a] with rank to LGI, by decree 14/4/1815.
Campaigns 1813, Saxony; 1814, France.

HESHUSIUS, Everhardus Henricus
[b] Nieveen, 12/5/1773; [s] Johannes H., clergyman, & Livina Bos; [d]
Tiel, 22/8/1822.
[e/v] 1st Batavian Hussars, 19/10/1798; embarked for Cape of Good
Hope, 1800; [pm] Cpl, 10/5/1801; Adj ranking as Sgt, Cape Dragoons,
12/5/1802; Lt-Adj, 14/10/1804; [t>] Dutch 1st Dragoons, 20/7/1806;
[a] as Lt to Dutch 3rd Hussars, 10/10/1809; [t>] Royal Horse Guards,
3/7/1810; [a] with rank to 2e CLGI, 30/10/1810. Lt Adj-M, 12/6/1811.
Left for Russia, 10/2/1812; crossed Rhine, 12/3/1812. [pm] Capt, Young
Guard, by decree 18/3/1813; [p] Leipzig, 18/10/1813. Capt in Dutch
Legion, 17/11/1813; Capt, Dutch 1st Dragoons,23/1/1814; served in
1815 campaign; Maj, Dutch 1st Cuirassiers, 16/8/1817; [d] in garrison at
Tiel, 22/8/1822.
Campaigns 1799, Holland; 1800-01, served under Gen Augéreau; 1804-

06, at Cape of Good Hope; 1806, Prussia; 1807, Pomerania; 1809, Zeeland; 1812, Russia; 1813, Saxony.
Awards Legionnaire, Legion of Honour, 14/4/1813; Knight, Military Order of William, 4th Class, 18/7/1815.

HOEVENAAR, Nicolas Ludolph
[b] Utrecht, 22/5/1772; [s] Adrien H., notary, & Marie Christine Oortman. SLt in Dutch Corps d'Artillerie, also known as "d'Avernold", on 1/7/1787; resigned, 26/10/1787; [a] to French Army as SM, 1/8/1792. Asst with staff of Gen Daendels, 6/1/1795; [a] as 2nd Lt to Batavian Dragoons, 9/7/1795; [pm] Lt, 8/1/1796; Capt-Adj, Dutch 3rd Hussars, 21/10/1806; Adj-M in 1808; [pm] Cd'E in Dutch Royal Guard Hussars, 29/4/1809; [a] with rank to 2e CLGI, 23/1/1811. [pm] Commandant d'armes, ranking as Col, by decree 18/3/1813. Right arm amputated as result of wounds; went on three months' leave, 23/4/1813; leave extended, 25/8/1813 and 30/11/1813; released from service in French Army, 22/6/1814; [r] as Col, 1/7/1814.
"Saved the life of his colonel, Roest van Alkemade, at Ciudad Rodrigo."
Campaigns 1787, in Holland against Prussia; 1792-95, Armée du Nord; 1796, Germany; 1799, Holland; 1800-01, Armée du Nord; 1805, embarked at Texel - 1805-07, Germany; 1808-10, Spain, with 4th Army Corps.
Awards Legionnaire, Legion of Honour, 24/4/1810; Knight, Order of the Union, 29/4/1809; Knight, Order of the Reunion, 7/3/1812.

HULOT, André
[b] Paris, 20/10/1789.
[e] 7e Chasseurs à cheval, 15/3/1808; [pm] Cpl, 20/11/1808; Sgt, 1/1/1809; SLt, 30/4/1809; Lt, 23/1/1812; Lt, ADC to Gen Ricard, 18/12/1812; [pm] by King of Naples, Capt in 7e Hussards, 8/1/1813; authorised to stay at depot, 14/4/1813; [a] as Capt to 2e CLGI, Young Guard, by decree 10/8/1813; [a] 5e Lanciers de Ligne, 6/6/1814.
Campaigns 1809, Austria; 1812, Russia; 1813, Saxony; 1814, France.
Awards Legionnaire, Legion of Honour, 28/11/1813.

I

IMBERT, Claude Edouard
[b] Buxerolles, near Poitiers (Vienne), 5/5/1791; [s] Gabriel Abraham I., landowner and former treasurer at Bureau des Finances, Poitiers, & Marie Modeste Durand.
S-Asst S-M in 7th Army Corps in Spain, 3/6/1809 to 10/10/1811; [a] to military hospitals of 10th Military Division, 10/10/1811 to 17/12/1811; [a] as S-Asst S-M to Ambulances de la Garde Impériale, 17/12/1811 to 26/5/1813; [pm] Asst S-M in 2e CLGI, Young Guard, by decree 26/5/1813; reported to regt 28/7/1813. On sick leave at military hospital of Dresden (or Torgau?), 27/8/1813; removed from muster roll. Cpl in Gardes du Corps, Compagnie de Luxembourg, in 1814. He later claimed to have been [pm] Lt in the Red Lancers on 27/9/1813.
Wounds Eight times during his military career.
Campaigns Took part in six campaigns.

J

JALY, François Médard
[b] Périgueux (Dordogne), 3/6/1784; [s] Jean J., notary, & Jeanne Albert. [d] 10/3/1819.
[e] Army as S-Asst S-M at military hospital of Grande Armée in Germany, 13/3/1807; director of military hospital in Pomerania, 20/10/1807 to 28/11/1807; [a] with rank to 6e Régiment d'Artillerie à cheval, 20/2/1809; responsible for three military hospitals in Bavaria, 18/5/1809 to 30/10 1809; [a] to military hospital at Eggenfelding, Bavaria, 1-15/12/1809; commanded evacuation post for wounded in Bavaria, 28/12/1809 to 1/3/1810; [a] as Asst S-M to military hospital at Metz, 1/4/1810; Asst S-M at depot of 13e Infanterie de Ligne, 12/7/1811; [a] with rank to 2e CLGI, Young Guard, by decree

26/5/1813; reported to regt 1/7/1813. Left for Angers, 3/1814; [a] 4e Lanciers de Ligne, 10/6/1814 (became Régiment de Monsieur, 1/8/1814). Asst S-M, Légion Départmentale de la Dordogne, 1/1/1816; removed from regt muster roll, 21/2/1816. [t>] Régiment de Carabiniers de Monsieur, 24/4/1816; [t>] Régiment de Chasseurs de l'Isère, 16/7/1816.
Wounds Bullet wound to belly at battle of Ratisbonne, 23/4/1809.
Campaigns 1807, Poland; 1808, Pomerania; 1809, Austria; 1814, France.
Awards Legionnaire, Legion of Honour, 5/4/1814.

JERZMANOWSKI, Jean Paul, Baron
[b] Mniewo, Poland, 25/6/1779; [s] François J., chief magistrate of Pridecz district, & Françoise Dobrska; [d] Paris, 15/4/1862.
[e/v] Légion Polonaise of French Army, 2/8/1800; SLt, 23/9/1800; Lt, 21/1/1801; resigned, 25/8/1801; ADC to Gen Ordener, 14/11/1804; ADC to Gen Duroc, 22/9/1806; [pm] Capt in Chevau-légers Lanciers Polonais de la Garde Impériale, 7/4/1807; Cd'E, 17/2/1811; Maj, by decree 15/3/1814.
    Embarked for Elba, 17/4/1814, as commander of Polish troops of Napoleon's escort. Returned to France with Napoleon, 1/3/1815; Maj commanding Polish squadron of LGI, 22/4/1815. Instructed to lead Polish troops home after Second Abdication; returned to his estates at Touraine in 1819. Recalled as Col of cavalry, 5/2/1831.
Wounds Wounded at Wagram, 6/7/1809; Craonne, 7/3/1814; and Waterloo, 18/6/1815.
Awards Legionnaire, Legion of Honour, 10/3/1809; Knight of the Empire, and annuity of 1,000 francs drawn on Canal du Midi, 15/3/1810; Officer, Legion of Honour, 14/4/1813; Baron of the Empire, 16/8/1813; Knight, Order of the Reunion, 28/11/1813; Commander, Legion of Honour, 11/4/1815 (confirmed, 28/11/1831).

DE JONGH, Cornelis
[b] Amsterdam, 18/3/1777; [s] Frederik d J., merchant, & Wilhelmina Sligter.
[e] Batavian Hussars, 30/6/1798; [pm] Cpl, 15/11/1801; QM, 21/4/1802; SM, 21/10/1805; 2nd Lt, 19/3/1809; [t>] Cavalry of Dutch Royal Guard, 6/10/1809; [a] as 2nd Lt to 2e CLGI, 30/10/1810. Left for Russia, 21/1/1812; crossed Rhine, 11/2/1812. Left regt without permission, 31/3/1814. [e] Dutch Army; Lt, 26/3/1815; [r] 1/2/1819.
"A mediocre officer."
Campaigns 1799, Holland; 1800, Germany; 1805-07, Prussia & Pomerania; 1809, Zeeland; 1812, Russia; 1813, Saxony; 1814, France.

JOUET, Louis François
[b] Tuboeuf (Orne), 3/5/1767.
[e] 14e Régiment de Cavalerie, 9/6/1788; [pm] Cpl, 1/4/1793; SM, 29/5/1799; Adj-NCO in 1?-2?/1804; Lt, 16/6/1807; Capt, Dragons de la Garde de Paris, 26/9/1812; [a] with rank to 2e CLGI, Old Guard, by decree 18/3/1813. Left for the army, 1/4/1813; crossed Rhine, 26/4/1813; [r] 10/8/1813; left regt, 1/3/1814.
Wounds Wounded at battle of Reichenbach, 22/5/1813.
Campaigns 1792-93, 1793-1800, 1809, with Armée d'Italie in Germany; 1813, Saxony; 1814, France.
Awards Legionnaire, Legion of Honour, 16/8/1813.

K

KERAVAL, Claude Mathurin
[b] Versailles, 10/9?-9/10?/1778; [s] Mathurin K., & Cécile Jaffray.
[e] 24e Chasseurs à cheval, 1/10/1793; [a] Chasseurs à cheval de la Garde des Consuls, 3/1/1800; [pm] Cpl, 15/10/1802; Sgt in Vélites, 18/12/1805; SM, 16/2/1807; S-Adj-M, 2nd Lt, 5/4/1809; Lt, 27/2/1813. [a] CRCLF, 5/8/1814; [a] LGI, 1/4/1815; [a] to Escadron de service at Waterloo, 6/1815; [ds] 21/12/1815.
Wounds Bullet wound to right arm at Brescia; sabre cuts to left side

and right hand; bullet wound to right leg in Piedmont; three sabre cuts at Benavente, 29/12/1808 - one cut nose in two, one to eyebrow, another to head.

Campaigns 1793-94, Pyrénées Orientales; 1795-1800, Italy; 1803-04, Coasts; 1805-06-07, Grande Armée; 1808, Spain; 1809, Austria; 1810-11, Spain; 1812, Russia; 1813, Saxony; 1814, France; 1815, Armée du Nord.

Awards Legionnaire, Legion of Honour, 14/4/1807; annuity of 500 francs, 1/1/1809.

L

LACROIX, ?

Surgeon-major, [a] from Dragons de Paris, 27/2/1813; could not join 2e CLGI as surgeon-major; [t>] Gendarmerie Impériale de Paris, 1/8/1813.

LADURELLE, Claude François

[b] Vouziers (Ardennes), 16/6/1782; [s] Joseph L. & Marie Barnier. [a] from Spanish Royal Guard as 2nd Lt to 2e CLGI, 1/2/1814; [a] 3e Lanciers de Ligne, 9/6/1814.

Campaigns 1814, France.

Awards Legionnaire, Legion of Honour, 3/4/1814.

DE LALAING D'AUDENARDE, Charles Eugène, Count

[b] Paris, 13/11/1779; [s] Viscount Eugène François Thérèse Fabien d L., Chamberlain to Empress Marie Thérèse of Austria & Grand-maâtre des cuisines at the Court of Brussels, & Agathe Sophie de Peyrac; [d] Paris, 4/3/1859.

Page at the Court of Vienna, 1795; SLt, 6th Dragoons de Melas, 1/4/1799; resigned, 15/10/1803. [t>] French Army as Capt, 112e Régiment d'Infanterie de Ligne, 28/6/1804; Cd'E of Dragons, 22/7/1805; Cd'E, 3e Cuirassiers, 5/9/1805; equerry to Empress Josephine in 1805 (his wife was lady-in-waiting to Josephine until the Empress's death in 1814). Maj, 3e Cuirassiers, 10/9/1807; commanded two sqns of Cavalerie de marche, Bayonne, 17/7/1808; supernumerary Col, 3e Cuirassiers, 29/1/1809; Col, 7/9/1811.

Gen of Brigade, 5/12/1812; Cpl, Escadron Sacré, during retreat from Moscow, 1812. [a] 3rd Cuirassier Division, 1st Cavalry Corps of the Grande Armée, 12/4/1813; commander, 1st Brigade, 3rd Heavy Cavalry Division, 15/8/1813; Maj in 2e CLGI, 26/12/1813; commander of Young Guard squadrons.

Lt, Gardes du Corps du Roi, Compagnie de Noailles, 1/6/1814. Followed Louis XVIII to Ghent, 20/3/1815, and was present at Duchess of Richmond's ball, Brussels, 15/6/1815. Instructed by King Louis to demand surrender of fortress of Cambrai, 25/6/1815. Lt Cdt, Gardes du Corps, 1/11/1815; commanded Gardes du Corps sqns which served in Spanish campaign with Armée des Pyrénées, 19/2/1823; LtGen, 30/7/1823; unattached, 1/2/1824; commander, 7th Military Division, 28/11/1824; unattached, 4/8/1830; [a] to General Staff, 7/2/1831; [r] 1848. Recalled to active service as member of General Staff, 1/1/1853; Senator, 4/3/1853.

Campaigns 1805, Germany; 1806, Prussia; 1807, Poland; 1809, Austria; 1812, Russia; 1813, Saxony; 1814, Belgium under Gen Maison; 1823, Spain.

Awards Legionnaire, Legion of Honour, 1805; Officer, Legion of Honour, 1809; Baron of the Empire, 15/10/1809; Commander, Legion of Honour, 22/8/1814; Knight, Military Order of St Louis, 10/7/1814; Commander, 1/5/1821; Grand Cross, Order of Charles III of Spain, 21/6/1824; Grand Cross, Order of St George of the Reunion of the Two Sicilies, 27/3?-5?/1830; Peer of France, 3/10/1837; Grand Cross, Legion of Honour, 19/8/1847.

LAMARCHE, Jean Baptiste

[b] Pesmes (Haute-Saône), 12/3/1789; [s] Jean Baptiste L., *bâtonnier en droit, ex-juge de paix du canton de Pesmes, membre du Corps électoral de l'arrondissement de Gray*, & Jeanne Charlotte Chevillet.

S-Asst-M in 26e Régiment d'Infanterie Légère, 10/1/1809; Asst S-M, military hospital at Groeningen, 18/8/1811; returned to 26e Léger, 21/5/1812; [t>] 7e Léger, 11/9/1814; Asst S-M, 9e Cuirassiers, 17/5/1815; [a] as S-Asst S-M to LGI, by decree 22/5/1815. Recalled as Asst S-M to the Line, 1/9/1815; [ds] 16/12/1815.

Campaigns 1809, Grande Armée; 1812, Russia; 1813, Saxony; 1814, France; 1815, France.

Awards Knight, Order of the Reunion, 19/11/1813.

LAMBERT, Christophe

[b] Ponsas (Drôme), 14/1?-25/2/1773; [s] Jacques L. & Marie Rey. [e] 13e Hussards, 14/5/1793; [a] Guides du Général Bonaparte, 9/6/1796; [pm] Cpl, 21/11/1796; [a] Chasseurs à cheval de la Garde des Consuls, 3/1/1800; Sgt, 25/6/1801; 2nd Lt, 18/12/1805; Lt, 3/8/1809; [t>] as Lt, S-Adj-M to CRCLF, 9/8/1814; [pm] Lt in LGI, by decrees 14/4/1815 & 22/5/1815; [ds] 21/12/1815.

Wounds Lance wound to face, Austerlitz, 2/12/1805; bullet and bayonet wounds to right leg, Eylau, 8/2/1807; bullet wound to right side and arm, on Danube, 1809.

Campaigns 1792-93, Alpes; 1793-96, Italy; 1797-98, Egypt; 1799-1800, Italy; 1803-04, Coasts; 1805, Austria; 1806-07, Prussia & Poland; 1808, Spain; 1809, Austria; 1812, Russia; 1813, Saxony; 1814, France; 1815, Armée du Nord.

Awards Legionnaire, Legion of Honour, 14/3/1806; annuity of 500 francs drawn on the Mont Napoléon, 1/1/1807; Officer, Legion of Honour, 15/8/1809.

LANDRIEVE, Pierre Paul

[b] Quebec, 29/6/1763.

[a] Garde du Corps ranking as Lt, 6/10/1784; [pm] Capt, 27e Chasseurs à cheval, 6/10/1806; [a] with rank to 2e CLGI, Old Guard, by decree 18/3/1813; reported to regt 26/4/1813. Left for the army, 5/6/1813; crossed Rhine, 28/6/1813; [p] 18/10/1813; [m] 11/11/1813; returned to France, 5/6/1814. [t>] CRCLF, 2/8/1814; [pm] supernumerary in LGI, by decree 14/4/1815; on sick leave in Paris, 1/7/1815; [ds] 22/12/1815.

"At the battle of Gebora, being captain of an elite company, he charged and routed three battalions of Spanish and Portugese infantry, killing or capturing most of them. He received the Legion of Honour for this brilliant action."

Wounds Bruised by bullet at battle of Töplitz, 17/9/1813; wounded 11/11/1813.

Campaigns 1807, Pomerania; 1808, Denmark; 1809-10, Spain.

Awards Legionnaire, Legion of Honour, 20/5/1811.

LANGRENOIS or LAGRENOIS, Louis François

[b] Paris, 28/1/1787; [s] Joseph L. & Catherine Salegard. [e] 22e Chasseurs à cheval, 8/11/1808; [pm] Cpl, 9/9/1810; [a] as Lancer to 2e CLGI, 17/3/1812. [pm] Cpl, 3/1/1813; Sgt, 6/8/1813; 2nd Lt, by decree 6/1/1814; [a] 2e Lanciers de Ligne, 24/6/1814.

Campaigns 1809, Austria; 1810-11, Spain; 1812, Russia; 1813, Saxony; 1814, France.

LANNOY, Antoine

[b] Laon (Aisne), 16/12/1774; [s] Jacques L. & Louisa Bodelance. [e] 1er Chasseurs à cheval, 24/9/1792; [pm] Cpl on battlefield of Hedelbourg; [a] Chasseurs à cheval de la Garde des Consuls, 9/12/1800; [t>] Dragons de la Garde de Paris, 28/8/1802; Cpl, 29/9/1805; Sgt, 6/1/1809; SM, 26/3/1812; SLt, 1/7/1812; [a] as 2nd Lt to 2e CLGI, 27/2/1813. Left for the army, 5/3/1813. Left for Angers, 3/1814; proposed for post in CRCLF, 31/7/1814, & [a] 2/8/1814. Placed on half pay and left regt, 10/12/1814.

Wounds etc. He had five horses killed under him.

Campaigns 1792-1800, Germany, Holland & Switzerland; 1805, Armée du Nord; 1813, Saxony; 1814, France.

LAROCHE, also known as ENJUBEAULT, Auguste Grégoire François
[b] Sablé-sur-Sarthe (Sarthe), 15/9?-24/12?/1777; [s] Joseph L. & Margueritte Hesse.
[e] 22e Chasseurs à cheval, 25/5/1794; [a] Chasseurs à cheval de la Garde, 9/5/1801; [pm] Cpl in Vélites, 18/12/1805; Sgt, 1/10/1806; 2nd Lt, 3/8/1809; Lt, 27/2/1813; [a] CRCLF, 5/8/1814. [a] LGI, by decree 14/4/1815; [p] Waterloo, 18/6/1815.
Wounds Lance wound at battle of Cremona; bullet wound to the knee in the Tyrol; bayonet wound to thigh at Eylau, 8/2/1807; wounded in thigh, battle of Dresden, 26/8/1813; wounded at Waterloo, 18/6/1815.
Campaigns 1793-94, Spain; 1795-97, Italy; 1798, Switzerland; 1799, Italy; 1800, Germany; 1803-04, Coasts; 1805-06-07, Grande Armée; 1808, Spain; 1809, Austria; 1810-11, Spain; 1812, Russia; 1813, Saxony; 1814, France; 1815, Armée du Nord.
Awards Legionnaire, Legion of Honour, 20/10/1802; presented with *carabine d'honneur.*

LAROUVIERE, Henry Félix
[b] Schanasen (Bas-Rhin), 28/9/1791.
[e] 2e Chasseurs à cheval, 1/10/1809; [pm] Cpl, 16/6/1810; [t>] 15e Chasseurs à cheval, 16/5/1811; QM, 18/10/1811; Sgt, 1/10/1812; SM, Chasseurs à cheval de la Garde Impériale, 1/3/1813; [pm] 2nd Lt, S-Adj-M into 1er éclaireurs de la Garde Impériale, 21/12/1813; [a] CRCLF, 10/8/1814; [a] LGI, by decree 14/4/1815; 2nd Lt, 1/9/1815; [ds] 9/11/1815.
Campaigns 1810-13, Spain; 1813, Saxony; 1814, France; 1815, Armée du Nord.
Awards Legionnaire, Legion of Honour, 27/2/1815.

LASSERRE, Martial
[b] Landes (Landes), 1/7/1783.
[t>] from Spanish Royal Guard to 2e CLGI as Capt, Old Guard, 1/2/1814; [a] 4e Lanciers de Ligne, 10/6/1814.
Campaigns 1814, France.
Awards Legionnaire, Legion of Honour, 3/4/1814.

DE LASTOURS, Charles
[b] Balene (Corrèze), 1770.
Page in service of King Louis XVI, 1782-92; Lt in (Royal) Chasseurs de Normandie, 16/9/1792; to Santo-Domingo as Lt in Dragons d'Orléans, 1793; [pm] Capt on Santo-Domingo, 1801; ADC to Gen Rochambeau, 1802; [pm] temporary Cd'E on battlefield of Cul de Sac, 1802; confirmed Capt on return to France, 1803; ADC to Gen Berthier, 1806. Cd'E in Chasseurs Ioniens on Corfu, 1/1/1808; [p] by British frigate between Corfu and Ancona, 18/3/1808; in captivity until 11/5/1812. On return to France, [a] as Capt, ADC to Marshal Augereau, 1812-13; [t>] as Cd'E into 2e CLGI, Young Guard, by decree 2/4/1813. Left for the army, 5/6/1813; crossed Rhine, 28/6/1813. Commanded Lancers of Young Guard in 1st Army Corps under Gen Maison, Belgium, 1814. [a] to Maison du Roi, 1/5/1814.
Campaigns 1793-1803, Santo-Domingo; 1806-08, Naples & Corfu; 1813, Saxony; 1814, Belgium.
Awards Legionnaire, Legion of Honour, 14/4/1813.

LAURILLARD DE FALLOT, George Jacob
[b] The Hague, 7/5/1781; [s] Antoine Laurillard a.k.a. Fallot, doctor, & Anne Bertaux; [d] of wounds, Moscow, 14/10/1812.
Descendant of family mainly of doctors and soldiers who left France to avoid religious persecution. Abandoned medical studies to enter Batavian Army. [e/v] Dutch Royal Guard Cavalry, 12/11/1806; [pm] Cpl in Vélites, 3/1/1807; Sgt, 4/4/1807; SM, 19/10/1807; [a] as Lt to the Line, 10/2/1808; [pm] Lt in 2e CLGI, 30/10/1810. Left Versailles for Russia as S-Adj-M. Martinien states that he was wounded at the

Moskowa, 7/9/1812, dying at the military hospital in Moscow, 14/10/1812.
"This officer knows his duty very well, and speaks both languages [Dutch & French] fluently. He serves with distinction, is industrious and very energetic; he is very worthy of becoming adjutant-major".

LEMAIRE, Jean Baptiste
[b] Paris, 14/5/1775; [s] Charles L. & Magdelaine Vernet; [d] of wounds, Torgau, 23/11/1813.
[e] Cavalry, 5/9/1793; [t>] 10e Dragons, 26/8/1794; [pm] Cpl, 18/9/1800; [a] Chasseurs à cheval de la Garde des Consuls, 14/5/1801; QM, 15/10/1802; Sgt, 27/8/1803; SM, 2/2/1804; 2nd Lt, 16/2/1807; [pm] Lt in 2e CLGI, by decree 14/1/1813. [a] Capt, Young Guard, by decree 18/3/1813; [m] at battle of Reichenbach, 22/5/1813; at military hospital, Dresden, 13/9/1813.
Wounds Bullet wound to left leg in the Vendée; wounded at Reichenbach, 22/5/1813.
Campaigns 1793, 1804-05, Austria; 1806, Prussia; 1807, Poland; 1808, Spain; 1809, Austria; 1812, Russia; 1813, Saxony.
Awards Legionnaire, Legion of Honour, 14/3/1806.

LESAGE, Louis
[b] Liry (Ardennes), 1/11/1776; [s] Pierre L. & Lucile Auge.
[a] as 2nd Lt to 2e CLGI, from Spanish Royal Guard, 1/2/1814; resigned, 1/5/1814.
Campaigns 1814, France.
Awards Legionnaire, Legion of Honour, 3/4/1814.

LESCAILER, Adrien Joseph
[b] Douai (Nord), 3/4/1774.
[e] 2e Cie de Grenadiers de Douai, 12/10/1792; [a] to 21e Chasseurs à cheval, 4/11/1794; [pm] Cpl, 28/7/1795; Sgt, 1/1/1799; [ds] due to wounds, 20/7/1803. [a] Dragons de la Garde de Paris, 19/8/1803; [pm] Cpl, 25/8/1804; Sgt, 2/10/1805; Adj-NCO, 1/12/1809; SLt, 1/7/1812; [t>] with rank into 2e CLGI, 27/2/1813, confirmed by decree 18/3/1813. [t>] CRCLF, 2/8/1814; placed on half pay, 25/8/1814; resigned, 10/12/1814.
Wounds Bullet wound to right thigh and sabre cut to head.
Campaigns 1792-93, Nord; 1795-98, France; 1799, Ouest; 1805, Nord; 1813, Saxony; 1814, France.

LETHUILLER, Jacques François
[b] St Martin-de-Boscherville (Seine-Inférieure), 4/4/1772.
[e] 11e Régiment de Cavalerie (former Royal Roussillon), 23/5/1794; [t>] Grenadiers de la Garde des Consuls, 5/5/1800; [pm] Cpl, 27/4/1803; Sgt in Grenadiers à cheval de la Garde Impériale, 22/12/1805; [a] as 2nd Lt to 2e CLGI, by decree 18/1/1813. Left for the army, 15/4/1813; crossed Rhine, 19/5/1813; returned to depot, 19/2/1814; left for Angers, 3/4/1814. [t>] CRCLF, 2/8/1814; second standard bearer, 19/11/1814; [a] LGI as 2nd Lt, eagle bearer, by decree 14/4/1815; Lt, 22/5/1815 *[see also Reckinger, Henry]*; commanded squadron of LGI during Hundred Days. [a] again as second standard bearer, 1/9/1815; proposed for retirement, 16/12/1815; [ds] 21/12/1815.
Wounds Sabre cut to thigh, near Chieti, 1798; bullet through right shoulder at battle of Hoogsträten, 10/1/1814; bullet wound to right hand, Waterloo, 18/6/1815.
Campaigns 1793-94, Rhine; 1795-99, Italy & Naples; 1803-05-06-07, Germany; 1808, Spain; 1809, Austria; 1813, Saxony; 1814, Belgium under Gen Maison; 1815, Armée du Nord.
Awards Legionnaire, Legion of Honour, 14/3/1805.

LEUTNER, Gregorius Frederik
[b] Breda, 21/7/1773; [s] Jeremias August L. & Antonia Hooynen.
[e] Dutch 1st Cavalry Regt, 9/10/1798; QM, 6/1/1800; Lt, 21/10/1806;

[t>] Dutch Royal Guard Cavalry, 25/8/1809; [a] as 2nd Lt to 2e CLGI, 30/10/1810. Lt, S-Adj-M, Old Guard, 18/3/1813; left for Holland, 1/5/1814; resigned, 30/7/1814.
"A good officer."
Campaigns 1797, embarked at Texel; 1799, Holland; 1807-09, Germany; 1812, Russia; 1813, Saxony; 1814, France.

LHOTTE, Joseph L.J.N.
[b] Phalsbourg (Moselle), 13/4/1786.
[e] 2e Carabiniers, 24/9/1803; [pm] Cpl, 4/12/1806; Sgt, 21/5/1807; [t>] 13e Cuirassiers, 21/10/1807; [t>] 8e Cuirassiers, 6/3/1811; [t>] as 2nd Lt into Grenadiers à cheval de la Garde Impériale, 9/2/1813; [a] CRCLF, 10/8/1814. [t>] as 2nd Lt into LGI, by decree 14/4/1815; [ds] 15/11/1815.
Wounds Wounded at battle of Waterloo, 18/6/1815.
Campaigns 1804, Coasts; 1805, Grande Armée; 1807, Grande Armée; 1808-11, Spain; 1812, Russia; 1813, Saxony; 1814, France; 1815, Armée du Nord.
Awards Legionnaire, Legion of Honour, 12/9/1813.

LIMBOURG, Louis
[b] Thionville (Moselle), 1/1776.
[e] 3e Hussards, 28/12/1793; [pm] Cpl, 20/5/1799; Sgt, 20/4/1800; Adj-NCO, 21/2/1805; 2nd Lt, 21/11/1808; Lt, Chasseurs à cheval de la Garde Impériale, 27/2/1813; [t>] as Capt, ranking as Lt, to CRCLF, 1/10/1814. [a] LGI, by decree 14/4/1815; proposed for retirement after Hundred Days; [ds] 9/11/1815.
Campaigns 1793-1800, Rhine; 1802-04, Ocean; 1805-06-07, Grande Armée; 1808-12, Spain; 1813, Saxony; 1814, France.
Awards Legionnaire, Legion of Honour, 14/9/1813; Officer, 27/2/1814.

VAN DER LINDEN, Hermanus
[b] Husem (Friesland), 5/3/1769; [s] Jan Otten v d L., horse dealer, & Catharina Hermans.
Trooper in Guard of the Stadtholder, 30/5/1788 to 25/3/1795; [t>] Dutch 2nd Hussars, 28/8/1796; [pm] Cpl, 8/1/1797; Sgt, 15/5/1801; [t>] Hussars of Dutch Royal Guard, 13/8/1806; Lt, 22/9/1806 (became Garde à cheval, 1808, & Guard Cavalry Regt, 1809). [a] as 2nd Lt to 2e CLGI, 30/10/1810. Served in 4e Esc, 1812; remained at depot for much of 1812 & 1813; later with army, but returned, 20/1/1814; left regt without permission, 31/3/1814.
"A good officer for garrison duties."
Campaigns 1793-94, Germany; 1797, embarked at Texel; 1799, Holland; 1800, Germany; 1805, embarked at Texel; 1805-06, Germany; 1809, Brabant; 1813, Saxony.
Awards Knight, Order of the Union, 1/1/1807; Knight, Order of the Reunion, 7/3/1812.

LORY, Louis
[b] Paris, 14/2/1783.
[e] 25e Chasseurs à cheval, 11/11/1801; [pm] Cpl, 31/9/1805; Sgt, 14/6/1806; [a] to service of King of Naples, later King of Spain, as SLt in Light Horse of Royal Guard, 9/8/1806; Lt, 14/6/1809; Capt Adj-M, 18/10/1809; [a] from Spanish Royal Guard to 2e CLGI, 1/2/1814; [a] as Capt, 4e Lanciers de Ligne, 28/7/1814.
Campaigns 1801-02, Camp de Boulogne; 1802-04, Camp de Bayonne; 1805, Germany, 7th Corps; 1806-09, Calabria, Armée de Naples; 1809-13, Spain; 1814, France.
Awards Legionnaire, Legion of Honour, 3/4/1814; Knight, Royal Order of the Two Sicilies, 18/5/1808; Knight, Royal Order of Spain, 22/3/1812.

M

MACARE, Cornelis Hendrik
[b] Middelburg, 7/3/1766; [s] Pieter Johan M. & Johanna Jacoba van Stooren.
[a] Cornet in Cavalry Regt of Hesse-Philipsthal, 1782; resigned 1786. Returned to army as Lt, 13/3/1791; Capt, 1793; resigned, 1/7/1795. Officer, Garde d'honneur, 1806; Capt, 3rd Hussars, 26/2/1807; [a] 2e CLGI, 8/4/1812; [r] 18/3/1813.
Campaigns 1793-94, Flanders & Brabant; 1807, Germany; 1808, Coasts & Spain; 1809, Spain.

MANHEIM, Michel
[b] Kaerlich, nr Koblenz, 19/6/1770; [s] Johannes M. & Anna Marie Anheier.
[e] Dutch Dragoons, 20/8/1790; [pm] Cpl, 21/8/1794; [ds] 1795; rejoined in Hussars, 8/8/1798; [pm] Cpl, 25/6/1799; Sgt, 14/9/1801; [a] as SM to Dutch Royal Guard, 14/7/1805; returned to Line as Lt-Adj, 9/5/1806; [t>] Royal Guard Hussars, 4/3/1807; Lt, 23/12/1808; [a] as Lt to 2e CLGI, 30/10/1810. [t>] as Capt to 22e Chasseurs à cheval, 10/9/1811, confirmed by decree 23/10/1811.
"A very good officer, both in garrison and on campaign; intelligent and very energetic."
Campaigns 1793-94, Brabant; 1799, Holland; 1800-01-06, Germany; 1809, Brabant.

MAREILHAC, Jean
[b] Bordeaux (Gironde), 30/4/1795; [s] Jean Baptiste M., wine merchant, *Magistrat consulaire*, Mayor of Bordeaux in 1796, member of *Conseil Général de la Gironde* 1800-07, & Jeanne Bonneau.
[a] St Germain Military School, by decree 15/5/1812, [e] 14/6/1812; [a] as SLt to 2e CLGI, by decree 18/3/1813. [a] 4e Lanciers de Ligne, 10/6/1814.
Campaigns 1813, Saxony; 1814, France.

MASCHECK, Carolus Paulus Cornelis
[b] Bergen-op-Zoom, 6/7/1787; [s] Gen Hendrik Joseph Carolus M., & Joanne Ijeke; [d] in battle, Quatre-Bras, 15/6/1815.
[e] Dutch 2nd Cavalry Regt as cadet, 30/8/1799; 2nd Lt, 21?-30?/7/1803; [t>] 2nd Dragoons, 8/8/1803; orderly officer; Lt, 2nd Cavalry Regt, 21/10?-12?/1806; Lt QM in Corps de Gendarmerie, 16/4/1807; Lt, 2nd Cuirassiers, 1807; [t>] Gardes Grenadiers, 29/8/1809; [t>] Gardes du Corps à cheval, 25/9/1809; Lt in Cavalry of Dutch Royal Guard, 12/5/1810; [t>] 2e CLGI, 30/10/1810. Capt, 22e Chasseurs à cheval, 10/9/1811, confirmed by decree 23/10/1811; [r] 30/6/1814. [e] Dutch 4th Light Dragoons as Capt; killed at Quatre-Bras.
"A good officer, a man of promise....He distinguished himself in Pomerania in 1806, capturing an enemy cannon, five officers and 80 troopers at Pasewalk."
Campaigns 1805-09, Germany; 1812-13, Spain.

MASCHECK, Joseph Hubertus Sigismundus
[b] 's Hertogenbosch, 29/11/1783; [s] LtCol Hubertus Sigismundus M., & Cornelia Jeanette Joanna Nolet (cousin of Charles M. above); [d] 1819.
[e] Dutch 2nd Cavalry Regt, 28/4/1798; [a] 2nd Lt, 2nd Dragoons, 26/10?-11?/1804; Lt, 26/2/1807; [a] 2e CLGI, 30/10/1810. Left for Russia, 10/2/1812; returned, 11/2/1812 & [e] military hospital, 3/3/1812; left hospital, 28/7/1812; [pm] Capt into 4e Lanciers de Ligne, 14/1/1813; left the regt, 23/3/1813; resigned, 1814. Capt in Dutch Army, 10/4/1815; Capt, Dutch 3rd Carabiniers.
Campaigns 1799, Holland; 1800-04-06, Germany; 1813, Saxony; 1814, France; 1815, Belgium.

MATHIS, Louis

[b] Sarre-Union (Bas-Rhin), 6/9/1777.
[e] 18e Régiment de Cavalerie, 11/3/1792; [pm] SLt, 21e Dragons, 3/1/1795; [t>] as Lt into 13e Dragons, 20/6/1803; Capt, 24/9/1803; [ds] 12/6/1804. Recalled into 25e Dragons, 4/4/1805; Cd'E, 24/6/1811; [t>] 18e Dragons, 12/8/1812; [pm] Cd'E, 2e CLGI, Young Guard, by decree 18/3/1813; reported to regt, 24/5/1813. [t>] as Maj to 13e Chasseurs à cheval, 28/11/1813, and served in that regt during Hundred Days.
Campaigns 1792-97, Armée du Rhin & Moselle, Sambre & Meuse; 1798-99, Switzerland; 1800, Germany; 1805-07, Grande Armée; 1808-12, Spain & Portugal.
Awards Legionnaire, Legion of Honour, 14/3/1806; Knight, Military Order of St Louis.

MAURIN, Jean Jacques Michel

[b] Montpellier (Hérault), 29/9/1779.
[e] 1er Régiment d'Artillerie Légère, 21/12/1798; [pm] Cpl, 9/8/1800; Sgt, 13/8/1800; SLt, Légion de la Loire, 7/9/1800; Lt, 22/9/1800; ADC to Gen Rostollant, 12/4/1802; [t>] as Lt into 24e Chasseurs à cheval, 21/1/1803; Adj-M, 25/12/1805; Capt, 26/6/1807; ADC to Gen Maurin, 30/6/1807; [a] as Capt to 2e CLGI, Old Guard, 14/1/1813, confirmed by decree 11/4/1813; reported to regt, 1/9/1813; [a] ADC to Gen Maurin, 5/5/1814.
"Captured in Portugal by guerrillas; imprisoned in England for four years."
Wounds Wounded 1/10/1813 during visit to advance-guard.
Campaigns 1798, Italy; 1799-01, Armée d'Ouest; 1804-06, Italy; 1807, Poland; 1808, Portugal.
Awards Legionnaire, Legion of Honour, 7/5/1807.

MERGELL, Karel George Eduard

[b] Felsberg, Westphalia, Lower Hesse, 27/4/1781; [d] 18/10/1851.
[e] Medical service, Army of Batavian Republic as Asst S-M, 3rd Bn, 1st Demi-Brigade, 18/5/1802; Asst S-M, 6th Artillery Co of 2nd Bn, on 19/6/1802; Asst S-M ranking as S-M, Batavian Dragoons, 16/9/1803; S-M, 3rd Hussars, 3/11/1809; [a] S-M in 2e CLGI, 30/10/1810. Took part in Russian campaign. Left from Fulda 14/2/1813, arrived Versailles 27/2/1813; S-M, Old Guard, 18/3/1813. Left for Holland, 11/5/1814; resigned, 30/7/1814. Inspector-general of Dutch Army medical service, 1815; director of medical service, Dutch 1st Corps, 5/4/1815; [a] to staff of Prince of Orange; [pm] Inspector of Dutch medical service, 18/5/1817; director of Leiden military hospital, 1/10/1819; [r] 27/4/1822.
Campaigns 28/7/ to 4/9/1805, embarked at Texel - Austria; 1806, Prussia; 1807, Prussia & Pomerania; 1808-10, Coasts & Spain; 1812, Russia; 1813, Saxony; 1814, France.
Awards Legionnaire, Legion of Honour, 5/4/1814; Knight, Order of the Reunion, 16/8/1813.

VAN MERLEN, Jean Baptiste, Baron

[b] Antwerp, 1/6/1773; [s] Bernard Joseph Antoine v M. & Isabelle Caroline Liégeois; [d] Waterloo, 18/6/1815.
[e/v] Army of United Belgian States, 17/3/1789; SLt, 21/3/1790; standard bearer, Régiment d'Anvers (No.5), 7/6/1790; SLt, Belgian 1st Regt, 15/7/1792; Capt, 11/8/1793. [t>] 5th Chasseurs-Tirailleurs, 1/1794; ADC to Gen Dumonceau, 1/1794. [e] Dutch Army, 6/1795; Lt, Batavian Hussars, 10/7/1795; Cd'E, 4/4/1798; LtCol, 3rd Hussars, 1/10/1806; [t>] 2nd Hussars, 18/10/1806; LtCol, Cavalry of Dutch Royal Guard, 15/10/1806; [t>] Hussars of the Guard, 23/10/1806; Maj, 6/4/1807; Col, Garde à cheval regt, 5/3/1808; & of 3rd Hussars, 21/3/1809; passed as supernumerary into 2e CLGI, 11/11/1810, but only reported from Dutch Hussars 8/4/1812.

Gen of Brigade, by decree 12/1/1813; left the regt, 16/1/1813. Commanded Chasseurs à cheval brigade in 1st Cavalry Corps of Grande Armée, 1/3/1813; commanded 2nd Cavalry Bde, 3rd Cavalry Division, 1st Cavalry Corps, 15/8/1813. Served under Marshal Marmont, 1/1814; fell from horse during charge, wounded, [p] 31/1/1814; released 4/1814; [r] 28/6/1814.
MajGen in Dutch Army, 10/7/1814; [a] to command 3rd Cavalry Bde of Dutch Field Army, Division Collaert, 25/3/1815. Fought at Waterloo at head of 5th Light Dragoons; wounded by bullet during charge, died two hours later. His body was stripped by plunderers; left naked and unidentified on the battlefield, he was buried in a mass grave.
Awards Knight, Order of the Union, 1/1/1807; Knight, Order of the Reunion, 7/3/1812; Legionnaire, Legion of Honour, 13/9/1813; Officer, 4/12/1813; Baron of the Empire, 5/4/1814.
Campaigns 1789-90, Belgium; 1792-94, Armée du Nord; 1795, France; 1797, embarked; 1799, Holland; 1800-05-06, Germany; 1809-12, Spain; 1813, Saxony; 1814, France; 1815, Belgium.

VAN DER MEULEN, Karel

[b] Zutphen, 23/5/1778; [s] Jan Carel v d M. & Charlotte Hedewig Ulrica Malapert; [d] near Vilna, Russia, 10?/12/1812.
[a] Cavalry Regt of Hesse-Philipsthal as cadet, 14/4/1792; 2nd Lt, 7/11/1795; Lt, 28/6/1805; [t>] Hussars of Dutch Royal Guard, 15/10/1806; Capt, 3/8/1808; [t>] as Capt into 2e CLGI, 30/10/1810. Left for Russia, 21/1/1812, with 1er Esc, 1ere Cie; crossed Rhine, 11/2/1812; [m] 10/12/1812, suffering from frostbite.
"Knows his job very well, but serves with nonchalance."
Campaigns 1794, Flanders; 1797, embarked at Texel; 1799-1806-08, Germany; 1809, Brabant; 1812, Russia.

DE MEY, Jan Frederik

[b] Breda, 3/10/1776; [s] Pieter Theodorus de M., LtCol of Regt van der Duyn, & Mensina Hubertina Pietronella de Witte.
[e] Régiment de Dopff as cadet, 16/9/1787; Lt, 10/7/1792; resigned, 2/7/1795; returned to army as Lt, 25/4/1807; served in Hussars of Dutch Royal Guard; [t>] as Lt into 2e CLGI, 30/10/1810. [a] to Gendarmerie, 15/4/1811.
Campaigns 1793, Holland & Brabant; 1808, Coasts & Spain; 1810, Spain.

MIERZEJEWSKI, ?

Polish Lancer of Napoleon's Elba squadron, former Sgt; [a] LGI, 25/4/1815; [pm] 2nd Lt, by decree 22/5/1815. [e] Russian Army, 1/10/1815.

MIOT DE MELITTO, René

[b] Paris, 23?-24?/6/1795; [s] André François M., Count of Mélitto, Commissioner of War, Chamberlain & Minister of Interior to King Joseph (1806-13), Conseiller d'Etat, & Adélaïde Joséphine Arcambal; [d] of wounds, 6/12/1815.
[e] Light Horse of Spanish Royal Guard, 9/12/1809; [pm] Cpl, 6/3/1810; Sgt, 10/11/1810; SLt, 7/3/1811; [t>] as 2nd Lt into 2e CLGI, 1/2/1814; ADC to Gen Jamin, 18/2/1814. Died from wounds received at Waterloo.
Campaigns 1810-13, Spain; 1814, France; 1815, Belgium.

MIRZA, "le petit Daniel"

[b] Choucha, Armenia, 15/6/1784.
[e] Syrian Janissaries, 20/6/1800; [t>] Mamelukes de la Garde des Consuls, 15/4/1802; [pm] Cpl, 18/12/1805; Sgt, 6/4/1807; 2nd Lt, 6/12/1811; [a] CRCLF, 5/8/1814; [a] LGI, by decree 14/4/1815; [ds] 21/12/1815.

Wounds Lance wound to waist, Altemburg, 27/9/1813 (horses killed under him at Dresden, Altembourg & Hanau).
Awards Legionnaire, Legion of Honour, 25/3/1806; annuity of 500 francs, drawn on Mont Napoléon.

MOLERAT DE GARSAULT, Arthur François Marie Hortense
[b] Nancy (Meurthe-et-Moselle), 25/11/1795; [s] Louis Charles M., Col of Garde Constitutionnelle, & Marie Thérèse Suzanne Lasalle.
[a] St Germain Military School, by decree 7/2/1812, [e] 16/7/1812; [a] as SLt to 2e CLGI, by decree 18/3/1813. [a] 4e Lanciers de Ligne, 10/6/1814; joined King Louis XVIII at Ghent, 1815; Lt, unattached, 20/6/1815. [a] as 2nd Lt to Dragons de la Garde Royale, 8/10/1815; removed from muster roll, 27/3/1816; [ds] 6/8/1816; recalled as Lt, Dragons du Rhône, 5/11/1816.
Wounds Wounded during campaign of France, 1814.
Campaigns 1813, Saxony; 1814, France.

MORETTI, Théodore
[a] St Germain Military School, by decree 9/7/1811; [e] 15/2/1812; [a] as SLt to 2e CLGI, by decree 18/3/1813; [a] to muster volonteers, 16/4/1813; [a] 4e Lanciers de Ligne, 10/6/1814.
Campaigns 1813, Saxony; 1814, France.

N

NAUDET, Marie Charles
[b] Paris, 5/5/1787; [s] François N. & Nicole Marie Louise Robadeuf; [d] Vienne (Isère), 19/2/1839.
[e] Fontainebleu Military School, 12/12/1803; [a] as SLt to 35e Régiment d'Infanterie de Ligne, 18/12/1804; SLt in 8e Chasseurs à cheval, 21/9/1805; Lt, 9/6/1809; Capt, 6/4/1812; [a] with rank to 2e CLGI, Young Guard, by decree 18/3/1813; reported to regt, 14/4/1813. Left for the army, 30/4/1813; crossed Rhine, 24/5/1813. [a] 4e Lanciers de Ligne, 10/6/1814.
Wounds Wounded on road to Mojaïsk, 8/9/1812.
Campaigns 1805, Grande Armée; 1809, Italy & Germany; 1812, Russia; 1813, Saxony; 1814, France; 1815, Belgium.
Awards Legionnaire, Legion of Honour, 11/10/1812.

DE NETTANCOURT, François Julien, Marquis
[b] Gondrecourt-le-Château (Meuse), 9/9/1783; [s] François Antoine d N., LtCol of Régiment de Guyenne, & Marie Labbé de Coussay; [d] Maisons, nr Bayeux (Calvados), 14/5/1860.
[e] 3e Hussards, 24/3/1803; [pm] Cpl, 5/9/1803; Sgt, 7/12/1803; SLt in 10e Hussards, 2/9/1805; Lt, 24/9/1809; [t>] as 2nd Lt into Grenadiers a chéval de la Garde Impériale, 6/12/1811; [pm] Lt in 2e CLGI, by decree 14/1/1813; reported to regt, 1/2/1813. Left for the army, 5/3/1813; crossed Rhine, 1/4/1813. [t>] as S-Asst-M into Gardes du corps du roi, 1/6/1814; became Col in cavalry.
Wounds Bullet wound to right shoulder, 11/10/1811.
Campaigns 1802-05; 1806-11; 1812, Russia; 1813, Saxony; 1814, France.
Awards Legionnaire, Legion of Honour, 14/9/1813; Officer; Knight, Military Order of St Louis.

O

OGER, Narcisse
[b] Château-du-Loir (Sarthe), 27/5/1794; [s] André Henri O. & Madelaine Serpin.
[e] St Germain Military School, 31/5/1812; [a] as SLt to 2e CLGI, by decree 25/12/1813; [a] 5e Lanciers de Ligne, 6/6/1814.
Campaigns 1814, France.

VAN OMPHAL, Antonie Frederik Jan Floris Jacob, Baron
[b] Tiel, 2/5/1788; [s] Alexander Diederik v O., Lord of Yzendoorn,

Sous-Préfet of Deventer, & Dame Wilhelmina Anna Cornelia Le Pagniet; [d] The Hague, 8/7/1863.
[e] Horse Grenadiers of Dutch Royal Guard as cadet-NCO, 28/1/1807; QM, 3/4/1807; Sgt, 21/10/1807; 2nd Lt in 3rd Hussars, 10/2?-29/7?/1808; [t>] Dutch Royal Guard, 3/4/1808?-11/1809?; 2nd Lt in 2e CLGI, 30/10/1810. Lt in Old Guard, 18/3/1813. Left for Holland, 15/6/1814; resigned, 30/7/1814. [t>] Dutch Army as Lt of Hussars, 23/12/1814; Capt-Adj to Gen Chassé, 4/5/1815; Cd'E, 1825; Maj, 2nd Cuirassiers, 20/12/1826; LtCol, 31/8/1831; Col, 3/1/1839; MajGen, 6/12/1843; [r] 1/8/1850. [a] ADC to King William I of Holland.
"A very good officer...distinguished himself at Ciudad Real [27/3/1809]."
Campaigns 1808-10, Spain; 1812, Russia; 1813, Saxony; 1814, France.
Awards Legionnaire, Legion of Honour, 14/9/1813; Knight, Order of the Reunion, 3/4/1814; Knight, Military Order of William, 4th Class, 11/8/1815.

P

PAATS VAN WIJCHEL, Adriaan Pierre
[b] Anloo (Drenthe), 15/12/1787; [s] Jan Geertsma v W., Lord of Hillum and Scheldewoude, & Johanna Paats; [d] in captivity, Saratov, Russia, 17/1/1813.
[e] 4th Chasseur Bn as cadet, 5?-6?/2/1800; [t>] Dutch cavalry, 28/6/1805, & [pm] Lt the same day; [a] as 2nd Lt to 2e CLGI, 30/10/1810. Left for Russia,10/2/1812; crossed Rhine, 12/3/1812; [p] Babinovitz, 27/7/1812.
Wounds Wounded at Babinovitz, 27/7/1812.
Campaigns 1806-07, Germany; 1808, Coasts; 1809, Spain; 1812, Russia.

PAILLARD, Jean Baptiste Henri Casimir
[b] Nemours (Seine-et-Marne), 9/3/1785; [s] Jean Baptiste P. & Sofie Cotte.
[e] Dragons de la Garde de Paris, 3/3/1806; [pm] Cpl, 15/4/1809; QM, 16/4/1809; [t>] 2e CLGI, Old Guard, 27/2/1813. Sgt, 28/2/1813; SM, 1/3/1813; SLt, Young Guard, 30/8/1813, confirmed 1/5/1814; [a] 2e Lanciers de Ligne, 18/8/1814. Placed on half pay, Paris, 2/12/1815.
Wounds Sabre cut to left hand, battle of Töplitz, 18/9/1813; lance wound to left thigh, 5/2/1814, nr Antwerp.
Campaigns 1813, Saxony; 1814, France.

PERRIN, Joseph Hyacinthe
[b] Gières (Isère), 12/1773.
[e] 1er Bataillon de l'Isère, 14/12 1791; [pm] QM, 21/1/1794; [a] 10e Chasseurs à cheval, 15/11/1796; Cpl, 14/7/1800; QM, 16/7/1800; Sgt, 10/1/1803; SM, 1/11/1806; Adj-NCO, 1/4/1807; SLt, 4e Chasseurs à cheval, 9/2/1813; Lt S-Adj-M, 1er Éclaireurs de la Garde Impériale, 21/12/1813; [a] as 2nd Lt to CRCLF, 10/8/1814. [t>] LGI, by decree 14/4/1815; on leave, 1/11/1815; removed from muster roll, 19/11/1815.
Wounds Five sabre cuts, 14/10/1806.
Campaigns 1792-94, Alpes; 1795-97, Italy; 1798-1800, Rhine; 1803-05, Coasts; 1806, Germany; 1807, Poland; 1808-12, Spain; 1813, Saxony; 1814, France.
Awards Legionnaire, Legion of Honour, 27/2/1815.

PETIET, Augustin Louis, Baron
[b] Rennes (Ille-et-Vilaine), 19/7/1784; [s] Claude Louis P., *Conseiller-secrétaire* to the king, *Inspecteur des revues*, *Conseiller d'Etat*, Minister of War (8/2/1796), Senator of the Empire (19/5/1806); & Anne Françoise Guillemette Le Liepvre du Bois de Pacé; [d] Paris, 1/8/1858.
[e] Army as cadet Commissioner of War, 3/6/1800; Asst in Armée de Réserve the same day; Asst with General Staff of Armée d'Italie, 7/10/1800; [t>] as SLt into 10e Hussards by order of the Consul, 8/10/1800. Military secretary to Gen Soult, 9/12/1803; Lt, 30/7/1804; ADC to Marshal Soult, 11/2/1805; [a] 8e Hussards, authorised by the

Emperor to remain with Marshal Soult; Capt, 8e Hussards, 9/5/1807; recalled as ADC to Marshal Soult, 22/10/1808; Cd'E, 19/5/1811; [a] as Capt to 2e CLGI, 18/1/1813.

[pm] Second Maj, awaiting vacancy in a light cavalry regt, 28/1/1813; [a] as Cd'E to 2e CLGI, by decree 18/3/1813. [pm] Adj-Cdt, Chief of Staff of Light Cavalry Division of Gen Piré, 5th Cavalry Corps, 6/11/1813; [a] to staff of 1st Military Division, 5/6/1814. At the disposal of HRH Monsieur, 6/3/1815; [a] to Imperial Headquarters, Armée du Nord, 13/5/1815. Maréchal de camp, 5/7/1815 - not confirmed by the king, placed on inactive list, 1/8/1815.

[a] as supernumerary Col to Corps Royal d'Etat-Major, 27/5/1818; unattached, 1/1/1819; exceptionally employed at Dépôt de la Guerre, 15/2/1822; Col in Corps Royal d'Etat-Major, 12/2/1823; [a] Dépôt, 21/3/1823; Chief of Staff to Supreme Commander of the Cavalry Camp, 7/3/1826; returned to Dépôt de la Guerre, 1/11/1826; member of Advisory Board to the Staff, 1827 & 1829. Chief of Staff, 3rd Division, for Algerian expedition, 23/3/1830. Maréchal de camp but unattached, 13/12/1830; commander, Department of Hérault, 18/4/1831; temporary commander, Department of Seine et Oise, 1/8/1833; commander, Department of Loiret, 13/9/1833; to General Staff Reserve, 20/7/1846; [r] 12/4/1848, on pension of 4,800 francs; recalled at own demand to General Staff Reserve, by decree 26/12/1852. Deputy in Corps Législatif, Department of Nièvre, elected 29/2/1852, re-elected 22/6/1857; Reporter to the Council of State; member of the General Council of Nièvre.

"At Austerlitz, 2/12/1805, Petiet charged three times at the head of a Dragoon division, and overran four cannon [his horse was killed under him].... At Friedland, 14/6/1807, he captured, at the head of his company, 300 Prussian horses and two cannon.... In Spain, 11/2/1811, the General in Chief of the Armée du Midi gave Petiet command of 200 Voltigeurs, with whom he took a fort near Badajoz defended by 400 men and four cannon."

Wounds Sabre cut to head and shoulder at Gebora, 19/2/1811; at Nangis, 17/2/1814, bullet wounds to right side and right leg.

Campaigns 1799-1814.

Awards Legionnaire, Legion of Honour, 14/3/1806; Officer, 16/8/1813; Baron of the Empire, by decree 17/1/1814; Commander, Legion of Honour, 23/5/1825; Grand Officer, 27/4/1846; Knight of the Iron Crown, 3/4/1814; Knight, Military Order of St Louis, 27/11/1814.

PIOTROWSKI, ?

Former SM in Polish Lancers of the Guard, and member of Napoleon's Elba squadron; [a] as supernumerary 2nd Lt to LGI, by decree 14/4/1815. [e] Russian Army, 1/10/1815.

PITEL, Jean Baptiste Félix

[b] Villedieu-les-Poêles (Manche), 22/2/1771; [s] Joseph P., coppersmith, & Denise Agathe Françoise P.

[e] 7e Dragons, 21/2/1790; [pm] QM, 1/10/1792; Sgt, 13/3/1794; SM, 7/4/1794; SLt, 21/12/1796; [p] Mantua, 31/7/1799; released 11/6/1800. Lt, 14/4/1804; Adj-M, 31/5/1806; [a] as Adj-M to Light Horse of Royal Guard of King of Naples, 9/8/1806; Cd'E, 17/10/1809; [a] with rank from Spanish Royal Guard to 2e CLGI, Young Guard, 1/1/1814; [a] 4e Lanciers Ligne, 10/6/1814.

Wounds Wounded before Verona, 5/4/1799.

Campaigns ? - incl.1799, Italy, & 1814, France.

Awards Knight, Royal Order of the Two Sicilies, 18/5/1808; Knight, Royal Order of Spain, 17/10/1809; Legionnaire, Legion of Honour, 3/4/1814; Knight, Military Order of St Louis, 7/8/1814.

PLATELET LAGRANGE DE LA TUILLERIE, Jean Baptiste

[b] Fort Royal (Martinique), 19/9/1794; [s] Jean Baptiste Jacques P. & Marie Jeanne Adélaïde Cools.

[e] St Germain Military School, 9/1/1812; [a] as SLt to 2e CLGI, by decree 18/3/1813; [a] 2e Lanciers de Ligne, 24/6/1814.

Wounds Wounded 1/2/1814 at battle of la Rothière.

Campaigns 1813, Saxony; 1814, France.

Awards Legionnaire, Legion of Honour, 5/4/1814.

POST, Jan

[b] Tiel, 28/8/1778; [s] Hermanus P. & Evarina van Riemsdijk; [d] Utrecht, 18/8/1841.

[e] Dutch 2nd Cavalry Regt as cadet, 15/6/1796; [pm] 2nd Lt, 15/2/1803; [t>] 2nd Batavian Hussars, 1805; [t>] Dutch Royal Guard, 1806; Lt, 17/3/1807; Capt, 7/4?-9?/1809; [t>] 2e CLGI, 30/10/1810. Left for Russia, 10/2/1812; crossed Rhine, 12/3/1812. Left Fulda 14/2/1813, arrived Versailles 25/2/1813. [pm] Cd'E in Young Guard, 18/3/1813; returned to depot, 20/1/1814; left for Angers, 3/1814; [t>] 2e Lanciers de Ligne, 24/6/1814; [r] 11/9/1814.

[e] Dutch Army; Maj, 6th Hussars, 25/1/1815; LtCol, 2/4/1815. 2nd Col commanding 3rd Cavalry Regt (later 3rd Cuirassiers), 27/8/1820; MajGen, 20/12/1826; commanded Dutch 1st Cavalry Brigade after Belgian Revolution; [r] 4/4/1836.

"He serves well."

Wounds Bullet wound at battle of Leipzig, 1813.

Campaigns 1797, embarked at Texel; 1799, Holland; 1805, embarked at Texel - Austria; 1806, Prussia; 1809, Zeeland; 1812, Russia; 1813, Saxony; 1814, France.

Awards Legionnaire, Legion of Honour, 14/4/1813; Knight, Military Order of William, 3th Class, 16/11/1830; Knight, Order of the Netherlands Lion, 19?-29?/2/1824.

DE POTIER, Jacques Charles

[b] Nancy (Meurthe-et-Moselle), 26/6/1782.

[e] 5e Hussards, 23/5/1800; [pm] Cpl in 8e Hussards; QM; Sgt, 2/3/1803; SLt, 10/3/1804; Lt, 22/11/1806; Capt, 26/4/1809; Cd'E, 10/8/1813;

[a] as Capt to 2e CLGI, Old Guard, by decree 11/8/1813. [t>] CRCLF, 2/8/1814; [a] LGI, by decree 14/4/1815; left regt without permission, 21/5/1815.

Wounds Bullet wound to left hand, Russia.

Campaigns 1799-1800, Rhine; 1801-04, Coasts; 1805, Grande Armée; 1806, Grande Armée; 1807, Poland; 1808, Spain; 1809, Austria; 1810-11, Corps d'Observation; 1812, Russia; 1813, Saxony; 1814, Brabant.

Awards Legionnaire, Legion of Honour, 21/8/1812; Knight, Military Order of St Louis, 12/1814.

POUPON, François Xavier

[b] Croupet (Jura), 27/5/1778.

[e] 9e Hussards, 2/5/1799; [pm] Cpl, 10/7/1802; Sgt, 11/11/1804; SM, 16/4/1808; SLt, 30/9/1811; Lt in 12e Hussards, 16/10/1813; [t>] 6e Lanciers de Ligne, 21/8/1814; [a] LGI, 19/5/1815. Commanded a Young Guard squadron, 22/5/1815.

Campaigns 1798-1805, 1806-1814.

R

RAFFACZINSKI, ?

Former SM of Polish Lancers of the Guard, member of Napoleon's Elba squadron; [a] as supernumerary 2nd Lt to LGI, by decree 14/4/1815. [e] Russian Army, 1/10/1815.

Awards Legionnaire, Legion of Honour, 15/4/1813.

RAPATEL, Augustin François Marie, Baron

[b] Rennes (Ille-et-Vilaine), 18/6/1775; [s] Jean Michel R., professor at Rennes medical school, & Jeanne Françoise Beauvais; [d] Rennes, 25/6/1839.

Medical officer at military hospital of Rennes, 18/6/1791; Cpl, Chasseurs Volontaires de Rennes, 14/8/1792 to 30/10/1792; Surgeon 3rd Class with Armée de la Moselle, 1/2/1793; at Rennes military hospital under

Armée des Côtes, 23/11/1794 to 19/9/1796; Lt Asst to Adj-Gen Trublier, 22/9/1796, & to Adj-Gen Simon, 23/3/1797; Capt, 21/3/1798. [p] aboard the ship *le Roche*, 12/10/1798; exchanged, 5/1799. [a] ADC to Gen Simon, 2/9/1799; [ds] with Gen Simon for his part in "Complot des Libelles", 10/8/1802; prisoner in the Temple; later allowed to live in Rennes under police surveillance.

Recalled as Capt in 4e Chasseurs à cheval, 5/10/1803; [a] with rank to Light Horse of Royal Guard of Naples, 9/8/1806; Cd'E, 18/1/1809; Maj, 27/11/1810; authorised to remain in Spanish Army, 14/7/1812; orderly officer to King Joseph, 1/1814; [a] as Maj to 2e CLGI, Young Guard, 1/2/1814. Col, Dragons du Roi (1er), 11/5/1814; on inactive list, 21/3/1815; resigned, 26/3/1815; recalled to serve with Staff of Minister of War, 16/6/1815. [a] as Maréchal de Camp to 1st Corps, Armée des Pyrénées, 11/8/1823; unattached, 1/1/1824; commander, Département du Nord, 16/10/1832; commander, Département de la Haute Saône, 28/2/1833; on inactive list, 18/6/1837.

Campaigns 1792-93, Armée du Nord; 1793-94, Armée de la Moselle; 1795, Armée de l'Ouest; 1796-98, Armée de Sambre & Meuse and Armée d'Angleterre; 1799-00, Armée de l'Ouest; 1805-07, Naples; 1808-13, Spain; 1814, France; 1823, Spain.

Awards Legionnaire, Legion of Honour, 4/1/1807; Knight, Royal Order of the Two Sicilies, 22/6/1808; Knight, Royal Order of Spain, 25/10/1809; Knight, Military Order of St Louis, 19/7/1814; Officer, Legion of Honour, 29/7/1814; Commander, Legion of Honour, 1/8/1821; Knight, Royal and Military Order of St Ferdinand, 4th Class. Made Baron, 2/3/1816, confirmed 2/4/1822.

RECKINGER, Henry
[b] Saarlouis, 3/6/1775.
[e] 7e Hussards, 21/12/1796; Grenadiers à cheval de la Garde Impériale, 17/6/1801; [pm] Cpl, 11/10/1802; Sgt, 26/2/1806; [a] as 2nd Lt to 2e CLGI, by decree 18/1/1813. Left for the army, 5/3/1813; crossed Rhine, 1/4/1813. [t>] CRCLF, 2/8/1814; [a] as 2nd Lt to LGI, by decree 14/4/1815; [pm] eagle bearer, by decree 22/5/1815 [*see also Lethuiller, Jacques*]; Lt, 1/9/1815; [ds] 21/12/1815.
"He distinguished himself near Antwerp in 1814, where at the head of 18 lancers he charged and routed a Prussian infantry regiment."
Wounds Wounded 13/1/1814 near Antwerp.
Campaigns 1796, Rhine; 1805-07, Grande Armée; 1808, Spain; 1809, Austria; 1813, Saxony; 1814, Armée du Nord et Brabant, under Gen Maison; 1815, Armée du Nord.
Awards Legionnaire, Legion of Honour, 14/3/1806; Officer, 16/1/1814.

REIAUTEY or REAUTEY, St Valéry
[b] Fervaques (Calvados), 19/9/1789.
[e] 8e Chasseurs à cheval, 22/12/1804; [pm] QM, 27/12/1807; Sgt, 25/9/1808; [a] as SLt to 1st Croatian Regt, 6/8/1811; Lt, 10/4/1812; [a] Grenadiers à cheval de la Garde Impériale, 7/1/1814; [t>] as 2nd Lt into CRCLF, 10/8/1814. [a] LGI, by decree 14/4/1815; at military hospital of Limoges from 12/10/1815; removed from muster roll, 22/12/1815.
Wounds Sabre cut to right hand, near the Piave, Italy; right foot fractured by explosion at battle of Raab, 14/6/1809; severely wounded by sabre in right side and two cuts to right thigh, Wagram, 5/7/1809; wounded at Waterloo, 18/6/1815.
Campaigns 1804, Holland; 1809, Austria; 1812, Russia; 1813, Saxony; 1814, France; 1815, Armée du Nord.
Awards Legionnaire, Legion of Honour, 24/11/1814.

RENAUX, Charles Hyppolite
[b] Perpignan (Pyrénées-Orientales), 10/12/1794.
[a] from Prytanée de la Flèche as cadet to St Germain Military School, by decree 21/11/1811, [e] 16/2/1812; [a] as SLt to 2e CLGI, by decree

18/3/1813. Left for the army, 30/6/1813; sent to Versailles, 1/12/1813; [a] 1er Éclaireurs de la Garde Impériale, 20/12/1813.
Campaigns 1813, Saxony; 1814, France.

RENNO, Jean
[b] St Jean-d'Acre, Syria, 5/5/1777; [s] François R., doctor to Djezzar Pasha, & Hélène; [d] Melun, 10/4/1848.
[a] as volunteer SLt ranking as S-Asst S-M to St Esprit military hospital, Rome, 25/9/1797; [a] to staff of Gen Desaix, later to staff of Armée d'Orient; [t>] as Lt into Mamelukes de la Garde des Consuls, 15/4/1802; Capt, 16/2/1807; [a] CRCLF, 5/8/1814. [a] LGI, by decree 14/4/1815; [ds] 22/12/1815.
"He served under Gen Maison, 26/3/1814, and was mentioned in Army despatches."
Campaigns 1797-1800, Egypt; 1803-04, Coasts; 1805-06-07, Austria, Prussia & Poland; 1808-11, Spain; 1812, Russia; 1813, Saxony; 1814, served under Gen Maison; 1815, Armée du Nord.
Awards Legionnaire, Legion of Honour, 15/6/1802; Officer, 14/3/1806; Knight, Order of the Reunion, 27/2/1814; Order of the Lily; Knight, Military Order of St Louis, 27/2/1815.

RETTERICH, Adam Jean Pierre
[b] Nijmegen, 10/3/1778; [s] Philippe R. & Everdine van Zuylen; [d] 25/1/1849.
[e] Dutch Army in Prince of Orange's Infantry Regt, 1/1/1789; [r] 20/10/1795. [e/v] Saxony-Gotha Infantry Regt, 10/12/1797; [r] 7/9/1805. [e/v] Dutch Royal Gendarmerie, 11/4/1807; [pm] Cpl, 24/4/1807; Sgt, 20/3/1807; [a] Dutch Royal Guard, 1/11/1809; SM, 1/12/1809; [t>] as sergeant into 2e CLGI, 21/9/1810; Lt, Young Guard, 18/3/1813. Left regt without permission, 31/3/1814; resignation accepted, 24/7/1818. [e] Dutch Army as Lt, 3rd Carabiniers; Capt, 21/7/1828; Maj, 3/1/1839; [r] 6/6/1840.
Wounds Lance wound to head and bullet wound to right leg during Russian campaign.
Campaigns 1793-94, Brabant; 1799, Holland; 1800-09, against the British; 1812, Russia; 1813, Saxony; 1814, France.

REYNTJES, Jean
[b] Raalte, 10/10/1779; [s] Bernard R. & Jeanne Ketting; [d] of wounds, Dresden, 6/6/1813.
[e] Dutch 1st Dragoons, 23/2/1801; [pm] Cpl, 23/8/1803; SM in Dutch Royal Guard, 29/4/1809; [t>] 2e CLGI, 8/4/1812. [pm] SLt Adj-M in Young Guard, 2/4/1813.
Wounds Seriously wounded at battle of Reichenbach, 22/5/1813.
Campaigns 1805, Austria; 1806, Prussia; 1808-12, Spain; 1812, Russia; 1813, Saxony.

ROGIER, Gabriel
[b] Allier (Allier), 15/12/1789; [s] Pierre R. & Jeanne l'Hermitte.
[e] St Germain Military School, 2/11/1812; [a] as SLt to 2e CLGI, Young Guard, 25/12/1813; [pm] SLt, by decree 19/2/1814; [a] 3e Lanciers de Ligne, 9/6/1814.

ROLLIN, Jacques
[b] Pont-de-Vaux (Ain), 9/3/1777; [s] Jean Baptiste R. & Anne Françoise Frèrejean.
[e] 6e Bataillon de l'Ain as SLt, 29/7/1792; [t>] as dragoon into 4e Dragons, 14/7/1799; [a] Chasseurs à cheval de la Garde des Consuls, 5/9/1802; [pm] Cpl, 27/8/1803; QM, 18/12/1805; SM, 25/8/1808; 2nd Lt, 20/8/1809; Lt, 27/2/1813; [a] CRCLF, 5/8/1814. [a] LGI, by decree 14/4/1815; proposed for retirement after Hundred Days; [ds] 15/11/1815.
"He received from the Government the ownership of a house in Paris that will be

his after the death of his father-in-law, M.Perneau, Usher to the Cabinet of Louis XVIII."

Wounds etc. Bullet wound to right leg at Petit St Bernard, 1793; bayonet wound to left cheek at Nuremberg, 1799; sabre cuts to right hand and nose; three lance wounds - one to right arm and two to right side - at Braine in 1814. (He had six horses killed under him, three in Spain and three in France.)

Awards Legionnaire, Legion of Honour, 14/3/1806; annuity of 500 francs, drawn on the Canal de l'Oing, 1/1/1809.

ROYEN, Henricus

[b] Delft, 4/1/1788; [s] Wilhelmus R., retired Capt, & Adriana Mathilda Huysmans; [d] Haarlem, 23/10/1859.

[e] Dutch 2nd Hussars, 21/10/1803; cadet, 15/10/1804; [pm] 2nd Lt, 8/4/1806; [t>] Hussars of Dutch Royal Guard, 4/3/1807; [t>] as Lt to Dutch Garde du Corps à cheval as Schildknaap, 25/9/1809;

[a] Dutch Garde à cheval, 14/5/1810; [t>] 2e CLGI, 30/10/1810. [pm] S-Adj-M; left for Russia, 10/2/1812; crossed Rhine, 12/3/1812. Left Fulda 14/2/1813, arrived Versailles 20/2/1813; [pm] Capt, Young Guard, 18/3/1813. Left regt without permission, 31/3/1814. [e] Dutch 4th Light Dragoons, 1/5/1814; [t>] 6th Hussars, 17/2/1815; [a] Capt, 10th Lancers; Maj, 22/7/1820; LtCol, 16/4/1830; Col, 3/1/1839; MajGen, 2/5/1842; [r] 21/10/1843.

"The colonel recommends that this officer be appointed adjutant, as Adjutant Schillings is crippled and unfit to continue in his duties."

Campaigns 1805, embarked at Texel - Germany; 1806, Prussia; 1807, Poland; 1809, Brabant; 1812, Russia; 1813, Saxony; 1814, France.

Awards Legionnaire, Legion of Honour, 14/4?-18/8?/1813; Knight, Military Order of William, 4th Class, 24/5/1821.

S

SALVETAT, Adolphe Pierre

[b] Paris, 5/4/1775; [s] Guillaume S. & Marie Margueritte S. (a cousin of Mlle Mars, a famous actress of the Théâtre-Français).

[e] Bataillon de Paris, 8/9/1792; [a] 2e Hussards, 23/4/1798; [pm] QM, 2/1/1800; [a] Chasseurs à cheval de la Garde des Consuls, 12/6/1800; [pm] Cpl, 23/9/1800; Sgt, 15/10/1802; SLt in 18e Dragons, 23/9/1805; Lt, 15/1/1809; Capt in 17e Dragons, 9/12/1812; [a] as Lt to 2e CLGI, by decree 18/1/1813. Left for the army, 5/3/1813; Capt, Young Guard, by decree 18/3/1813; crossed Rhine, 1/4/1813; [p] 22/5/1813; returned to France, 29/9/1814. [pm] supernumerary Capt ranking as Cd'E, CRCLF, by order 24/11/1814. [a] as supernumerary to LGI, by decree 14/4/1815; [ds] 16/11/1815.

Wounds Sabre cut to head near Frankfurt-am-Main, 1798; three lance wounds at battle of Reichenbach, 22/5/1813.

Campaigns 1792-93; 1793-1800; 1813, Saxony.

Awards Legionnaire, Legion of Honour, 11/3/1806.

SCHNEITHER, Jean Jacques Adolphe

[b] Leiden, 11/1/1779; [s] Jean Jacques S. & Catharina Maria Wrist; [d] 3/9/1849.

[e] Dutch Army as 2nd Lt, 16/6/1795; [pm] Lt, 7/9/1799; ADC to Gen Quaita, 1805; ADC to Gen Daendels, 1806; Lt-Asst with General Staff, 1/3/1807; Capt, 25/3/1808; returned with rank to Line, 2/11/1808; [a] Dutch Royal Guard, 6/10/1809; [a] as Capt to 2e CLGI, 30/10/1810. Left Fulda 14/2/1813, arrived Versailles 25/2/1813; Cd'E in Young Guard, 18/3/1813. Left for Angers, 3/1814; [a] 3e Lanciers de Ligne, 9/6/1814; inactive, 11/1814. [e] Dutch Army; Maj, 18/4/1820; LtCol, 16/4/1830; Col, 3/1/1839; [r] 16/6/1840.

"He comes from the infantry, and does not know the cavalry very well."

Wounds Wounds to chest and left arm in Holland, 9/1799.

Campaigns 1796, Germany; 1797, embarked at Texel; 1799, Holland; 1805, Germany; 1809, Brabant; 1812, Russia; 1813, Saxony; 1814, France.

Awards Legionnaire, Legion of Honour, 14/4/1813.

SCHONENDALL D'ARIMONT, ?
[pm] SLt in 2e CLGI, 28/6/1813, effective from 10/4/1813; did not join the regiment.

SCHULTZ, ?

Polish Lancer of Napoleon's Elba squadron; [pm] Capt in LGI, by decree 14/4/1815. [e] Russian Army, 1/10/1815.

SENNEPART, Frédéric Jean

[b] Toulouse (Haute-Garonne), 4/9/1781; [s] Denis S. & Gabrielle Poulard.

[e] 22e Chasseurs à cheval, 23/1/1802; [pm] Cpl, 25/4/1802; QM, 29/4/1802; Sgt, 8/11/1803; SM, 11/4/1805; Adj-NCO, 22/11/1806; SLt, 28/6/1807; Lt, 20/9/1809; Capt, 5e Dragons, 28/1/1813; [a] as Capt into 2e CLGI, by decree 18/3/1813. [a] 2e Lanciers de Ligne, 24/6/1814; returned home and placed on half pay, 2/12/1815.

Wounds Sabre cut to left arm, battle of Warnemühl, 1/11/1805.

Campaigns 1805, Austria; 1806, Prussia; 1807, Poland; 1808-09, Spain & Portugal; 1813, Saxony; 1814, France; 1815, Belgium.

Awards Legionnaire, Legion of Honour, 1/10/1807.

SENNO, Fortunato

Former orderly officer of Napoléon; [a] as 2nd Lt to LGI, by decree 15/4/1815; removed from muster roll, 1/8/1815.

SERAN, Alphonse

[b] Lyon (Rhône), 31/5/1784.

[e] 22e Dragons, 29/7/1805; [pm] Cpl, 30/10/1807; QM, 7/3/1808; Sgt, 11/9/1808; SM, 1/10/1809; SLt-QM, Dragons de Paris, 8/10/1812, by decree 4/9/1812; Lt-QM, 1/3/1813; [a] as Lt to 2e CLGI, Young Guard, by decree 18/3/1813. [t>] CRCLF, 2/8/1814; [a] as 2nd Lt paymaster to LGI, by decree 14/4/1815; [ds] 22/12/1815.

Wounds Lance wound to left thigh, 26/2/1806; sabre cut to head, 15/5/1809; wounded, and horse killed under him, at battle of Töplitz, 17/9/1813.

Campaigns 1805-06-08, Germany; 1809-10, Spain & Portugal; 1813, Saxony; 1814, served under Gen Maison.

Awards Legionnaire, Legion of Honour, 5/4/1814.

SKOWRONSKI, ?

Polish Lancer of Napoleon's Elba squadron; [a] as Lt to LGI, by decree 14/4/1815. [e] Russian Army, 1/10/1815.

SMITH, Jean Marie Emerie

[b] Paris, 26/2/1791.

Asst S-M in 10e Hussards, 27/3/1813 to 2/4/1813; Asst S-M, 2e Régiment d'Infanterie Légère, 3/4/1813 to 26/5/1813; Asst S-M, Young Guard, at Versailles depot, by decree 26/5/1813. [t>] CRCLF; [a] 3e Lanciers de Ligne. 1839, requested post as surgeon with Garde Municipale de Paris.

Campaigns 1813, Saxony; 1814, France.

SOUFFLOT DE MAGNY ET DE PALOTTE, Pierre Jules

[b] Auxerre (Yonne), 13/12/1793; [s] Germain André S. d M., Conseiller général de l'Yonne, & Jeanne Marie Julie Boyard; [d] Paris, 2/6/1893.

[e] 20e Chasseurs à cheval as QM, aged 17, on 26/1/1810; [pm] Sgt, 15/8/1810; SLt, 20/7/1811; [a] 13e Chasseurs à cheval, 12/1811; returned to 20e Chasseurs à cheval, 5/1812. Present at Valladolid, Spain,

where he was almost murdered by a drunken gendarme; took a British standard in battle at Guarda in the Mondego valley; commanded Marshal Marmont's escort. Lt, 22/5/1813; Capt, 11/4/1814; ADC to Gen Maurin at Champaubert and Vauchamps, 1814; [a] as Lt to LGI, by decree of 22/5/1815. Placed on half pay, 1/9/1815. (Member of the Sabretache, 1893.)
Campaigns 1810-11, Spain & Portugal; 1812, Russia; 1813, Saxony; 1814, France; 1815, Belgium.
Awards Legionnaire, Legion of Honour, 1811 [senior living member of the Legion of Honour, 1893]; St Helena Medal.

SPIES, Johan Christiaan
[b] Laasphe-Wittgenstein, Westphalia, 25/2/1787; [s] Johan Ludwig Carel S., & Maria Renno; [d] - or [p]? - at battle of Craonne, 7/3/1814.
[e] Dragoons as cadet, 8/6/1800; [pm] Lt, 28/6/1805; [t>] Dutch Royal Guard, 3/11/1809; [a] as 2nd Lt to 2e CLGI, 30/10/1810; Lt, 18/3/1813.
"I do not know him at all - his colonel speaks highly of him."
Campaigns 1805-07, Germany; 1808-09, Spain; 1812, Russia; 1813, Saxony; 1814, France.
Awards Legionnaire, Legion of Honour, 14/4/1813.
[See below]

SPIES, Johan Frederik
[b] Laasphe-Wittgenstein, Westphalia, 19/12/1779; [s] Johan Ludwig Carel S. & Maria Renno.
[e] Dutch 1st Cavalry Regt, 27/10/1801; [pm] Cpl, 11/1/1805; [t>] Dutch Royal Guard, 23/8/1806; Sgt, 7/9/1806; Lt-Adj in Dutch 3rd Hussars, 6/9/1809; [a] as 2nd Lt to 2e CLGI, 30/10/1810. Left for Russia, 10/2/1812; crossed Rhine, 12/3/1812. [p] 24/12/1812? - or entered military hospital at Königsberg, 30/12/1812? - did not return to regiment.
"He is adjutant, but does not understand his duties; a good officer for a company, however."
Campaigns 1801-06, Germany; 1809, Brabant; 1812, Russia.
[See above & below]

SPIES, Johan Werner Carel
[b] Laasphe-Wittgenstein, Westphalia, 15/12/1784; [s] Johan Ludwig Carel S. & Maria Renno; [d] 15/3/1818.
[e] Dutch 1st Cavalry, 27/10/1800; [t>] as Cpl to Dutch Royal Guard, 26/4/1806; Sgt, 7/12/1806; SM, 1/6/1809; 2nd Lt, 7/9/1809; [t>] 2e CLGI, 30/10/1810. Lt, 9/7/1813; left for Holland, 26/6/1814; resignation accepted, 30/7/1814. [e] Dutch Army; Capt, 15/2/1815.
"An average officer."
Campaigns 1805, Germany; 1806, Prussia; 1809, Brabant; 1812, Russia; 1813, Saxony; 1814, France.
Awards Legionnaire, Legion of Honour, 14/9/1813; Order of the Lily, 4/3/1814.
[See above]

VAN STENIS or STEENIS, Cornelis Johannes
[b] Utrecht, 20/6/1787; [s] Gert v S. & Antonia Brevelt.
Cadet at military hospital, Leiden, 2/9/1805; [pm] Surgeon 3rd Class, 29/8/1808; surgeon in Dutch Royal Guard, 31/7/1809; [a] Imperial Guard, 19/7/1810; S-Asst S-M in 2e CLGI, 1/10/1810. [pm] Asst S-M in the five Old Guard squadrons, 26/5/1813. Left for Holland with permission from Gen Maison, 11/5/1814, but did not return to regiment.
Campaigns 1809, Zeeland; 1812, Russia; 1813, Saxony; 1814, France.

STERKE, Lambertus Everardus
[b] Kampen, 2/12/1780?-81?; [s] Nicolaas S., retired Capt, & Ammarentia Johanna de Vries; [d] 9/7/1824.
[e] Dutch 2nd Cavalry Regt as cadet, 1/10/1795; 2nd Lt, 1?-3?/2/1801;

Lt-Adj, 21/10/1806; Lt, 1?-26?/2/1807; [t>] 2e CLGI, 30/10/1810. Capt, by decree 22/6/1811; left for Russia, 10/2/1812; crossed Rhine, 12/3/1812; [m] suffering from frostbite, Königsberg, 15/12/1812, but survived. [e] Dutch Army; LtCol, 2/9/1815; Col, 28/7/1822.
Wounds Wounded at battle of the Beresina, 28/11/1812.
Campaigns 1797, embarked at Texel; 1799, Holland; 1805-07, Germany; 1808-09, Spain; 1812, Russia.

DE STUERS, Hubert Joseph Jean Lambert, Knight
[b] Roermond, 16/11/1789; [s] Pierre Jean Joseph Bernard d S., Knight, & Petronille Jeanne Alouisa de la Cour; [d] Maastricht, 13/4/1861.
[e] 18th Light Infantry Bn as cadet, 2/7/1803; Lt in 1st Bn, 6th Line Infantry Regt, 27/10/1806; [a] ADC to Gen Carteret, 26/6/1809; ADC to Gen Dumonceau; [t>] Dutch 3rd Hussars, 17/9/1809; [t>] Cuirassiers of Royal Guard, 6/10/1809; [t>] as Lt into 2e CLGI, 30/10/1810.
Lt S-Adj-M in 1812. Left Fulda 14/2/1813, arrived at Versailles 20/2/1813; [pm] Capt Adj-M, 18/3/1813; Cd'E, 21/6/1813. [t>] CRCLF, 2/8/1814; [a] LGI, by decree 14/4/1815; resigned, 5/7/1815.
Returned to Dutch Army; LtCol, 11/8/1815; to Sumatra as LtCol, 17/10/1817; [r] due to bad health, 22/2/1818. Supernumerary LtCol; returned to Dutch Indies, arrived Batavia 29/12/1820; [a] as supernumerary to 7th Hussars; commander of Souracarta; chief of staff to infantry & cavalry commander, 3/9/1821; adjutant to Governor-General of Dutch Indies, 15/6/1822; Col, 24/7/1824; military commander of Padang, 2/11/1824; MajGen and C-in-C Army of the Indies, 16/11/1830; returned to Holland, 1830; [r] 1835.
Campaigns 1805, Germany; 1809, Austria; 1812, Russia; 1813, Saxony; 1814, France; 1815, Belgium.
Awards Legionnaire, Legion of Honour, 15/4/1813; Officer; Knight, Order of the Reunion, 3/4/1814; Knight, Military Order of William, 3rd Class, 27/5/1824; Knight, Order of the Netherlands Lion, 25/2/1831; Commander, 8/10/1834.

STUTTERHEIM, Gerhardus Petrus
[b] The Hague, 7/8/1785; [s] Gerhardus S., & Anna Maria Frederika Brileman.
Apprentice surgeon in 1st Bn, Dutch 5th Demi-Brigade, 12/7/1802; [t>] Dutch Royal Guard, 26/10/1806; [a] to Garde Impériale, 19/7/1810; S-Asst S-M in 2e CLGI, 1/10/1810. Left for Russia, 10/2/1812; crossed Rhine, 12/3/1812. Left Fulda 14/2/1813, arrived Versailles, 26/2/1813; Aide-M in Old Guard, 26/5/1813. Left for Holland, 26/6/1814; resignation accepted, 30/7/1814.
Campaigns 1805-09, Westphalia & Zeeland; 1812, Russia; 1813, Saxony; 1814, France.
Awards Knight, Order of the Reunion, 3/4/1814.

LE SUEUR, Petrus Ludovicus
[b] at Cape of Good Hope, 7/10/1783; [s] Hendrik le S., garrison surgeon, & Dorothea Scheller; [d] 8/10/1830?-20/9/1842?
[a] Cape Dragoons as cadet, 1803; took part in all campaigns at the Cape; 2nd Lt, 16/8/1804; Lt, 25/2/1807; [a] from Dutch 3rd Hussars in Spain to 2e CLGI, 8/4/1812. Left for Russia, 5/6/1812. Left Fulda 14/2/1813, arrived Versailles 27/2/1813; Capt, Young Guard, 18/3/1813; left regt without permission, 31/3/1814. [e] Dutch Army; Maj, 20/11/1814; LtCol in Army of Indies, 8/10/1816; [r] 5/9/1826?-12/10/1830?
Campaigns 1805, Germany; 1808-11, Spain; 1812, Russia; 1813, Saxony; 1814, France.
Awards Legionnaire, Legion of Honour, 14/4/1813.

T

DE TARLE, Amédée Paulin Benoît
[b] Paris, 4/4/1790; [s] Benoît Joseph d T., Intendant with army of Gen Rochambeau, Knight of Military Order of St Louis and Order of

Cincinnatus, & Jeanne Antoinette Françoise d'Aure; [d] Versailles, 28/12/1877.

[e] Fontainebleu Military School as cadet; SLt, 4e Hussards, 2/1806; Lt, 1812; [pm] Lt S-Adj-M in 2e CLGI, by decree 18/3/1813. [pm] Capt, 5e Hussards, 18/9/1813; [a] Chasseurs à cheval de la Garde Impériale during Hundred Days. Placed on inactive list, 1817 and 1822. In Egypt, 11/1824 to 8/1826; returned as chief instructor to Egyptian cavalry of Mohammed-Ali, 5/1827 to 1831. [pm] Capt, 5e Lanciers; Cd'E, 6e Dragons; commander of reserves of Côte d'Or at Dijon; left army in 1849; [a] to Châlons sur Marne as paymaster to treasury.

"On 11/4/1813 at the battle of Yécla he charged the enemy at the head of soldiers under his command with great fury and devotion, contributing to the success of the affair; he was wounded and lost his horse in this action."

Wounds Lance wound before Valencia, Spain.

Campaigns 1806, Spain; 1809, Austria; 1810-13, Spain; 1813, Saxony; 1814, France.

Awards Legionnaire, Legion of Honour, 1814; Officer, 1835.

THUROT, Nicolas

[b] Bressolles (Allier), 29/3/1773; [s] Jean Turau T., tenant farmer, & Marie Besson; [d] Haguenau (Bas-Rhin), 19/11/1835.

[e/v] 34e Régiment d'Infanterie, 3/3/1791; Grenadier,16/4/1792; [t>] 6e Hussards, 20/3/1793; [pm] Cpl, 15/4/1793; [p] at battle of Marchiennes, 31/10/1793; escaped, 8/2/1794. Sgt, 31/5/1796; SLt in Légion des Francs, 22/9/1796; embarked on ship le Nestor for abortive Irish expedition, 12/1796 to 1/1797. SLt in Guides de l'Armée d'Allemagne, 26/10/1797; [t>] 8e Hussards, 11/9/1798; Lt, 20/2/1800; Capt, 19/8/1802; Cd'E, 22/10/1808; [t>] 1er Hussards; [a] as Cd'E to 2e CLGI, 29/12/1812; reported to regt, 1/4/1813.

[pm] Col, 8e Hussards, 15/10/1813 at age of 40, and after 22 years' military service - confirmed by decree, 28/11/1813. [a] to Strasbourg garrison, under siege. [pm] provisional Gen of Brigade by Röderer; [a] extraordinary Imperial commissioner for 5th Military Division, 5/3/1814, but not confirmed under First Restoration; placed on inactive list, 1/8/1814. [a] as supernumerary to 14e Dragons, 18/10/1814; recalled as Col, 12e Cuirassiers, 19/4/1815; distinguished himself at battle of Waterloo during charges on English squares, 18/6/1815.

Placed on inactive list, 18/1/1816; [r] by Ordinances of 11/10/1820, effective from 10/3/1820; [pm] honorary Maréchal de Camp, 23/5/1825. Returned to active service under July Monarchy; Col, 14e Légion de Gendarmerie, Carcassonne, 23/4/1831; [r] by Ordinances of 8/5/1835, effective from 24/1/1835. Mayor of Haguenau, 8/1820 to 8/1830; Baron of the Empire according to the epitaph on his grave.

Wounds Bullet wound to thigh at battle of la Grisuelle, 11/6/1792; bullet wound to right leg at battle of Valmy, 20/9/1792; bullet wound to left thigh at battle of Marchiennes, 31/10/1793; canister shot wound to left thigh near Nijmegen, 8/11/1794; bullet wound to left shoulder at attack on Fort St André, Isle of Bommel, 12/12/1794; bullet wound to chest at battle of Zürich, 25/9/1799; canister shot wound to right thigh at battle of Jena, 14/10/1806; bullet wound to head at battle of Eylau, 7/2/1807; bullet wound to left leg at battle of Heilsberg, 10/6/1807; sabre cuts to forehead and left hand, Königsberg, 15/6/1807; wounded at battle of Sabugal, 3/4/1811; bullet wound to right thigh at battle of Leipzig, 16/10/1813 *[thirteen recorded wounds in total]*.

Campaigns 1792-94, Armée du Nord; 1794, Holland; 1797, Germany; 1798-99, Armée du Danube et de la Suisse; 1800, Armée du Rhin; 1805-07, Grande Armée; 1810-13, Spain & Portugal; 1813, Saxony; 1814, France; 1815, Armée du Nord.

Awards Legionnaire, Legion of Honour, 14/6/1804; Officer, 25/8/1811; Knight, Military Order of St Louis, 20/8/1814.

DE TIECKEN, Marie Michel Balthazar

[b] Tongeren, 11/1/1777; [s] Pierre Michel T. & Anne Cathérine Kempeneers; [d] Tongeren, 8/7/1848.

[a] as cadet to Dutch 2nd Hussars, 10/9/1795; SM, 1795; SLt, 28/4/1800; Lt, 10/9/1805; Capt Adj, 21/10/1806; Capt Adj-M, 1807; Capt, instructor in Cuirassiers of Dutch Royal Guard, 25/1/1807; Capt in Gardes à cheval, 1808; Capt, 6e Cie, Garde Cavalerie, 1809; Cd'E, 7/9/1809; [t>] with rank into 2e CLGI, 30/10/1810. Left for Russia, 10/2/1812; crossed Rhine, 12/3/1812. Left Fulda 14/2/1813, arrived Versailles 25/2/1812. [t>] CRCLF under First Restoration, 1814; [a] Cd'E in LGI, by decree 14/4/1815; Col, 1/7/1815; submitted resignation, 5/7/1815.

[e] Dutch Army as LtCol, 11/8/1815; [a] 4th Dragoons; [pm] Col, 5th Dragoons, 27/8/1820; Col, 10th Lancers, 22/3/1823; [r] as MajGen, 16/4/1830. Honorary Gen in Belgian Army, 27/12/1830; commanded Armée de l'Escaut during Belgian Revolt; later commanded Belgian 3rd, 2nd, & again 3rd Military Divisions; ADC to King Leopold I; [r] 3/7/1835. Baron of Terhove, 10/9/1847.

"A very good officer, serving with distinction; he understands his duties perfectly."

Wounds, etc. Canister shot bruise to chest at Brienne; wounded at Rheims; had horses killed under him at Mojaïsk, Bautzen, Brienne, Craonne and Laon.

Campaigns 1796, Germany; 1797, embarked at Texel; 1799, Holland; 1800-01, Germany; 1805, embarked at Texel - Germany; 1806, Prussia; 1807, Swedish Pomerania; 1809, Brabant & Zeeland; 1812, Russia; 1813, Saxony; 1814, France; 1815, Belgium & France.

Awards Legionnaire, Legion of Honour, 14/4/1813; Officer, 27/2/1814; Knight, Order of the Union, 25/11/1807; Knight, Order of the Reunion, 7/3/1812; Knight, Military Order of St Louis, 27/12/1814; Knight, Order of Leopold, 15/12/1833; Officer, 17/7/1840.

TIMMERMAN, Jan Theodoor

[b] Geysteren, 8/5/1761; [s] Joannes Theodorus T., retired Maj, & Sophia Lambertina Remis; [d] Russia, 15?/12/1812.

[e] Cavalry Regt of Hesse-Philipsthal as cadet, 10/10/1772; standard bearer, 18/5/1778; Adj, 10/6/1784; Lt, 5/5/1788; resigned, 8/7/1795. Returned as Capt, Dutch 3rd Hussars, 26/2/1807; [a] as Capt to 2e CLGI, 8/4/1812. Left for Russia, 5/5/1812; [m] 15/12/1812.

Wounds Wounded, 14/12/1812, and lost on road to Kovno.

Campaigns 1793-94, Brabant & Flanders; 1807, Germany; 1808, Coasts & Spain; 1809-11, Spain; 1812, Russia.

TOPY, Nicolas

[b] Naples, 15/3/1777.

[e] Navy of Naples, 1/1/1792; [t>] French service in Légion Italienne, 5/2/1799; sent home sick when Legion disbanded, 20/4/1801. Velite in Royal Guard of Naples, 10/4/1806; [pm] Cpl, 15/9/1807; Sgt, 1/5/1808; SLt in Spanish Royal Guard, 18/9/1809; [a] to 2e CLGI, 1/2/1814; [t>] 4e Lanciers de Ligne, 10/6/1814.

Wounds Sabre cut to right arm, 1799; two canister shot wounds at battle of Arrizzo, 1799; sabre cut to head at battle of Ocana, 19/11/1809.

Campaigns 21/5/1797 to 15/9/1798, naval operations against Algeria; 1807, Calabria; 1808-13, Spain; 1814, France.

TOURNEL, Joseph

[b] Vidauban (Var), 1786.

[e] Army as S-Asst S-M in 26th Military Division, 15/11/1806; [a] Armée de l'Espagne, 20/11/1808; temporary Asst S-M, 16/3/1809; [a] 6e Bataillon Auxilaire du Train d'Artillerie, 2nd Army Corps, 6/6/1810; [a] Headquarters, 1/1/1812; [pm] Asst S-M in 2e CLGI, Young Guard, by decree 26/5/1813. Left for the army, 30/6/1813; crossed Rhine, 24/7/1813. Stationed at Angers, 6/7/1814; [a] CRCLF, 2/8/1814; [a] LGI, by decree 14/4/1815; [ds] 16/12/1815.

Campaigns 1806-07, Germany; 1808-11, Spain & Portugal; 1812-13,

Spain & Saxony; 1814, France.
Awards Legionnaire, Legion of Honour, 24/11/1814.

TROUBLET DE NERMONT, Laurent
[b] Ile de France, 28/2/1796; [s] Laurent T. & Victoire Elisabeth Gillette Etienne Bolgerd.
[e] St Germain Military School, 27/12/1813; [pm] SLt in 2e CLGI, by decree 19/2/1814; [a] 5e Lanciers de Ligne, 6/6/1814.
Campaigns 1814, France.

TRZEBIATOWSKI, ?
Former SM of Polish Lancers of the Guard, member of Napoleon's Elba squadron; [a] LGI, 25/4/1815; [pm] 2nd Lt, 22/5/1815. [e] Russian Army, 1/10/1815.
Awards Legionnaire, Legion of Honour, 27/2/1814.

TULLEKEN, François Oswald
[b] Hattem (Yssel Supérieur), 1/3/1777; [s] Oswald T., Mayor of Hattem, & Françoise Greven; [d] Hattem, 19/5/1842.
[e] Dutch Army as standard bearer in Orange-Friesland Cavalry Regt, 20/7/1792; Lt, 28/7/1795; Capt, 3rd Hussars, 28/6/1805; [t>] as Capt to 2e CLGI, 30/10/1810. Left for Russia with 3e Esc, 7e Cie, 10/2/1812; crossed Rhine 12/3/1812. Left Fulda 14/2/1813, arrived Versailles 25/2/1813; [r] by decree 18/3/1813, left regt 6/7/1813.
"Distinguished himself in Spain at battles of 27 & 28/3/1809 [Ciudad Real]."
Campaigns 1793-94, Brabant; 1796, Germany; 1797, embarked at Texel; 1805-06, Germany; 1808-09, Coasts & Spain; 1812, Russia.
Awards Legionnaire, Legion of Honour, 15/3/1813.

U

UBAGHS, Henri François
[b] Maastricht, 29/10/1787?-1789?; [s] Jean Hubert U. & Marie Jesse.
Velite in Grenadiers à pied de la Garde Impériale, 11/9/1806; SLt in 4e Tirailleurs de la Garde Impériale, 25/3/1809; Lt, 8/6/1811; [a] as Lt to 2e CLGI, 18/3/1813. Capt, ADC to Gen Rottembourg, 2/2/1814; on sick leave from 26/8/1814; resigned, 10/1/1815 - Capt in Hussards de Croy, 11/11/1814.
Wounds Wounded at battle of la Rothière, 1/2/1814, and at Waterloo, 18/6/1815.
Awards Legionnaire, Legion of Honour; Knight, Order of the Reunion, 3/4/1814.

V

VALLERY, Syriague
[b] Versailles, 25/7/1789. Lt, [t>] from Spanish Royal Guard, 1/2/1814; passed as ADC, 19/2/1814.

VANTINI, Zénon Ruffin Luc
[b] Porto Ferrajo, Corsica, 18/10/1797.
Page in service of Grand Duchess Elisa of Tuscany, 4/1811 to 12/1813; SLt in National Guard of Elba, 1/1814; [pm] orderly officer to Napoleon, 20/5/1814. [a] as 2nd Lt to LGI during Hundred Days, and present at Waterloo. Followed the army to the Loire, then returned to Elba, 1/8/1815. [pm] Lt in 46e Régiment d'Infanterie de Ligne, 1830; disapeared in mysterious circumstances at Morbihan, 9/9/1832, and presumed dead; he had, however, emigrated to England, where he acquired naturalised citizenship.

VELDHUYS, Jean
[b] Hoorn, 9/7/1777; [s] Jean V. & Cathérine Buis; [d] 1828.
[e] Dutch cavalry, 1/8/1793; [a] Batavian Hussars, 1795; [t>] Dutch Royal Guard, 14/8/1806; [pm] Cpl, 26/9/1806; Sgt, 19/12/1806; [a] as SM to 2e CLGI, 30/10/1810. [pm] Lt, Young Guard, 18/3/1813; left

regt without permission, 31/3/1814. [e] Dutch Army as 2nd Lt, 16/8/1815; Lt, 16/8/1817; [r] 17/5/1828.
Campaigns 1794, Brabant; 1805, embarked at Texel; 1806, Prussia; 1809, Brabant; 1813, Saxony; 1814, France.

VERHAEGEN, Jan Willem
[b] Kampen, 3/2/1787; [s] Henri Rudolph V., lawyer, & Catharina Susanne Jeanne Duclos de Corselles; [d] 21/4/1818.
[e] Dutch 2nd Cavalry Regt as cadet, 11/3/1799; 2nd Lt, 15/9/1803; [t>] Grenadiers of Dutch Royal Guard, 1/11/1806; Lt, 1/5/1807; [t>] the Line, 7/10/1807; returned with rank to Royal Guard, 6/10/1809; [pm] Lt in 2e CLGI, 30/10/1810; eagle bearer, by decree 30/10/1811;
left regt without permission, 31/3/1814. [e] Dutch Army, 1814; Capt, 15/4/1815.
"A good officer on campaign, but not very strict in garrison."
Campaigns 1805-06, Germany; 1808-10, Spain; 1812, Russia; 1813, Saxony; 1814, France.

VERMAESEN, George
[b] Schoorl (Zuyderzee), 19/8/1781; [s] Laurens V., retired Lt, & Antoinette de Bunge; [d] 28/11/1871.
[e] Dutch 2nd Cavalry Regt as cadet, 17/7/1796; Lt, 19/1/1803; Lt, 1/5/1807; [t>] Cavalry of Dutch Royal Guard, 6/10/1809; [a] as Lt to 2e CLGI, 30/10/1810. Left for Russia, 10/2/1812; crossed Rhine, 12/3/1812. Left regt without permission, 31/3/1814. [e] Dutch Army; Capt, 2/9/1815; [r] 17/5/1828.
"A good officer."
Campaigns 1796-97, Germany; 1799, Holland; 1805-07, Germany; 1809, Germany; 1812, Russia; 1813, Saxony; 1814, France.
Awards Legionnaire, Legion of Honour, 14/4/1813.

VERRON, ?
Lt in 5e Chasseurs à cheval; became 2nd Lt in 2e CLGI, 18/3/1813, but preferred to stay with the Line where he had just been promoted captain, 21/4/1813.

VIALA, Louis
[b] Le Vigan (Gard), 14/10/1773?-16/5/1775?; [s] Louis V. & Marie Martin.
[e/v] Compagnie franche du département du Leman, 9/9/1792; [a] Guides du Gen Bonaparte, 21/5/1796; [pm] Cpl, 12/1/1799; [a] Chasseurs à cheval de la Garde des Consuls, 3/1/1800; Sgt, 6/8/1801; SM, 15/10/1802; SLt, standard bearer, 22/1/1804; 2nd Lt, Chasseurs à cheval de la Garde Impériale, 23/9/1804; Lt, 1/5/1806; [t>] CRCLF, 5/8/1814. [a] LGI, by decree 14/4/1815; [ds] 22/12/1815.
Wounds etc. Bullet wound to left leg at battle of Alcared, 1793; two sabre cuts to head at battle of Wagram, 6/7/1809; horses killed under him at Wagram, Leipzig and Bautzen.
Campaigns 1792, Alps; 1793, Spain; 1794, Pyrénées Orientales; 1795-97, Italy; 1798, Switzerland; 1799, Italy; 1800, Germany; 1803-04, Coasts; 1805-06-07, Grande Armée; 1808, Spain; 1809, Austria; 1812, Russia; 1813, Saxony; 1814, France; 1815, Armée du Nord.
Awards Legionnaire, Legion of Honour, 15/6/1804; Officer, 28/11/1813.

DE LA VILLASSE D'AUDIBERT, Joseph Marie Hyacinthe Siffrin Exupert Eleazard, Marquis
[b] Carpentras (Vaucluse), 21/2/1786.
[e] French Navy as trainee helmsman [master's mate], 17/10/1798; Midshipman, 1800; SLt with General Staff, 1801; Gendarme d'ordonnance, 19/11/1806; [pm] Cpl, 23/2/1807; Sgt, 16/7/1807; Lt in 7e Cuirassiers, 18/2/1808; Capt, 3/6/1809; Cd'E, 19/11/1812; [t>] Éclaireurs de la Garde Impériale, 4/12/1813; placed on half pay under

First Restoration; [pm] as Cd'E into LGI, by decree 22/5/1815. Present at Waterloo, 18/6/1815; [ds] 22/12/1815.

Wounds Bullet wound to left ankle at Tiberon; sabre cuts to neck and left hand at Essling, 21/5/1809; bullet bruise to right hand at Wagram, 5/7/1809; bullet wound to side at the Beresina, 28/11/1812; lance wound to right arm, 1813; bullet wound to forehead at Laon, 1814.

Awards Legionnaire, Legion of Honour, 13/8/1809; Officer, 16/5/1813; Knight, Order of the Reunion, 16/3/1814.

VIRAVAUD, Jean

[b] Auch du Coin (Cantal), 20/3/1778; [s] François V. & Jeanne Vige.
[a] from Spanish Royal Guard into 2e CLGI as 2nd Lt, 1/2/1814; [a] 4e Lanciers de Ligne, 10/6/1814.

Awards Legionnaire, Legion of Honour, 3/4/1814.

W

DE WACKER VAN SON, George Theodoor Zeeger Constant

[b] Utrecht, 11/10/1785; [s] Petrus d W. & Theodora Adriana Falck;
[d] in battle, Russia, 25/9/1812.
[e] Waldeck Regt as cadet, 1803; NCO in cavalry, 26/3/1807; QM in Cuirassiers of Dutch Royal Guard, 26/2/1808; Lt in Dutch 3rd Hussars, 3/7/1808; [t>] as 2nd Lt into 2e CLGI, 30/10/1810. Left for Russia with 2e Esc, 6e Cie, 10/2/1812; crossed Rhine, 12/3/1812; killed during a reconnaissance, 25/9/1812.

Campaigns 1812, Russia.

DE WATTEVILLE, Albert, Baron

[b] Berne, Switzerland, 15/3/1787; [s] Charles Emmanuel, Baron of Belp, & Charlotte de Watteville; [d] near Vilna, Russia, 7/12/1812.
Swiss officer in French Army; Capt in 2nd Swiss Regt and [a] ADC to Marshal Lannes, 1809; orderly officer of Napoleon, 22/6/1809; [pm] Cd'E in 2e CLGI, 13/1/1811.

Awards Baron of the Empire, 23/7/1810; annuity of 5,000 francs drawn on Hanover, by Imperial decree.

WEERTS TEN BRINK, Jacob Wolter

[b] Deventer, 28/2/1788; [s] Johan & Diederica ten Brink; [d] Russia, 1812.
[e] Dragoons of Batavian Guard as 2nd Lt, 28/11/1805; Lt, 23/9/1806; [a] as 2nd Lt to 2e CLGI, 30/10/1810. Left for Russia with 1er Esc, 1ere Cie, 10/2/1812; crossed Rhine, 12/3/1812; dismissed by decree, 9/7/1812. Tried by court martial at Vilna for plundering and insubordination, he returned to his regiment without suffering any serious penalty; but Gen Colbert refused to readmit him to the Red Lancers, and he took refuge in the 11e Hussards. He died during the retreat from Moscow.

"He knows his job well enough, but lacks energy."

Campaigns 1806, Germany; 1809, Brabant; 1812, Russia.

WERNER, Henrik

[b] Maastricht, 18/3/1768; [s] Hendrik W., retired soldier, & Anna Maria Remmers.
[e] Van Bylandt Regt as drummer, 26/5/1780; [pm] Cpl, 15/4/1785; Sgt, 18/6/1789; Lt, 7/12/1795; Lt, 25/3/1802; Capt, 25/8/1809; [a] from Dutch 3rd Hussars in Spain as Capt into 2e CLGI, 30/10/1810. Served in 4e Esc, 8e Cie, 1812; [a] as Cd'E to 3e Chasseurs à cheval, by decree 14/1/1813 (but remained in Red Lancers). Officier d'habillement, 1813; [t>] CRCLF, 2/8/1814; resigned, 21/9/1814.

"He serves with distinction, and is favourably noticed."

Campaigns 1787, Holland; 1793, Brabant; 1796, Germany; 1797, embarked at Texel; 1799, Holland.

Awards Legionnaire, Legion of Honour, 5/4/1814; Order of the Lily.

WILLICH, Carel

[b] The Hague, 1/4/1770; [s] Jacob W. & Leonora Goethuisen; [d] 30/9/1824.
[e] Cavalry Regt of Hesse-Philipsthal, 12/11/1788; [pm] Cpl, 25/4/1791; 2nd Lt, 1/7/1799; [t>] as Lt-instructor into Dutch Royal Guard, 28/6/1806; [t>] the Line, 7/10/1807; returned to Royal Guard, 9/6/1809; [a] as 2nd Lt to 2e CLGI, 30/10/1810. [pm] Lt, Old Guard, 18/3/1813; left regt without permission, 31/3/1814. [e] Dutch Army; Capt, 1/4/1815.

"A very good instructor."

Wounds Wounded near Carbeck, 1794.

Campaigns 1793-94, Brabant; 1797, embarked at Texel; 1799, Brabant.

Z

ZIEGLER, Arend Jansse

[b] Namur, 23/4/1764; [s] Pieter Z., retired soldier, & Johanna van Dijk; [d] 29/12/1835.
[e] Dutch Army as dragoon, Prince of Hesse-Cassel Regt, 15/2/1779; [pm] Cpl, 4/6/1783; QM, 11/3/1791; Sgt, 14/8/1793; SM, 14/8/1795; 2nd Lt, 13/4/1798; Lt, 28/6/1805; [pm] as Lt into 2e CLGI, 30/10/1810, but apparently reported to regt from Dutch 3rd Hussars in Spain only on 8/4/1812. Left for Russia, 14/4/1812; crossed Rhine, 3/5/1812. Left Fulda 14/2/1813, arrived Versailles 25/2/1813; [pm] Capt, Old Guard, 18/3/1813; left regt without permission, 31/3/1814. [e] Dutch Army; Capt, 28/4/1814; Maj, 18/4/1820; LtCol, 16/4/1830; [r] 3/9/1835.

Campaigns 1787, Holland; 1793-94, Brabant & Flanders; 1796, Germany; 1799, Holland; 1805-07, Germany; 1808-11, Spain; 1812, Russia; 1813, Saxony; 1814, France.

Awards Legionnaire, Legion of Honour, 18/3/1813; Knight, Military Order of William, 10/9/1831.

ZIEGLER, Pieter Arend

[b] The Hague, 2/6/1787; [s] Arend Jansse Z. (see above) & Anna Geertruida Schnepp; [d] Haarlem, 27/11/1860.
[e] Batavian Dragoons as cadet, 15/10/1804; 2nd Lt in Dutch 3rd Hussars, 26/2/1807; [a] as 2nd Lt to 2e CLGI, on 30/10/1810. Left for Holland, 26/6/1814; resignation accepted, 30/7/1814. [e] Dutch Army; 2nd Lt in Carabiniers of National Militia (became 9th Cuirassiers), 4/1815; Lt, 10/1/1816; Capt, 28/12/1826; [r] 5/12/1835.

Campaigns 1805, Austria; 1806-07, Prussia & Pomerania; 1808-10, Spain; 1812, Russia; 1813, Saxony; 1814, France.

Awards Legionnaire, Legion of Honour, 14/4/1813; Knight, Military Order of William, 4th Class, 16/11/1830.

VAN ZUYLEN VAN NYEVELT, Arnaud Jacob, Baron

[b] Kampen, 29/11?-9/12?/1788; [s] Philip Julius v Z., Count of the Empire, LtGen, Maître des cérémonies to the King of Holland, & Clara Helena de Wacker van Son; [d] Batavia, 11/10/1821.
[e] Waldeck Regt as cadet, 12/11/1803; [t>] Dragoons, 19/10/1804; [t>] as 2nd Lt into Dutch Royal Guard, 28/6/1805; Lt in Gardes du Corps à cheval, 25/9/1809; [a] as Lt to 2e CLGI, 30/10/1810. Left for Russia, 10/2/1812; crossed Rhine, 12/3/1812; [p] Russia, 27/7/1812. Returned to Holland after First Restoration; [a] as Capt into Dutch cavalry, 13/12/1814; [pm] Maj in Army of the Indies, 1/2/1820.

"Of fragile health, but well trained and full of energy."

Wounds Wounded and captured while with the advance-guard in Russia, 27/7/1812.

Campaigns 1806, Germany; 1809, Brabant; 1812, Russia.

APPENDIX IV

Muster Roll of the Dutch troopers and non-commissioned officers who served under King Louis and who were assigned to the 2nd Light Horse Lancers of the Imperial Guard between 21 September 1810 and 1 June 1811

The notes on the service of individuals preserved in the Muster Roll are neither comprehensive nor entirely consistent. This alphabetical listing employs the following abbreviations of terms used in the original:

[b]	born
[d]	died or killed
[m]	missing (the roll makes a distinction between "went missing" and "fell behind", though the practical result must have been almost invariably the same)
[p]	prisoner of war
[wd]	wounded
[dst]	deserted (the roll distinguishes between this and the next notation:)
[lwp]	left regiment without permission
[ds]	dismissed from service
[d/d]	dismissed on disciplinary grounds
[d/h]	dismissed on health grounds
[d/u]	dismissed as unfit for duty
[dm]	demoted
[t>]	transferred to, passed into
[r]	retired

Ranks & appointments:
All listed individuals served as Lancers unless other ranks or appointments are indicated, by these abbreviations:

Trpt	Trumpeter
TM	Trumpet-Major
Fr	Farrier
MFr	Master-Farrier
Cpl	Corporal
QM	Quartermaster (*fourrier* - a corporal's appointment)
Sgt	Sergeant
SM	Sergeant-Major
Adj-NCO	Adjutant (non-commissioned)
SLt	Sub-lieutenant

Units:

CRCLF	Corps Royal des Chevau-légers lanciers de France - the Red Lancers under the First Restoration
Lanciers de Ligne	The corps of numbered Line Lancer regiments created in 1811 were not individually titled e.g. "3e Régiment de Chevau-légers lanciers de Ligne"; but we use the term here for clarity of distinction from the Guard Lancers.

Note that a number of individual enlisted men were transferred to other Imperial Guard cavalry, Line cavalry and Line infantry regiments. The abbreviations in most cases make clear whether this was a punishment for bad behaviour (e.g. "[d/d] [t>] 126e Inf de Ligne"); a posting to a newly raised unit as cadre, or to an existing unit as a replacement (e.g."[t>] with rank, 1er Lanciers de Ligne"); or a transfer on promotion to commissioned rank (e.g. "[t>] as SLt into Inf de Ligne"). It is noteworthy that enlisted ranks might be posted to a Colonial Battalion as a punishment, while sub-lieutenants' commissions appear to have been offered as an inducement to serve in the disease-ridden Indies.

A

Abrams, Pierre, [b] Utrecht 16/3/1783; Cpl, 19/2/1812; [p] Russia, 27/7/1812

Agterberg, Adrien, [b] Reenen 12/5/1783; removed from muster roll 30/6/1811 for long absence - on charge from 3/8/1810

Ainsi, Jean Pierre, [b] Dormel 1/4/1781; [d/d] [t>] 11e Hussards, 23/7/1811

Albers, Gerard, [b] Grave 2/11/1788; [m] Russia, 28/10/1812

Albert, Albert, [b] Deventer 28/3/1784; [m] Russia, 28/11/1812

Albertz, Jacques, [b] Arnhem 1/5/1786; [p] Russia, 27/7/1812

Aldenhosen, Casmir, [b] Ruisburg 2/2/1779; Cpl, 4/6/1811; [dm] Lancer 21/9/1811; [r] 3/12/1811

Alexandre, Jean, [b] Bastogne 18/10/1761; Cpl, 22/11/1810; Sgt, 5/3/1813; [t>] CRCLF, 2/8/1814

van Alfen, Samuel, [b] Buren 6/5/1788; [d/h] [r] 1/8/1811

Allardt, Lambert, [b] Maastricht 10/4/1781; [m] Russia, 25/11/1812

Ameiden, Pierre, [b] Dordrecht 3/3/1786; [dst] 10/4/1811

Anemaat, Sebastien, [b] Zeevenbergen 17/4/1791; [t>] as SLt into 63e Inf de Ligne, 1/6/1811

Anten, Crétien, [b] Utrecht 25/10/1791; [d] in hospital, Brussels, 23/3/1812

Antonius, Gerard, [b] Tilburg 15/6/1789; [m] Russia, 5/12/1812

Appelman, Nicolas, [b] Bommel 8/8/1792; [m] Russia, 11/12/1812

Arends, Everard, [b] Astenburg 16/2/1786; [ds] 1/3/1811

Arends, Gerard, [b] Milligen 15/4/1783; [m] Russia, 30/11/1812

Arends, Henry, [b] Brummen 7/7/1781; Cpl, 21/9/1810; [dm] Lancer, 30/9/1810; [m] Russia, 5/12/1812

Arends, Pierre, [b] Amsterdam 12/8/1782; Cpl, 1/6/1813; [dm] Lancer, 23/9/1813; [ds] 11/7/1814

Ariens, Roger, [b] Minderschaa 9/2/1787; Cpl, 21/9/1810; [d/d] [t>] 11e Hussards, 10 /8/1811

van Asten, Aubert, [b] 's Hertogenbosch 6/12/1788; Cpl, 23/2/1813; [ds] 12/7/1814

Aus, Frédéric, [b] Emden 17/8/1788; [m] Russia, 3/12/1812

van Auw, Jean, [b] Kampen 19/1/1787; [p] 10/10/1812

B

van Baardewijk, Corneille, [b] Vlijmen 14/5/1781; [lwp] 2/4/1814

Baars, Jacques Jean, [b] Zutphen 20/12/1789; [d] in hospital, Paris, 15/4/1812

de Baas, Arnaud, [b] Leiden 16/12/1789; [t>] 126e Inf de Ligne, 18/4/1811

Baas, Sebastien, [b] Leiden 13/11/1787; Cpl, 6/2/1810; [dm] Lancer, 11/11/1810; [d/d] [t>] 31e Chasseurs à cheval, 23/7/1811

Backhuysen, Jean, [b] Bommel 1/5/1792; [m] Russia, 20/11/1812

Bakker, Daniel, [b] Kampen 10/4/1789; [m] Russia, 29/11/1812

Bakker, François, [b] Loonaken 20/9/1762; [d/h] [r] 1/12/1811

Balthoff, Jean, [b] Breda 10/7/1789; [m] Russia, 27/11/1812

Balvoord, Henry, [b] Arnhem 14/4/1778; [m] Russia, 6/12/1812

Baron, Jean Lambert, [b] Urle Romain 15/7/1781; [d/h] [r] 26/6/1811

van Bart, Edouard, [b] Schiedam 17/9/1787; Cpl, 16/5/1808; QM, 13/2/1811; [d] in hospital, Brussels, 14/3/1812

Basset, Frédéric, [b] Haarlem 18/12/1792; [m] Russia, 25/11/1812

van Bast, Jean, [b] Kampen 10/2/1786; [lwp] 31/3/1814

Bauman, François, [b] Sgt, 9/9/1809; *see Appendix III, Officers*

Bauman, Frédéric, [b] Gravesande 10/10/1775; QM, 30/10/1806; Sgt, 1/2/1813; SM, 10/2/1813; Vaguemestre, 26/2/1813; [lwp] 31/3/1814

Bax, Jean, [b] Aalburg 15/8/1785; removed from muster roll 2/8/1814, in hospital

Beck, Godefroy, [b] Eysennach, Saxony, 4/5/1778; [t>] 126e Inf de Ligne, 18/4/1811

Beckers, Lambert, [b] Bierharen 6/4/1781; [d] in hospital, Versailles, 25/12/1811

Beerends, Bernard, [b] Volberg 25/3/1784; [p] Russia, 15/11/1812

Beerends, Gerard, [b] Vooren 20/7/1776; [lwp] 31/3/1814

Beerends, Jean, [b] Doesburg 6/10/1786; [lwp] 31/3/1814

Behrens, Frédéric, [b] Berlin 18/7/1789; Cpl; Sgt, 26/6/1813; [lwp] 31/3/1814

Belflamme, Martin Jacques, [b] Charneux 16/3/1784; [d] in hospital, Moscow, 12/9/1812

van Benthum, Pierre, [b] Utrecht 11/6/1784; [m] Russia, 13/11/1812

Berden, Thomas, [b] Leeuwen 15/10/1785; [d] of wounds, 25/11/1812

van den Berg, Gerard, [b] Amsterdam 16/5/1785; [m] Russia, 14/11/1812

van den Berg, Guillaume, [b] The Hague 30/3/1783; [m] Russia, 27/10/1812

van den Berg, Jacques, [b] Antwerp 20/8/1786; [d/d] [t>] 11e Hussards, 23/7/1811

van den Berg, Jean, [b] Tilburg 6/8/1786; Cpl, 1/11/1808; [dm] Lancer, 4/8/1812; [m] Russia, 21/11/1812

van den Berg, Pierre, [b] Amersfoort 2/1/1785; [d] in hospital, Versailles, 10/2/1811

Bergers, Jean, [b] Ysselsteyn 29/4/1787; Sgt, 21/9/1810; SM, 1/2/1813; [ds] 11/7/1814

Berghausen, Pierre, [b] Bechem 10/3/1785; [t>] Lanciers du Grand Duché de Berg, 12/3/1811

Bergmans, Everard, [b] Nijmegen 16/10/1791; [lwp] 12/7/1814

Berk, Adam, [b] Krolingen 30/7/1790; [m] Russia, 13/12/1812

Berke, Arnaud, [b] Amsterdam 18/3/1788; [m] Russia, 12/10/1812

Berkers, Balthasar, [b] Eindhoven 7/5/1791; [m] Russia, 3/10/1812

Betram, Jean, [b] Heusden 2/9/1778; [m] Russia, 28/11/1812

de Beus, Henry, [b] Amersfoort 6/11/1776; Cpl, 11/9/1809; [r] 24/7/1811

Biemans, Martin, [b] Rotterdam 26/5/1782; Cpl, 20/10/1806; [t>] Vétérans, 17/4/1811

de Bies, Jean Jacob, [b] Putt 11/1/1785; [r] 1/12/1811

van der Bint, Jacques, [b] The Hague 28/2/1782; [d] in hospital, Brussels, 26/10/1811

Bischop, Philippe, [b] Durlen 21/7/1777; [t>] 11e Hussards, 23/7/1811

Blankers, Jacques, [b] Luyt 24/7/1789; [m] Russia, 15/11/1812

Blankesteyn, Pierre, [b] Beuskom 15/3/1787; [m] Russia, 21/11/1812

Bleeterswijk, Guillaume, [b] Zoele 17/9/1790; [m] Russia, 28/12/1812

van den Blerk, Antoine, [b] Maalwijk 13/7/1791; Fr, 11/4/1813; [dst] 10/1/1814

Blikman, Jean, [b] Woort 5/8/1788; [d/d] put at disposal of Minister of War, 28/7/1812

Blokman, Jean, [b] Utrecht 4/5/1788; [m] Russia, 13/10/1812

Blom, Antoine, [b] Zwolle 6/6/1785; [lwp] 2/4/1814

Blom, Henry, [b] Niekerk 27/9/1784; [p] Russia, 17/11/1812

de Boer, Bernard, [b] Oldenhoven 17/2/1787; [m] Russia, 28/11/1812

Boers, Frédéric Guillaume, [b] Leeuwarden 2/2/1792; [lwp] 31/3/1814

van den Bogaard, Jean, [b] Schiedam 16/2/1789; [lwp] 2/4/1814

Bokke, Guillaume, [b] Maastricht 6/11/1785; [m] Russia, 26/11/1812

Boll, Frédéric, [b] Noordwijk 14/5/1784; Cpl,1/8/1809; [dm] Lancer, 7/10/1810

Bolle, Jean, [b] Mechelen 24/6/1782; [m] Russia, 12/12/1812

Bollermans, François, [b] Oldenbourg 10/9/1782; [m] Russia, 16/11/1812

Bonebakker, Henry, [b] Arnhem 9/7/1786; [lwp] 31/3/1814

de Bons, Sibert, [b] Leeuwarden 4/9/1786; [m] Russia, 18/12/1812

Boom, Thomas, [b] Gorcum 25/12/1785; [m] Russia, 22/11/1812

Boomhout, Jean, [b] Utrecht 15/1/1785; [d] in hospital 24/8/1811

Boone, ?, [b] Saxony 2/5/1785; Fr; [m] Russia, 16/11/1812

Boortmans, Valentin, [b] Vlijmen 25/10/1785; [p] Russia, 27/7/1812

Bootermans, Jean, [b] Baardewijk 5/10/1787; [m] Russia, 28/11/1812

Booyen, Gerard, [b] Kronenburg 1/5/1787; [m] Russia, 3/10/1812

Borgmans, Armand, [b] Amsterdam 22/8/1788; [d] in hospital, Danzig, 2/12/1812

van der Borst, Jean, [b] Etten 20/9/1786; [p] 4/10/1812

van den Bosch, Dideric, [b] Zwolle 14/7/1786; [p] Russia, 16/9/1812

Bosch, Etienne, [b] Evello 7/4/1777; [p] Russia, 12/9/1812

van den Bosch, Guillaume Joseph, [b] Roermond 26/5/1786; [m] Russia, 2/12/1812

Bosch, Jacques, [b] Nijmegen 28/3/1780; Cpl, 29/6/1811; [m] Russia, 5/12/1812

van den Bosch, Joachim, [b] Schideam 7/11/1792; [d/h] 10/2/1812

Bosche, François, [b] Middelburg 20/10/1772; [t>] Vétérans, 17/4/1811

de Bosson, Jean Gerard, [b] Oosterhout 8/3/1793; [m] Russia, 24/11/1812

Botterleuw, Jean, [b] Amsterdam 13/4/1782; [m] Russia, 18/11/1812

Boulard, Nicolas, [b] Wijk-bij-Duurstede 21/6/1788; [m] Russia, 30/11/1812

Bourdeaux, Louis Guillaume, [b] Berlin 2/4/1791; Cpl, 21/9/1810; [t>] as SLt to the Indies, 7/12/1811

Boxmeer, Gilles, [b] Delst 20/3/1780; [lwp] 30/3/1814

Brackmans, André, [b] Antwerp 25/3/1773; SM, 21/9/1810; [m] Russia, 13/11/1812

Brand, Jean, [b] Echfeld 11/1/1787; Cpl Trpt, 27/2/1813; [lwp] 31/3/1814

Brand, Jean Armand, [b] Amsterdam 25/11/1775; Sgt, 7/12/1806; [lwp] 31/3/1814

Brands, Gerard Jean, [b] Rheenen 10/12/1790; [m] Russia, 20/11/1812

Brandt, ?, [b] Nijmegen 5/3/1785; [d/h] [r] 1/3/1811

Brandt, Charles Louis Auguste, [b] Nijmegen 26/6/1786; [t>] as SLt to the Indies, 27/1/1811

Brandwijk, Adrien, [b] Gouda 15/1/1791; [t>] 4e Bataillon Colonial, 29/6/1812

Breedenkamp, Gerard, [b] Amsterdam 21/2/1786; [m] Russia, 4/12/1812

Breekers, Antoine, [b] Tergoes 16/7/1786; [m] Russia, 3/12/1812

Breukelmans, Gerard, [b] Loon op Zand 26/5/1775; [m] Russia, 30/11/1812

van Brinen, Teunis, [b] Alphen 18/11/1790; [lwp] 9/3/1814

Vanden Brink, Henri Hendriks, [b] Yssel 29/4/1788; [lwp] 31/3/1814

van den Brink, Henry, [b] Augermin 11/1/1782; [m] Russia, 3/11/1812

Broeckhuysen, Lambert, [b] Amsterdam 3/1/1780; [m] Russia, 5/8/1812

van de Broek, François, [b] Noodorp 7/3/1787; [m] Russia, 27/11/1812

van den Broek, Jean Baptiste, [b] Antwerp 31/8/1773; [d/u] 1/3/1811

Broeks, Jean, [b] The Hague 25/1/1783; [m] Russia, 14/7/1812

Bron, Barend, [b] Canton of Vollenhoven 19/6/1778; [t>] Vétérans, 17/4/1811

Brugmans, Antoine, [b] Canton of Breda 26/3/1789; [d/d] [t>] 11e Hussards, 2/12/1811

Bruin, Jean, [b] Breda 6/5/1786; [m] Russia, 31/10/1812
Bruinoog, Abraham, [b] Waterland 10/10/1777; [d/h] 10/2/1812
Bruins, Matthieu, [b] Voorberg 28/3/1787; [d/d] [t>] 30e Chasseurs à cheval, 23/7/1811
Bruls, Hubert, [b] Eysden 15/7/1775; [m] Russia, 11/12/1812
Bruy, Jean, [b] Wiese 12/9/1786; Cpl, 23/2/1812; [m] Russia, 2/12/1812
Bruyere, Jean, [b] Canton of Milleu 29/5/1781; Fr; MFr, 8/10/1811; [ds] 12/7/1814
Bruyn, Gerard Paul, [b] Monnikendam 21/5/1791; [t>] as SLt to the Indies, 27/1/1811
de Bruyn, Henry, [b] Kerkdriel 30/5/1792; stayed in Russia, as [p] 29/10/1812
de Bruyn, N., [b] Woerden 3/2/1784; [m] Russia, 5/11/1812
Bruyns, Henry, [b] Amsterdam 22/9/1787; [d/u] 1/3/1811
Buchner, George Jacques, [b] Tergoes 29/11/1790; [t>] as SLt into 54e Inf de Ligne, 25/6/1811
Buffart, Andre, [b] Gorinchem 24/10/1788; [d] 17/9/1813
Bulsing, Antonie, [b] Dentiechem 2/2/1780; Cpl, 21/9/1810; [dst] 6/2/1812
van den Burg, Corneil, [b] Utrecht 18/1/1777; [lwp] 2/4/1814
van den Burg, Henry, [b] Voorburg 18/9/1785; [p] 13/9/1812
Burgens, Jean Guillaume, [b] Sittard 2/10/1782; [m] Russia, 24/10/1812
Burgers, Pierre, [b] Amsterdam 1/1/1783; [d] of fever in hospital, Danzig, 20/3/1813
Burghard, Jérime, [b] Middelbourg 18/11/1787; [d/h] [r] 1/3/1811
Buskeo, Bernard, [b] Zwolle 14/5/1792; [d/d] [t>] 126e Inf de Ligne, 9/4/1811
Busker, Antoine, [b] Nijmegen 1/10/1785; Cpl, 1/1/1809; [m] Russia, 28/12/1812
Butter, Jean, [b] Wesep 8/5/1778; Cpl, 31/1/1811; [ds] 11/7/1814
Butterling, Catien, [b] Velsen 15/10/1783; Cpl, 21/9/1810; [m] Russia, 14/12/1812
Buys, Frédéric, [b] Amersfoort 1/1/1781; [m] Russia, 12/12/1812
Buys, Gerard Jean, [b] Nijmegen 22/1/1788; *see Appendix III, Officers*

C

van Campen, Gerard Jean, [b] Stravesand 12/6/1777; Cpl, 12/8/1811; QM, 3/1/1813; [ds] 12/7/1814
Canis, Jean, [b] Amsterdam 16/1/1790; Cpl, 21/9/1810; [dm] Lancer 30/8/1811; [m] Russia, 28/11/1812
Carron, Henry, [b] Ferten 20/10/1788; [m] Russia, 2/12/1812
van Casteren, Jean, [b] Moergestel 24/3/1784; [m] Russia, 5/12/1812
Chambras, Jean, [b] Canton of Strasbourg 13/2/1772; [m] Russia, 4/11/1812
Champagna, Alexandre, [b] Munster 14/5/1787; Cpl, 21/9/1810; [dm] Lancer 19/2/1811; [m] Russia, 30/10/1812
Chavet, Pierre François, [b] Zart 10/5/1770; [m] Russia, 28/11/1812
Classen, Jean Charles, [b] The Hague 9/6/1788; Master Spurrier, 10/2/1812; [m] Russia, 2/12/1812
Coenders, Jean, [b] Steenderen 3/10/1781; Cpl, 21/9/1810; Sgt, 12/2/1813; [lwp] 31/3/1814
Colla, Jean, [b] Maastricht 22/3/1793; Trpt, 11/9/1810; [m] Russia, 29/11/1812
Cols, Pierre, [b] Haastert 16/10/1786; [m] Russia, 7/11/1812
Colson, Jean Antoine, [b] Zutphen 4/9/1789; [t>] into Inf de Ligne as SLt, 27/1/1811
Cooze, Corneil, [b] Haardrech 7/10/1786; [d] in hospital, Paris, 15/1/1812
Corbeek, Henry, [b] Genderingen 10/3/1795; [m] Russia, 10/12/1812
Corber, Henry, [b] Disheim 10/4/1787; [m] Russia, 20/11/1812
Coster, André, [b] Middelburg 6/7/1787; [t>] into Inf de Ligne as SLt, 27/1/1811
Courtoy, Lambert, [b] Overhespen 1/11/1771; [d/h] [r] 26/6/1811
Croissand, Paul, [b] Heuste l3/2/1786; Sgt, 21/9/1810; [p] 26/3/1814

D

van Dalen, Guillaume, [b] Tergoed 19/2/1785; [p] Russia, 27/7/1812
van Dam, Jacob, [b] Garnveld 15/12/1787; [m] Russia, 25/11/1812
Damans, Frédéric, [b] Graaf 9/12/1787; [lwp] 31/3/1814
Danens, Jean, [b] Gouda 30/10/1782; [lwp] 31/3/1814
Debbens, Jean Bernard, [b] Nijmegen 30/1/1785; [lwp] 31/3/1814
Debie, Crétien, [b] Rotterdam 28/12/1792; [d/u] 15/10/1810
Deckers, Guillaume, [b] Utrecht 1/5/1787; [p] Russia, 4/11/1812
Deegelink, Adam, [b] Enkhuysen 10/1/1790; [d/u] 25/7/1811
Dekkers, Henry, [b] Drenthen 17/4/1788; [d] in hospital, Paris, 23/11/1811

Dekkers, Herman, [b] 's Hertogenbosch 8/4/1776; [m] Russia, 2/12/1812
Dekkers, Jacques, [b] Geul 20/6/1760; [r] 1/12/1811
Dekkers, Pierre, [b] Cologne 1/1/1787; [p] 24/11/1812
Delhoe, Pierre, [b] Ijsden 12/10/1782; [t>] Vétérans, 17/4/1811
van Dello, Antonie, [b] Kuylenburg 15/12/1789; [m] Russia, 15/11/1812
Demaire, Gerard, [b] Breukelen 20/10/1785; [m] Russia, 17/11/1812
Denhartog, Abraham, [b] Kuylenburg 19/3/1784; [d/u] 15/10/1810
Deschosin, Godefroy, [b] Roermond 22/12/1782; Sgt, 12/3/1808; [p] 25/9/1812
Devilleneuve, Guillaume, [b] Waalwijk 17/10/1787; [t>] into Inf de Ligne as SLt, 25/3/1811
Devisé, André, [b] Lautermagne 8/9/1772; Sgt, 5/4/1810; [t>] as SLt into 1er Cuirassiers, 8/2/1813
Devries, François, [b] Delft 15/9/1786; [m] Russia, 28/11/1812
Dienjes, Henry, [b] Maastricht 10/4/1782; [m] Russia, 6/11/1812
Dierstok, Jean Henry, [b] Enschede 5/6/1788; [m] Russia, 26/10/1812
van Dijk, Arie, [b] Rotterdam 9/11/1785; [m] Russia, 1/12/1812
van Dijk, Guillaume, [b] Utrecht 15/1/1782; Sgt, 21/9/1810; [m] Russia, 11/12/1812
van Dijk, Jean, [b] Reenen 24/11/1774; Cpl, 13/10/1811; [m] Russia, 2/12/1812
Dijke, Regnier, [b] Hilversum 20/1/1787; [dst] 6/3/1814
Dirks, Guillaume, [b] Hees 10/3/1777; [m] Russia, 5/12/1812
Dirkse, Gerard Jean, [b] Coverden 22/4/1777; [r] 1/12/1811
van der Donck, R., [b] Greffen 14/10/1779; [d/u] 1/3/1811
Donders, Jean, [b] Thoorn 12/4/1783; Cpl, 21/9/1810; [m] Russia, 21/12/1812
Donders, Pierre, [b] Tilburg 11/2/1775; [d/d] 24/7/1811
Doorissen, Arend, [b] Cleves 10/10/1778; Cpl, 13/4/1810; [m] Russia, 9/11/1812
van Dorst, Jacques, [b] Breda 6/12/1779; Cpl, 19/2/1811; Sgt, 17/2/1813; [ds] 12/7/1814
Draasel, Guillaume, [b] Voorburg 30/7/1785; [t>] 30e Chasseurs à cheval, 23/7/1811
van Driell, Gysbert, [b] Waardenburg 24/10/1790; [lwp] 31/3/1814
Duchène, Walter, [b] Liège 1/5/1771; [r] 24/7/1811
Duits, Henry, [b] Haarlem 28/9/1787; [m] Russia, 1/12/1812
Dupont, François, [b] Flexen 10/4/1778; [d/h] [r] 24/7/1811
Duprez, Pierre Charles, [b] Liège 13/3/1780; [d] in battle 25/10/1812
Duyghuysen, [b] Batenburg 15/6/1780; Sgt, 11/9/1809; [p] Russia, 15/9/1812
Duyndam, Jean, [b] Oegstgeest 28/6/1784; [m] Russia, 10/10/1812
Duytsch, Henry, [b] Nijmegen 7/5/1783; Cpl, 3/1/1813; fell behind, 18/5/1813
van Dyck, Everard, [b] Arnhem 20/5/1780; [m] Russia, 17/11/1812

E

van Eck, Gerard, [b] The Hague 2/4/1791; [d/d] [t>] 30e Chasseurs à cheval, 23/7/1811
van Eck, Henry, [b] Gameren 10/5/1786; [p] 10/9/1812
van Eck, Jean, [b] Utrecht 12/5/1786; [d/d] [t>] 30e Chasseurs à cheval, 23/7/1811
van Eck, Pierre, [b] Gammeren 1/6/1791; [p] Russia, 1/11/1812
van Eersel, Corneil, [b] Amsterdam 3/4/1781; [m] Russia, 11/12/1812
Elbert, George, [b] Bessenbach 4/1/1777; Cpl, 16/3/1810; [m] Russia, 2/12/1812
Elooy, Jean, [b] Haagje 18/6/1783; [lwp] 30/3/1814
Elsman, Jean, [b] Utrecht 15/1/1785; Cpl, 27/2/1807; [m] Russia, 2/12/1812
Emmerick, Joseph Martin, [b] The Hague 22/5/1785; Cpl, 24/2/1813; [lwp] 30/3/1814
Emons, Gerard, [b] Rekem 2/8/1784; Cpl, 28/11/1806; [m] Russia 1/12/1812
Emou, Frédéric, [b] Schiedam 3/3/1775; [m] Russia, 6/12/1812
van Emst, Jean, [b] Ype 1/7/1784; [m] Russia, 17/11/1812
Ender, Theophile, [b] Schellembourg 25/4/1775; [m] Russia, 9/12/1812
Endevoets, Joseph Adolphe, [b] Esck 15/4/1781; [m] Russia, 29/11/1812
Engelbert, Jean Henry, [b] Amsterdam 15/2/1793; [m] Russia, 5/9/1812
van Engelen, Theodore, [b] Ouderkerk 12/9/1789; [d/h] 15/10/1810
van Erk, Pierre, [b] Ettenburg 25/12/1784; [t>] 1er Lanciers de Ligne, 28/6/1812
van Ermelen, Herman, [b] Vurgten 6/8/1789; [p] Russia, 12/9/1812
van Es, Jacques, [b] Canton of Dordrecht 19/5/1787; [m] Russia, 10/12/1812
van Es, Pierre, [b] Dordrecht; [lwp] 31/3/1814
Eschweiler, Jean; Sgt, 1/11/1806; *see Appendix III, Officers*
Eskes, Henry, [b] Arnhem 11/9/1784; Cpl, 21/9/1810; [m] Russia, 29/11/1812

Esman, Guillaume, [b] Doetichem 20/9/1786; [e/v] Royal Guard 3/4/1807; [dst] 17/10/1807; returned 3/9/1810; [t>] 126e Inf de Ligne, 18/4/1811
Everts, Corneil, [b] Bedme 7/8/1785; [p] 24/11/1812
Everts, Evert, [b] Oosterbeek 8/11/1774; [d/h] 1/3/1811
Everts, Gerard [1], [b] Barneveld 2/5/1787; [p] Russia, 24/11/1812
Everts, Gerard [2], [b] Bikbergen 1/8/1786; [t>] 14e Cuirassiers, 27/12/1811
Eyk, Bartholemie, [b] Amsterdam 16/7/1778; [t>] 31e Chasseurs à cheval, 27/12/1811
Eykelenkamp, Jean, [b] Utrecht 19/6/1785; [m] Russia, 28/11/1812
Eykenboom, Louis, [b] Schiedam 24/12/1787; [p] Russia, 23/9/1812
Eyrich, Guillaume Leonard, [b] Rokersheim 12/5/1769; [d/h] [r] 24/7/1811
Eysbreeker, Henry, [b] Nijmegen 10/1/1788; [ds] 12/7/1814
van Eyssult, Paul, [b] Amsterdam 12/2/1787; [m] Russia, 16/9/1812

F

Faaes, Adrien Jean, [b] Meel 1/8/1791; [m] Russia, 22/12/1812
Fendel, Guillaume, [b] The Hague 8/8/1783; [lwp] 31/3/1814
Fennema, Jacques, [b] Oosterwijk 11/7/1787; [lwp] 20/4/1814
Fheelinngs, Jacob, [b] IJsselmuiden 23/4/1786; [m] Russia, 4/11/1812
Florin, Jacques, [b] Boertange 14/1/1782; [d] in hospital, Versailles, 2/6/1811
Fobel, Jean, [b] Bengheim 2/3/1786; Cpl, 6/4/1807; [m] Russia, 2/12/1812
Fokkens, Herman, [b] Wageningen 1/9/1780; Cpl, 21/9/1810; [m] Russia, 12/12/1812
Fournier, André, [b] Delfshaven 5/11/1782; QM, 10/7/1809; SM, 3/1/1813; [ds] 11/7/1814
Fox, Josué, [b] Dordrecht 10/1/1777; Cpl, 17/10/1806; [d] Russia, 4/12/1812
Frank, F., [b] Groll 10/8/1786; [p] Russia, 27/7/1812
Franken, Henry, [b] Beverwijk 27/2/1790; [m] Russia, 10/10/1812
Franken, Otto, [b] Leer 17/5/1769; [m] Russia, 23/9/1812
Franssen, Jean, [b] Tongeren 8/1/1770; Cpl, 6/6/1808; [r] 24/7/1811
Frederiks, Nicolas, [b] Neustad 1/5/1788; [m] Russia, 5/10/1812
Frekenius, Jean Henry, [b] Amsterdam 13/1/1783; [d/d] [t>] 124e Inf de Ligne, 9/4/1811
Fréquin, Guillaume, [b] Urleromain 13/5/1775; [wd] Lützen, 2/5/1813; [t>] CRCLF, 2/8/1814
Freyberg, Jean, [b] Zendershausen 14/10/1782; Cpl Tptr, 21/9/1810; [d] in hospital, Paris, 11/1/1812

G

van Gaalen, Henry, [b] Utrecht 12/4/1782; [p] Russia, 16/9/1812
van Galen, Henry Jean, [b] Deventer 28/6/1789; [t>] as SLt into Régiment de Walcheren, 25/3/1811
van Galen, Jacques, [b] Wateringen 12/9/1791; [lwp] 31/3/1814
van Gasteven, Corneil, [b] Kuylenburg 4/12/1792; [m] Russia, 5/10/1812
Geeresteyn, Jacques, [b] Canton of Wijk-bij-Duurstede 20/12/1792; [m] Russia, 28/10/1812
van Geffen, Gerard, [b] Hurne 1/11/1784; [ds] from regt. by order of Duke of Istria, 28/7/1812
van Geffen, Leonard, [b] Oss 20/10/1781; [m] Russia, 8/12/1812
van Geffen, Matthieu, [b] Heteren 1/10/1781; [m] Russia, 17/11/1812
Geimbergs, Martin, [b] Breda 1/1/1787; [ds] 11/7/1814
Genietz, Jean Bernard, [b] Amsterdam 17/8/1792; Cpl, 21/9/1811; [m] Russia, 10/12/1812
van Gent, Pierre, [b] Breda 3/3/1785; [d] in hospital, Paris, 1/4/1812
Gerlach, Bernard, [b] Maastricht 8/3/1784; [p] Russia, 23/9/1812
Gerrits, Hubert, [b] Rotterdam 25/11/1785; [m] Russia, 29/9/1812
Gerritsen, Gerard, [b] Harwelt 10/10/1784; [m] Russia, 20/10/1812
Gerritzen, Diederic, [b] Zalk 26/3/1768; Cpl, 30/11/1811; Sgt, 10/2/1813; fell behind, 22/5/1813
Gerritzen, Jean, [b] Barneveld 6/12/1773; [p] Russia, 27/7/1812
Gertner, Samuel Jacques, [b] The Hague 18/10/1790; [t>] as SLt into Inf de Ligne, 25/6/1811
Geurts, Guillaume, [b] Veldwezel 30/5/1788; [m] Russia, 27/11/1812
Van Geyn, Herman, [b] Maarssen 18/3/1787; [d] in hospital, Versailles, 5/5/1813
van Geyn, Nicolas, [b] Maarssen 18/3/1787; removed from muster roll, 31/3/1814
Geysbers, Jacques, [b] Spaarndam 11/12/1789; [m] Russia, 10/12/1812
Geysen, Louis, [b] Veldweesel 20/9/1778; [m] Russia, 28/12/1812

Geyssen, Rogier, [b] Loosdrecht 20/9/1788; [t>] 30e Chasseurs à cheval, 23/7/1811
Gieben, Gerard, [b] Elst 15/3/1775; [p] Russia, 25/10/1812
van Giesen, Gilbert, [b] Hulst 10/10/1784; [p] 3/2/1814
Gilles, Joseph, [b] Liäge 10/11/1770; [d/h] [r] 1/12/1811
Gillet, Franáois, [b] Lar 3/2/1783; [d/d] [t>] 11e Hussards, 23/7/1811
Gillissen, Jean Guillaume, [b] 's Hertogenbosch 16/9/1785; [p] Russia, 25/10/1812
Gilmer, Jean Crétien, [b] Saxony 16/3/1782; Trpt; [m] Russia, 6/12/1812
Gisser, Jacques, [b] The Hague 28/11/1779; *see Appendix III, Officers*
Gitshoven, [b] Valkenswaard 14/11/1784; [p] Russia, 27/7/1812
Goliath, François, [b] Sparendam 10/11/1782; Fr; [m] Russia, 23/11/1812
Gooyers, Henry, [b] Rotterdam 11/5/1782; [m] Russia, 24/11/1812
van Gorkom, Diederic, [b] Utrecht 22/9/1782; [m], sick, 23/11/1812
van Goudoever, Louis, [b] Utrecht 12/9/1786; SM, 21/9/1810; [d] 5/12/1812
de Graaf, Hubert, [b] Nieuwkuyk 14/10/1786; Cpl, 20/9/1806; Sgt, 1/4/1813; [ds] 12/7/1814
de Graaff, Corneil, [b] Kraslingen 24/11/1782; Cpl, 1/1/1809; Sgt, 9/1/1813; removed from muster roll 31/3/1814 while in hospital
Greven, Bezard, [b] Wilp 11/5/1790; [m] Russia, 30/10/1812
Grisart, Henry, [b] Laaren 12/3/1787; Cpl, 21/9/1810; [p] Russia, 6/12/1812
Grissart, Jean Joseph, [b] Breda 7/2/1785; Cpl, 21/9/1810; [p] Russia, 6/12/1812
Grobé, Jean Jacques, [b] The Hague 15/2/1775; Sgt, 4/8/1805; removed from muster roll for long absence, 22/11/1813
Grobé, Jean Volkmaar, [b] Groshamer 17/5/1783; Trpt; [p] Russia, 16/9/1812
van Groen, Jacques, [b] Westervoor 10/10/1787; [m] Russia, 15/11/1812
Groen, Jean, [b] Kuyk 12/3/1788; [m] Russia, 25/11/1812
Groenenberg, Joseph, [b] Groningen 10/5/1793; [m] Russia, 10/12/1812
Groenhuysen, Jacques, [b] Venendaal 14/5/1782; Sgt, 21/9/1810; Légion d'Honneur, 14/9/1813; [ds] 11/7/1812
de Groot, François; Sgt, 21/9/1810; *see Appendix III, Officers*
de Groot, Jacques, [b] Amsterdam 8/3/1789; Fr, 10/2/1811; [d] Russia, 24/11/1812
de Groot, Paul, [b] Utrecht 29/4/1784; Cpl, 11/9/1809; Sgt, 3/1/1813; removed from muster roll 31/3/1814 while in hospital
de Groot, Philippe, [b] Utrecht 29/9/1787; [m] Russia, 28/10/1812
Groothuyzen, Guillaume, [b] Gendt 14/1/1769; [lwp] 31/3/1814
Grootveld, Henry, [b] Utrecht 12/7/1789; [m] Russia, 15/11/1812

H

Haanen, Bernard, [b] Rugten 16/4/1789; [d/u] 20/10/1810
van Haaren, Gerard, [b] Nijmegen 23/2/1785; [m] Russia, 10/10/1812
van Haarlem, Adrien, [b] Vianen 1/10/1773; Sgt, 21/9/1810; [ds] 12/7/1814
de Haas, Henry, [b] Utrecht 17/6/1788; [p] 25/10/1812
Haasen, Lambert, [b] Orhelen 1/12/1786; [m] Russia, 14/11/1812
Hagemans, Henry, [b] Styn 11/11/1778; Cpl, 21/9/1810; [d/m] Lancer at own request, 14/7/1811; [m] Russia, due to sickness, 6/11/1812
Hageraat, Ferdinand, [b] The Hague 9/8/1783; Cpl, 9/12/1806; [dm] Lancer, 6/1/1811; Cpl, 2/6/1811; [dm] Lancer, 26/3/1812; [p] 30/1/1814
Hakkenberg, Jacques, [b] Nijmegen 1/10/1788; [m] Russia, 15/11/1812
Halkers, Everard, [b] Schiedam 1/4/1788; [m] Russia, 2/11/1812
van den Ham, Corneil, [b] Kuylenburg 8/3/1790; [lwp] 31/3/1814
Hamers, Antoine, [b] Gillen 20/3/1785; [ds] 11/7/1814
Hamerslag, Henry, [b] 's Hertogenbosch 19/12/1787; Cpl, 10/6/1807; [m] Russia, 16/9/1812
Hansen, Martin, [b] Canton of Horst 6/5/1783; [lwp] 31/3/1814
Harms, Roelof, [b] Zuidhoorn 25/9/1772; [t>] Vétérans, 17/4/1811
Harmse, Leonard, [b] Elst 20/3/1787; [d] in hospital, Paris, 16/3/1812
Havelaar, Jean, [b] Amsterdam 4/6/1788; [d/d] [t>] 124e Inf de Ligne, 9/4/1811
la Haye, Laurent, [b] Sint-Truiden 1/1/1780; [wd] sabre cut to right arm, Austria; lost both legs, Leipzig, 16/10/1813; Légion d'Honneur, 16/8/1813; [t>] CRCLF, 2/8/1814
Heemskerk, Jean, [b] Delst 10/10/1784; Cpl, 21/9/1810; [d] in hospital, Versailles, 23/11/1810

Heinneman, George, [b] Hessencassel 1/3/1790; Cpl, 1/4/1813; [p] 31/3/1814
Heinneman, Jean, [b] Niedemyssen 4/5/1772; Cpl, 7/10/1810; Sgt, 28/5/1813; [p] 20/3/1814
Hekelenburg, Jean, [b] Nassau 15/3/1781; Trpt; [m] Russia, 11/12/1812
D'Helis, Henry, [b] Helen 15/3/1782; Cpl, 23/2/1813; [lwp] 9/5/1814
Hellaad, Jean Baptiste, [b] Antwerp 5/10/1787; [m] 2/12/1812
Hellers, Jean, [b] The Hague 9/10/1789; [ds] 12/7/1814
Helling, Jacques, [b] Terwolde 26/3/1788; [lwp] 31/3/1814
Hendriks, Henry, [b] Zutphen 25/5/1785; [m] Russia, 5/12/1812
Hendriks, Matthieu, [b] Leeuwarden 2/3/1778; [p] Russia, 23/9/1812
Hendriks, Pierre Henry, [b] Arnhem 6/10/1785; [lwp] 31/3/1814
Henke, Henry, [b] Emael 18/2/1784; [d/h] 19/9/1811
Hennus, Bartholemi, [b] Klimmen 20/10/1781; [d] in hospital, Vilna, 24/10/1812
Hensepeeter, Jean, [b] Drempt 28/7/1783; Cpl, 24/2/1813; [lwp] 1/4/1814
Herbich, Jean, [b] Puy l9/8/1788; [t>] as SLt into Inf de Ligne, 25/3/1811
Hermans, F. Matthieu, [b] Rotterdam 21/9/1785; [m] Russia, 1/12/1812
van Herp, Gerard, [b] Herp 12/8/1778; [t>] Vétérans 17/4/1811
Herting, Jean, [b] 's Hertogenbosch 17/9/1785; [m] Russia, 24/7/1812
Hesenman, Jean, [b] Kekendom 17/8/1788; [lwp] 2/4/1814
Hess, Jacob, [b] Cubatz, Saxony, 10/3/1771; TM, 1/5/1801; [d] in his room, 20/1/1811
Hesschenmulder, Jean, [b] Rotterdam 1/3/1780; SM, 10/2/1807; [m] Russia, 4/12/1812
van Hesse, R., [b] Harde 15/3/1784; [p] Russia, 8/12/1812
Hessen, Jean Crétien, [b] Rotterdam 20/3/1791; [t>] 11e Hussards, 23/7/1811
Hesters, Crétien, [b] Tongeren 9/1/1778; Sgt, 11/9/1809; [p] Russia, 25/9/1812
Hette, Diederic, [b] Kolle 2/5/1777; [d/m] [r] 1/12/1811
Heuneman, Chrétien, [b] Amsterdam 24/2/1786; [m] Russia, 27/11/1812
van den Heuvel, Gerard, [b] Nerrewijnen 22/7/1779; [m] Russia, 30/10/1812
Hey, Jean Albert, [b] Wijk-bij-Duurstede 29/8/1790; [m] Russia, 3/10/1812
Heymans, Corneile, [b] The Hague 13/6/1790; [m] Russia, 9/12/1812
Heymans, François, [b] Haassen 20/4/1787; [p] Russia, 27/7/1812
Heymans, Gilles, [b] Rotterdam 2/7/1782; [d/u] 1/8/1811
Heyne, Guillaume, [b] Saxony 27/5/1779; [d] 7/11/1812
Heyne, Leonard, [b] Barneveld 14/5/1792; [d/d] [t>] 124e Inf de Ligne, 9/4/1811
Heynekink, Crétien, [b] 's Hertogenbosch 29/9/1787; [dst] from depot in Holland, 13/11/1810
Hinfelaar, Jacques, [b] The Hague 13/3/1784; Cpl, 9/9/1809; [d] in hospital, Versailles, 3/2/1811
Hirschfeld, Auguste, [b] Grussen 12/5/1786; Trpt; [d/d] [t>] 11e Hussards, 10/8/1811
Hoekstra, Eypen, [b] Leeuwarden 29/3/1785; [lwp] 31/3/1814
Hoepeling, Philippe, [b] Oegstgeest 10/12/1789; QM, 21/9/1810; [dm] Lancer, 18/4/1811; [p] Russia, 27/7/1812
Hofman, Gerard, [b] Kevelaar 6/4/1783; [m] Russia, 21/10/1812
Hofmeyer, Guillaume Frédéric, [b] Nieuweschans 16/8/1786; [t>] 11e Hussards, 23/7/1811
Holleboom, Gerard, [b] Berkum 21/11/1784; [p] Russia, 23/10/1812
Holtman, Gerard, [b] Amsterdam 11/2/1789; [m] Russia, 20/11/1812
Homan, Jean, [b] Helderhausen 18/7/1782; Trpt; [d] 20/10/1812
Homots, François, [b] Groningue 15/12/1776; Sgt, 21/9/1810; [m] Russia, 27/10/1812
Hoofs, Frédéric Norbert, [b] Tilburg 15/3/1791; [ds] 12/7/1814
Hoogeveen, Jacques, [b] Scheveningen 6/4/1777; Sgt, 2/11/1806; [ds] 15/10/1810
van Hoorn, Jacques, [b] Maastricht 3/5/1776; [m] Russia, 10/10/1812
Hopman, Henry, [b] Haarlem 6/6/1784; [d] Warsaw 25/1/1813
Hoppenbrouwer, Gerard, [b] Heusden 5/11/1781; [m] Russia, 4/12/1812
Horn, Valentin, [b] Leyderdorp 26/3/1785; [t>] as SLt into Inf de Ligne, 1/6/1811
Houenschild, André, [b] Koningsdalen 14/4/1785; [m] Russia, 26/8/1812
Houkens, François, [b] Utrecht 1/10/1791; [m] Russia, 4/12/1812
Hout, Henry, [b] Delft 20/3/1788; [m] Russia, 23/10/1812
Houtkamp, Augustin, [b] Groningue 27/10/1769; [r] 24/7/1811
Houwerling, Corneil, [b] Overschie 15/3/1789; [m] Russia, 28/10/1812
van Hove, Nicolas, [b] Schoonhoven 6/12/1787; [m] Russia, 5/11/1812

Hovestadt, Elise, [b] Doesburg 12/7/1793; [m] Russia, 28/11/1812
Hubert, Joseph, [b] Othe 10/5/1783; Cpl, 21/9/1810; [d] in battle, 25/10/1812
Hubertus, Joseph, [b] Rosendaal 8/11/1790; [m] Russia, 2/12/1812
Huisman, Theodore, [b] Narderwijk 17/11/1787; [p] Russia, 27/7/1812
van der Hul, Lambert, [b] Barneveld 24/6/1772; Sgt, 26/2/1808; [m] Russia, 18/11/1812
Hulsman, Everard, [b] Kampen 28/10/1785; removed from muster roll 31/3/1814 – in hospital since 1/4/1813
Hulsman, Henry, [b] Westronen 25/12/1791; [m] Russia, 2/12/1812
Hunselaar, Bartholomie, [b] Heteren 26/5/1783; [m] Russia, 7/12/1812
Hupker, Jacques, [b] Petershagen 10/10/1778; [d/h] 1/3/1811
Huppelschote, Requin, [b] Amersfoort 6/10/1778; Cpl, 5/2/1807; [d/h] [r] 26/6/1811
Huster, Joseph, [b] Amsterdam 24/2/1785; [m] Russia, 12/11/1812
Huyghens, Balden Ysbrand, [b] Amsterdam 9/11/1790; Cpl, 18/4/1811; [t>] as SLt into 95e Inf de Ligne, 10/1/1811
Huynsbergen, Martin, [b] Deusersen 7/1/1783; Fr; [d] in hospital, Versailles, 15/12/1810
Huysen, Guillaume, [b] Amsterdam 4/3/1776; Sgt, 5/9/1807; [m] Russia, 5/12/1812
Huysman, Jean, [b] Briel 22/7/1784; [d] in hospital, Nancy, 2/1/1814

I

Ichterhausen, Ernst, [b] Luna, Saxony, 24/6/1786; Trpt; removed from muster roll 1/2/1814 - in hospital since 1/6/1813
Iliohan, Jean Diederic, [b] Zutphen 10/5/1777; [d/h] 1/3/1811
Imhoff, Jean, [b] Sassenhaussen 4/4/1775; SM, 1/12/1805; [r] 1/12/1811
Inderheyden, Jean François, [b] Breda 9/10/1777; Sgt, 2/9/1809; Sub-instructor SM, 18/3/1812; [ds] 11/7/1814
van Ingen, Christophe, [b] Tilburg 29/8/1787; Sgt, 10/5/1807; [dm] Cpl, 2/6/1811; [m] Russia, 2/12/1812
Itterson, Lambert, [b] Oud Heusden 6/5/1785; [d] in hospital, Paris, 10/3/1812

J

Jacquet, Joseph, [b] Liège 15/4/1770; Cpl, 16/2/1808; [d/h] [r] 24/7/1811
Jacquet, Toussaint, [b] Juprelle 1/1/1785; Fr; Asst-veterinary, 1/9/1813; [ds] 12/7/1814
Jagers, François, [b] Wijk bij Duurstede 26/7/1786; Cpl, 21/9/1810; Sgt, 28/2/1813; [lwp] 31/3/1814
Jamsen, Valérie, [b] Burta 20/3/1787; [m] Russia, 10/12/1812
Jansen, Adriaan, [b] Nemdel 12/8/1784; [lwp] 29/3/1814
Jansen, François, [b] Driel 12/7/1783; [m] Russia, 6/12/1812
Jansen, Gerard, [b] Amsterdam 1/6/1790; [m] Russia, 23/10/1812
Jansen, Henry, [b] Canton of Groningue 1/5/1787; [lwp] 20/4/1814
Jansen, Herman, [b] Nieuwkerk 16/5/1788; [m] Russia, 23/11/1812
Jansen, Hubert, [b] Canton of Cleves 17/4/1787; [p] Russia, 25/9/1812
Jansen, Jacques, [b] Dordrecht 23/7/1783; Trpt, 21/9/1810; [d/h] [r] 1/12/1811
Jansen, Jean, [b] Nijmegen 21/5/1786; fell behind, 18/5/1813
Jansons, Antoine, [b] Zierikzee 5/10/1787; [m] Russia, due to sickness, 27/11/1812
Janssen, Jacques, [b] Wildendorp 2/2/1762; SM, 1/5/1801; [t>] Vétérans, 17/4/1811
Janssen, Jean Jacques, [b] Nijmegen 21/3/1794; Trpt, 21/9/1810; [p] Russia, 25/10/1812
Janssen, Louis, [b] Echt 12/3/1789; [d/u] 1/3/1811
Janssen, Thimothé, [b] Wageningen 30/10/1780; Sgt, 1/2/1809; [d] 9/12/1812
Janssens, Armand, [b] Reusel 23/4/1777; Sgt, 21/9/1810; [m] Russia, 5/12/1812
Jobay, Pierre, [b] Canton of Dordrecht 19/9/1789; [m] Russia, 23/10/1812
Joly, François, [b] Principality of Neufchâtel 27/2/1786; QM, 7/9/1809; [t>] as SLt into 4e Chevau-légers de Ligne, 8/2/1813; left Red Lancers 1/3/1813
Jonemans, André, [b] Schewede 7/7/1783; Cpl, 15/3/1806; [m] Russia, 6/11/1812
de Jong, ?, [b] Gouda 3/3/1793; [lwp] 20/4/1814
De Jong, Adrien [1], [b] Vianen 4/9/1782; [lwp] 31/3/1814
De Jong, Adrien [2], [b] Vianen 12/5/1791; [m] Russia, 6/12/1812
Jongbloed, Jean, [b] Enscheeve 17/3/1780; [dst] 22/3/1810; returned 3/9/1810; [d/d] [t>] 126e Inf de Ligne, 9/4/1811
de Jongh, Corneil, [b] The Hague 6/7/1788; [dst] 15/12/1810
Joost, Henry, [b] Heidelberg 17/1/1785; removed from muster roll 1/1/1813 - on leave since 27/12/1811
Joosten, Jean [1], [b] Gendt 1/1/1786; [lwp] 15/5/1814
Joosten, Jean [2], [b] Lommel 22/1/1780; Cpl, 13/7/1809; [m] Russia, 2/11/1812

Jordens, Rudolphe, [b] Wohlen 10/3/1787; [m] Russia, 26/8/1812

Jorissen, Chrétien, [b] Vlijlingen 15/10/1784; Cpl, 21/9/1810; [dm] Lancer, 9/10/1810; [p] Russia, 25/9/1812

Jorissen, Henry, [b] The Hague 30/8/1782; [m] Russia, 28/9/1812

K

Kahl, Guillaume, [b] Volst 16/4/1786; Sgt, 21/9/1810; [wd] [m] Russia, 2/12/1812

Kallenberg, Pierre, [b] Leiden 11/11/1792; [dst] 15/12/1810

Kalter, Arnoult, [b] Yselmuyde 6/10/1786; [d] in battle, 25/10/1812

Kamphens, Marie, [b] Bergen-op-Zoom 2/1/1790; Cpl, 10/2/1813; fell behind, 4/2/1814

de Kamps, André, [b] Alcoude 18/11/1789; [m] Russia, 10/12/1812

van Karnebeek, Jean, [b] Amsterdam 19/2/1788; [t>] as SLt into Inf de Ligne, 27/1/1811

Karsens, Diederic, [b] Woubrugge 15/7/1789; [ds] 12/7/1814

Kastermans, Pierre, [b] Hees 1/5/1785; [m] Russia, 6/12/1812

Kastricum, Adrien, [b] Haarlem 16/7/1789; [d/d] [t>] 126e Inf de Ligne, 18/4/1811

de Kat, Herman Jacques, [b] Amsterdam 23/2/1790; [m] Russia, 1/12/1812

Kattenbach, Jean Godefroy, [b] Aalsfel 18/4/1783; Trpt; [ds] 11/7/1814

Kauffman, J., [b] Haug 31/12/1782; Trpt Cpl, 21/9/1810; TM, 21/2/1813; fell behind, 18/10/1813; [d] in battle, Reichenbach

van Keeken, Guillebert, [b] Liège 25/7/1785; Cpl, 14/7/1812; [p] 27/7/1812

Keer, Guillaume, [b] Emmerick, Lippe, 11/3/1790; [p] Russia, 25/9/1812

van Keers, Henry, [b] Luttichhausen 9/1/1782; [m] Russia, 20/11/1812

Keetel, Antoine, [b] Woudenberg 29/4/1789; [m] Russia, 15/11/1812

Kelhoven, André, [b] The Hague 11/7/1784; [m] Russia, 18/12/1812

Kempkes, Arie, [b] Driel 16/7/1787; [m] Russia, 19/11/1812

Kempkes, Gerard, [b] Driel 1/1/1786; [t>] 124e Inf de Ligne, 17/12/1813

Kempkes, Pierre, [b] Valburg 12/1/1795; [t>] 124e Inf de Ligne, 9/4/1811

Kerkhoff, Arnold, [b] Doesburg 14/1/1786; Cpl, 1/4/1808; [m] Russia, 5/12/1812

van Kesteren, Pierre, [b] Nijmegen 6/5/1788; [m] Russia, 16/10/1812

De Keyzer, Armand, [b] Bommel 10/2/1788; [m] Russia, 19/11/1812

Keyzer, Guillaume, [b] Wassenach 11/8/1783; [m] Russia, 27/11/1812

Khule, Corneil; Master-spurrier; Asst-veterinary, 1/9/1810; [r] 1/12/1811

Kiezinger, Jean, [b] Amsterdam 11/2/1788; [m] Russia, 11/11/1812

Klaasen, Diederic, [b] Hoevelaak 7/1/1787; [p] Russia, 21/9/1812

van der Klaashorst, ?, [b] The Hague 1/8/1787; [p] Russia, 27/7/1812

Klaassen, Martin, [b] Alken 7/3/1777; [m] Russia, 8/12/1812

Klaassen, Pierre, [b] Ruiseveen 25/5/1783; Cpl, 1/2/1813; [lwp] 31/3/1814

van der Klasthorst, Guillaume, [b] The Hague 21/7/1781; [m] Russia, 6/12/1812

van der Kleiberg, Lucas, [b] Hellevoort 4/12/1774; [d/d] [t>] 11e Hussars, 23/7/1811

de Klerk, Jean Martin, [b] Dordrecht 17/2/1787; [d/h] 1/10/1811

Klinkhamer, Arnould, [b] Brakelen 24/4/1773; [m] Russia, 7/12/1812

Klippers, Jean Adolphe, [b] The Hague 11/6/1782; [d] in hospital, Versailles, 14/8/1811

Klosner, Charles Frédéric, [b] 's Hertogenbosch 2/11/1792; [m] Russia, 12/12/1812

Knoote, Abraham, [b] Leiden 6/6/1786; Sgt, 8/9/1809; [m] Russia, 15/12/1812

Knotsenburg, Guillaume, [b] Kulenborg 23/4/1787; [lwp] 2/4/1814

Koch, Leonard Henry, [b] Batsveld 25/12/1785; Cpl, 16/7/1810; removed from muster roll 8/8/1811 for long absence

Kock, Conrad Ignace, [b] The Hague 21/12/1779; Sgt, 2/12/1809; [m] Russia, 6/12/1812

Koek, Antoine, [b] Erpenzeel 1/1/1790; [m] Russia, 4/12/1812

Koelensmit, Antoine Rudolphe, [b] Utrecht 27/1/1784; [d/d] put at disposal of Minister of War, 30/11/1810

Koenders, Guillaume, [b] Steenderen 7/3/1785; Cpl, 1/11/1809; [p] 12/9/1812

de Koff, Daniel, [b] Wijk-bij-Duurstede 23/9/1788; [d/h] 4/8/1811

Kok, Mathieu, [b] The Hague 11/1/1783; [m] Russia, 25/11/1812

Koks, Lambert, [b] Rekem 16/9/1780; [p] Russia, 25/7/1812

van der Kolk, Jean, [b] Grip 2/8/1790; [lwp] 31/3/1814

Kollemberg, Henry, [b] Schoonhoven 24/5/1783; [d] in hospital, Versailles, 24/1/1811

de Koning, Gauthier, [b] Dordrecht 5/8/1784; Cpl, 21/9/1810; [dm] Lancer, 19/2/1811; [m] Russia, 4/12/1812

Kook, Corneil, [b] Utrecht 1/9/1788; [m] Russia, 2/11/1812

Kools, Laurent, [b] Ginniken 7/10/1791; [m] Russia, 1/9/1812

Koster, André, [b] Schummest 5/8/1788; [m] Russia, 3/11/1812

Kouwenberg, Jean, [b] Hallen 25/5/1780; [p] 25/10/1812

Kouwer, Jean Jacques, [b] The Hague 1/6/1780; [m] Russia, 12/10/1812

Kraaft, Theodore François, [b] The Hague 3/10/1791; Cpl, 7/1/1812; [m] Russia, 2/12/1812

Kraak, Jean, [b] Oud-Beyerland 23/7/1780; [t>] 11e Hussards 23/7/1811

Kraamer, Jean, [b] Bruindermoer 10/12/1790; [m] Russia, 25/11/1812

Kragten, Jean, [b] Utrecht 24/3/1791; [d] Russia, 1/11/1812

Kreft, Stephane, [b] Leiden 10/2/1783; [m] Russia, 8/11/1812

Kreyne, Jean, [b] Palbourg 1/11/1789; [lwp] 31/3/1814

Krisveld, Guillaume Auguste, [b] Maastricht 23/1/1790; [t>] as SLt to the Indies, 27/1/1811

Kroh, Charles Frédéric, [b] Wageningen 13/4/1786; [m] Russia, 11/8/1812

Kruisweg, Herman Henry, [b] Zwolle 27/4/1783; Cpl, 21/9/1812; [m] Russia, 26/11/1812

Kruyt, Jean, [b] Oosterwijk 1/3/1789; [t>] as SLt to the Indies, 27/1/1811

Kuchleo, George Charles, [b] Cape of Good Hope 24/9/1788; [t>] as SLt to the Indies, 27/1/1811

Kuhl, Guillaume Henry, [b] Zutphen 10/6/1787; [ds] 11/7/1814

Kuhl, Henry Guillaume, [b] Zutphen 2/9/1790; [m] Russia, 2/12/1812

Kuilenburg, Adam, [b] Maastricht 25/11/1787; [lwp] 31/3/1814

Kuipen, Guillaume, [b] Hengelo 28/10/1782; [t>] Vétérans, 17/4/1811

Kuypers, Corneel, [b] Hilversum 14/8/1786; [m] Russia, 6/12/1812

Kuypers, Jean, [b] Enkhuizen 5/2/1779; [lwp] 26/6/1814

L

van Laaer, Thierry, [b] Vaesen 28/4/1785; [m] Russia, 30/11/1812

de Laan, Gauthier, [b] Bokhoven 1/11/1784; [d/d] [t>] 31e Chasseurs à cheval, 23/7/1811

van Laar, Christophe, [b] Wageningen 1/5/1773; [m] Russia, 11/11/1812

Lambert, Pierre Godefroy, [b] Maastricht 2/1/1791; [t>] as SLt to the Indies, 27/1/1811

Lambrechts, Jean Louis, [b] Tongeren 19/8/1795; SM, 9/9/1809; [d] in battle, 25/10/1812

Langenbach, Henry, [b] Duchy of Berg 16/1/1782; [m] Russia, 30/11/1812

Langenikel, Chrétien, [b] Mulhausen 4/4/1780; Trpt; [t>] 11e Hussards, 13/5/1812

Langeveld, Jean, [b] The Hague 16/4/1787; [ds] 11/7/1814

Lans, Gerard, [b] Zwolle 8/11/1781; [t>] as SLt to the Indies, 27/1/1811

Lauren, Arie, [b] Briel 28/1/1786; [d/d] [t>] 1er Bataillon Colonial, 1/8/1812

Laurens, Pierre, [b] Briel 13/3/1789; [ds] 12/7/1814

Leeber, Guillaume, [b] Middelbourg 11/5/1783; [t>] 11e Hussards, 1/8/1812

Leenaards, Nicolas, [b] Emel 19/5/1787; [m] Russia, 1/12/1812

Leenders, Jean, [b] Dissen 1/12/1782; [p] Russia, 23/9/1812

van Leer, Antoine, [b] Utrecht 26/5/1780; [d/d] [t>] 124e Inf de Ligne, 9/4/1811

Leers, Henry, [b] Zutphen 15/8/1787; [p] Russia, 25/9/1812

van Leersum, Gilbert, [b] Loenen 17/11/1789; [m] Russia, 4/12/1812

Leesmans, Pierre, [b] Breda 1/1/1784; [lwp] 31/3/1814

van Leeuwen, Corneil, [b] Gouda 6/3/1793; [m] Russia, 7/12/1812

van Leeuwen, Jean, [b] The Hague 17/12/1778; Sgt, 9/9/1809; [m] Russia, 8/12/1812

Lehr, Jacques, [b] Rokel 17/4/1783; [m] Russia, 9/12/1812

Leicher, Nicolas, [b] The Hague 1/9/1778; removed from muster roll, 2/8/1814 - in hospital

Lelie, Jean, [b] Amsterdam 4/8/1782; [t>] 31e Inf de Ligne, 23/7/1811

Lens, Jean Baptiste, [b] Bergen-op-Zoom 4/7/1787; [lwp] 31/3/1814

Lethman, Jean, [b] Schoonhoven 12/2/1785; [p] Russia, 25/9/1812

Leverland, Jean, [b] Leeuwarden 17/5/1787; [m] Russia, 26/11/1812

Lick, Herman, [b] Bremen 20/3/1790; [m] Russia, 9/12/1812

De Liefde, Steven, [b] Hussen 10/4/1788; [m] Russia, 4/12/1812

Lieffeling, Gerard, [b] Utrecht 18/5/1781; [m] Russia, 19/11/1812

Lieshout, François, [b] 's Hertogenbosch 20/9/1789; [d/d] [t>] 124e Inf de Ligne, 9/4/1811

Lijsenaar, Gerard, [b] Gameren 7/10/1791; [lwp] 30/3/1814

van der Linden, Gerard, [b] Nijmegen 28/6/1784; [m] Russia, 12/12/1812

Lindt, Jean Franáois, [b] Muyden 22/12/1787; fell behind, 19/9/1813

Lindt, Jean Pierre, [b] The Hague 26/11/1786; [p] Russia, 27/7/1812

Linsing, Corneil, [b] Brandt 15/10/1783; [ds] 11/7/1814

van Lit, Nicolas, [b] Heemstede 10/5/1786; [m] Russia, 12/12/1812

van Litt, Antoine, [b] Wagenooden 20/1/1786; [d/d] [t>] 30e Chasseurs à cheval, 23/7/1811

van Litt, François, [b] Wagenoode 20/2/1792; [m] Russia, 23/10/1812

van Litt, Pierre, [b] Waardenogen 22/6/1789; [p] Russia, 25/9/1812

van Lochem, Pierre, [b] Schoonhoven 4/10/1790; [m] Russia, 13/11/1812

Lodestein, Christophe, [b] Groningue 23/4/1786; [m] Russia, 2/12/1812

Loeff, Pierre, [b] Heessel 17/2/1780; [p] Russia, 27/7/1812

van Loenen, Corneil, [b] Amsterdam 21/9/1777; Cpl, 4/1/1711; [m] Russia, 2/12/1812

Lokmans, Pierre, [b] The Hague 20/7/1791; [m] Russia, 4/12/1812

Lombar, François, [b] Amsterdam 2/1/1782; Sgt, 10/10/1809; [ds] 19/10/1810

Lonbar, Thomas Leopold, [b] Amsterdam 28/5/1791; Cpl, 14/7/1811; QM, 12/8/1811; [m] Russia, 24/11/1812

Lookermans, Pierre, [b] Velsen 14/6/1780; Cpl, 10/3/1807; [m] Russia, 3/12/1812

Loosdrecht, Jean, [b] Wijk bij Duurstede 18/4/1778; [lwp] 31/3/1814

Loostermans, Corneil, [b] Meer 3/4/1785; QM, 6/4/1807; [m] Russia, 27/11/1812

Lorffer, Laurent, [b] Steinfort 4/10/1786; [p] Russia, 15/11/1812

Louis, Gerard Bol, [b] Velsen 16/8/1788; [d] in hospital, Paris, 25/3/1812

Loup, Jean Abraham, [b] Utrecht 13/11/1790; [d/d] [t>] 126e Inf de Ligne, 18/4/1811

Louterbach, Conrad, [b] Westphalia 1/11/1784; Trpt, 21/9/1810; [m] Russia, 30/11/1812

Luttenberg, Gerard, [b] Zwolle 9/7/1785; [m] Russia, 2/12/1812

M

Maaler, Martin, [b] Amsterdam 17/12/1790; [t>] 11e Cuirassiers, 11/9/1811

Maas, Henry, [b] Utrecht 2/2/1793; [ds] 6/10/1810

Maas, Martin, [b] Amsterdam 14/2/1787; [d/h] 1/10/1811

Maas, Mathis Jean, [b] Oud Valkenburg 9/7/1784; Sgt, 17/11/1806; [m] Russia, 2/11/1812

Maasbach, Jean, [b] Thiel 8/4/1790; [m] Russia, 6/11/1812

Maase, Jean, [b] Wardensveld 7/6/1776; [t>] Vétérans, 17/4/1811

Maasland, Jacques, [b] Vianen 15/10/1782; [p] Russia, 27/7/1812

Machiels, Pierre, [b] Barnasten 4/5/1788; [m] Russia, 20/11/1812

Magrée, Herman, [b] Harderwijk 8/3/1785; Cpl, 1/10/1809; Sgt, 3/1/1813; [ds] 11/7/1814

Manders, Pierre, [b] Baak 14/3/1784; Cpl, 11/9/1809; [d/h] 11/2/1812

Marcelis, Jean, [b] Grooslinde 8/2/1779; [m] Russia, 10/11/1812

Marks, Jean, [b] Zelst 16/12/1786; [m] Russia, 1/11/1812

Marps, Jean, [b] Bergen-op-Zoom 15/5/1788; [m] Russia, 11/11/1812

Martens, [b] Tessen 4/1/1779; Sgt, 21/9/1812; [ds] 12/7/1814

Martijn, Pierre, [b] Neurrout 23/4/1783; [p] Russia, 27/7/1812

Martijn, Pierre Guillaume, [b] Zierikzee 30/6/1790; [t>] as SLt to the Indies, 27/1/1811

Marx, George, [b] Mulh 17/12/1783; [m] Russia, 8/12/1812

Mathieu, Emelie Marie, [b] Putting 1/4/1788; Cpl, 21/1/1811; [t>] as SLt into Inf de Ligne, 10/3/1811

Matinius, D. François, [b] Archauger (Archangel?), Russia, 12/6/1782; [m] Russia, 17/11/1812

Mauss, George Auguste Alexandre, [b] Liège 21/5/1776; SM, 1/11/1809; [m] Russia, 8/12/1812

Medema, J.J., [b] , Garnveld 23/3/1787; [p] Russia, 16/10/1812

Meelis, Nicolas Jean, [b] Kolm 12/7/1779; [p] 2/2/1814

Meemeling, Rudolf, [b] Warseveld 10/1/1782; [m] Russia, 26/11/1812

Meerbeek, Pierre, [b] Dort 7/3/1783; [m] Russia, 20/11/1812

Meimers, Jean, [b] Courveld 13/6/1773; Cpl, 2/9/1809; [m] Russia, 22/11/1812

Meinder, Diederic, [b] Heteren 8/1/1779; [lwp] 31/3/1814

Meisner, Charles Auguste, [b] Dresden, Saxony, 19/12/1784; [d/u] 15/10/1810

Mellis, Antoine, [b] Raskerd 18/6/1786; [d] in hospital, Versailles, 30/3/1813

Melser, Fréderic, [b] The Hague 6/10/1779; [p] 25/9/1812

Mensch, Nicolas, [b] Maastricht 21/10/1783; [d] 16/2/1813

Menso, Corneille Henry, [b] Venlo 14/5/1793; [t>] as SLt into Inf de Ligne, 8/6/1811

Menso, Walter, [b] Utrecht 19/5/1786; [t>] as SLt into Inf de Ligne, 8/6/1811

Menten, Jean, [b] Zatendaal 15/5/1776; [ds] 11/7/1814

Mentink, Caspar, [b] The Hague 14/8/1791; [m] Russia, 3/12/1812

Mes, Jean, [b] Delft 10/12/1777; fell behind in Russia, 15/12/1812

Mespoulier, Adrien, [b] Tilburg 10/5/1778; [p] Russia, 11/12/1812

van Meuwen, Henry, [b] Tilburg 2/10/1784; [m] Russia, 8/12/1812

Meyer, Henry, [b] Zoeterwoude 24/3/1789; [m] Russia, 19/11/1812

Meyer, Jean, [b] Amersfoort 8/11/1781; [m] Russia, 31/10/1812

Meyer, Jean Henry, [b] Hengelo 15/5/1781; [dst] 16/7/1813

van Meyeren, Adriaan, [b] Bergenbach 31/12/1790; [m] Russia, 15/8/1812

Mezand, Cesar, [b] Hirson 14/8/1784; Cpl, 21/9/1810; [dm] Lancer, 15/3/1812; [m] Russia, 24/10/1812

Minnoltz, Jean Nicolas, [b] The Hague 3/11/1776; Cpl, 23/2/1812; [m] Russia, 3/10/1812

Moerkerk, Laurens, [b] Gorcum 15/3/1780; [d/h] 1/10/1811

Moesbach, Jean Jacques, [b] Saxony 7/8/1787; TM, 21/9/1810; probably regimental kettledrummer, 1810 to 1812; [d] at home, 19/2/1813

Moesman, Antoine, [b] Amersfoort 16/4/1792; [m] Russia, 12/11/1812

de Mol, Louis, [b] Maarsen 22/12/1793; [m] Russia, 6/11/1812

Mol, Paul, [b] Oudenbosch 10/3/1785; [p] Russia, 27/11/1812

Moor, Philippe, [b] Breda 26/7/1789; Cpl, 19/4/1812; [r] 15/1/1814 - absent on leave since 18/10/1813

Mooren, Guillaume, [b] Beugen 6/1/1783; [p] Russia, 27/7/1812

Morgenrood, Frédéric, [b] Utrecht 16/1/1786; [m] Russia, 19/11/1812

Moritz, Everard, [b] Nassau 17/9/1782; Trpt; fell behind, 23/8/1813

Morsser, Jean, [b] Oldenzaal 16/10/1780; [m] Russia, 28/11/1812

Mourik, Jean, [b] Zoelmonde 6/1/1773; [m] Russia, 12/11/1812

Mous, [b] Noordhorn 2/3/1786; [d/h] [r] 1/3/1811

Mulder, George, [b] Leen 25/9/1785; [m] Russia, 27/11/1812

Mulders, Jacques, [b] Bunzen 15/1/1790; [ds] 11/7/1814

Mullekes, Pierre, [b] Steyn 8/3/1786; [lwp] 31/3/1814

Muller, Charles, [b] Prussia 29/12/1764; [t>] 11e Hussards, for being a foreigner, 30/3/1811

Mumsen, Jean, [b] The Hague 24/8/1784; [p] Russia, 27/7/1812

van der Muts, Gilbert, [b] Amersfoort 1/2/1775; [m] Russia, 22/11/1812

Muys, Nicolas G., [b] Gouda 19/10/1791; [m] Russia, 6/12/1812

Muyselaar, Gerard, [b] The Hague 8/3/1786; [p] Russia, 25/10/1812

N

Nap, Jean, [b] Leeuwarden 26/4/1786; [m] Russia, 2/12/1812

Nastert, Jean, [b] Zeyl 6/7/1788; [d] in battle, 25/10/1812

Neerpel, Corneil, [b] Voorberg 1/5/1786; [d] in hospital, Stettin, 20/4/1812

Nelissen, Jean Pierre, [b] Driebergen 1/5/1782; [p] Russia, 27/7/1812

Neys, Jacob, [b] Heusen 20/10/1772; [m] Russia, 5/12/1812

Neyssen, Henry, [b] Haarlem 4/2/1784; [p] Russia, 25/7/1812

Nicasie, Adrien, [b] Amsterdam 16/3/1788; fell behind, Russia, 4/12/1812

Nicolas, Jean Henry, [b] Maastricht 22/11/1779; Cpl, 10/1/1805; [ds] 15/10/1810

Nieuwenhuis, François, [b] Wesel 3/4/1883; [p] 24/9/1812

Nieuwkampen, Antoine, [b] Canton of Amersfoort 13/11/1788; [lwp]2/4/1814

Nohen, Jean, [b] Steinbach, Austria, 12/10/1781; removed from muster roll for long absence, 1/11/1810; returned to regiment, 27/3/1811; [d/d] [t>] 1er Bataillon Colonial, Flushing, 30/5/1811

Nollé, Guillaume, [b] Amsterdam 10/1/1779; Cpl, 7/2/1807; [ds] 15/10/1810

van der Noort, Roelof, [b] Enkhuysen 2/3/1785; [dst] 18/12/1810; returned, 28/12/1810; [p] Russia, 18/7/1812

Noot, Oswald François, [b] Hellevoetsluys 9/9/1792; Cpl, 7/2/1811; QM, 13/4/1811; [t>] as SLt into Inf de Ligne, 22/6/1811

O

Oerlemans, Guillaume, [b] The Hague 30/10/1789; [m] Russia, 31/12/1812

van Oers, Corneil, [b] Delft 17/10/1785; [p] Russia, 24/9/1812

van Ooeyen, Jean Henry, [b] Thiel 2/4/1787; [lwp] 31/3/1814

Oostenrychère, Jean, [b] Salsdorf 5/6/1778; Cpl, 30/3/1807; [m] Russia, 8/11/1812

Oosthout, Corneil, [b] The Hague 22/6/1789; [t>] as SLt to the Indies, 27/1/1811

van Ooyen, Antoine, [b] Oud Bergerland 12/9/1760; [r] 26/6/1811

van Osch, Guillaume, [b] Canton of Tiel 20/4/1789; [m] Russia, 10/12/1812

van Otterloo, Henry, [b] Voorst 15/1/1787; Sgt, 16/4/1807; [wd] Germany, 17/9/1813 - lance thrust to left side and leg shot away by ball; Légion d'Honneur, 16/8/1813; [t>] CRCLF, 2/8/1814; [t>] Invalides, 1815

Otterloo, Jean, [b] Scherpenzee l9/10/1778; [d/h] 1/8/1811

Otto, Jean, [b] Utrecht 3/5/1783; [p] Russia, 25/9/1812

Oudhaarlem, Pierre, [b] Maassluis 17/4/1789; [t>] 126e Inf de Ligne, 18/4/1811

Oudshoorn, Corneil, [b] Zuysburg 11/3/1784; [m] Russia, 27/9/1812

Ouwenschek, Jean, [b] Berlin 10/1/1786; [t>] 11e Hussards, 30/3/1811, for being a foreigner

Overeem, Christophe, [b] Ameringen 20/8/1791; [d/d] [t>] 124e Inf de Ligne, 9/4/1811

Overeem, Henry, [b] Scherpenzeel 15/1/1786; [p] 9/12/1812

Overgauw, Gierlof, [b] Delfshaven 20/1/1787; [m] Russia, 26/10/1812

P

Paalmans, F., [b] Deventer 14/11/1782; [d/d] [t>] 124e Inf de Ligne, 9/4/1811

Pajooie, Joseph, [b] Breda 10/8/1781; [d/u] 1/3/1811

Palmaden, Gerard, [b] Wijhe 17/11/1783; [d] in battle, 25/10/1812

Parré, Adrien, [b] Delft 22/12/1776; [m] Russia, 1/12/1812

Passu, Jacques, [b] Roermond 10/6/1785; Cpl, 24/2/1810; [m] Russia, 1/12/1812

Pauw, Jean, [b] The Hague 24/5/1777; Cpl, 1/11/1809; [m] Russia, 4/12/1812

Pechtholt, Jean, [b] Willemstad 10/11/1788; [m] Russia, due to sickness, 16/12/1812

Peeters, Jean, [b] Nijmegen 25/12/1785; [t>] Gendarmerie Impériale, 16/12/1811

Peeters, Pierre, [b] Nijmegen 15/8/1785; [m] Russia, 30/12/1812

Pelser, Paul, [b] The Hague 24/12/1788; Cpl, 21/9/1810; Sgt, 19/3/1814; [lwp] 31/3/1814

Penders, Arnould, [b] Kosta 13/3/1785; [p] Russia, 22/9/1812

Person, Jacques, [b] Monster 13/6/1782; [m] Russia, 17/12/1812

Petit Jean, Paul Auguste, [b] Berlin 3/4/1785; [t>] 11e Hussards, 30/3/1811, for being a foreigner

Pheiffer, Louis, [b] Kuck 4/10/1790; Cpl, 10/2/1811; [t>] as SLt into 69e Inf de Ligne, 1/6/1811

Picaard, Jean, [b] Arnhem 30/3/1777; Sgt, 5/1/1807; [lwp] 31/3/1814

Picaerd, Godefroy, [b] Hasselt 1/7/1774; Sgt, 1/11/1807; [ds] 15/10/1810

Pieters, Godefroy, [b] Maastricht 24/1/1783; [m] Russia, 8/12/1812

Pieters, Peter, [b] Arnhem 10/1/1787; [d/d] [t>] 126e Inf de Ligne, 18/4/1811

Pieters, Pierre, [b] Viesselinks 3/5/1785; Cpl, 18/7/1809; [m] Russia, 12/12/1812

Piets, Jean, [b] Bechel 12/5/1788; [m] Russia, 16/11/1812

van der Pijl, Floris, [b] Gorinchem 20/12/1786; [ds] 12/7/1814

Pijpers, Henry, [b] Groningue 14/1/1783; [m] Russia, 5/12/1812

Pijzel, Frédéric, [b] The Hague 2/4/1786; Cpl, 6/11/1811; [lwp] 20/4/1814

Pliester, Diederic R., [b] Borger 23/4/1790; [m] Russia, 12/11/1812

van der Pluim, Guillaume, [b] Geertruidenberg 2/5/1784; [m] Russia, 2/12/1812

van der Pluym, Adrien, [b] Breda 16/12/1785; [m] Russia, 29/10/1812

Pluys, Adrien, [b] Maaslandsluis 11/4/1787; [m] Russia, 10/12/1812

van der Poel, Corneil, [b] Bommel 18/12/1780; [d/h] 15/10/1810

van der Pol, Frédéric, [b] Voorthuysen 2/2/1787; [m] Russia, 26/10/1812

Pommer, Jean, [b] Well 1/4/1782; [m] Russia, 3/12/1812

van Poolsumbooy, Pierre, [b] Utrecht 13/3/1790; [t>] as SLt into 116e Inf de Ligne, 23/7/1811

Poorters, Charles, [b] 's Hertogenbosch 5/10/1784; Cpl, 31/10/1805; [m] Russia, 6/12/1812

Porst, Abraham, [b] Oud-Beyerland 7/7/1781; [p] Russia, 27/7/1812

Post, David Pierre, [b] The Hague 30/3/1790; [m] Russia, 5/12/1812

Post, Gerard, [b] Eemnes 29/10/1780; [m] Russia, 12/11/1812

Poulie, Leonard, [b] Rotterdam 17/10/1785; Cpl, 21/9/1810; [dm] Lancer, 25/2/1811; [d/d] [t>] 11e Hussards, 2/12/1811

Privé, Jacques, [b] Leiden 17/6/1778; Sgt, 10/10/1808; [lwp] 31/3/1814

Proest, Guillaume, [b] Bergen-op-Zoom 15/10/1791; [m] Russia, 28/10/1812

Pruyssers, Isidor, [b] Waalwijk 26/2/1785; Cpl, 11/9/1809; Sgt, 3/1/1813; fell behind, 18/5/1813

van der Putt, Frédéric Louis, [b] Maastricht 5/6/1785; SM, 25/12/1806; [lwp] 31/3/1813

R

Raabe, Joseph Frédéric, [b] Lycra, Russia, 25/4/1774; SM, 1/11/1809; [d/h] [r] 1/12/1811

de Raad, Adrien, [b] Delft 1/9/1785; Sgt, 1/11/1809; [m] Russia, 11/12/1812

van Raay, Corneille, [b] Waalwijk 7/3/1786; [m] Russia, 10/12/1812

van Raay, Matthieu, [b] Geertrudenberg 24/10/1782; [ds] 12/7/1814

Rams, Jean, [b] Veen 1/5/1784; [m] Russia, 7/12/1812

Rasch, Conrad, [b] Heldesheim 17/11/1783; [m] Russia, 10/12/1812

van Rees, Abraham Corneil, [b] Vught 10/10/1788; Cpl; [d] in hospital, Stettin, 7/5/1812

van Rees, Philippe, [b] Leiden 1/8/1777; [d] in hospital, Paris, 15/12/1811

Retterich, Adam Jean Pierre, [b] Nijmegen 10/3/1778; see *Appendix III, Officers*

van Reulh, Pierre Joseph, [b] Tilburg 12/7/1780; Cpl, 20/3/1807; [ds] 1/3/1811

Reyckel, Regnier, [b] Halmael 9/10/1775; Cpl, 20/9/1809; Sgt, 30/11/1810; [m] Russia, 10/12/1812

Reykers, Jean, [b] Zutphen 15/12/1785; [p] Russia, 23/9/1812

Reynders, Corneil, [b] Amersfoort 17/3/1783; [p] Russia, 25/9/1812

Reynders, Pierre, [b] Wageningen 14/8/1784; [m] Russia, 10/11/1812

Reyndert, Corneil, [b] Gatik 28/3/1784; Cpl, 1/1/1809; [dm] Lancer, 8/6/1811

Reyne, Diederic, [b] Wychem 2/2/1781; [m] Russia 3/11/1812

Reynen, Guillaume, [b] Maastricht 5/4/1785; Sgt, 1/12/1806; [dm] Lancer 15/4/1813; Cpl, 25/1/1814; Sgt, 26/1/1814; [ds] 11/7/1814

van Reyzen, Jean, [b] Haarlem 16/6/1784; [p] Russia, 25/10/1812

van Rhee, Martin, [b] Hoorn 2/2/1790; [m] Russia, 15/11/1812

van Rhenen, Bernard, [b] Bilt 15/5/1785; [p] Russia, 27/7/1812

van Rhenen, Walter, [b] Venendaal 22/2/1773; [p] Russia, 27/7/1812

van Rhijn, Guillaume, [b] Alphen 1/9/1778; [d/d] [t>] 11e Hussards, 23/7/1811

van Rhijn, Jean, [b] Delft 27/3/1785; [p] Russia, 27/7/1812

de Ridder, Jean, [b] Buurmalsen 22/11/1787; [d] in battle, 25/10/1812

Riems, David, [b] The Hague 27/2/1789; [m] Russia, 13/11/1812

van der Rijden, Henry, [b] Wageningen 4/1/1786; [m] Russia, 30/9/1812

Rijgenbach, Antoine, [b] Zwolle 22/5/1789; fell behind in Russia, 6/11/1812

Rijkman, Martin, [b] Leer 6/4/1786; [m] Russia, 2/12/1812

van Rijn, Henry, [b] Leidschendam 22/4/1787; [m] Russia, 28/11/1812

van Rijn, Herman, [b] Utrecht 27/8/1788; [m] Russia, 20/11/1812

Rijswijk, Nicolas, [b] Ween 7/7/1782; Cpl, 26/9/1806; [dm] Lancer, 4/4/1812; [m] Russia, 21/11/1812

Rits, Pierre, [b] 's Hertogenbosch 23/5/1784; [d/d] [t>] 126e Inf de Ligne, 18/4/1811

Ritter, Jean, [b] Magdebourg 2/9/1783; Trpt; [m] Russia, 30/11/1812

Roelands, Jacques, [b] Breda 17/5/1787; [p] Russia, 27/7/1812

Roelofse, Hermanus, [b] Opheusden 20/11/1785; [m] Russia, 10/12/1812

Roelofsen, Guillaume, [b] Delft 30/7/1791; [m] Russia, 22/12/1812

Roeters, Pierre, [b] Omersade 29/1/1782; Cpl, 11/9/1809; [d/h] 11/2/1812

Rolandus, Thomas Doleguis, [b] Schoonhoven 1/9/1784; [t>] as SLt into Inf de Ligne, 1/6/1811

Rom, Jacques Jean, [b] Heusden 12/2/1790; [t>] as SLt to the Indies, 27/1/1811

Rombout, Jean, [b] Bergen-op-Zoom 22/4/1783; [ds] 12/7/1814

De Rooy, Henry, [b] Voorburg 20/5/1789; [m] Russia, 12/12/1812

de Rooyen, Pierre, [b] Zevenbergen 20/9/1786; [ds] 12/7/1814

van Rossen, Jean Bernard Auguste, [b] Dunkerque 12/10/1791; [t>] as SLt into 63e Inf de Ligne, 1/6/1811

van Rossum, Herman, [b] Breda 1/5/1790; [m] Russia, 12/11/1812

van Rossum, Jean, [b] Utrecht 4/6/1788; [m] Russia, 14/11/1812

van Rossum, Martinus, [b] Driel 2/8/1781; Sgt, 1/9/1809; [lwp] 30/3/1814

Rousseau, Lambert, [b] Middelbourg 22/12/1787; Cpl, 3/1/1813; [lwp] 2/4/1814

de Rouville, Guillaume Henry, [b] Drunen 22/12/1787; [t>] as SLt into Inf de Ligne, 6/6/1811

Ruighard de Maire, Conrad, [b] Schiedam 18/2/1783; [d/h] [r] 1/3/1811 de Ruyter, Leonard, [b] Katwijk 2/10/1782; [m] Russia, 10/11/1812

S

Salmons, Frédéric, [b] The Hague 7/4/1777; [d/u] 1/3/1811
Samplion, Jean, [b] Montfoort 11/4/1781; [ds] 11/7/1814
Samplion, Nicolas, [b] Monfoort 17/9/1786; Cpl, 24/2/1813; [dm] Lancer, 1/8/1813; [lwp] 31/3/1814
Samson, André, [b] Lexmond 6/11/1777; [m] Russia, 9/12/1812
Schaaf, André, [b] Halleren 17/3/1781; [wd] [m] Russia, 25/11/1812
Schaffels, Jean, [b] Dordrecht 8/9/1790; [lwp] 31/3/1814
Scheepers, Guillaume, [b] Mersem 15/3/1775; [r] 1/12/1811
Scheepmaker, Abraham, [b] Amsterdam 17/10/1785; [t>] 126e Inf de Ligne, 18/4/1811
Scheer, Pierre, [b] 's Hertogenbosch 14/3/1774; [r] 1/8/1811
Schefsky, Jean Nicolas, [b] Warsaw, Poland, 10/10/1784; [lwp] 31/3/1814
Schilperoort, Guillaume Jean Olivier, [b] Rotterdam 7/11/1786; [ds] 1/3/1811
Schleicher, Martin, [b] Krombach 6/2/1782; Trpt; [t>] 14e Cuirassiers, 24/2/1812
Schmell, Isaac, [b] The Hague 8/10/1789; [d] in hospital, Versailles, 17/8/1811
Schneiter, Charles Leonard, [b] Leiden 25/7/1790; Sgt, 21/9/1810; [m] Russia, 7/12/1812
Schnell, Michel, [b] Volksheim 10/11/1772; Sgt, 14/2/1807; [r] 24/7/1811
Schneyders, Gerard, [b] Panhiel 22/8/1783; [p] Russia, 27/7/1812
Schnoek, Jean, [b] Flushing 11/4/1784; [d/u] 1/3/1811
Scholten, Guillaume, [b] Gouda 10/2/1792; Cpl, 24/2/1813; [lwp] 31/3/1814
Scholten, Jacques, [b] Gouda 5/2/1791; [lwp] 31/3/1814
Schonenveld, Bernard, [b] Canton of Aurich 10/10/1783; [d] in hospital, Versailles, 8/4/1811
Schoor, Luc, [b] Amsterdam 28/7/1784; Cpl, 21/10/1806; [dm] Lancer, 14/5/1811; Cpl, 9/2/1812; [p] Russia, 27/7/1812
Schouten, Barthelomy, [b] Leiden 25/3/1785; [p] Russia, 23/9/1812
Schouten, Jean Henry, [b] Arnhem 20/5/1782; Cpl, 21/9/1810; Sgt, 3/1/1813; [dst] 6/1/1814
Schreuder, Jean, [b] Leiden 8/9/1797; fell behind sick, 4/12/1812
Schreuder, Jean Melchior, [b] Venlo 22/6/1792; left behind in hospital, Görlitz, 23/8/1813
Schrijven, Pierre, [b] Neefstrek 20/5/1789; [m] Russia, 12/11/1812
Schrijver, E., [b] Leiden 15/11/1792; [m] Russia, 28/11/1812
Schudt, Nicolas, [b] Utrecht 25/5/1788; Cpl, 17/6/1811; [p] 28/1/1814
Schults, Frédéric Guillaume, [b] Bexterhouden 1/3/1790; [t>] 11e Hussards, 27/12/1811
Schupp, Jean Guillaume, [b] Bergen-op-Zoom 5/4/1786; [d/h] [r] 1/12/1811
Schutten, Gerard Jean Antoine, [b] Raalden 1/8/1786; [lwp] 20/4/1814
Schuurmans, Adrien, [b] Alken 10/8/1783; [m] Russia, 9/12/1812
Schuurmans, Aubert, [b] Alleken 12/3/1787; [m] Russia, 6/11/1812
Seybel, Michel Diederic, [b] Haarlem 15/8/1792; [m] Russia, 27/11/1812
Seyffert, Henry, [b] The Hague 6/12/1778; Sgt; [dm] Lancer, 3/1/1811
Seyller, François, [b] Mainz 2/5/1786; Cpl, 1/2/1813; Sgt, 28/2/1813; [lwp] 31/3/1814
Siebe, Jean Crétien, [b] Obersitsk, Silesia, 18/10/1785; Cpl, 28/9/1808; [t>] 11e Hussards, 30/3/1811, for being a foreigner
van Silva, Jean, [b] Elloch 17/9/1784; [dst] 26/3/1811
Sitler, Crétien, [b] Prusse 10/10/1784; [p] Russia, 5/9/1812
van der Slaak, Guillaume, [b] Voorburg 9/10/1784; [lwp] 31/3/1814
Slaay, Jean, [b] Dentighem 25/4/1781; [m] Russia, 26/7/1812
Slagter, Gerard, [b] Campen 15/2/1780; [m] Russia, 1/11/1812
Slegthelm, Jean, [b] Overschie 28/12/1784; [p] Russia, 16/9/1812
Slettering, Gerard Joseph, [b] Laag Keppel 25/3/1785; Cpl, 4/10/1810; [m] Russia, 2/12/1812
van der Sloot, Abraham, [b] Schiedam 9/1/1788; [t>] as SLt into 116e Inf de Ligne, 20/7/1811
van der Sloot, Nicolas, [b] Rotterdam 14/8/1793; [m] Russia, 4/12/1812
Sluyterman, Herman, [b] The Hague 11/2/1778; [ds] 11/7/1814
Sluyters, Théodore, [b] 's Hertogenbosch 3/5/1774; Sgt, 13/2/1807; [d/u] 15/10/1810
Smeets, Henry, [b] Mijsewijk 7/4/1779; [d] in hospital, Versailles, 24/1/1812
Smit, Christian, [b] Liège 22/9/1779; [d] in hospital, Versailles, 25/2/1811
Smit, Diederic, [b] Amsterdam 19/9/1774; [m] Russia, 13/10/1812

Smit, François, [b] Aix-la-Chapelle 16/9/1782; [d/d] [t>] 30e Chasseurs à cheval, 23/7/1811
Smit, Jean, [b] Overschie 13/7/1789; [m] Russia, 28/10/1812
Smit, Mathieu, [b] Doorwerth 20/12/1783; [p] Russia, 25/10/1812
Smit, Nicolas Corneil, [b] Laaren 15/3/1790; [d/u] 1/3/1811
Smith, Jacques, [b] Valburg 14/2/178?; [m] Russia, 6/12/1812
Smitsz, Theodore, [b] The Hague; [dst] 5/9/1810
Smulders, Pierre, [b] Tilburg 24/3/1784; [d/d] [t>] 124e Inf de Ligne, 9/4/1811
Snaters, Jean, [b] Sluyswijk 12/3/1787; [t>] Gendarmerie Impériale, 16/12/1811
Snijders, J., [b] Saxony 1/6/1785; [lwp] 31/3/1814
Soeters, Jean Albert, [b] Zutphen 14/6/1787; [d] in Gros Caillou hospital, 13/6/1811
Soiron, Nicolas, [b] Osemond 5/6/1792; [m] Russia, 9/12/1812
Sol, Henry, [b] Oud Loosdrecht 28/3/1787; [lwp] 2/4/1814
Solting, Jean, [b] Voorburg 24/8/1788; [m] Russia, 13/11/1812
Spaarman, Henry, [b] Heusden 5/7/1774; [m] Russia, 25/11/1812
Spieler, Jean, [b] Kronenburg 8/3/1774; [m] Russia, 26/10/1812
Spies, Jean, [b] Canton of Assen 1/1/1790; [m] Russia, 12/10/1812
Sprengers, Corneil, [b] Breda 15/9/1790; [p] Russia, 10/10/1812
Sprok, Jean, [b] Paderborn 10/12/1779; [m] Russia, 8/12/1812
Staaten, Conrad, [b] Leur 8/3/1781; [d/d] [t>] 11e Hussards, 23/7/1811
Staats, Pierre, [b] Haacht 12/10/1783; Cpl, 21/4/1812; Sgt, 3/1/1813; [dm] Lancer, 17/11/1813; [lwp] 31/3/1814
van Staaveren, Henry, [b] Weye 1/11/1782; Cpl, 21/9/1810; [dm] Lancer at own request, 19/7/1811; [lwp] 31/3/1814
Stadman, Jean, [b] Haarlem 20/4/????; [p] Russia, 25/10/1812
Stam, Herman, [b] Nalburg 1/6/1788; [m] Russia, 6/12/1812
Stassen, Theodore Henry, [b] Braaselem 2/9/1784; [d] in battle, 25/10/1812
van der Steeg, Jean, [b] Sint-Truiden 4/3/1777; Cpl, 21/9/1810; [m] Russia, 21/11/1812
Steekeleburg, Pierre, [b] Montfoort, 2/7/1782; [m] Russia, 30/11/1812
Steenbergen, Jean, [b] Woerden 15/6/1779; [p] Russia, 23/9/1812
Steenis, Antoine Juste, [b] Utrecht 15/3/1790; [m] Russia, 12/12/1812
Steevens, Diederic, [b] Doesburg 4/5/1784; Fr, 21/9/1810; Lancer, 3/5/1811; Fr, 9/5/1811; [dst] 2/11/1813
Steevens, Gerard, [b] Dordrecht 20/1/1788; [m] Russia, 8/11/1812
Steevens, Jacques, [b] Emmerie 10/9/1782; Cpl, 15/9/1809; [d] in hospital, Versailles, 19/1/1811
Steindjes, Gerard, [b] Welle 9/3/1779; [t>] 126e Inf de Ligne, 18/4/1811
Steingutter, Jean, [b] Zykensaxen 15/1/1772; Cpl, 21/9/1810; [d] of wounds, 2/11/1812
Sterrenberg, Ange, [b] Heluw 1/12/1780; [m] Russia, 11/11/1812
Stolker, Pierre, [b] Bergambach 8/7/1792; [m] Russia, 7/12/1812
van Straalen, Antoine, [b] Amersfoort 11/2/1790; [p] 29/1/1814
Straatman, Jean, [b] Warbourg 10/6/1786; [d] in hospital, Paris, 23/2/1812
Straus, Louis, [b] Oldenburg 15/7/1775; Sgt, 28/10/1806; [ds] 12/7/1814
Stroothuys, Jean, [b] Vollenhoven 22/7/1785; Cpl, 21/1/1809; [m] Russia, 25/11/1812
Stuivesand, Jacques, [b] Ysselmunde 8/4/1788; [m] Russia, 7/11/1812
Swibel, Abraham, [b] The Hague 26/2/1785; [p] Russia, 25/9/1812

T

van Talma, Adrien Dominique, [b] Amsterdam 25/11/1784; Sgt, 21/9/1810; [dm] 30/12/1811; [t>] 1er Lanciers de Ligne, 28/6/1812
Telders, Pierre, [b] Rotterdam 22/9/1792; [m] Russia, 11/12/1812
Tenhunsveld, Guillaume, [b] Amsterdam 20/3/1788; [p] Russia, 27/7/1812
Terwint, Pierre, [b] Gendt 17/9/1785; [m] Russia, 28/11/1812
Teunissen, Guillaume, [b] Rotterdam 20/4/1785; [d] 17/9/1813
Teunissen, Jean, [b] Wageningen 18/5/1784; [m] Russia, 30/10/1812
Thalman, Joseph, [b] Namur 4/10/1780; [m] Russia, 4/12/1812
Theulinge, André, [b] Bezoyen 8/7/1791; [p] Russia, 23/9/1812
Theunisse, Henry, [b] Olst 28/5/1788; [p] Russia, 25/10/1812
Theunissen, Gilles, [b] Nijmegen 20/8/1779; Cpl, 19/4/1812; [m] Russia, 4/12/1812
Theunissen, Jacques, [b] Nijmegen 12/9/1787; [m] Russia, 1/12/1812
Theunissen, Pierre, [b] Walsen 3/5/1786; [m] Russia, 20/9/1812
Thibau, Toussaint, [b] Fréloup 2/3/1782; Cpl, 1/1/1810; Sgt, 21/9/1810; [t>] CRCLF, 2/8/1814
Thieleman, Henry, [b] Flushing 24/1/1780; [m] Russia, 30/11/1812

van Thielen, Jean Frédéric, [b] Bredenvoort 21/3/1791; [t>] as SLt into Inf de Ligne, 23/6/1811
van der Thien, Thierry, [b] Utrecht 3/3/1787; [m] Russia, 24/7/1812
Thirion, Nicolas, [b] Breda 25/7/1778; [t>] as Lt into 1er Carabiniers, 1/3/1813
Thoma, Antoine Bernard, [b] Bergen-op-Zoom 21/4/1784; Sgt, 16/7/1810; Légion d'Honneur; [m] Russia, 6/12/1812
Thomas, Jean Ernest, [b] Bergen-op-Zoom 1/6/1787; QM, 16/7/1810; Sgt, 3/1/1811; [d] in the army, 4/8/1813
Thomasse, Corneille, [b] Meerkerk 20/5/1789; [m] Russia, 10/12/1812
Thomassen, Jean, [b] Noorkerk 15/1/1785; [m] Russia, 17/11/1812
Thooft, Jean Philippe, [b] Vollenhoven 18/11/1788; Cpl, 21/9/1810; QM, 29/6/1811; [m] Russia, 28/11/1812
van Thour, Philippe, [b] The Hague 24/1/1784; [p] Russia, 27/7/1812
Tijm, Jean, [b] Canton of Alkmaar 4/10/1788; [m] Russia, 20/11/1812
Timmermans, Nicolas, [b] Varik 15/3/1785; [m] Russia, 21/10/1812
Tindas, Thomas, [b] Utrecht 14/4/1787; [p] Russia, 27/7/1812
van Toll, Jean, [b] Utrecht 10/2/1785; removed from muster roll for long absence, 30/6/1811 - on charge from 11/4/1810
Tolsma, Martin, [b] Amsterdam 10/4/1788; Cpl, 12/8/1811; [d/h] 11/2/1812
Tomhoff, Guillaume, [b] Laasphel 18/8/1784; Sgt, 1/11/1805; [m] Russia, 6/12/1812
Tookelenburg, Adrien Thierry, [b] Canton of Weesp 18/8/1787; [d] 20/11/1812
Trillekes, Henry, [b] Schiedam 20/5/1791; [p] Russia, 8/11/1812
van Trompen, Matthieu, [b] Briel 12/4/1789; [p] Russia, 24/10/1812
Tropp, Crétien, [b] Weldungen 15/4/1778; Cpl, 21/9/1809; [m] Russia, 4/12/1812
Tuinders, Leonard, [b] Moordrecht 23/11/1783; [d/d] [t>] 30e Chasseurs à cheval, 23/7/1811
Tulkhoff, Pierre, [b] Delft 5/9/1785; [m] Russia, 20/10/1812
van der Tuyn, Nicolas, [b] The Hague 27/1/1783; Cpl, 26/5/1810; [m] Russia, 30/11/1812

U

van Uchelen, Henry Guillaume, [b] Didam 31/7/1790; Sgt, 15/7/1809; [m] Russia, 8/12/1812
Udoo, Henry, [b] Emkom 7/3/1789; [m] Russia, 20/11/1812
Udoo, Stevin, [b] Beusekom 13/11/1789; [m] Russia, 11/11/1812

V

de Vaan, Arnold, [b] Kuylenburg 20/8/1790; [d/d] [t>] 126e Inf de Ligne, 18/4/1811
Vaesen, Pierre, [b] Maastricht 5/4/1781; [lwp] 31/3/1814
Valck, Louis Frédéric, [b] Boxmeer 8/1/1791; [t>] as SLt to the Indies, 27/1/1811
van der Valk, Arend, [b] Poeldijk 16/2/1782; [m] Russia, 28/11/1812
Vanaggelen, Etienne, [b] Wageningen 10/9/1789; [d] on road to Moscow, 4/6/1812
Vanbatem, Pierre, [b] Utrecht 1/12/1788; [m] Russia, 28/11/1812
Vandenhoven, Abraham, [b] Hellevoetsluis 19/4/1780; [d] in hospital, Versailles, 14/1/1811
Vanderaa, Jean Henry, [b] Lemmer 18/5/1782; [d/d] put at disposal of Minister of War, 30/11/1810
Vanderhorst, Adrien, [b] Zwijndrecht 22/5/1780; [m] Russia, 26/11/1812
Vanderhorst, Bernard, [b] Doesburg 11/2/1788; [m] Russia, 25/11/1812
Vanderhorst, Gilbert, [b] Zwijndrecht 26/11/1784; [m] Russia, 6/12/1812
Vanderkop, Corneil, [b] Tijl 3/4/1789; [m] Russia, 12/9/1812
Vandermeer, Guillaume, [b] Delfshaven 1/1/1788; [m] Russia, 28/11/1812
Vanderson, Jean, [b] Amsterdam 4/7/1786; Sgt, 22/2/1809; [t>] as Lt into 20e Chasseurs à cheval, 10/9/1811
Vanderwall, Lambert, [b] Zuysdijk 11/8/1786; Cpl, 21/9/1810; [m] Russia, 30/11/1812
Vanderwist, Pierre, [b] Amerongen 25/10/1780; fell behind, 1/4/1813
Vanderzanden, Jacques, [b] Burzen 4/5/1789; Cpl, 10/2/1813; [t>] with rank, 1er Lanciers de Ligne, 10/4/1813
Vandrumel, Gerard, [b] The Hague 29/12/1788; [p] Russia, 25/9/1812
Vanheertem, Jean, [b] Canton of 's Hertogenbosch 7/2/1790; [lwp] 31/3/1814
Vanhemmen, Jean, [b] Oyen 11/8/1783; removed from muster roll 2/8/1814 - in hospital since 26/3/1814
Vanhoorn, Pierre, [b] Beekbergen 27/4/1780; [d] Russia, 15/11/1812
Vanhorsen, Rombout, [b] Aalst 5/3/1787; [p] Russia, 12/9/1812

Vanijzendijk, Eli, [b] Amsterdam 2/3/1792; [m] Russia, 29/11/1812

Vankerk, Jean, [b] Kuylenburg 29/10/1785; Cpl, 3/1/1813; [lwp] 31/3/1814

Vanmaanen, Charles, [b] Rotterdam 8/10/1782; Cpl, 11/9/1809; [dm] Lancer, 7/1/1812; [m] Russia, 24/10/1812

Vanooijen, Jean, [b] Asperen 20/5/1783; [m] Russia, 4/12/1812

Vanschie, Guillaume, [b] Noordwijk 10/8/1792; [d/d] [t>] 126e Inf de Ligne, 18/4/1811

Vansebach, Alexandre, [b] Saxony 18/4/1777; Sgt, 16/6/1808; [t>] Vétérans, 17/4/1811

Vanstokkum, Jean, [b] Rotterdam 13/2/1781; Fr; [m] Russia, 20/10/1812

Vanuffeld, Guillaume, [b] Roemond 12/8/1782; Cpl, 6/2/1811; [m] Russia, 30/11/1812

Vanveen, Elias, [b] Jaarsveld 19/2/1784; [m] Russia, 19/10/1812

Vanweynen, Adrien, [b] Kerkdriel 5/10/1790; [m] Russia, 28/11/1812

Vanwouw, Guillaume, [b] Voorschoten 1/5/1793; [ds] 19/10/1810

Vanzuijdam, F, [b] Canton of Bomme 16/12/1789; [lwp] 31/3/1814

Vanzwelm, B., [b] Gendt 14/11/1787; [t>] 124e Inf de Ligne, 9/4/1811

Veen, Armand, [b] Vianen 15/3/1794; [t>] 124e Inf de Ligne, 9/4/1811

Veen, Jacques, [b] Amsterdam 5/11/1789; [m] Russia, 20/11/1812

Veenendaal, Guillaume, [b] Utrecht 8/3/1792; [m] Russia, 28/10/1812

Vander Velden, Arie, [b] Kortenhoef 15/10/1787; [lwp] 31/3/1814

van Velden, Jean, [b] Oven 10/1/1787; [d/u] 1/3/1811

Veldhuisen, Antoine, [b] Zeyvenne 9/3/1787; removed from muster roll for long absence, 1/1/1813 - in hospital at Helder since 2/11/1811

Veldhuys, Jean, [b] Hoorn 9/7/1777; Sgt, chief instructor, 21/9/1810; SM, 30/10/1810; see Appendix III, Officers

Veldkamp, Everard, [b] Jermon 12/3/1784; [lwp] 31/3/1814

van Velp, Aubert, [b] Nijmegen 10/3/1785; [d] in hospital, Versailles, 1/2/1811

Vels, Pierre, [b] Delft 16/11/1789; [lwp] 31/3/1814

Velte, Pierre, [b] Rotterdam 17/12/1789; Cpl, 21/9/1810; [d] in battle, 25/10/1812

Verbiesen, Henry, [b] The Hague 14/8/1768; [d/u] 1/3/1811

Verbundt, Arnould, [b] Oosterhout 30/3/1787; [lwp] 30/3/1814

Verhaar, Corneil, [b] Utrecht 19/1/1790; [m] Russia, 19/11/1812

Verhagen, Diederic, [b] Utrecht 6/5/1785; [m] Russia, 12/11/1812

Verheul, Creyn, [b] Monster 10/5/1784; Sgt, 21/9/1810; [d] in battle, 25/10/1812

Verhoeff, Jean, [b] Utrecht 11/7/1793; [d/d] put at disposal of Minister of War, 30/11/!810

Verhoeven, Guillaume, [b] Tilburg 2/2/1788; [t>] 124e Inf de Ligne, 9/4/1811

Verkerk, Antoine, [b] Nieuwenbrug 2/6/1790; [m] Russia, 29/11/1812

Verkroost, Jean, [b] Utrecht 1/1/1790; [m] Russia, 7/11/1812

Verlee, Diederic, [b] Kuylenburg 26/2/1787; [m] Russia, 28/11/1812

Vermaak, Corneil, [b] Utrecht 19/12/1789; [m] Russia, 2/12/1812

Verschuur, Jean, [b] Haagje 24/6/1785; [m] Russia, 27/11/1812

Verschuur, Pierre, [b] Tilburg 9/12/1784; [m] Russia, 1/11/1812

Versteeg, Adrien, [b] Kerkbriel 7/1/1790; [m] Russia, 15/11/1812

Versteeg, Antoine, [b] Zoetermere 12/9/1785; Cpl, 21/9/1810; [dm] Lancer at own request, 2/10/1811

de Vett, Dominique, [b] Maastricht 22/2/1779; [m] Russia, 30/10/1812

Vetter, Jean, [b] Bengel 27/5/1766; Master-Fr, 26/10/1810; [ds] 22/7/1814

Vewer, Jean, [b] Hoorn 21/4/1786; Cpl, 7/12/1807; [m] Russia, 14/12/1812

Viegen, Pierre, [b] Amersfoort 7/7/1785; Cpl, 21/9/1810; [m] Russia, 5/11/1812

Viering, Martin, [b] The Hague 27/3/1778; Sgt, 1/11/1807; [m] Russia, 3/12/1812

Vijfjaar, Jacob, [b] Maassluis 1/11/1788; [m] Russia, 27/11/1812

Vink, Jean Paul, [b] Oegstgeest 27/5/1772; [t>] 14e Cuirassiers, 27/12/1811

Visseo, F, [b] Dunkerque 27/1/1779; [m] Russia, due to sickness, 2/11/1812

Visser, Jacques [1], [b] Kerkwijk 1/12/1777; [p] Russia, 27/7/1812

Visser, Jacques [2], [b] Maarsen 20/1/1788; [m] Russia, 14/11/1812

van der Vliet, Guillaume, [b] Wardragen 9/10/1782; Cpl, 14/6/1810; [d/d] put at disposal of Minister of War, 28/7/1812

Vlot, Mathieu, [b] Zaandam 17/3/1784; [d/h] [r] 1/12/1811

Voogt, Sebastien, [b] Schiedam 13/2/1785; [d] in hospital, Utrecht, 10/2/1812

van Voorst, Jean, [b] Wageningen 14/8/1784; [d] in battle, 13/9/1812

Voorthuysen, Antoine, [b] Beuskom 16/5/1784; [d] from sickness, 4/10/1812

Voorts, Jean Inglebert, [b] Amsterdam 19/4/1787; [m] Russia, 3/11/1812

Vos, Frédéric, [b] Amsterdam 24/9/1786; [t>] 14e Cuirassiers, 27/12/1811

Voskamp, Albert, [b] Zwolle 20/7/1789; [m] Russia, 7/12/1812

de Vreede, Guillaume, [b] Maastricht 26/10/1784; [m] Russia, 1/12/1812

Vreesen, Jacques, [b] Rotterdam 7/4/1786; [d/h] 28/2/1812

Vridags, Jean, [b] Houpertingen 16/4/1783; [m] Russia, 9/10/1812

Vrie, Pierre, [b] The Hague 7/7/1789; [ds] 11/7/1814

de Vries, Gerard, [b] Beek 10/7/1784; [m] Russia, 7/11/1812

de Vries, Guillaume, [b] Dordrecht 20/9/1787; fell behind sick, 24/11/1812

de Vries, Jean, [b] Buk 27/12/1785; [wd] [m] Russia, 10/10/1812

Vroom, Pierre, [b] Hogeveen 23/4/1789; [p] Russia, 22/9/1812

van Vught, Henry, [b] Heerssensdam, 7/9/1787; [dst] 18/12/1810

van Vugt, Adrien, [b] Druuren 9/12/1787; [m] 31/3/1813

van Vuuren, Antoine, [b] Kuilenburg 1/5/1789; [d/d] [t>] 31e Chasseurs à cheval, 23/7/1811

Vuurpeyl, Engelbert, [b] Leiden 28/1/1788; [m] Russia, 5/11/1812

Vuyst, Jean Guillaume, [b] Naarden 9/5/1783; [m] Russia, due to sickness, 20/11/1812

W

van der Waard, Jean, [b] Naarden 11/8/1783; [lwp] 31/3/1814

Waardenburg, Jean, [b] Lytooyen 20/1/1792; [m] Russia, 2/12/1812

van Waasbergen, Pierre, [b] Rotterdam 23/4/1793; [d/h] 15/10/1810

Wagner, Chrétien Emanuel, [b] Rotterdam 2/1/1788; Cpl, 6/2/1811; [t>] as SLt into Inf de Ligne, 25/3/1811

Wagtman, Henry, [b] Voorhelm 20/5/1782; [d/u] 1/3/1811

Walesen, Jean, [b] Canton of Nijmegen 25/2/1780; Cpl, 8/9/1809; [p] Russia, 20/9/1812

van der Wall, Pierre, [b] Haarlem 22/8/1784; [d] in hospital, Versailles, 24/6/1811

Walstijn, Jean, [b] Maarsen 25/4/1790; [m] Russia, 4/12/1812

Warnaer, Jean, [b] Niekerk 27/11/1788; [t>] as SLt to the Indies, 27/1/1812

Weeda, Guillaume, [b] Maassluis 10/10/1791; [m] Russia, 10/11/1812

van Weelden, Guillaume, [b] Canton of Bommel 17/2/1782; [d/d] put at disposal of Minister of War, 3/11/1810

Weening, Albert, [b] Velpen 13/4/1788; [p] Russia, 7/11/1812

van Weerdt, Corneil, [b] Slijdingen 10/5/1787; [m] Russia, 29/11/1812

Weillaar, Dominique, [b] Scherpenseel 12/6/1777; [ds] 11/7/1814

Weller, Guillaume, [b] Groningen 28/1/1790; [d/d] [t>] 1er Bataillon Colonial, 30/5/1811

Welters, Henry, [b] Leiden 14/2/1783; [m] Russia, 18/12/1812

Wentzel, Adolphe, [b] Lunebourg 10/8/1790; [t>] 11e Hussards, 30/3/1811, for being a foreigner

Vander Werf, Arie, [b] Jorwerd 15/4/1789; Cpl; [d] in battle, 25/10/1812

van der Werf, Arnould, [b] Jorwerd 5/11/1787; Cpl, 1/1/1809; [ds] 11/7/1814

Werlotte, Lambert, [b] Velswesel 10/10/1786; Cpl, 1/3/1814; [ds] 12/7/1814

Werner, Frédéric Henry, [b] Breda 2/2/1794; Sgt, 21/9/1810; [m] Russia, 25/11/1812

Wertmiller, Emanuel Charles, [b] Maastricht 15/4/1788; [t>] as SLt to the Indies, 27/1/1811

Wertmuller, Denis, [b] The Hague 13/7/1788; [lwp] 31/3/1814

Wessels, Guillaume, [b] Arnhem 17/1/1785; [lwp] 31/3/1814

van Westerloo, Arend, [b] Amsterdam 19/3/1785; Cpl, 21/9/1810; [m] Russia, 23/10/1812

Westerveld, Corneil, [b] Zoest 1/10/1782; [m] Russia, 5/12/1812

Wettig, François, [b] Amsterdam 6/6/1781; Cpl, 8/10/1808; Sgt, 12/2/1813

Wex, George, [b] "Hertfort, England", 19/11/1786; [p] Russia, 12/11/1812

Weyers, Auguste F., [b] Nassau 29/5/1791; [p] Russia, 12/11/1812

Weyers, François, [b] Rotterdam 3/3/1781; [ds] 12/7/1814

Wieck, Jacques, [b] Massenhausen 29/9/1776; [t>] CRCLF, 2/8/1814

Wiekenkamp, Gerard, [b] Burkalor 6/10/1766; [ds] 11/7/1814

Wiensmeyer, Jean Henry, [b] Krenstadt 14/12/1769; [p] Russia, 21/9/1812

Wientjes, Pierre, [b] Boxmeer 20/5/1789; [lwp] 31/3/1814

Wigmans, Pierre, [b] Rotterdam 20/5/1787; Cpl, 3/1/1813; [lwp] 31/3/1814

Wildemans, Abraham, [b] Maassluis 15/3/1788; [p] Russia, 25/10/1812

Wildenburg, Corneil, [b] Langeraar 1/6/1788; [d/u] 1/3/1811

Wildert, Jacques, [b] Canton of Thiel 17/5/1784; [m] Russia, 6/11/1812

Wilhelm, Jean Daniel, [b] Buurmassen 19/8/1792; [m] Russia, 5/12/1812

Willekes, Jean, [b] Groningen 9/5/1786; [m] Russia, 6/12/1812

Willems, Pierre, [b] Vught 1/1/1789; [m] Russia, 4/12/1812

Willemsen, Jean, [b] Arnhem 7/8/1788; [p] Russia, 25/10/1812

Wilmotte, Joseph, [b] Canton de Liège 20/5/1779; Master-saddler; [t>] CRCLF, 2/8/1814

Winnekers, Guillaume, [b] Emmerik, 20/2/1783; [m] Russia, 20/10/1812

Winters, Everhard, [b] Wijnbergen 17/4/1780; [m] Russia, 30/11/1812

Witlijn, Martin, [b] Schiedam 15/12/1785; [m] Russia, 27/11/1812

de Witt, Corneil, [b] Purmerinde 13/11/1787; QM, 10/11/1809; [m] Russia, 6/12/1812

Witte, Herman, [b] Geertvliet 2/5/1780; [m] Russia, 20/10/1812

Wolters, Theodore, [b] Mars 23/3/1788; [p] Russia, 23/9/1812

Woordman, Henry, [b] Rotterdam 1/1/1784; [m] Russia, 28/11/1812

Woordman, Jean, [b] Haarlem 17/9/1786; [d/u] 1/3/1811

Wouters, Henry, [b] Grootassen 12/5/1779; [p] Russia, 29/9/1812

Wouters, Jean, [b] Groot Hasselt 16/2/1777; [m] Russia, 10/11/1812

Wulfers, Guillaume, [b] Delft 19/12/1779; [m] Russia, due to sickness, 25/11/1812

Y

van Ykelschot, Jean, [b] Antwerp 15/7/1790; [d] in hospital, Metz, 25/11/1813

Z

Zadelhoff, Thierry, [b] 10/5/1785; Cpl, 20/3/1814; [lwp] 31/3/1814

Zandvoort, Jean Guillaume, [b] Berkel 25/6/1786; [m] Russia, 10/10/1812

van der Zant, Antoine, [b] The Hague 1/10/1790; [d/h] 31/8/1811

van Zanten, Abraham, [b] Buren 19/8/1784; Cpl, 1/1/1809; [t>] as SLt into 6e Lanciers de Ligne, 1/5/1813

Zee, Joseph, [b] Worms 11/5/1790; [p] Russia, 27/7/1812

van Zeegen, Leonard, [b] Vlaardingen 1/1/1786; [t>] 14e Cuirassiers, 27/12/1811

Zeeventrik, Guillaume, [b] Trieste 14/1/1782; [m] Russia, 30/11/1812

van Zetten, Frédéric, [b] Grossum 21/4/1787; [d] in hospital, Versailles, 26/1/1813

van Zetten, Roelof, [b] Beuskom 22/2/1778; [m] Russia, 2/12/1812

van Zeyl, Nicolas, [b] Egmond 3/8/1790; [ds] 12/7/1814

van Zeylst, Simon, [b] Sprange 27/4/1787; [lwp] 31/3/1814

Ziell, Thomas, [b] Breda 8/3/1787; Cpl, 21/9/1810; [p] Russia, 25/11/1812

van den Zilver, Hubert, [b] Tilburg 6/7/1789; [d/h] 1/10/1811

van Zoelen, Guillaume, [b] Goldermalsen 1/1/1786; [m] Russia, 12/12/1812

van Zoelen, Silvain, [b] Bommel 27/3/1787; [m] Russia, 11/8/1812

van Zoest, Armand, [b] Leiden 17/8/1791; [p] Russia, 25/9/1812

Zoet, Jacques, [b] Thiel 17/11/1775; Sgt, 21/9/1810; [dm] Lancer, 21/2/1814; [ds] 11/7/1814

Zondermans, Bernard, [b] Obergom 20/11/1781; Cpl, 20/2/1803; Cpl, 29/7/1811; [d] in battle, 25/10/1812

Zonnemans, Jean, [b] Weert 25/12/1787; [m] Russia, 30/10/1812

Zoutendijk, Pierre, [b] Hoorn 2/8/1787; [p] Russia, 28/9/1812

Zurich, Guillaume Frédéric, [b] Amsterdam; Cpl, 23/1/1811; [t>] as SLt into 25e Inf de Ligne, 1/6/1811

van Zuyl, Pierre, [b] Utrecht 10/11/1783; [m] Russia, 7/12/1812

Zwaan, Jean Joseph, [b] Venlo 5/1/1785; [t>] as SLt to the Indies, 27/1/1811

Vander Zwaleuwe, Joseph, [b] Wemel 1/1/1776; [p] Russia, 17/9/1812

Zwart, Corneil, [b] Egmond-aan-Zee 24/3/1783; [d/u] 1/9/1811

Zwartz, Mathieu, [b] Weyen 8/5/1788; [dst] 20/4/1814

van Zwelm, Jean, [b] Arnhem 6/6/1779; [ds] 1/3/1811

Zwieren, Stefan, [b] 's Hertogenbosch 1/12/1781; [m] Russia, 16/11/1812

Zwigt, Pierre Thierry, [b] Olsenmark 24/2/1791; [m] Russia, 8/12/1812

Zwijts, Leonard, [b] Schiedam 24/5/1791; [m] Russia, 24/11/1812

APPENDIX V

Muster Roll of troopers and non-commissioned officers formerly of the Dutch 3rd Hussars who were assigned to the 5th Squadron, 2nd Light Horse Lancers of the Imperial Guard on 5-8 April 1812.
(Note that some were immediately transferred to other units - see also Appendix II.)

Abels, Albert, [b] Amsterdam 16/5/1786; [m] Russia, 25/12/1812
Alexis, ?; Fr; [m] Russia, 9/12/1812

Bauer, Godfroy, [b] Silesia 1775; [t>] Chasseurs à cheval de la Garde Impériale, 9/4/1812
Beerends, Eberhard, [b] Reukum 2/2/1788; [ds] 12/7/1812
van Beers, Gerard, [b] Elshout 22/5/1786; fell behind, 14/10/1813
Beerts, Antoine, [b] Vlijtingen 18/11/1780; [t>] Chasseurs à cheval de la Garde Impériale, 9/4/1812
Bergman, Gerard, [b] Arnhem 15/3/1786; Trpt; [m] Russia, 28/11/1812
Blijs, Godefroy, [b] Grochewechte 5/2/1780; [m] Russia, 5/9/1812
Bloemenberg, Joseph, [b] Pampsperingen 3/5/1785; [m] Russia, 6/12/1812
Bochems, Henry, [b] Gronsveld 1/1/1782; [m] Russia, 6/12/1812
van den Braak, Leonard, [b] Driel 15/8/1787; QM, 1/5/1808; [pm] SLt into 3e Lanciers de Ligne, 1/3/1813
Bregt, Chrétien, [b] Ritmer 10/3/1786; [m] Russia, 1/12/1812
Broers, Anthoine, [b] Thiel 5/11/1785; [ds] 12/7/1814
Broestvlek, André, [b] Lanterode 1/7/1784; [p] 23/10/1813
Bronkhorst, Albert, [b] Arnhem 12/11/1778; [m] Russia, 6/12/1812

Camuse, François, [b] Rotterdam 22/2/1776; Cpl; [t>] Grenadiers à cheval de la Garde Impériale, 9/4/1812
Claas, Gerard, [b] Heerden 2/9/1780; [m] Russia, 14/12/1812

Dammans, Jean, [b] 's-Hertogenbosch 20/3/1785; [lwp] 20/4/1814
Deveer, Eberhard, [b] Arnhem 7/5/1782; QM, 4/5/1807; [d] of wounds, 12/11/1812
van Diest, Bernard, [b] Leiden 15/10/1784; Cpl; [t>] Chasseurs à cheval de la Garde Impériale, 9/4/1812
Dillissen, Eberhard, [b] Arnhem 14/7/1782; Sgt, 1/5/1808; [d] in hospital, Versailles, 13/10/1812
Dirks, Martin, [b] Ude 1/11/1785; ; Cpl, 24/2/1813; [dst] 5/5/1813
Doyen, Lambert, [b] Gronsveld 6/8/1778; ; Cpl, 28/11/1806; Sgt, 29/5/1813; fell behind, 26/2/1814

van Engelen, Jean, [b] The Hague 31/3/1787; [m] Russia, 13/12/1812
Erhard, Louis, [b] Burgdorp 21/3/1779; Cp, 4/5/1807; Sgt, 3/3/1814; [ds] 12/7/1814

Fies, Jean, [b] Atteurs 3/8/1786; [p] Russia, 28/9/1812

Gehenis, André, [b] Smeermaas 10/4/1786; [m] Russia, 30/10/1812
Gerritz, Henry; [m] Russia, 6/12/1812
Gerritzen, Pierre, [b] Bergen-op-Zoom 9/2/1781; Sgt, 6/4/1807; [d] in hospital, 11/6/1813
Gijsberts, Jacques, [b] Owerde 8/3/1785; [d] Russia, 1/12/1812
Gijzelaar, Christophe, [b] Utrecht 17/5/1785; Cpl, 28/11/1806; [t>] Grenadiers à cheval de la Garde Impériale, 9/4/1812
Gijzelaar, Pierre, [b] Arnhem 2/3/1784; [t>] Grenadiers à cheval de la Garde Impériale, 9/4/1812
Goovaards, Adrien, [b] Bergen-op-Zoom 6/1/1788; [m] Russia, 30/10/1812
Gorissen, Gerard, [b] Bergen-op-Zoom 12/2/1787; Cpl, 6/4/1807; [t>] Grenadiers à cheval de la Garde Impériale, 9/4/1812
van der Grind, Pierre, [b] Orten 5/1784; [m] Russia, 5/12/1812
Guers, Christian, [b] Smeermaas 12/1786; Cpl, 17/2/1813; [ds] 12/7/1814

Ham, Jean, [b] Gorinchem 12/3/1793; Trpt; [m] Russia, 28/11/1812
Hamers, Gerard, [b] Maersemme 20/6/1778; fell behind, 22/5/1813
Hamers, Staats, [b] Geleen 7/5/1784; [ds] 11/7/1814
Hartman, Jean, [b] Keurenberg 22/5/1789; Cpl, 3/1/1813; [p] 25/10/1813
van Helden, Hubert, [b] Veen 21/2/1786; [m] Russia, 4/12/1812
Hendriks, Joseph, [b] 's-Hertogenbosch 1/4/1791; [m] Russia, 11/12/1812
Heugen, Herman, [b] Appeldoorn 1/1/1784; [m] Russia, 1/12/1812
Heyers, Leonard, [b] Boorsten 5/3/1781; [m] Russia, 18/12/1812
Houberks, Pierre, [b] Rutten 1/4/1785; [m] Russia, 7/11/1812

van Huis, Theodore, [b] Wolterswijk 13/2/1787; [m] Russia, 1/12/1812
Janssen, Chrétien, [b] Blesterwijk 20/5/1771; [m] Russia, 4/12/1812
Janssen, Jean, [b] Diepenheim 18/7/1774; Cpl; [dm] Lancer, 28/11/1812; [m] Russia, 10/12/1812
Janssen, Jean, [b] Doesburg 15/1/1783; [t>] Chasseurs à cheval de la Garde Impériale, 9/4/1812
Janssen, Pierre, [b] Nijmegen 15/5/1786; removed from muster roll 2/8/1814 - in hospital since 22/9/1813
Josten, Germain, [b] Frennigue 1/1/1780; [t>] Chasseurs à cheval de la Garde Impériale, 9/4/1812

Kampers, Henry, [b] Zulberg 26/1/1787; [m] Russia, 7/12/1812
Kleevers, Pierre, [b] Tilburg 15/3/1784; [m] Russia, 15/11/1812
Kluts, Gilles, [b] Maastricht 24/6/1770; [p] Russia, 3/9/1812
Kroon, Henry, [b] Loon-op-Zand 12/5/1787; [m] Russia, 9/11/1812
Kultz, Lambert, [b] Heukeloom; fell behind, 4/10/1813

Lagman, Joseph, [b] Silesia 29/8/1783; [m] Russia, 30/11/1812
Le Suisse, Louis, [b] Liège 25/2/1777; Sgt, 6/4/1807; [m] Russia, 9/12/1812
Libert, Lambert, [b] Liège 12/1/1777; [t>] CRCLF, 2/8/1814

Machiels, Pierre, [b] Hops 10/4/1789; [p] 4/11/1813
Marchand, Gérard, [b] Amiens 1/8/1787; [m] Russia, 30/11/1812
Mergel, Conrad, [b] Maastricht 12/3/1784; [t>] Chasseurs à cheval de la Garde Impériale, 9/4/1812
Mertens, Martin, [b] Guus 3/5/1786; [m] Russia, 3/12/1812
Moors, Mathieu Joseph, [b] Vleeron 25/10/1781; [t>] Chasseurs à cheval de la Garde Impériale, 9/4/1812

Nap, Jean, [b] Doorewaard 1/1/1782; [t>] Grenadiers à cheval de la Garde Impériale, 9/4/1812

Opduin, Bartholomé, [b] Dalsen 3/1778; [m] Russia, 3/11/1812
d'Or, Denis, [b] Vleeron 1/3/1783; [t>] Chasseurs à cheval de la Garde Impériale, 9/4/1812
van Os, Henry, [b] Zuid Bommel 12/8/1783; Cpl, 28/11/1808; [dm] Lancer, 12/10/1812; Cpl, 25/5/1813; [ds] 12/7/1814

Paqué, Gilles, [b] Dalen 6/5/1784; fell behind, 4/10/1813
Pastork, Jean, [b] Silesia, 9/12/1771; [p] 22/10/1813
Peeper, Servaas, [b] Maastricht 3/9/1777; Sgt, 1/7/1809; [m] Russia, 1/12/1812
Plooy, Martin, [b] Schiedam 17/12/1785; Sgt, 1/10/1809; [pm] Lt into 2e Carabiniers, 1/3/1813

Rebalen, Louis Marie, [b] Bretagne; Fr; [t>] 7e Dragons, 28/6/1812
Reyntjes, Jean, [b] Raalte 10/10/1779; see Appendix III, Officers
van Rhijen, Antoine, [b] Etten 28/11/1788; Cpl; [ds] 12/7/1814
Rietbergen, Jacques, [b] Kam 3/5/1785; [m] Russia, 20/11/1812
Romsée, François, [b] Xhine 1/4/1771; Sgt, 3/8/1795; [m] Russia, 9/12/1812
de Ruyter, Henry, [b] Weesp 2/9/1785; [d] in hospital, Paris, 20/9/1812
de Ruyter, Jean, [b] Weesp 10/3/1786; [t>] Chasseurs à cheval de la Garde Impériale, 9/4/1812

Schaap, Jean, [b] Aaltz 3/1/1784; [ds] 12/7/1814
Schruers, Pierre, [b] Meersen 1/7/1785; [t>] Chasseurs à cheval de la Garde Impériale, 9/4/1812
Slot, Thierry, [b] Maassluys 27/11/1787; [t>] Chasseurs à cheval de la Garde Impériale, 9/4/1812
Speltie, Chrétien Joseph, [b] The Hague 11/4/1782; SM, 16/3/1807; [lwp] 31/3/1814
van Straaten, Martin, [b] Nijmegen 1783; [t>] Chasseurs à cheval de la Garde Impériale, 9/4/1812

Tasquin, Thomas, [b] Verviers 20/7/1775; Cpl, 28/11/1806; Sgt, 16/8/1813; [ds] 12/7/1814
Thibau, Joseph, [b] Richel 2/8/1781; [lwp] 20/4/1814
Thies, Henry, [b] Bulzengen 20/10/1770; [d] in hospital, Versailles, 2/9/1813

Veldkamp, Henry, [b] Kerpel 8/2/1771; [m] Russia, 1/1/1813
Velling, Guillaume, [b] Utrecht 20/8/1786; [m] Russia, 1/12/1812

Wagelmans, Denis, [b] Maastricht 21/3/1782; fell behind, 18/8/1813
Wagter, Jean, [b] Danzig, 20/5/1789; [m] Russia, 8/11/1812
Wendich, Henry, [b] Dissen, Saxony, 17/2/1777; [t>] Chasseurs à cheval de la Garde Impériale, 9/4/1812
Westkamp, Bernard, [b] Kleinaarden 14/4/1783; [m] Russia, 12/11/1812
Willemsen, Gilbert, [b] Rotterdam 11/9/1779; Cpl; Sgt, 3/1/1813; Legionnaire, Legion of Honour, 5/4/1814; [ds] 11/7/1814
Windhold, Arnoud, [b] Wageningen 16/12/1779; Fr; [lwp] 20/4/1814
de Wolf, Antoine George, [b] Lubeck; Cpl, 3/5/1808; Sgt, 12/2/1813; [d] 6/11/1813

APPENDIX VI

Troopers and non-commissioned officers serving with the regiment in 1815 who were members of the Legion of Honour

Aubier, Charles, Sergeant. Legionnaire, 6/8/1811. Removed from muster roll 9/11/1815 - on leave since 26/9/1815.
Auvray, Thomas. Legionnaire, 27/2/1815. Corporal, 1/7/1815.

Balthasard, Jacques, Trumpet Major. Legionnaire, 28/11/1813. Killed at Waterloo, 18/6/1815.
Barthe, Jean. Legionnaire, 14/9/1813. Retired, 14/12/1815.
Bataille, François, Corporal. Legionnaire, 24/11/1814. Removed from muster roll, 1/9/1815 - in Gros Caillou hospital since 18/6/1815.
Baudet, Pierre, Corporal (since 1809). Legionnaire, 20/6/1809.
Becker, Nicolas. Legionnaire, 19/3/1815. Dismissed, 16/11/1815.
Becquer, Thibault, Corporal (since 9/4/1813). Legionnaire, 19/3/1815. Dismissed, 9/11/1815.
Bernard, Félix, Quartermaster. Legionnaire, 19/3/1815. Sergeant, 1/7/1815. Sent to the department where he lived, 22/12/1815.
Berry, Jean Baptiste, Corporal. Legionnaire, 5/4/1814. Fell behind, 18/6/1815.
Berthaux, Jean. Legionnaire, 6/1/1814. Dismissed, 21/12/1815.
Bertheleau, Pierre. Legionnaire, 30/4/1815. Killed at Waterloo, 18/6/1815.
Berthier, Sergeant-Major. Legionnaire, 14/9/1813. Dismissed, 16/11/1815.
Besson, Pierre Philibert, Sergeant-Major. Legionnaire, 5/4/1814. Sent to the department where he lived, 22/12/1815.
Bonnard, Dominique Raphaël, Quartermaster. Legionnaire, 30/4/1815. Fell behind, 6/7/1815.

Caillet, André, Corporal. Legionnaire, 27/2/1815. Dismissed, 9/11/1815.
Carpentier, François Honoré, Sergeant (since 29/9/1813). Legionnaire, 19/3/1815. Dismissed, 9/11/1815.
Cataux, Pierre François. Legionnaire, 24/11/1814. Corporal, 1/7/1815. Dismissed, 13/12/1815.
Chaumont, François, Sergeant. Legionnaire, 24/11/1814. Dismissed, 21/12/1815.
Cocuelle, Jean Charles Louis. Legionnaire, 30/4/1815. Removed from muster roll, 1/9/1815 - in hospital since 23/6/1815.
Colet, Laurent. Legionnaire, 27/2/1814. Corporal, 16/7/1815. Dismissed, 16/11/1815.
Colombé, Charles, Sergeant-Major. Legionnaire, 27/2/1814. Dismissed, 22/12/1815.
Commun, Pierre, Trumpeter (1er Escadron, 1ere Compagnie). Legionnaire, 24/11/1814. Removed from muster roll, 1/10/1815 - in hospital at Versailles since 29/6/1815.
Corbin, Louis. Legionnaire, 28/11/1813. Dismissed, 21/12/1815.
Couchot, Maurice. Legionnaire, 24/11/1814. Corporal, 1/7/1815. Dismissed, 9/11/1815.
Coulpotin, Pierre Simon. Legionnaire, 24/11/1814. Dismissed, 16/11/1815.
Couturier, Alexandre Mathieu, Sergeant. Legionnaire, 19/3/1815. Dismissed, 13/12/1815.

Daraux, Casimir, Sergeant. Legionnaire, 24/11/1814. Retired, 14/12/1815.
Darmstad, Sébastien, Corporal. Legionnaire, 30/4/1815. Deserted, 11/7/1815.
Dehaye, François Auguste, Corporal. Legionnaire, 5/4/1814. Removed from muster roll, 21/12/1815 - on leave since 16/7/1815.
Deher, Claude, Corporal. Legionnaire, 24/11/1814. Dismissed, 21/12/1815.
Delahaye, Balthasard, Sergeant. Legionnaire, 30/4/1815. Passed into Gendarmerie, 21/12/1815.
Delille, André. Legionnaire, 5/4/1814. Deserted, 7/7/1815.
Denieport, Pierre, Sergeant (since 16/2/1814). Legionnaire, 28/11/1813. Dismissed, 21/12/1815.
Deteg, Joseph, Quartermaster. Legionnaire, 19/3/1814. Fell behind, 18/6/1815.
Drion, Antoine, Corporal. Legionnaire, 24/11/1814. Dismissed, 16/11/1815.
Dubarbé, Pierre. Legionnaire, 30/4/1814. Corporal, 1/7/1815. Passed into Hussards de la Garde Royale, 5/12/1815.
Duchemin, Henry François. Legionnaire, 19/3/1815. Dismissed, 21/12/1815.
Dumas, Charles. Legionnaire, 27/2/1815. Fell behind, 18/6/1815.
Duval, Jean François Auguste, Corporal. Legionnaire, 24/11/1814. Fell behind, 16/6/1815.
Duval, Louis Philippe, Sergeant (since 16/2/1814). Legionnaire, 3/4/1814. Dismissed, 9/11/1815.

Essé, Jean, Corporal (since 15/3/1814). Legionnaire, 19/3/1815. Dismissed, 16/11/1815.

Fondu, Louis Henry, Corporal (since 27/11/1813). Legionnaire, 30/4/1815. Fell behind, 18/7/1815.

Foulleux, Jean Baptiste, Sergeant-Major. Legionnaire, 5/4/1815. Dismissed, 21/12/1815.

Fram, Louis, Sergeant. Legionnaire, 24/11/1814. Fell behind, 16/6/1815.

Fréquin, Guillaume. Assigned to the Corps, 21/9/1810. Legionnaire, 24/11/1814. Removed from muster roll, 22/12/1815 - on leave since 18/7/1815.

Gageot, Joseph, Sergeant (since 29/1/1813). Legionnaire. Dismissed, 13/12/1815.

Gambray, Jacques Pierre, Corporal. Legionnaire, 24/11/1814. Deserted, 5/7/1815.

Godefroy, Bernardin. Legionnaire, 19/3/1815. Deserted, 5/7/1815.

Gouat, Pierre, Corporal (since 7/3/1813). Legionnaire, 19/3/1815. Retired, 14/12/1815.

Gourju, Joseph Alexis Benjamin, Corporal (since 1/3/1813). Legionnaire, 24/11/1814. Passed into Gendarmerie, 21/12/1815.

Gris, Jean Jacques Barthélemy, Sergeant. Legionnaire, 28/11/1813. Passed into Invalides, 14/12/1815.

Griset, Jean François, Sergeant. Legionnaire, 24/11/1814. Dismissed, 21/12/1815.

Guidet, Jean Claude, Sergeant (since 12/1812). Legionnaire, 3/4/1814. Dismissed, 9/11/1815.

Guillaume, Pierre, Quartermaster (since 1/3/1813). Legionnaire, 30/4/1815. Dismissed, 9/11/1815.

Guinot, François, Sergeant (since 1/11/1809). Legionnaire, 5/4/1814. Retired, 14/12/1815.

Harras, Pierre Augustin. Legionnaire, 27/2/1814. Deserted, 10/10/1815.

Harrault, François Joseph. Legionnaire, 19/3/1815. Removed from muster roll, 1/9/1815 - in hospital since 29//6/1815.

la Haye, Laurent. Assigned to the corps, 21/9/1810. Legionnaire, 16/8/1813. Passed into Invalides, 16/7/1815.

Isambart, Jean Louis, Corporal. Legionnaire, 24/11/1814. Dismissed, 21/12/1815.

Jacob, Mathieu. Legionnaire, 14/9/1813. Passed into Hussards de la Garde Royale, 5/12/1815.

Jourdan, ?, Lancer. Legionnaire, 30/4/1815. Deserted, 6/7/1815.

Jourdan, Jacques François, Lancer-Vélite. Legionnaire, 30/4/1815. Dismissed, 21/12/1815.

Klebaut, Ferdinand Louis, Sergeant. Legionnaire, 24/11/1814. Dismissed, 16/11/1815.

Köhl, Henry. Legionnaire, 19/3/1815. Dismissed, 9/11/1815.

Krapeller, Jean Pierre. Legionnaire, 14/9/1813. Dismissed, 21/12/1815.

Laauchers, Jean. Legionnaire, 26/5/1803. Dismissed, 6/11/1815.

Lacour, Charles René Louis, Vélite, Sergeant-Major (since 17/3/1814). Legionnaire, 5/4/1814. Dismissed, 21/12/1815.

Laforge, Nicolas Jean Baptiste, Corporal (since 25/2/1813). Legionnaire, 5/4/1814. Removed from muster roll, 22/12/1815 - in hospital since 4/7/1815.

Lafoureade, Gratien, Quartermaster. Legionnaire, 30/4/1815. Dismissed, 21/12/1815.

Lahalle, Joseph. Legionnaire, 30/3/1815. Deserted, 9/7/1815.

Laidelin, Michel, Sergeant. Legionnaire, 24/11/1814. Passed into Gendarmerie, 21/12/1815.

Lambert, François, Corporal. Legionnaire, 30/4/1815. Sergeant, 1/7/1815. Dismissed, 16/11/1815.

Lantaigne, Pierre François, Corporal. Legionnaire, 24/11/1814. Deserted, 16/10/1815.

Laredde, Charles Nicolas, Corporal. Legionnaire, 19/3/1815. Dismissed, 21/12/1815.

Lasalle, Léonard. Legionnaire, 14/4/1807. Fell behind, 18/6/1815.

Lebrun, Gervais, Sergeant. Legionnaire, 24/11/1814. Deserted, 5/7/1815.

Leclerc, Pierre Marie, Corporal. Legionnaire, 24/11/1814. Deserted, 11/7/1815.

Leduc, François, Sergeant (since 28/9/1813). Legionnaire, 24/11/1814. Sent to the department where he lived, 22/12/1815.

Lemoine, Bastien, Sergeant. Legionnaire, 24/11/1814. Died, 30/10/1815.

Lenoble, Georges, Corporal (since 17/1/1813). Legionnaire, 24/11/1814. Dismissed, 9/11/1815.

Lenoir Despinasse, Isaac Joseph, Vélite, Sergeant (since 15/3/1813). Legionnaire, 24/11/1814. Removed from muster roll, 1/10/1815 - on leave since 29/6/1815.

Leroux, Alexandre Benoist Guillaume, Quartermaster. Legionnaire, 30/4/1815. Sergeant, 1/7/1815. Dismissed, 21/12/1815.

Letestu, Georges Joseph, Corporal (since 18/8/1813). Legionnaire, 30/4/1815. Removed from muster roll 2/8/1814 - on sick leave since 2/5/1814. Returned to the corps, 1/3/1815. Deserted, 5/7/1815.

Levecque, Pierre, Corporal (since 10/4/1814). Legionnaire, 30/4/1815. Dismissed, 21/12/1815.

Livret, Pierre, Corporal (since 1/3/1813). Legionnaire, 5/4/1814. Removed from muster roll, 21/12/1815 - on leave since 16/7/1815.

Ménescal, Jacques, Sergeant. Legionnaire, 24/11/1814. Dismissed, 9/11/1815.

Mertens, Jean Pierre. Legionnaire, 24/11/1814. Removed from muster roll, 11/8/1815.

Mervaillé, Louis Clément, Sergeant (since 10/2/1813). Legionnaire, 19/3/1815. Retired, 21/12/1815.

Milan, Joseph, Sergeant. Legionnaire, 24/11/1814. Dismissed, 13/12/1815.

Morand, Jean Louis, Sergeant. Legionnaire, 19/3/1815. Fell behind, 30/6/1815.

Moreau, Louis. Legionnaire, 5/4/1814. Dismissed, 21/12/1815.

Mothiron, Jean, Sergeant. Legionnaire, 24/11/1814. Dismissed, 16/11/1815.

Muller, Louis Philippe, Corporal. Legionnaire, 27/2/1815. Fell behind, 30/6/1815.

Nimier, François Lubin, Sergeant-Major. Legionnaire, 28/10/1813. Dismissed, 9/11/1815.

Noël, Laurent, Sergeant. Legionnaire, 19/3/1815. Dismissed, 15/7/1815.

van Otterloo, Henry, Sergeant. Assigned to corps, 21/9/1810. Legionnaire, 16/8/1813. Passed into Invalides, 1815.

Papillon, ?. Legionnaire, 5/4/1814. Dismissed, 21/12/1815.

Parisse, François. Legionnaire, 2/4/1814. Deserted, 5/7/1815.

Pennet, Philibert. Legionnaire, 19/3/1815. Corporal, 1/7/1815. Dismissed, 9/11/1815.

Petit, Evrard. Legionnaire. Fell behind, 19/6/1815.

Picard, François. Legionnaire, 24/11/1814. Dismissed, 16/11/1815.

Podevin, Louis Laurent, Sergeant (since 16/2/1814). Legionnaire, 24/11/1814. Dismissed, 21/12/1815.

Poulet, Hubert, Sergeant. Legionnaire, 24/11/1814. Dismissed, 16/11/1815.

Poussigue, ?, Corporal. Legionnaire, 5/4/1814. Dismissed, 9/11/1815.

Reyboul, Ferdinand, Sergeant. Legionnaire, 30/4/1815. Dismissed, 13/12/1815.

Rigaux, Jean François, Sergeant-Major (since 3/3/1813). Legionnaire, 24/11/1814. Dismissed, 16/11/1815.

Roussel, Pierre Joseph, Corporal (since 1/3/1813). Legionnaire, 5/4/1814. Deserted, 5/7/1815.

Rozier, Charles Gabriel, Corporal. Legionnaire, 24/11/1814. Deserted, 5/7/1815.

Ruin, Jean Baptiste, Corporal (since 27/2/1813). Legionnaire, 5/4/1814. Removed from muster roll, 1/9/1815 - in hospital since 18/6/1815.

Schroeder, Fréderick, Sergeant-Major. Legionnaire, 27/5/1814. Returned home, 13/12/1815.

Solgne, Jean Baptiste, Corporal. Legionnaire, 24/11/1814. Dismissed, 16/11/1815.

Thibault, Toussaint, Sergeant. Assigned to corps, 21/9/1810. Legionnaire, 28/11/1813. Dismissed, 16/11/1815.

Thirard, Jean Louis, Corporal (since 1/4/1815). Legionnaire, 30/4/1815. Deserted, 10/10/1815.

Vallet, Louis Melchior, Corporal (since 1/3/1813). Legionnaire, 24/11/1814. Dismissed, 9/11/1815.

Valette, Benoist. Legionnaire, 28/9/1813. Dismissed, 13/12/1815.

Vathé, Claude, Corporal. Legionnaire, 24/11/1814. Deserted, 24/6/1815.

Vienne, Jean. Legionnaire, 30/4/1815. Fell behind, 5/7/1815.

Vilde, Joseph, Corporal. Legionnaire, 19/2/1815. Dismissed, 9/11/1815.

Villas, Jean, Corporal. Legionnaire, 24/11/1814. Passed to Garde du Roi, 21/12/1815.

Vitry, Pierre Marie Michel, Veterinary. Assigned to corps, 21/9/1810. Order of the Lily, 18/6/1814; Legionnaire, 30/4/1815. Removed from corps, 22/12/1815 - in hospital at Chartres since 15/8/1815.

Wampach, Theodore, Sergeant. Legionnaire, 30/4/1815. Dismissed, 16/11/1815.

INDEX OF PLACE NAMES